Table of Contents

Introduction

What Is Air Frying?

First, a quick explanation of what air frying is and isn't. They don't fry food at all. They are more like a self-contained convection oven than a deep fat fryer. Most units have one or more heating elements, along with a fan or two to circulate the hot air. These appliances quickly heat and circulate the hot air around and through the food in the tray. This cooking method takes advantage of the heat and the drying effect of the air to cook foods quickly, leaving them crisp and browned on the outside but still moist inside. While the results can be similar to using a deep fryer, they are not identical.

What Are The Pros And Cons Of An Air Fryer?

While the enthusiasm about these products may be a bit overblown, there are some solid benefits to using an air fryer, as well as some major downsides.

Pros Of An Air Fryer

1. Healthier Meals

You do not need to use much (or any) oil in these appliances to get your food crispy and browned! Most users just spritz a little oil on the item and then proceed to the cooking cycle. The hot air takes advantage of the little bit of oil, and any excess oil just drains away from the food. This makes these devices ideal for making fresh and frozen fries, onion rings, mozzarella sticks, chicken wings, and nuggets. Unlike a traditional oven, air frying items are cooked faster and the excess oil doesn't soak into your food. So the claims that they use less oil and make healthier meals are true!

2. Quicker, More Efficient Cooking

Air fryers take just minutes to preheat, and most of the heat stays inside the appliance. Foods cook faster than in an oven or on a stovetop because this heat is not lost to the surrounding air. Even frozen foods are quickly cooked because the effect of the heat is intensified by the circulating air. These units are also more energy-efficient than an oven. Using a fryer will not heat your house in the summer, and the cost of the electricity used is just pennies. Since the cooking cycle is also shorter, you can see that using a fryer makes most cooking faster and more efficient than traditional appliances!

3. Versatility

You can use them to air fry, stir fry, reheat, bake, broil, roast, grill, steam, and even rotisserie in some models. Besides the fries and nuggets, you can make hot dogs and sausages, steak, chicken breasts or thighs, grilled sandwiches, stir-fried meats and veggies, roasted or steamed veggies, all kinds of fish and shrimp dishes, even cakes and desserts. If your unit is large enough, you can even bake a whole chicken or small turkey, or do a beef or pork roast. They are more than just a fryer!

4. Space-Saving

Most units are about the size of a coffee maker. Some models are small and super-compact, making them perfect for small kitchens, kitchenettes, dorm rooms, or RVs. An air fryer can replace an oven in a situation that lacks one and can be more useful than a toaster oven or steamer. If you use it frequently you will likely be happy to give it a home on your kitchen counter!

5. Easy To Use

Most fryers are designed to be easy to use. Just set the cooking temperature and time, put your food in the basket, and walk away. Of course, you will get better results if you shake your food once or twice during the cooking cycle, especially for things like fries, chips, wings, and nuggets. This ensures even browning and perfect results. Many air fryer enthusiasts have even taught their children to use them for making after school snacks or quick lunches!

Cons Of An Air Fryer

1. Quality Issues

Air fryers are mostly made from plastic and inexpensive metal parts. They may or may not bear up after months or years of use. The heating elements, controls, and fans tend to go out eventually, and once they do your unit is useless. The metal cooking baskets and pans do not tend to last very long and often need to be replaced. Print on the dials or control panels can wear off. Even expensive units can have these issues, and some brands seem to have a lot of reported problems. These are not sturdy, long-lasting kitchen appliances overall.

2. Takes Up Space

Ok, I had "Space Saver" listed as a pro...how can it be a con as well? Easy! They do take up space, either on your counter or stored away in a cabinet. If you use it frequently this might not be a problem...but if you only drag it out to make the occasional batch of wings then the loss of space might not make it worth it to you. It depends on how and if you use it. Some units are fairly heavy as well, and might not be very easy to move around. They have the potential to be just another appliance you use a few times and then sell at a yard sale.

3. Not Ideal For Large Families

You will see some fryers advertised for "large families" but what does that mean? Most air fryers are best suited to making food for 1-4 people (depending on the capacity). There are very few that can handle making food for more than 4, and they often still require cooking in batches. For large families, a true convection air frying oven would probably be a better choice.

A medium-sized fryer with a capacity of 3.5 quarts can usually handle the main dish for two or a main and side dish for one. A large unit with a capacity of 5.8 quarts can handle the main dish like a whole chicken...which theoretically means enough to serve 4 people, as long as you cook the rest of the food in another appliance. So these are ideal for smaller families or single users, or a dorm or office snack maker.

4. Learning Curve

They ARE easy to use, but there is still a learning curve. Each unit has its peculiarities that you will have to figure out. They come with cooking guides and recipes, but those are more recommendations rather than firm instructions. It may take a few trials before you get the results that you want. Luckily the internet is filled with users who have shared their experiences, so finding tips is pretty easy.

5. Limitations

For all their versatility, air fryers have limitations as well. You are limited by the size and shape of the basket. Your frozen taquitos may not fit into some models, and you might be limited to a 6-inch pie pan in another. Food sometimes gets stuck to the cooking pans, meaning a more difficult clean-up for you. Even with accessories like elevated cooking racks and kabob skewers, you will still have to cook in batches or use another appliance if you are making food for multiple people. You also have to wait for the unit to cool off before cleaning and storing it away. For some people, these limitations might be too much to make an air fryer worth it.

Air Fryer Benefits

- An air fryer has many benefits to offer its customers.
- Low-fat meals
- Easy cleanup
- Uses hot-air circulation, the air fryer cooks your ingredients from all angles- with no oil needed.
- This ultimately produces healthier foods than most fryers and spares you from that unwanted aroma of fried foods in your home.
- To make sure you get the most out of your appliance, most fryers are accompanied by a recipe book to help you get started right away on your journey of fast, yet healthy meal preparations.
- Whether your favorite dish is french fries, muffins, chips, chicken tenders, or grilled vegetables, an air fryer can prepare it all.

Is An Air Fryer Useful?

At the tip of your fingers, you can have an appliance that specializes in making delicious, healthy meals that look and taste just like the ones made in oil fryers. The air fryer serves up many ways to be useful in your life.

Consider:

- Do you find yourself short on time to cook?
- Are you having a hard time letting go of those fatty foods, but still want to lose weight?
- Are you always seeking to get a bang for your buck?

If you answered yes to any of these questions, then an air fryer may be for you.

Why You Should Use An Air Fryer

An air fryer can pretty much do it all. And by all, we mean fry, grill, bake, and roast. Equipped with sturdy plastic and metal material, the air fryer has many great benefits to offer.

Air Fryers Can:

- Cook multiple dishes at once
- Cut back on fatty oils
- Prepare a meal within minutes
- While every appliance has its cons, the air fryer doesn't offer many.
- The fryer may be bulky in weight, but its dimensions are slimmer than most fryers. An air

fryer can barely take up any counter space.

- If you need fast, healthy, convenient, and tasty, then once again, an air fryer may be for you.

Air Fryer - Healthier

The biggest quality the air fryer offers is healthier dishes

In comparison to other fryers, air fryers were designed to specifically function without fattening oils and to produce food with up to 80 percent less fat than food cooked with other fryers. The air fryer can help you lose the weight, you've been dying to get rid of. While it can be difficult to let go of your favorite fried foods, an air fryer will let you have your cake and eat it too. You can still have your fried dishes, but at the same time, still conserve those calories and saturated fat. The air fryer can also grill, bake, and roast foods as well. Offering you an all in one combination, the air fryer is the perfect appliance for anyone looking to switch to a healthier lifestyle.

Fast And Quick

- If you're on a tight schedule, you may want to use an air fryer.
- Within minutes you can have crunchy golden fries or crispy chicken tenders.
- This fryer is perfect for people who are constantly on the go and do not have much time to prepare meals.
- With most air fryers, french fries can be prepared within 12 minutes.
- That cuts the time you spend in the kitchen by a tremendous amount.

Features

1. Temperature And Timer

- Avoid the waiting time for your fryer to decide when it wants to heat up.
- With an air fryer, once you power it on, the fryer will instantly heat.
- When using the appliance cold, that is, right after it has been off for a while (since last use) all you have to do is add three minutes to your cooking time to allow for it to heat up properly.
- The appliance is equipped with adjustable temperature control that allows you to set the temperature that can be altered for each of your

meals.
- Most fryers can go up to 200-300 degrees.
- Because the fryer can cook food at record times, it comes with a timer that can be pre-set with no more than 30 minutes.
- You can even check on the progress of your foods without messing up the set time. Simply pull out the pan, and the fryer will cause heating. When you replace the pan, heating will resume.
- When your meal is prepared and your timer runs out, the fryer will alert you with its ready sound indicator. But just in-case you can't make it to the fryer when the timer goes, the fryer will automatically switch off to help prevent your ingredients from overcooking and burning.

2. Food Separator

Some air fryers are supplied with a food separator that enables you to prepare multiple meals at once. For example, if you wanted to prepare frozen chicken nuggets and french fries, you could use the separator to cook both ingredients at the same time, all the while avoiding the worry of the flavors mixing. An air fryer is perfect for quick and easy, lunch and dinner combinations. It is recommended to pair similar ingredients together when using the separator. This will allow both foods to share a similar temperature setting.

3. Air Filter

Some air fryers are built with an integrated air filter that eliminates those unwanted vapors and food odors from spreading around your house. No more smelling like your favorite fried foods, the air filter will diffuse that hot oil steam that floats and sticks. You can now enjoy your fresh kitchen smell before, during, and after using your air fryer.

4. Cleaning

- No need to fret after using an air fryer, it was designed for hassle-free cleaning.
- The parts of the fryer are constructed of non-stick material.
- This prevents any food from sticking to surfaces that ultimately make it hard to clean.
- It is recommended to soak the parts of the appliances before cleaning.
- All parts such as the grill, pan, and basket are removable and dishwasher friendly.
- After your ingredients are cooked to perfection,

you can simply place your parts in the dishwasher for a quick and easy clean.

Tips On Cleaning An Air Fryer:

- Use detergent that specializes in dissolving oil.
- For a maximum and quick cleaning, leave the pan to soak in water and detergent for a few minutes.
- Avoid using metal utensils when cleaning the appliance to prevent scuffs and scratches on the material.
- Always let the fryer cool off for about 30 minutes before you wash it.

5. Cost-effective

Are there any cost-effective air fryers? For all that they can do, air fryers can be worth the cost. It has been highly questionable if the benefits of an air fryer are worth the expense. When you weigh your pros and cons, the air fryer surely leads with its pros. There aren't many fryers on the market that can fry, bake, grill and roast; and also promise you healthier meals. An air fryer saves you time, and could potentially save you money. Whether the air fryer is cost-effective for your life, is ultimately up to you.

The air fryer is a highly recommendable appliance to anyone starting a new diet, parents with busy schedules, or individuals who are always on the go. Deciding whether the investment is worth it, is all up to the purchaser. By weighing the air fryer advantages and the unique differences the air fryer has, compared to other fryers, you should be able to decide whether the air fryer has a lot to bring to the table.

1. Air Fryer Breakfast Recipes

1. Ham and Cheese Mini Quiche

Prep Time: 30 minutes

Ingredients

- 1 shortcrust pastry
- 3 oz. chopped ham
- ½ cup grated cheese
- 4 eggs, beaten
- 3 tbsp. greek yogurt
- ¼ tsp. garlic powder
- ¼ tsp. salt
- ¼ tsp. black pepper

Instructions

Preheat the air fryer to 330 degrees F. Take 8 ramekins and sprinkle them with flour to avoid sticking. Cut the shortcrust pastry into 8 equal pieces to make 8 mini quiches. Line your ramekins with the pastry. Combine all of the other **Ingredients** in a bowl. Divide the filling between the ramekins. Cook for 20 minutes

Nutrition Facts

Calories 365.7, Carbohydrates 21.4 g, Fat 20.4 g, Protein 8.9 g

2. Breakfast Banana Bread

Prep Time: 50 minutes

Ingredients

- 1 cup plus
- 1 tbsp. flour
- ¼ tsp. baking soda
- 1 tsp. baking powder
- 1/3 cup sugar
- 2 mashed bananas
- ¼ cup vegetable oil
- 1 egg, beaten
- 1 tsp. vanilla extract
- ¾ cup chopped walnuts
- ¼ tsp. salt
- 2 tbsp. peanut butter2 tbsp. sour cream

Instructions

Preheat the air fryer to 330 degrees F. Spray a small baking dish with cooking spray or grease with butter. Combine the flour, salt, baking powder, and baking soda in a bowl. In another bowl combine bananas, oil, egg, peanut butter, vanilla, sugar, and sour cream. Combine both mixtures gently. Stir in the chopped walnuts. Pour the batter into the dish. Bake for 40 minutes. Let cool before serving.

Nutrition Facts

Calories 438, Carbohydrates 58 g, Fat 21 g, Protein 7.6

3. Baked Kale Omelet

Prep Time: 15 minutes

Ingredients

- 3 eggs
- 3 tbsp. cottage cheese
- 3 tbsp. chopped kale
- ½ tbsp. chopped basil
- ½ tbsp. chopped parsleySalt and pepper, to taste
- 1 tsp. olive oil

Instructions

- Add oil to your air fryer and preheat it to 330 degrees F.
- Beat the eggs with some salt and pepper, in a bowl.
- Stir in the rest of the **Ingredients**. Pour the mixture into the air fryer and bake for 10 minutes

Nutrition Facts

Calories 294, Carbohydrates 3.9 g, Fat 19.5 g, Protein 24.7 g

4. Tasty Baked Eggs

Preparation time: 10 minutes Cooking time: 20 minutes

Ingredients:

- 4 eggs
- 1 pound baby spinach, torn
- 7 ounces ham, chopped
- 4 tablespoons milk
- 1 tablespoon olive oil

- Cooking spray
- Salt and black pepper to the taste

Instructions:

- Heat up a pan with the oil over medium heat, add baby spinach, stir cook for a couple of minutes and take off heat.
- grease 4 ramekins with cooking spray and divide baby spinach and ham in each.
- Crack an egg in each ramekin, also divide milk, season with salt and pepper, place ramekins in preheated air fryer at 350 degrees F and bake for 20 minutes.
- Serve baked eggs for breakfast.

Nutrition Facts:

calories 321, fat 6, fiber 8, carbs 15, protein 12

---

5. Breakfast Egg Bowls

Preparation time: 10 minutes Cooking time: 20 minutes

Ingredients:

- 4 dinner rolls, tops cut off and insides scooped out
- 4 tablespoons heavy cream
- 4 eggs
- 4 tablespoons mixed chives and parsley
- Salt and black pepper to the taste
- 4 tablespoons parmesan, grated

Instructions:

- Arrange dinner rolls on a baking sheet and crack an egg in each.
- Divide heavy cream, mixed herbs in each roll and season with salt and pepper.
- Sprinkle parmesan on top of your rolls, place them in your air fryer and cook at 350 degrees F for 20 minutes.
- Divide your bread bowls on plates and serve for breakfast.

Nutrition Facts:

calories 238, fat 4, fiber 7, carbs 14, protein 7

---

6. Delicious Breakfast Soufflé

Preparation time:10 minutes Cooking time: 8 minutes

Ingredients:

- 4 eggs, whisked
- 4 tablespoons heavy cream
- A pinch of red chili pepper, crushed
- 2 tablespoons parsley, chopped
- 2 tablespoons chives, chopped
- Salt and black pepper to the taste

Instructions:

- In a bowl, mix eggs with salt, pepper, heavy cream, red chili pepper, parsley and chives, stir well and divide into 4 soufflé dishes.
- Arrange dishes in your air fryer and cook soufflés at 350 degrees F for 8 minutes.
- Serve them hot.

Nutrition Facts:

calories 300, fat 7, fiber 9, carbs 15, protein 6

---

7. Air Fried Sandwich

Preparation time: 10 minutes Cooking time: 6 minutes

Ingredients:

- 2 English muffins, halved
- 2 eggs
- 2 bacon strips
- Salt and black pepper to the taste

Instructions:

- Crack eggs in your air fryer, add bacon on top, cover and cook at 392 degrees F for 6 minutes.
- Heat up your English muffin halves in your microwave for a few seconds, divide eggs on 2 halves, add bacon on top, season with salt and pepper, cover with the other 2 English muffins and serve for breakfast.

Nutrition Facts:

calories 261, fat 5, fiber 8, carbs 12, protein 4

---

8. Rustic Breakfast

Preparation time: 10 minutes Cooking time: 13 minutes

Ingredients:

- 7 ounces baby spinach
- 8 chestnuts mushrooms, halved
- 8 tomatoes, halved
- 1 garlic clove, minced
- 4 chipolatas
- 4 bacon slices, chopped
- Salt and black pepper to the taste
- 4 eggs
- Cooking spray

Instructions:

- Grease a cooking pan with the oil and add tomatoes, garlic and mushrooms.
- Add bacon and chipolatas, also add spinach and crack eggs at the end.
- Season with salt and pepper, place pan in the cooking basket of your air fryer and cook for 13 minutes at 350 degrees F.
- Divide among plates and serve for breakfast.

Nutrition Facts:

calories 312, fat 6, fiber 8, carbs 15, protein 5

9. Egg Muffins

Preparation time: 10 minutes Cooking time: 15 minutes

Ingredients:

- 1 egg
- 2 tablespoons olive oil
- 3 tablespoons milk
- 3.5 ounces white flour
- 1 tablespoon baking powder
- 2 ounces parmesan, grated
- A splash of Worcestershire sauce

Instructions:

- In a bowl, mix egg with flour, oil, baking powder, milk, Worcestershire and parmesan, whisk well and divide into 4 silicon muffin cups.
- Arrange cups in your air fryer's cooking basket, cover and cook at 392, degrees F for 15 minutes.
- Serve warm for breakfast.

Nutrition Facts:

calories 251, fat 6, fiber 8, carbs 9, protein 3

10. Polenta Bites

Preparation time: 10 minutes Cooking time: 20 minutes

Ingredients:

- For the polenta:
- 1 tablespoon butter
- 1 cup cornmeal
- 3 cups water
- Salt and black pepper to the taste
- For the polenta bites:
- 2 tablespoons powdered sugar

Instructions:

- In a pan, mix water with cornmeal, butter, salt and pepper, stir, bring to a boil over medium heat, cook for 10 minutes, take off heat, whisk one more time and keep in the fridge until it's cold. Scoop 1 tablespoon of polenta, shape a ball and place on a working surface.
- Repeat with the rest of the polenta, arrange all the balls in the cooking basket of your air fryer, spray them with cooking spray, cover and cook at 380 degrees F for 8 minutes.
- Arrange polenta bites on plates, sprinkle sugar all over and serve for breakfast.

Nutrition Facts:

calories 231, fat 7, fiber 8, carbs 12, protein 4

11. Delicious Breakfast Potatoes

Preparation time: 10 minutes Cooking time: 35 minutes

Ingredients:

- 2 tablespoons olive oil
- 3 potatoes, cubed
- 1 yellow onion, chopped
- 1 red bell pepper, chopped
- Salt and black pepper to the taste
- 1 teaspoon garlic powder
- 1 teaspoon sweet paprika
- 1 teaspoon onion powder

Instructions:

- Grease your air fryer's basket with olive oil, add potatoes, toss and season with salt and pepper.
- Add onion, bell pepper, garlic powder, paprika and onion powder, toss well, cover and cook at

370 degrees F for 30 minutes.

- Divide potatoes mix on plates and serve for breakfast.

Nutrition Facts:

calories 214, fat 6, fiber 8, carbs 15, protein 4

12. Breakfast Sandwich

Prep Time: 10 minutes

Ingredients

- 1 egg
- 1 English muffin
- 2 slices of bacon
- Salt and pepper, to taste

Instructions

- Preheat the air fryer to 395 degrees.Crack the egg into a ramekin.Place the muffin, egg and bacon in the air fryer.
- Cook for 6 minutes.Let cool slightly so you can assemble the sandwich.
- Cut the muffin in half.Place the egg on one half and season with salt and pepper.
- Arrange the bacon on top.Top with the other muffin half.

Nutrition Facts

Calories 240.7, Carbohydrates 25.5 g, Fat 8.8 g, Protein 13.3 g

13. Prosciutto, Mozzarella and Egg in a Cup

Prep Time: 20 minutes

Ingredients

- 2 slices of bread
- 2 prosciutto slices, chopped
- 2 eggs
- 4 tomato slices¼ tsp. balsamic vinegar
- 2 tbsp. grated mozzarella¼ tsp. maple syrup
- 2 tbsp. mayonnaise
- Salt and pepper, to taste

Instructions

- Preheat the air fryer to 320 degrees.grease two

large ramekins.Place one bread slice in the bottom of each ramekin.

- Arrange 2 tomato slices on top of each bread slice.Divide the mozzarella between the ramekins.
- Crack the eggs over the mozzarella
- .Drizzle with maple syrup and balsamic vinegar.Season with some salt and pepper.
- Cook for 10 minutes, or until desired.

Nutrition Facts

Calories 291.3, Carbohydrates 12.9 g, Fat 20.5 g, Protein 13 g

14. Air Fried Shirred Eggs

Prep Time: 20 minutes

Ingredients

- 2 tsp. butter, for greasing
- 4 eggs, divided
- 2 tbsp. heavy cream4 slices of ham
- 3 tbsp. Parmesan cheese
- ¼ tsp. paprika
- ¾ tsp. salt
- ¼ tsp. pepper
- 2 tsp. chopped chives

Instructions

- Preheat the air fryer to 320 degrees F.grease a pie pan with the butter.
- Arrange the ham slices on the bottom of the pan to cover it completely.Use more slices if needed (or less if your pan is smaller).
- Whisk one egg along with the heavy cream, salt and pepper, in a small bowl.Pour the mixture over the ham slices.Crack the other eggs over the ham.
- Sprinkle the Parmesan cheese.
- Cook for 14 minutes.Sprinkle with paprika and garnish with chives.Serve with bread.

Nutrition Facts

279.9, Carbohydrates 1.8 g, Fat 20 g, Protein 20.8 g

15. Very Berry Breakfast Puff

Prep Time: 20 Minutes

Ingredients

- 3 pastry dough sheets
- 2 tbsp. mashed strawberries
- 2 tbsp. mashed raspberries
- ¼ tsp. vanilla extract2 cups cream cheese1 tbsp. honey

Instructions

- Preheat the air fryer to 375 degrees F.Divide the cream cheese between the dough sheets and spread it evenly.In a small bowl combine the berries, honey and vanilla.
- Divide the mixture between the pastry sheets.Pinch the ends of the sheets, to form puff.
- You can seal them by brushing some water onto the edges, or even better, use egg wash. Place the puffs on a lined baking dish.Place in the air fryer and cook for 15 minutes

Nutrition Facts

Calories 255.9, Carbohydrates 24.5 g, Fat 15.7 g, Protein 4.3

16. Cheese Air Fried Bake

Preparation time: 10 minutes Cooking time: 20 minutes

Ingredients:

- 4 bacon slices, cooked and crumbled
- 2 cups milk
- 2 and ½ cups cheddar cheese, shredded
- 1 pound breakfast sausage, casings removed and chopped
- 2 eggs
- ½ teaspoon onion powder
- Salt and black pepper to the taste
- 3 tablespoons parsley, chopped
- Cooking spray

Instructions:

In a bowl, mix eggs with milk, cheese, onion powder, salt, pepper and parsley and whisk well.

grease your air fryer with cooking spray, heat it up at 320 degrees F and add bacon and sausage.

Add eggs mix, spread and cook for 20 minutes.

Divide among plates and serve.

Nutrition Facts:

calories 214, fat 5, fiber 8, carbs 12, protein 12

17. Biscuits Casserole

Preparation time: 10 minutes Cooking time: 15 minutes

Ingredients:

- 12 ounces biscuits, quartered
- 3 tablespoons flour
- ½ pound sausage, chopped
- A pinch of salt and black pepper
- 2 and ½ cups milk
- Cooking spray

Instructions:

- grease your air fryer with cooking spray and heat it over 350 degrees F.Add biscuits on the bottom and mix with sausage.
- Add flour, milk, salt and pepper, toss a bit and cook for 15 minutes.
- Divide among plates and serve for breakfast.

Nutrition Facts:

calories 321, fat 4, fiber 7, carbs 12, protein 5

18. Turkey Burrito

Preparation time: 10 minutes Cooking time: 10 minutes

Ingredients:

- 4 slices turkey breast already cooked
- ½ red bell pepper, sliced
- 2 eggs
- 1 small avocado, peeled, pitted and sliced
- 2 tablespoons salsa
- Salt and black pepper to the taste
- 1/8 cup mozzarella cheese, grated
- Tortillas for serving

Instructions:

- In a bowl, whisk eggs with salt and pepper to the taste, pour them in a pan and place it in the air fryer's basket.
- Cook at 400 degrees F for 5 minutes, take pan out of the fryer and transfer eggs to a plate.
- Arrange tortillas on a working surface, divide eggs on them, also divide turkey meat, bell pepper, cheese, salsa and avocado.
- Roll your burritos and place them in your air fryer after you've lined it with some tin foil.
- Heat up the burritos at 300 degrees F for 3 minutes, divide them on plates and serve.

Nutrition Facts:

calories 349, fat 23, fiber 11, carbs 20, protein 21

19. Tofu Scramble

Preparation time: 5 minutes Cooking time: 30 minutes

Ingredients:

- 2 tablespoons soy sauce
- 1 tofu block, cubed
- 1 teaspoon turmeric, ground
- 2 tablespoons extra virgin olive oil
- 4 cups broccoli florets
- ½ teaspoon onion powder
- ½ teaspoon garlic powder
- 2 and ½ cup red potatoes, cubed
- ½ cup yellow onion, chopped
- Salt and black pepper to the taste

Instructions:

- Mix tofu with 1 tablespoon oil, salt, pepper, soy sauce, garlic powder, onion powder, turmeric and onion in a bowl, stir and leave aside. In a separate bowl, combine potatoes with the rest of the oil, a pinch of salt and pepper and toss to coat.
- Put potatoes in your air fryer at 350 degrees F and bake for 15 minutes, shaking once.
- Add tofu and its marinade to your air fryer and bake for 15 minutes.
- Add broccoli to the fryer and cook everything for 5 minutes more.

Nutrition Facts:

calories 140, fat 4, fiber 3, carbs 10, protein 14

20. Oatmeal Casserole

Preparation time: 10 minutes Cooking time: 20 minutes

Ingredients:

- 2 cups rolled oats
- 1 teaspoon baking powder
- 1/3 cup brown sugar
- 1 teaspoon cinnamon powder
- ½ cup chocolate chips
- 2/3 cup blueberries
- 1 banana, peeled and mashed
- 2 cups milk
- 1 eggs
- 2 tablespoons butter
- 1 teaspoon vanilla extract

Instructions:

- In a bowl, mix sugar with baking powder, cinnamon, chocolate chips, blueberries and banana and stir.
- In a separate bowl, mix eggs with vanilla extract and butter and stir.
- Heat up your air fryer at 320 degrees F, grease with cooking spray and add oats on the bottom.
- Add cinnamon mix and eggs mix, toss and cook for 20 minutes. Stir one more time, divide into bowls and serve for breakfast.

Nutrition Facts:

calories 300, fat 4, fiber 7, carbs 12, protein 10

21. Ham Breakfast

Preparation time: 10 minutes Cooking time: 15 minutes

Ingredients:

- 6 cups French bread, cubed
- 4 ounces green chilies, chopped
- 10 ounces ham, cubed
- 4 ounces cheddar cheese, shredded
- 2 cups milk

- 5 eggs
- 1 tablespoon mustard

Salt and black pepper to the taste

Instructions:

- Heat up your air fryer at 350 degrees F and grease it with cooking spray. In a bowl, mix eggs with milk, cheese, mustard, salt and pepper and stir.
- Add bread cubes in your air fryer and mix with chilies and ham. Add eggs mix, spread and cook for 15 minutes.

Nutrition Facts:

calories 200, fat 5, fiber 6, carbs 12, protein 14

22. Tomato and Bacon Breakfast

Preparation time: 10 minutes Cooking time: 30 minutes

Ingredients:

- 1 pound white bread, cubed
- 1 pound smoked bacon, cooked and chopped ¼ cup olive oil
- 1 yellow onion, chopped
- 28 ounces canned tomatoes, chopped
- ½ teaspoon red pepper, crushed
- ½ pound cheddar, shredded
- 2 tablespoons chives, chopped
- ½ pound Monterey jack, shredded
- 2 tablespoons stock
- Salt and black pepper to the taste
- 8 eggs, whisked

Instructions:

- Add the oil to your air fryer and heat it up at 350 degrees F. Add bread, bacon, onion, tomatoes, red pepper and stock and stir.
- Add eggs, cheddar and Monterey jack and cook everything for 20 minutes.
- Divide among plates, sprinkle chives and serve.

Nutrition Facts:

calories 231, fat 5, fiber 7, carbs 12, protein 4

23. Tasty Hash

Preparation time: 10 minutes Cooking time: 15 minutes

Ingredients:

- 16 ounces hash browns
- ¼ cup olive oil
- ½ teaspoon paprika
- ½ teaspoon garlic powder
- Salt and black pepper to the taste
- 1 egg, whisked
- 2 tablespoon chives, chopped
- 1 cup cheddar, shredded

Instructions:

- Add oil to your air fryer, heat it up at 350 degrees F and add hash browns.
- Also add paprika, garlic powder, salt, pepper and egg, toss and cook for 15 minutes.
- Add cheddar and chives, toss, divide among plates and serve.

Nutrition Facts:

calories 213, fat 7, fiber 8, carbs 12, protein 4

24. Creamy Hash Browns

Preparation time: 10 minutes Cooking time: 20 minutes

Ingredients:

- 2 pounds hash browns
- 1 cup whole milk
- 8 bacon slices, chopped
- 9 ounces cream cheese
- 1 yellow onion, chopped
- 1 cup cheddar cheese, shredded
- 6 green onions, chopped
- Salt and black pepper to the taste
- 6 eggs
- Cooking spray

Instructions:

- Heat up your air fryer at 350 degrees F and grease it with cooking spray.

- In a bowl, mix eggs with milk, cream cheese, cheddar cheese, bacon, onion, salt and pepper and whisk well.
- Add hash browns to your air fryer, add eggs mix over them and cook for 20 minutes.

Nutrition Facts:

calories 261, fat 6, fiber 9, carbs 8, protein 12

---

25. Blackberry French Toast

Preparation time: 10 minutes Cooking time: 20 minutes

Ingredients:

- 1 cup blackberry jam, warm
- 12 ounces bread loaf, cubed
- 8 ounces cream cheese, cubed
- 4 eggs
- 1 teaspoon cinnamon powder
- 2 cups half and half
- ½ cup brown sugar
- 1 teaspoon vanilla extract

Instructions:

- grease your air fryer with cooking spray and heat it up at 300 degrees F.
- Add blueberry jam on the bottom, layer half of the bread cubes, then add cream cheese and top with the rest of the bread.
- In a bowl, mix eggs with half and half, cinnamon, sugar and vanilla, whisk well and add over bread mix.
- Cook for 20 minutes, divide among plates and serve for breakfast.

Nutrition Facts:

calories 215, fat 6, fiber 9, carbs 16, protein 6

---

26. Smoked Sausage Breakfast Mix

Preparation time: 10 minutes Cooking time: 30 minutes

Ingredients:

- 1 and ½ pounds smoked sausage, chopped and browned A pinch of salt and black pepper

- 1 and ½ cups grits
- 4 and ½ cups water
- 16 ounces cheddar cheese, shredded
- 1 cup milk
- ¼ teaspoon garlic powder
- 1 and ½ teaspoons thyme, chopped
- Cooking spray
- 4 eggs, whisked

Instructions:

- Put the water in a pot, bring to a boil over medium heat, add grits, stir, cover, cook for 5 minutes and take off heat. Add cheese, stir until it melts and mix with milk, thyme, salt, pepper, garlic powder and eggs and whisk really well.
- Heat up your air fryer at 300 degrees F, grease with cooking spray and add browned sausage.
- Add grits mix, spread and cook for 25 minutes.
- Divide among plates and serve for breakfast.

Nutrition Facts:

calories 321, fat 6, fiber 7, carbs 17, protein 4

---

27. Delicious Potato Frittata

Preparation time: 10 minutes Cooking time: 20 minutes

Ingredients:

- 6 ounces jarred roasted red bell peppers, chopped
- 12 eggs, whisked
- ½ cup parmesan, grated
- 3 garlic cloves, minced
- 2 tablespoons parsley, chopped
- Salt and black pepper to the taste
- 2 tablespoons chives, chopped
- 16 potato wedges
- 6 tablespoons ricotta cheese

Instructions:

- In a bowl, mix eggs with red peppers, garlic, parsley, salt, pepper and ricotta and whisk well. Heat up your air fryer at 300 degrees F and grease it with cooking spray.
- Add half of the potato wedges on the bottom and sprinkle half of the parmesan all over.

- Add half of the egg mix, add the rest of the potatoes and the rest of the parmesan. Add the rest of the eggs mix, sprinkle chives and cook for 20 minutes.
- Divide among plates and serve for breakfast.

Nutrition Facts:

calories 312, fat 6, fiber 9, carbs 16, protein 5

---

28. Asparagus Frittata

Preparation time: 10 minutes Cooking time: 5 minutes

Ingredients:

- 4 eggs, whisked
- 2 tablespoons parmesan, grated
- 4 tablespoons milk
- Salt and black pepper to the taste
- 10 asparagus tips, steamed

Instructions:

- In a bowl, mix eggs with parmesan, milk, salt and pepper and whisk well.
- Heat up your air fryer at 400 degrees F and grease with cooking spray.
- Add asparagus, add eggs mix, toss a bit and cook for 5 minutes.
- Divide frittata on plates and serve for breakfast.

Nutrition Facts:

calories 312, fat 5, fiber 8, carbs 14, protein 2

---

29. Breakfast Muffins

Prep Time: 15 minutes

Ingredients

- 1 cup flour¼ cup mashed banana
- ¼ cup powdered sugar
- 1 tsp. milk
- 1 tsp. chopped walnuts
- ½ tsp. baking powder
- ¼ cup oats¼ cup butter,

Instructions

- Preheat the air fryer to 320 degrees F.
- Place the sugar, walnuts, banana, and butter in a bowl and mix to combine. In another bowl, combine the flour, baking powder and oats.
- Combine the two mixtures together and stir in the milk. Grease a muffin tin and pour the batter in. Bake in your air fryer for 10 minutes. Enjoy.

Nutrition Facts

Calories 214.1, Carbohydrates 24.3 g, Fat 12.7 g, Protein 2.7 g

---

30. Easy, Crispy, And Perfect Air Fryer Bacon

Cook Time: 10 minutes

Total Time: 10 minutes

Servings: 2

Ingredients

- 6 slices Bacon

Instructions

- Line the air fryer basket with parchment paper. Parchment paper will soak up the grease and prevent the air fryer from smoking. Place the bacon on top of the paper. It's ok for the bacon to touch. I do not recommend stacking the bacon.
- Some air fryer brands may need a trivet placed on top of the bacon. If you have an air fryer that is older or is very loud, you may need a trivet to hold the bacon down. I did not need this while using a Power Air Fryer.
- Cook the bacon for 10 minutes at 380 degrees. I did not flip the bacon. Cook for additional time as necessary to reach your desired level of crunch.

Nutrition Facts

- Calories: 75kcal | Protein: 6g | Fat: 6g

---

31. Air Fryer Bacon And Egg Bite Cups (Keto Low-Carb)

Prep Time: 10 Minutes

Cook Time: 15 Minutes

Total Time: 25 Minutes

Ingredients

- 6 large eggs
- 2 tablespoons of heavy whipping cream or milk (any is fine)
- Salt and pepper to taste
- ¼ cup chopped green peppers
- ¼ cup chopped red peppers
- ¼ cup chopped onions
- ¼ cup chopped fresh spinach
- ½ cup shredded cheddar cheese
- ¼ cup shredded mozzarella cheese
- 3 slices of cooked and crumbled bacon

Instructions

- Add the eggs to a large mixing bowl.
- Add in the cream, salt, and pepper to taste.
- Whisk to combine. Sprinkle in the green peppers, red peppers, onions, spinach, cheeses, and bacon. I like to add only half of the ingredients here.
- Whisk to combine.
- I recommend you place the silicone molds in the air fryer before pouring in the egg mixture.
- This way you don't have to move the filled cups. Pour the egg mixture into each of the silicone molds. I didn't need to spray mine and they didn't stick. If you have not used your molds yet, you may want to spray with cooking spray first to be sure.
- Sprinkle in the remaining half of all of the veggies.
- Cook the egg bites cups for 12-15 minutes at 300 degrees. You can test the center of one with a toothpick.
- When the toothpick comes out clean, the eggs have set.

Nutrition Information

- Calories: 119|Total Fat: 9g|Carbohydrates: 2g|Protein: 8g

32. Quick And Easy Air Fryer Sausage

Cook Time: 20 Minutes

Total Time: 20 Minutes

Servings: 5

Ingredients

5 raw and uncooked sausage links

Instructions

- Line the air fryer basket with parchment paper. Parchment paper will soak up the grease and prevent the air fryer from smoking. Place the sausage on top of the paper. It's ok for the sausages to touch.
- Cook for 15 minutes at 360 degrees. Open and flip and cook an additional 5 minutes or until the sausage reaches an internal temperature of 160 degrees. Use a meat thermometer. You can also flip halfway through.
- Cool before serving.

Nutrition Facts

- Calories: 260kcal | Carbohydrates: 3g | Protein: 14g | Fat: 21g

33. Easy Air Fryer French Toast Sticks

Prep Time: 10 minutes

Cook Time: 12 minutes

Total Time: 22 minutes

Ingredients

- 4 slices Texas Toast bread I used Sarah Lee
- 1 tablespoon melted butter measured solid
- 1 egg beaten
- 2 tablespoons sweetener
- 1 teaspoon ground cinnamon
- 1/4 cup milk
- 1 teaspoon vanilla

Instructions

- Cut each slice of bread into 3 strip pieces.
- Add the beaten egg, sweetener, cinnamon, milk, and vanilla to the bowl with the melted butter. Stir to combine.
- Spray the air fryer basket with cooking oil spray.
- Dredge each piece of bread in the French toast batter. Be careful not to dredge each stick in too much batter. You may run out of batter if so.
- Place the French toast sticks in the air fryer basket. Do not overcrowd.
- Spray with cooking oil.
- Air Fry for 8 minutes at 370 degrees.

- Open the air fryer and flip the French toast. Cook for an additional 2-4 minutes or until crisp.

Nutrition Facts

- Calories: 52kcal | Carbohydrates: 7g | Protein: 2g | Fat: 2g

34. Rarebit

Prep Time: 15 minutes

Ingredients:

- 3 slices of bread
- 1 tsp. smoked paprika
- 2 eggs1 tsp. Dijon mustard
- 4 ½ oz. cheddar cheese, grated
- Salt and pepper, to taste

Instructions

- Toast the bread in the air fryer to your liking. In a bowl, whisk the eggs.
- Stir in the mustard, cheddar and paprika.+
- Season with some salt and pepper.Spread the mixture on the toasts.
- Cook the bread slices for about 10 minutes at 360 degrees

Nutrition Facts

Calories 401.5, Carbohydrates 15.4 g, Fat 27.2 g, Protein 26.9

35. Paleo Crispy Air Fryer Sweet Potato Hash Browns

Prep Time: 10 minutes

Cook Time: 20 minutes

Soak in water: 20 minutes

Total Time: 50 minutes

Ingredients

- 4 sweet potatoes peeled
- 2 garlic cloves minced
- 1 teaspoon cinnamon
- 1 teaspoon paprika
- salt and pepper to taste
- 2 teaspoons olive oil

Instructions

- Grate the sweet potatoes using the largest holes of a cheese grater.
- Place the sweet potatoes in a bowl of cold water. Allow the sweet potatoes to soak for 20-25 minutes. Soaking the sweet potatoes in cold water will help remove the starch from the potatoes. This makes them crunchy.
- Drain the water from the potatoes and dry them completely using a paper towel.
- Place the potatoes in a dry bowl. Add the olive oil, garlic, paprika, and salt and pepper to taste. Stir to combine the ingredients.
- Add the potatoes to the air fryer.
- Cook for ten minutes at 400 degrees.
- Open the air fryer and shake the potatoes. Cook for an additional ten minutes.
- Cool before serving.

Nutrition Facts

- Calories: 134kcal

36. Easy Air Fryer Hard Boiled Eggs

Cook Time: 16 minutes

Cooling: 5 minutes

Total Time: 21 minutes

Ingredients

- 6 large eggs You can use whatever size eggs you want and however many you want that will fit in the air fryer basket without stacking.

Instructions

- Place the eggs on the air fryer basket.
- Air fryer for 16 minutes at 260 degrees.
- Open the air fryer and remove the eggs. Place them in a bowl with ice and cold water.
- Allow the eggs to cool for 5 minutes.
- Peel and serve.

Nutrition Facts

- Calories: 72kcal | Protein: 6g | Fat: 5g

37. Easy Air Fryer Cherry Turnovers

Prep Time: 15 minutes

Cook Time: 10 minutes

Total Time: 25 minutes

Ingredients

- 17 oz package puff pastry 4 sheets
- 10 oz can of cherry pie filling
- 1 egg beaten
- 2 tablespoons water
- cooking oil I use olive oil.

Instructions

- Lay the pastry sheets on a flat surface.
- Unfold both sheets of the puff pastry dough. Cut each sheet into 4 squares, making 8 squares total.
- Beat the egg in a small bowl along with the water to create an egg wash.
- Use a cooking brush or your fingers to brush along the edges of each square with the egg wash.
- Load 1 to 1 1/2 tablespoons of cherry pie filling into the middle of each square sheet. Do not overfill the pastry.
- Fold the dough over diagonally to create a triangle and seal the dough. Use the back of a fork to press lines into the open edges of each turnover to seal.
- Make 3 slits into the top of the crust to vent the turnovers.
- Brush the top of each turnover with the egg wash. (You can also do this step after you have placed them in the air fryer basket.)
- Spritz the air fryer basket with cooking oil and add the turnovers. Make sure they do not touch and do not stack the turnovers. Cook in batches if needed.
- Air fry at 370 degrees for 8 minutes. I did not flip.
- Allow the pastries to cool for 2-3 minutes before removing them from the air fryer. This will ensure they do not stick.

Nutrition Facts

- Calories: 224kcal | Carbohydrates: 27g | Protein: 4g | Fat: 12g

---

38. Air Fryer Blueberry Muffins

Prep Time: 10 minutes

Cook Time: 15 minutes

Total Time: 25 minutes

Ingredients

- 1 1/2 cups all-purpose or white whole wheat flour
- 3/4 cup old-fashioned oats (oatmeal)
- 1/2 cup brown sweetener Light brown sugar can be used if preferred
- 1 tablespoon baking powder
- 1/2 teaspoon cinnamon
- 1/2 teaspoon salt
- 1 cup milk
- 1/4 cup melted unsalted butter (at room temperature)
- 2 eggs (at room temperature)
- 2 teaspoons vanilla
- 1 cup blueberries You can use fresh or frozen blueberries. If using frozen, do not thaw.

Instructions

- Combine the flour, rolled oats, salt, cinnamon, brown sweetener, and baking powder in a large mixing bowl. Mix.
- Combine the milk, eggs, vanilla, and butter in a separate medium-sized bowl. Mix using a silicone spoon.
- Add the wet ingredients to the dry ingredients in the mixing bowl. Stir.
- Fold in the blueberries and stir.
- Divide the batter among 12 silicone muffin cups and add them to the air fryer. Spraying the liners with oil is optional. The muffins generally don't stick.
- Place the air fryer at 350 degrees. Monitor the muffins closely for proper cook time, as every model will cook differently. The muffins will need to cook for 11-15 minutes. Insert a toothpick into the middle of a muffin, if it returns clean the muffins have finished baking. Mine was ready at about 13 minutes.

Nutrition Facts

- Calories: 121kcal | Carbohydrates: 13g | Protein: 3g | Fat: 5g

---

39. Air Fryer Loaded Hash Browns

Prep Time: 10 minutes

Cook Time: 20 minutes

Soak in water: 20 minutes

Total Time: 50 minutes

Ingredients

- 3 russet potatoes
- 1/4 cup chopped green peppers
- 1/4 cup chopped red peppers
- 1/4 cup chopped onions
- 2 garlic cloves chopped
- 1 teaspoon paprika
- salt and pepper to taste
- 2 teaspoons olive oil

Instructions

- Grate the potatoes using the largest holes of a cheese grater.
- Place the potatoes in a bowl of cold water. Allow the potatoes to soak for 20-25 minutes. Soaking the potatoes in cold water will help remove the starch from the potatoes. This makes them crunchy.
- Drain the water from the potatoes and dry them completely using a paper towel.
- Place the potatoes in a dry bowl. Add the garlic, paprika, olive oil, and salt and pepper to taste. Stir to combine the ingredients.
- Add the potatoes to the air fryer.
- Cook for ten minutes at 400 degrees.
- Open the air fryer and shake the potatoes.
- Add the chopped peppers and onions. Cook for an additional ten minutes.
- Cool before serving.

Nutrition Facts

- Calories: 246kcal | Carbohydrates: 42g | Protein: 6g | Fat: 3g

40. Air Fryer Homemade Strawberry Pop-Tarts

Prep Time: 15 minutes

Cook Time: 10 minutes

Total Time: 25 minutes

Ingredients

- 2 refrigerated pie crusts I used Pillsbury.
- 1 teaspoon cornstarch

- 1/3 cup low-sugar strawberry preserves I used Smucker's.
- Cooking oil I used olive oil.
- 1/2 cup plain, non-fat vanilla Greek yogurt
- 1 oz cream cheese I used reduced-fat.
- 1 tablespoon sweetener
- 1 teaspoon sugar sprinkles

Instructions

- Lay the pie crust on a flat working surface. I used a bamboo cutting board.
- Using a knife or pizza cutter, cut the 2 pie crusts into 6 rectangles (3 from each pie crust). Each should be fairly long as you will fold it over to close the pop tart.
- Add the preserves and cornstarch to a bowl and mix well.
- Add a tablespoon of the preserves to the crust. Place the preserves in the upper area of the crust.
- Fold each over to close the pop tarts.
- Using a fork, make imprints in each of the pop tarts, to create vertical and horizontal lines along the edges.
- Place the pop tarts in the Air Fryer. Do not stack, cook in batches if needed. Spray with cooking oil.
- Cook on 370 degrees for 10 minutes. You may want to check in on the Pop-Tarts for around 8 minutes to ensure they aren't too crisp for your liking.
- Combine the Greek yogurt, cream cheese, and sweetener in a bowl to create the frosting.
- Allow the Pop-Tarts to cool before removing them from the Air Fryer. This is important. If you do not allow them to cool, they may break.
- Remove the pop tarts from the Air Fryer. Top each with the frosting. Sprinkle sugar sprinkles throughout.

Nutrition Facts

- Calories: 274kcal | Carbohydrates: 32g | Protein: 3g | Fat: 14g

41. Quick And Easy Air Fryer Grilled Cheese

Prep Time: 5 minutes

Cook Time: 7 minutes

Total Time: 12 minutes

Ingredients

- 4 slices of bread I used 100% Whole Wheat
- 1 tablespoon butter melted
- 2 slices mild cheddar cheese
- 5-6 slices cooked bacon Optional
- 2 slices mozzarella cheese

Instructions

- Heat the butter in the microwave for 10-15 seconds to soften.
- Spread the butter onto one side of each of the slices of bread.
- Place a slice of buttered bread (butter side down) onto the air fryer basket.
- Load the remaining ingredients in the following order: a slice of cheddar cheese, sliced cooked bacon, a slice of mozzarella cheese, and top with another slice of bread (butter side up).
- If you have an air fryer that is very loud, you will likely need to use a layer rack or trivet to hold down the sandwich to keep it from flying. My Power Air Fryer does not need this, but my louder Black + Decker air fryer requires this to anchor the sandwich and keep it from flying around inside the air fryer.
- Cook for 4 minutes at 370 degrees.
- Open the air fryer. Flip the sandwich. Cook for an additional 3 minutes.
- Remove and serve.

Nutrition Facts

- Calories: 486kcal | Carbohydrates: 25g | Protein: 25g | Fat: 26g

---

42. Air Fryer Sweet Potato Hash

Prep Time: 10 minutes

Cook Time: 25 minutes

Total Time: 35 minutes

Ingredients

- 3 medium sweet potatoes Chopped into chunks about 1 inch thick.
- 1/2 cup diced white onions
- 3 slices bacon cooked and crumbled.
- 1/2 cup chopped green peppers

- 2 garlic cloves minced
- 1/3 cup diced celery
- 1 tablespoon olive oil
- 1 teaspoon Tony Chachere Lite Creole Seasoning
- 1/2 teaspoon paprika
- 1/2 teaspoon dried chives

Instructions

- Combine the sweet potato chunks, onions, celery, green peppers, and garlic in a large bowl.
- Drizzle the olive oil throughout and then sprinkle the Tony Chachere Lite Creole Seasoning and paprika. Stir and mix well to combine.
- Add the sweet potato mix to the air fryer basket. Do not overcrowd the basket. Cook in batches if needed.
- Air fry for 10 minutes at 400 degrees.
- Open the air fryer and shake the basket. Air fry for an additional 2-7 minutes until the sweet potatoes are crisp on the outside and tender to touch when pierced with a fork.
- Sprinkle the crumbled bacon and dried chives throughout.

Nutrition Facts

- Calories: 167kcal | Carbohydrates: 19g | Protein: 4g | Fat: 7g

---

43. Easy Air Fryer Roasted Potatoes

Prep Time: 10 minutes

Cook Time: 15 minutes

Total Time: 25 minutes

Ingredients

- 2 russet potatoes peeled and sliced into large chunks.
- 1 teaspoon olive oil
- 2 sprigs of fresh rosemary, use 1 sprig if you prefer a hint of rosemary flavor.
- 2 minced garlic cloves
- 1/2 teaspoon onion powder
- salt and pepper to taste
- cooking oil I use olive oil.

Instructions

- Drizzle the potatoes with olive oil and season

with garlic, onion powder, salt, and pepper to taste.

- Spray the air fryer basket with cooking oil.
- Add the potatoes to the air fryer basket along with the thyme. Do not overfill the basket. Cook in batches if needed.
- Air fry for 10 minutes at 400 degrees.
- Open the air fryer and shake the basket. Air fry for an additional 2-7 minutes until the sweet potatoes are crisp on the outside and tender to touch when pierced with a fork.
- Cool before serving.

Nutrition Facts

- Calories: 68kcal | Carbohydrates: 13g | Protein: 2g | Fat: 1g

44. Air Fryer Cinnamon Sugar Donuts

Prep Time: 5 minutes

Cook Time: 16 minutes

Total Time: 21 minutes

Ingredients

- 8 oz can of biscuits
- 1 teaspoon ground cinnamon
- 1-2 teaspoons stevia 1/4 cup of table sugar can be substituted
- cooking oil spray I used avocado oil

Instructions

- Lay the biscuits on a flat surface. Use a small circle cookie cutter or a biscuit cutter to cut holes in the middle of the biscuits. I used a protein powder scoop
- Spray the air fryer basket with oil.
- Place the donuts in the air fryer. Spray the donuts with oil. Do not stack the donuts. Cook in two batches if needed.
- Cook for 4 minutes at 360 degrees.
- Open the air fryer and flip the donuts. Cook for an additional 4 minutes.
- Repeat for the remaining donuts.
- Spritz the donuts with additional oil.
- Add the cinnamon and sugar to separate bowls.
- Dip the donuts in the cinnamon and sugar. Serve!

Nutrition Facts

- Calories: 186kcal | Carbohydrates: 25g | Protein: 3g | Fat: 9g

45. Air Fryer Fried Pork Chops Southern Style

Prep Time: 5 minutes

Cook Time: 20 minutes

Optional marinate: 30 minutes

Total Time: 25 minutes

Ingredients

- 4 pork chops (bone-in or boneless)
- 3 tbsp buttermilk I used fat-free
- 1/4 cup all-purpose flour
- Seasoning Salt to taste You can also use either a chicken or pork rub.
- pepper to taste
- 1 Ziploc bag
- cooking oil spray

Instructions

- Pat the pork chops dry.
- Season the pork chops with the seasoning salt and pepper.
- Drizzle the buttermilk over the pork chops.
- Place the pork chops in a Ziploc bag with the flour. Shake to fully coat.
- Marinate for 30 minutes. This step is optional. This helps the flour adhere to the pork chops.
- Place the pork chops in the air fryer. I do not recommend you stack. Cook in batches if necessary.
- Spray the pork chops with cooking oil.
- Cook the pork chops for 15 minutes at 380 degrees. Flip the pork chops over to the other side after 10 minutes.

Nutritional Facts

- Calories: 173kcal | Carbohydrates: 7g | Protein: 22g | Fat: 6g

46. Ninja Foodi Low-Carb Breakfast Casserole {Air Fryer}

Prep Time: 10 Minutes

Cook Time: 15 Minutes

Total Time: 25 Minutes

Ingredients

- 1 LB Ground Sausage
- 1/4 Cup Diced White Onion
- 1 Diced Green Bell Pepper
- 8 Whole Eggs, Beaten
- 1/2 Cup Shredded Colby Jack Cheese
- 1 Tsp Fennel Seed
- 1/2 Tsp Garlic Salt

Instructions

- If you are using the Ninja Foodi, use the saute function to brown the sausage in the pot of the food. If you are using an air fryer, you can use a skillet to do this.
- Add in the onion and pepper and cook along with the ground sausage until the veggies are soft and the sausage is cooked.
- Using the 8.75-inch pan or the Air Fryer pan, spray it with non-stick cooking spray.
- Place the ground sausage mixture on the bottom of the pan.
- Top evenly with cheese.
- Pour the beaten eggs evenly over the cheese and sausage.
- Add fennel seed and garlic salt evenly over the eggs.
- Place the rack in the low position in the Ninja Foodi, and then place the pan on top.
- Set to Air Crisp for 15 minutes at 390 degrees.
- If you are using an air fryer, place the dish directly into the basket of the air fryer and cook for 15 minutes at 390 degrees.
- Carefully remove and serve.

Nutrition Information

- Calories:282|Totalfat:23g|Saturatedfat:8g|Transfat:12g|Cholesterol:227mg|Sodium: 682mg|Carbohydrates: 3g|Sugar: 2g|Protein: 15g

---

47. Air Fryer Donuts

Prep Time: 10 Mins

Cook Time: 5 Mins

Total Time: 15 Mins

Ingredients

- 16 oz refrigerated flaky jumbo biscuits
- 1/2 c. Granulated white sugar
- 2 tsp ground cinnamon
- 4 tbsp butter melted
- Olive or coconut oil spray

Instructions

- Combine sugar and cinnamon in a shallow bowl; set aside.
- Remove the biscuits from the can, separate them and place them on a flat surface. Use a 1-inch round biscuit cutter (or similarly-sized bottle cap) to cut holes out of the center of each biscuit.
- Lightly coat the air fryer basket with olive or coconut oil spray. Do not use a non-stick spray like Pam because it can damage the coating on the basket.
- Place 4 donuts in a single layer in the air fryer basket. Make sure they are not touching.
- Air Fry at 360 degrees F for 5 minutes or until lightly browned.
- Remove donuts from Air Fryer, dip in melted butter then roll in cinnamon sugar to coat. Serve immediately.

Nutrition Facts

- Calories: 316kcal
- Carbohydrates: 42g
- Protein: 3g
- Fat: 15g
- Saturated Fat: 5g
- Cholesterol: 15mg
- Sodium: 585mg
- Potassium: 127mg
- Fiber: 1g
- Sugar: 16g
- Vitamin A: 175IU
- Calcium: 36mg
- Iron: 1.9mg

---

48. Air Fryer Breakfast Sausage

Prep Time: 10 Minutes

Cook Time: 10 Minutes

Total Time: 20 Minutes

Ingredients

- 1 lb ground pork
- 1 lb ground turkey
- 2 tsp fennel seeds
- 2 tsp dry rubbed sage
- 2 tsp garlic powder
- 1 tsp paprika
- 1 tsp sea salt
- 1 tsp dried thyme
- 1 tbsp real maple syrup

Instructions

- Begin by mixing the pork and turkey in a large bowl. In a small bowl, mix the remaining ingredients: fennel, sage, garlic powder, paprika, salt, and thyme. Pour spices into the meat and continue to mix until the spices are completely incorporated.
- Spoon into balls (about 2-3 tbsp of meat), and flatten into patties. Place inside the air fryer, you will probably have to do this in 2 batches.
- Set the temperature to 370 degrees, and cook for 10 minutes. Remove from the air fryer and repeat with the remaining sausage.

Nutritional Value

- Calories: 68kcal
- Carbohydrates: 13g
- Protein: 2g
- Fat: 1g
- Sodium: 400g

---

49. Crispy Bacon In The Air Fryer

Cook Time: 10 Minutes

Total Time: 10 Minutes

Ingredients

- 1 Pound of Bacon

Instructions

- Add bacon into the air fryer basket, evenly. This may take 2 batches to cook all of the bacon, depending on size.
- Cook at 350 degrees for 5 minutes.
- Turn bacon and cook an additional 5 minutes or until your desired crispiness.

- Remove bacon with tongs and place on a paper towel-lined plate.
- Let cool and serve.

Nutrition Information

- Calories:177|Totalfat:33g|Saturatedfat:5g|Transfat:0g|Cholesterol:37mg|Sodium: 637mg|Carbohydrates: 1g|Sugar: 0g|Protein: 13g

---

50. Air Fryer Breakfast Stuffed Peppers

Prep Time: 5 minutes

Cook Time: 13 minutes

Total Time: 18 minutes

Servings: 2

Ingredients

- 1 bell pepper halved, middle seeds removed
- 4 eggs
- 1 tsp olive oil
- 1 pinch salt and pepper
- 1 pinch sriracha flakes for a bit of spice, optional

Instructions

- Cut bell peppers in half lengthwise and remove seeds and middle leaving the edges intact like bowls.
- Use your finger to rub a bit of olive oil just on the exposed edges (where it was cut).
- Crack two eggs into each bell pepper half. Sprinkle with desired spices.
- Set them on a trivet inside your Ninja Foodi or directly inside your other brand of the air fryer.
- Close the lid on your air fryer (the one attached to the Ninja Foodi machine).
- Turn the machine on, press the air crisper button at 390 degrees for 13 minutes (times will vary slightly according to how well done you like your egg but this was perfect for us).
- Alternatively, if you'd rather have your bell pepper and eggless brown on the outside add just one egg to your pepper and set the air fryer to 330 degrees for 15 minutes. (for an over hard egg consistency)

Nutrition Facts

- Fat: 10g
- Saturated Fat: 3g
- Cholesterol: 327mg
- Sodium: 146mg
- Potassium: 246mg
- Carbohydrates: 4g
- Fiber: 1g
- Sugar: 2g
- Protein: 11g
- Vitamin C: 76mg
- Calcium: 49mg
- Iron: 1.8mg

51. Air Fryer Bacon And Egg Breakfast Biscuit Bombs

Prep Time: 35 Mins

Cook Time: 15 Mins

Total: 50 MIN

Ingredients

- Biscuit Bombs
- 4 slices bacon, cut into 1/2-inch pieces
- 1 tablespoon butter
- 2 eggs, beaten
- 1/4 teaspoon pepper
- 1 can (10.2 oz) Pillsbury Grands! Southern Homestyle refrigerated Buttermilk biscuits (5 biscuits)
- 2 oz sharp cheddar cheese, cut into ten 3/4-inch cubes
- Egg Wash
- 1 egg
- 1 tablespoon water

Instruction

- Prevent your screen from going dark while you cook.
- Cut two 8-inch rounds of cooking parchment paper. Place one round at bottom of the air fryer basket. Spray with cooking spray.
- In 10-inch nonstick skillet, cook bacon over medium-high heat until crisp. Remove from pan; place on paper towel. Carefully wipe skillet with a paper towel. Add butter to skillet; melt over medium heat. Add 2 beaten eggs and pepper to skillet; cook until eggs are thickened but still moist, stirring frequently. Remove from heat; stir

in bacon. Cool 5 minutes.
- Meanwhile, separate dough into 5 biscuits; separate each biscuit into 2 layers. Press each into a 4-inch round. Spoon 1 heaping tablespoonful of egg mixture onto the center of each round. Top with one piece of cheese. Gently fold edges up and over filling; pinch to seal. In a small bowl, beat the remaining egg and water. Brush biscuits on all sides with egg wash.
- Place 5 of the biscuit bombs, seam sides down, on parchment in the air fryer basket. Spray both sides of the second parchment round with cooking spray. Top biscuit bombs in a basket with a second parchment round, then top with remaining 5 biscuit bombs.
- Set to 325°F; cook 8 minutes. Remove top parchment round; using tongs, carefully turn biscuits, and place in basket in a single layer. Cook 4 to 6 minutes longer or until cooked through (at least 165°F).

Nutrition Information

- Calories: 200
- Total Fat: 12g
- Saturated Fat: 6g
- Cholesterol: 85mg
- Sodium: 440mg
- Potassium: 50mg
- Total Carbohydrate: 17g
- Sugars: 3g
- Protein: 7g

52. Air Fryer Sausage Breakfast Casserole

Prep Time: 10 Minutes

Cook Time: 20 Minutes

Total Time: 30 Minutes

Ingredients

- 1 Lb Hash Browns
- 1 Lb Ground Breakfast Sausage
- 1 Green Bell Pepper Diced
- 1 Red Bell Pepper Diced
- 1 Yellow Bell Pepper Diced
- 1/4 Cup Sweet Onion Diced
- 4 Eggs

Instructions

- Foil line the basket of your air fryer.
- Place the hash browns on the bottom.
- Top it with the uncooked sausage.
- Evenly place the peppers and onions on top.
- Cook on 355* for 10 minutes.
- Open the air fryer and mix up the casserole a bit if needed.
- Crack each egg in a bowl, then pour right on top of the casserole.
- Cook on 355* for another 10 minutes.
- Serve with salt and pepper to taste.

Nutrition Information

- Calories:517|Totalfat:37g|Saturatedfat:10g|Transfat:0g|Cholesterol:227mg|Sodium: 1092mg|Carbohydrates:27g|Sugar: 4g|Protein: 21g

---

53. Air Fryer Baked Egg Cups w/ Spinach & Cheese

Prep Time: 5 mins

Cook Time: 10 mins

Total Time: 15 mins

Ingredients

- 1 large egg
- 1 tablespoon (15 ml) milk or half & half
- 1 tablespoon (15 ml) frozen spinach, thawed (or sautéed fresh spinach)
- 1-2 teaspoons (5 ml) grated cheese
- Salt, to taste
- Black pepper, to taste
- Cooking spray, for muffin cups or ramekins

Instructions

- Spray inside of silicone muffin cups or ramekin with oil spray.
- Add egg, milk, spinach, and cheese into the muffin cup or ramekin.
- Season with salt and pepper. Gently stir ingredients into egg whites without breaking the yolk.
- Air Fry at 330°F for about 6-12 minutes (single egg cups usually take about 6 minutes - multiple or doubled up cups take as much as 12. As you add more egg cups, you will need to add more time.)

- Cooking in a ceramic ramekin may take a little longer. If you want runny yolks, cook for less time. Keep checking the eggs after 5 minutes to ensure the egg is to your preferred texture.

Nutrition Facts

- Calories: 115kcal | Carbohydrates: 1g | Protein: 10g | Fat: 7g | Saturated Fat: 2g | Cholesterol: 216mg | Sodium: 173mg | Potassium: 129mg | Sugar: 1g | Vitamin A: 2040IU | Calcium: 123mg | Iron: 1.3mg

---

54. Airfryer French Toast Sticks Recipe

Prep Time: 5 minutes

Cook Time: 12 minutes

Total Time: 17 minutes

Ingredients

- 4 pieces bread (whatever kind and thickness desired)
- 2 Tbsp butter (or margarine, softened)
- 2 eggs (gently beaten)
- 1 pinch salt
- 1 pinch cinnamon
- 1 pinch nutmeg
- 1 pinch ground cloves
- 1 tsp icing sugar (and/or maple syrup for garnish and serving)

Instructions

- Preheat Airfryer to 180* Celsius.
- In a bowl, gently beat together two eggs, a sprinkle of salt, a few heavy shakes of cinnamon, and small pinches of both nutmeg and ground cloves.
- Butter both sides of bread slices and cut into strips.
- Dredge each strip in the egg mixture and arrange it in Airfryer (you will have to cook in two batches).
- After 2 minutes of cooking, pause the Airfryer, take out the pan, making sure you place the pan on a heat-safe surface and spray the bread with cooking spray.
- Once you have generously coated the strips, flip and spray the second side as well.

- Return pan to the fryer and cook for 4 more minutes, checking after a couple of minutes to ensure they are cooking evenly and not burning.
- When the egg is cooked and the bread is golden brown, remove it from Airfryer and serve immediately.
- To garnish and serve, sprinkle with icing sugar, top with whip cream, drizzle with maple syrup, or serve with a small bowl of syrup for dipping.

Nutrition Facts

- Calories:178Kcal|Totalfat:15g|Saturatedfat:8g| Transfat:12g|Cholesterol:194mg|Sodium: 193mg|Carbohydrates: 2g|Sugar: 1g|Protein: 5g| Iron: 0.8mg| Calcium: 25mg

55. Air Fryer Breakfast Frittata

Prep Time: 15 mins

Cook Time: 20 mins

Total Time: 35 mins

Ingredients

- ¼ pound breakfast sausage fully cooked and crumbled
- 4 eggs, lightly beaten
- ½ cup shredded Cheddar-Monterey Jack cheese blend
- 2 tablespoons red bell pepper, diced
- 1 green onion, chopped
- 1 pinch cayenne pepper (Optional)
- cooking spray

Direction

- Combine sausage, eggs, Cheddar-Monterey Jack cheese, bell pepper. onion, and cayenne in a bowl and mix to combine.
- Preheat the air fryer to 360 degrees F (180 degrees C). Spray a nonstick 6x2-inch cake pan with cooking spray.
- Place egg mixture in the prepared cake pan.
- Cook in the air fryer until frittata is set, 18 to 20 minutes.

Nutrition Facts

Calories: 380| Protein 31.2g| Carbohydrates 2.9g| Fat 27.4g| Cholesterol 443mg| Sodium 693.5mg| Vitamin A

Iu: 894.6IU|Vitamin B6: 0.3mg|Vitamin C: 13.4mg|Calcium:69.2mg|Iron:3mg|Magnesium:26.7mg |Potassium:328.4mg| Sodium: 693.5mg|Thiamin: 0.1mg

56. Breakfast Potatoes In The Air Fryer

Prep Time: 2 minutes

Cook Time: 15 minutes

Total Time: 17 minutes

Servings: 2

Ingredients

- 5 medium potatoes, peeled and cut to 1-inch cubes (Yukon Gold works best)
- 1 tbsp oil
- Breakfast Potato Seasoning
- 1/2 tsp kosher salt
- 1/2 tsp smoked paprika
- 1/2 tsp garlic powder
- 1/4 tsp black ground pepper

Instructions

- Preheat the air fryer for about 2-3 minutes at 400F degrees. This will give you the crispiest potatoes.
- Meanwhile, toss the potatoes with breakfast potato seasoning and oil until thoroughly coated.
- Spray the air fryer basket with a nonstick spray. Add the potatoes and cook for about 15 minutes, stopping and shaking the basket 2-3 times throughout to promote even cooking.
- Transfer to a plate and serve right away.

Nutrition Facts

- Calories: 375
- Fat: 7g
- Sodium: 635mg
- Potassium: 2199mg63
- Carbohydrates: 67g
- Fiber: 13
- Protein: 13g
- Vitamin A: 245IU
- Vitamin: C 60.7mg
- Calcium: 160mg
- Iron: 17.4mg

57. Air-Fried Breakfast Bombs Are A Portable Healthy Meal

Active Time: 20 Mins

Total Time: 25 Mins

Yield: Serves 2

Ingredients

- 3 center-cut bacon slices
- 3 large eggs, lightly beaten
- 1 ounce 1/3-less-fat cream cheese, softened
- 1 tablespoon chopped fresh chives
- 4 ounces fresh prepared whole-wheat pizza dough
- Cooking spray

How To Make It

Step 1

Cook bacon in a medium skillet over medium until very crisp, about 10 minutes. Remove bacon from pan; crumble. Add eggs to bacon drippings in pan; cook, stirring often, until almost set but still loose, about 1 minute. Transfer eggs to a bowl; stir in cream cheese, chives, and crumbled bacon.

Step 2

Divide dough into 4 equal pieces. Roll each piece on a lightly floured surface into a 5-inch circle. Place one-fourth of the egg mixture in the center of each dough circle. Brush outside edge of dough with water; wrap dough around egg mixture to form a purse, pinching together dough at the seams.

Step 3

Place dough purses in a single layer in an air fryer basket; coat well with cooking spray. Cook at 350°F until golden brown, 5 to 6 minutes, checking after 4 minutes.

Nutritional Information

- Calories: 305
- Fat: 15g
- Sat fat: 5g
- Unsatfat: 8g
- Protein: 19g
- Carbohydrate: 26g
- Fiber: 2g
- Sugars: 1g
- Added sugars: 0g
- Sodium: 548mg

58. Air Fryer Scrambled Eggs

Prep Time: 3 Minutes

Cook Time: 9 Minutes

Total Time: 12 Minutes

Ingredients

- 1/3 tablespoon unsalted butter
- 2 eggs
- 2 tablespoons milk
- Salt and pepper to taste
- 1/8 cup cheddar cheese

Instructions

- Place butter in an oven/air fryer-safe pan and place inside the air fryer.
- Cook at 300 degrees until butter is melted, about 2 minutes.
- Whisk together the eggs and milk, then add salt and pepper to taste.
- Place eggs in a pan and cook it at 300 degrees for 3 minutes, then push eggs to the inside of the pan to stir them around.
- Cook for 2 more minutes then add cheddar cheese, stirring the eggs again.
- Cook 2 more minutes.
- Remove pan from the air fryer and enjoy them immediately.

Nutrition Information

- Calories:126Kcal|Totalfat:9g|Saturatedfat:4g|Transfat:0g|Cholesterol200mg|Sodium: 275mg|Carbohydrates: 1g|Sugar: 1g|Protein: 9g| Iron: 0.8mg| Calcium: 4mg

59. Air Fryer Banana Bread

Prep Time: 10 minutes

Cook Time: 28 minutes

Total Time: 38 minutes

Servings: 8

Ingredients

- 3/4 c all-purpose flour
- 1/4 tsp baking soda

- 1/4 tsp salt
- 1 egg
- 2 bananas overripe, mashed
- 1/2 tsp vanilla
- 1/4 c sour cream
- 1/4 c vegetable oil
- 1/2 c sugar
- 7" bundt pan

Instructions

- Mix dry ingredients in one bowl and wet in another. Slowly combine the two until flour is incorporated, do not overmix.
- Spray inside of 7" bundt pan with nonstick spray and pour in batter.
- Place inside air fryer basket and close. Set to 310 degrees for 28 minutes.
- Remove when done and allow to sit in the pan for 5 minutes. Then gently flip over on a plate. Drizzle melted frosting on the top, slice, and serve.

Nutrition Facts

- Calories: 198
- Fat: 9g
- Saturated Fat: 7g
- Cholesterol: 24mg
- Sodium: 121mg
- Potassium: 136mg
- Carbohydrates: 28g
- Fiber: 1g
- Sugar: 16g
- Protein 2g
- Vitamin A: 93IU
- Vitamin C: 3mg
- Calcium: 14mg
- Iron: 1mg

60.   Easy Air Fryer Breakfast Frittata

Prep Time: 5 min

Cook Time: 10 min

Total Time: 15 minutes

Yield: 4 servings

Ingredients

- 4 eggs
- ½ cup shredded sharp cheddar cheese
- ¼ cup fresh spinach, chopped
- 2 scallions, chopped
- 2 tablespoons half and half
- salt and pepper to taste

Instructions

- In a medium bowl, beat eggs with half and half.
- Stir in cheese, spinach, scallions, salt, and pepper.
- Spray a 6" cake pan with cooking spray (very important). Pour mixture into the pan.
- Air fry at 350 degrees (F) for 10-14 minutes. A toothpick inserted will come out clean when done.
- Let cool for 5 minutes before removing from pan and serving.

Nutritional Value

- Calories:178Kcal|Totalfat:15g|Saturatedfat:8g| Transfat:12g|Cholesterol:194mg|Sodium: 193mg|Carbohydrates: 2g|Sugar: 1g|Protein: 5g| Iron:0.8mg| Calcium: 25mg

61.   Air Fryer Breakfast Pizza

Prep Time: 5 Minutes

Cook Time: 15 Minutes

Total Time: 20 Minutes

Ingredients

- Crescent Dough
- 3 scrambled eggs
- crumbled sausage
- 1/2 chopped pepper
- 1/2 cup cheddar cheese
- 1/2 cup mozzarella cheese

Instructions

- Spray Pan with oil, Spread dough in the bottom of a Fat daddio or springform pan. Place in the air fryer on 350 for 5 minutes or until the top is slightly brown
- Remove from the air fryer . Top with Eggs, sausage, peppers, and cheese, Or use your favorite toppings.

- Place in the air fryer for an additional 5-10 minutes or until the top is golden brown.

Nutrition Information

Calories:250Kcal|Totalfat:19g|Saturatedfat:9g|Transfat:0g|Cholesterol:167mg|Sodium: 193mg|Carbohydrates: 2g|Sugar: 2g|Protein: 14g| Iron: 1mg| Calcium: 13mg

62. Air Fryer Breakfast Sweet Potato Skins

Prep Time: 7 Minutes

Cook Time: 23 Minutes

Total Time: 30 Minutes

Ingredients

- 2 medium sweet potatoes
- 2 tsp. olive oil
- 4 eggs
- 1/4 c. whole milk
- salt and pepper
- 4 slices cooked bacon
- 2 green onions, sliced

Instructions

- Wash the sweet potatoes and add 3-4 cuts to the potatoes. Microwave for 6-8 minutes, depending on their size until they are soft.
- Using an oven mitt, slice the potatoes in half lengthwise. Scoop out the potato flesh, leaving 1/4 inch around the edges. Save the scooped sweet potato for another use.
- Brush the potato skins with olive oil and sprinkle with sea salt. Arrange the skins in your Air Fryer basket and cook at 400° (or the highest available temp) for 10 minutes.
- Meanwhile, add the eggs, milk, salt, and pepper to a non-stick skillet. Cook the mixture over medium heat, stirring constantly, until there are no longer any visible liquid eggs.
- Top each cooked potato skin with 1/4 of the scrambled eggs and 1 slice of crumbled bacon. Cover with shredded cheese and cook for 3 minutes, or until the cheese is melted.
- Serve topped with green onion.

Nutritional Value

- Calories:208Kcal|Totalfat:12g|Saturatedfat:4g| Transfat:0g|Cholesterol:199mg|Sodium: 367mg|Carbohydrates: 14g|Sugar: 5g|Protein: 12g| Iron: 2mg|

63. Air Fryer French Toast Sticks

Prep Time: 7 Minutes

Cook Time: 8 Minutes

Total Time: 15 Minutes

Ingredients

- 12 slices Texas Toast
- 1 cup milk
- 5 large eggs
- 4 tbsp. butter, melted
- 1 tsp. vanilla extract
- 1/4 cup granulated sugar
- 1 tbsp. cinnamon
- Maple syrup, optional

Instructions

- Slice each bread slice into thirds.
- In a bowl, add the milk, eggs, butter, and vanilla. Whisk until combined.
- In a separate bowl, add the cinnamon and sugar.
- Dip each breadstick quickly into the egg mixture.
- Sprinkle the sugar mixture onto both sides.
- Place into the air fryer basket and cook at 350°F for about 8 minutes or until just crispy.
- Remove from basket and allow to cool. Serve with maple syrup, if desired.

Nutrition Information

- Calories: 170| Total Fat: 8g| Saturated Fat: 4g| Cholesterol: 90mg| Sodium: 183mg| Fiber: 1g| Sugar: 7g| Protein: 6g

64. Air Fryer Breakfast Taquitos Recipe

Prep Time: 25 mins

Cook Time: 6 mins

Total Time: 31 mins

Ingredients

- pound ground turkey sausage

- 2 teaspoons onion powder
- 2 cloves garlic minced
- ½ teaspoon salt
- ½ teaspoon pepper
- 6 large eggs
- 16 small low carb flour or whole wheat tortillas
- 1 cup fat-free shredded Mexican blend or cheddar cheese
- 2 tablespoons I Can't Believe It's Not Butter Melted

Instructions

Preheat oven to 400 F degrees. Lightly spray a 9x13 baking dish with coconut oil

In a large skillet, cook sausage until it's is no longer pink. Drain. Add garlic and cook until soft. Season with onion powder, salt, and pepper. In a bowl, whisk eggs and pour into the skillet and cook until eggs are scrambled. Remove skillet from the stovetop. Add mixture to a bowl and set aside. Add tortillas to the microwave for 20 seconds. This softens them and makes it easier to roll them. On a flat surface, top a tortilla with 2 tablespoons of the skillet mixture. Top with a sprinkle of cheese. Roll the tortilla tightly and place in the baking dish. Brush with melted butter. Repeat until the remaining tortillas are filled. Pre-heat Air Fryer to 350° for 1 minute. Bake for 3 minutes and turn, and bake for an additional 2-3 minutes or until tortillas are golden brown and crispy.

Serve with your favorite toppings!

Nutritional Facts

Calories:178Kcal|Totalfat:15g|Saturatedfat:8g|Transfat:12g|Cholesterol:194mg|Sodium: 193mg|Carbohydrates: 2g|Sugar: 1g|Protein: 5g| Iron: 0.8mg| Calcium: 25mg

65. Air Fryer French Toast

Prep Time: 5 mins

Cook Time: 9 mins

Total Time: 14 mins

Ingredients

- 2 eggs

- 2 TBS milk, cream, or half and half
- 1/2 tsp ground cinnamon
- 1/2 tsp vanilla extract
- 1 loaf challah or brioche bread, cut into 8 thick slices

Instructions

- In a medium bowl, add egg, milk, vanilla, and cinnamon; whisk to combine completely; set aside
- Make an assembly line: set up whisked egg mixture and bread next to each other.
- Spray the air fryer basket with nonstick oil spray
- Dip the slices of bread into the egg mixture being sure to flip and coat both sides. Lift out of the mixture and allow to drip for a few seconds, then place into the air fryer basket. Repeat for remaining slices
- Close the Air Fryer. Set to 400 degrees and 5 minutes. After 5 minutes, open the basket and carefully flip the french toast slices. Close the air fryer and cook for 3-4 more minutes at 400 degrees. *Time may vary slightly depending on the air fryer model.
- Remove the french toast when finished and then cook the remaining french toast slices.
- Serve with warm maple syrup and powdered sugar or your favorite toppings!

Nutrition Facts

- Calories:150Kcal|Totalfat:12g|Saturatedfat:4g| Transfat:0g|Cholesterol:160mg|Sodium: 200mg|Carbohydrates: 4g|Sugar: 1g|Protein: 3g| Iron: 2mg|

66. Air Fryer Breakfast Pockets

Prep Time: 30 minutes

Cook Time: 15 minutes

Ingredients

- 1 lb of ground pork
- 4 whole eggs
- 1 whole egg for egg wash
- 1/3 + 1/4 c of whole milk
- 1-2 ounces of Velveeta cheese
- Salt and pepper to taste
- 2 packages of Pillsbury pie crust 2 crusts to a

- package
- 2-gallon ziplock bags
- parchment paper
- Cooking spray

Instructions

- Remove pie crusts from the refrigerator.
- Brown and drain the pork.
- Heat 1/4 c milk and cheese in a small pot until melted.
- Whisk 4 eggs, season with salt and pepper, and add remaining milk.
- Scramble eggs in a skillet until almost fully cooked.
- Mix the meat, cheese, and eggs.
- Roll out your pie crust and cut it into a 3-4 inch circle (about the size of a cereal bowl).
- Whisk one egg to make an egg wash.
- Place about 2 tbsps of mix into the middle of each circle.
- Egg wash all edges of the circle.
- Fold the circle creating a moon shape.
- Crimp the folded edges with a fork.
- Layer the pockets in parchment paper and place them in a plastic ziplock bag overnight.
- Once ready to cook, pre-heat your Air Fryer to 360 degrees.
- Spray each side of the pocket with cooking spray.
- Place pockets in pre-heated Air Fryer for 15 minutes or until golden brown.
- Remove from Air Fryer and allow to cool for a few minutes before serving.

Nutrition Facts

- Calories:140Kcal|Totalfat:15g|Saturatedfat:8g| Transfat:2g|Cholesterol:160mg|Sodium: 180mg|Carbohydrates: 2g|Sugar:2g|Protein: 10g| Iron: 2mg| Calcium: 13mg

---

67. Air Fryer Cheesy Baked Eggs

Prep Time: 4 minutes

Cook Time: 16 minutes

Total Time: 20 minutes

Servings: 2

Ingredients

- 4 large Eggs
- 2 ounces Smoked gouda, chopped
- Everything bagel seasoning
- Salt and pepper to taste

Instructions

- Spray the inside of each ramekin with cooking spray. Add 2 eggs to each ramekin, then add 1 ounce of chopped gouda to each. Salt and pepper to taste. Sprinkle your everything bagel seasoning on top of each ramekin (as much as you like). Place each ramekin into the air fryer basket. Cook for 400F for 16 minutes, or until eggs are cooked through. Serve.

Nutrition

- Calories: 240kcal | Carbohydrates: 1g | Protein: 12g | Fat: 16g

---

68. Low-Carb Air Fryer Bacon And Egg Cups

Prep Time: 10 Minutes

Cook Time: 10 Minutes

Total Time: 20 Minutes

Ingredients

- 3 slices bacon, sliced in half
- 6 large eggs
- 1 bunch green onions, optional
- salt and pepper, optional

Instructions

- Arrange 6 baking cups (silicone or paper) in the air fryer basket. Spray with nonstick cooking spray.
- Line cups with bacon slice. Carefully crack an egg into each cup. Season with salt and pepper, if desired.
- Turn the air fryer on to 330° and cook for 10 minutes, until eggs are set. Carefully remove from air fryer and garnish with desired toppings.

Nutrition Information

- Calories:115Kcal|Totalfat:9g|Saturatedfat:3g|Transfat:0g|Cholesterol:10mg|Sodium: 160mg|Carbohydrates: 0g|Sugar: 0g|Protein: 8g| Iron: 2mg|

69. Air Fryer English Breakfast

Prep Time: 3 mins

Cook Time: 15 mins

Total Time: 18 mins

Ingredients

- 6 English Sausages
- 6 Bacon Rashers
- 2 Large Tomatoes
- 4 Black Pudding
- ½ Can Baked Beans
- 2 Large Eggs
- 1 Tbsp Whole Milk
- 1 Tsp Butter
- Salt & Pepper

Instructions

- Crack your eggs into a ramekin and stir in butter, milk, and salt and pepper. Place in the air fryer. Add to the air fryer bacon rashers, black pudding, and sausages. Slice tomatoes in half and season the top with salt and pepper.
- Close the air fryer basket, making sure first that there is room for each of the breakfast items to cook. Then cook for 10 minutes at 180c/360f. Though at the 5-minute interval stir your eggs with a fork.
- When the air fryer beeps, check to make sure the eggs are scrambled and remove the scrambled eggs with a kitchen glove or kitchen tongs. Replace the ramekin space with a ramekin of cold baked beans. Cook for a further 5 minutes at the same temperature.
- When it beeps load your English breakfast ingredients onto a plate and enjoy.

Nutrition

- Calories: 1496kcal | Carbohydrates: 22g | Protein: 70g | Fat: 124g | Saturated Fat: 42g | Cholesterol: 463mg | Sodium: 3005mg | Potassium: 1564mg | Fiber: 6g | Sugar: 4g | Vitamin A: 1579IU | Vitamin C: 21mg | Calcium: 117mg | Iron: 6mg

70. Air Fryer Bacon And Egg Toast

Prep Time: 1 Minute

Cook Time: 9 Minutes

Total Time: 10 Minutes

Ingredients

- Butter (if desired)
- 1 slice of bread
- 1 slice of bacon
- 1 egg
- Salt & pepper to taste

Directions

- Butter a slice of bread and place it in the air fryer. Add a slice of bacon around the top of the bread. Add an egg in the middle.
- Close the air fryer and cook for 9 minutes at 340 degrees, or until the desired doneness. Salt & pepper to taste. Enjoy!

Nutritional Value

- Calories:178Kcal|Totalfat:15g|Saturatedfat:8g|Transfat:0g|Cholesterol:194mg|Sodium: 193mg|Carbohydrates: 2g|Sugar: 1g|Protein: 5g| Iron: 0.8mg| Calcium: 25mg

71. How To Make Bacon In Your Air Fryer

Prep Time: 5 minutes

Cook Time: 10 minutes

Ingredients: Basic Air Fryer Bacon

- 4 pieces of thick-cut bacon
- 2 eggs
- 1 tablespoon butter
- 2 croissants sliced
- 1/2 cup ketchup
- 2 tablespoons apple cider vinegar
- 1 tablespoon molasses
- 1 tablespoon brown sugar
- 1/4 teaspoon mustard powder
- 1/4 teaspoon onion powder
- 1/2 tablespoon Worcestershire sauce
- 1/4 teaspoon liquid smoke

Instructions: Basic Air Fryer Bacon

- Preheat your Air fryer to 200 degrees C (or 390 degrees F)

- Lay the bacon strips of your choice flat on the Air fryer tray.
- Cook for 4-5 minutes, then flip the bacon.
- Cook for another 4-5 minutes until the desired doneness is reached.
- Air Fryer Bacon With BBQ Sauce Croissants
- Preheat your Air fryer to 200 degrees C (or 390 degrees F)
- Whisk together in a small saucepan the ketchup, apple cider vinegar, molasses, brown sugar, mustard powder, onion powder, Worcestershire sauce, and liquid smoke. Place on medium heat and bring to a simmer, cooking until the sauce thickens slightly.
- Lay the bacon flat on the Airfryer tray and brush with BBQ sauce. Cook for 4-5 minutes, then flip the bacon and brush the other side of the bacon with sauce. Cook for an additional 5 minutes or until the desired doneness is reached.
- Place the croissants into your toaster and toast lightly.
- Melt the butter in a medium-sized frying pan and fry the eggs until they reach your desired doneness. (over-easy is best).
- Place an egg on the bottom of one croissant, followed by two bacon slices and the croissant top. Repeat with the other croissant.
- Serve and enjoy!

Nutrition Information

- Calories: 656kcal, Carbohydrates: 57g, Protein: 16g, Fat: 39g, Saturated Fat: 17g, Cholesterol: 246mg, Sodium: 1262mg, Potassium: 584mg, Fiber: 1g, Sugar: 33g, Vitamin A: 1145IU, Vitamin C: 3mg, Calcium: 76mg, Iron: 3mg

72. Air Fryer Bacon

Prep Time: 2 Minutes

Cook Time: 10 Minutes

Total Time: 12 Minutes

Ingredients

- 8 ounces bacon about 8 strips
- Water

Instructions

- Preheat the air fryer at 350F for about 5 minutes.
- Pour ¼ cup of water into the bottom of the air fryer to minimize smoke. Make sure the water is not touching the basket or bacon. (You can also place a layer of bread in the bottom of the air fryer.)
- Place bacon in a single layer into the preheated air fryer basket. Feel free to cut bacon strips in half or even in thirds to make it fit nicely.
- Cook for 8 to 10 minutes for thinner bacon and 12 to 15 minutes for thicker cut bacon.

Nutrition

- Calories: 236kcal | Carbohydrates: 1g | Protein: 7g | Fat: 23g | Saturated Fat: 8g | Cholesterol: 37mg | Sodium: 375mg | Potassium: 112mg | Vitamin A: 21IU | Calcium: 3mg | Iron: 1mg

73. Air Fryer Egg Cups

Prep Time: 5 minutes

Cook Time: 12 minutes

Total Time: 17 minutes

Yield: 8

Ingredients

- 6 large eggs
- 1/2 cup of heavy cream
- (use low-fat milk for WW)
- 1/2 cup of cheddar
- 1/2 pound of breakfast sausage
- 1 tsp of olive oil
- 1 tsp of garlic
- 2 cups of spinach

Instructions

- Heat a nonstick skillet to medium-low.
- Add ground breakfast sausage and cook for 12-16 minutes or until cooked through and browned. Crumble the sausage with a wooden spoon or cooking utensil of choice.
- Remove the breakfast sausage from the skillet. Let the sausage cool.
- Add 1 tsp of olive oil and garlic to the skillet. Cook until the garlic is fragrant and Add the spinach to the skillet and cover; allow to cook 5 minutes. Take the spinach out of the pan let it cool as you

did with the sausage.

- In a medium bowl add the eggs and milk and whisk until combined. Fold in the cheddar, breakfast sausage, and spinach.
- Place the silicone muffin cups into the air fryer basket and set the temperature to 300 degrees. Fill the cups with the egg mixture (do not overfill). I used a measuring cup to fill the muffin cups.
- Set the air fryer time to 12 minutes.
- I had egg mixture left over after only cooking six egg cups at a time. My air fryer basket only fit 6 muffin cups in there without overflowing. Will have to cook in batches if there is any leftover.

Nutrition Value

Calories:230|Sugar:1g|Fat:19g|Sat Fat: 7g|Unsaturated Fat: 4g|Carbohydrates: 4g| Fiber: 0g| Protein: 10g

74. Air Fryer Quiche

Yield: makes 1

Prep time: 10 minutes

Cook time: 10 minutes

Total time: 20 minutes

Ingredients

- 1 egg
- 3-4 tbsp (45ml-60ml) of heavy cream
- 4-5 tiny broccoli florets
- 1 tbsp (15ml) finely grated cheddar cheese

Instructions

- Whisk together egg and cream. Lightly grease a 5" (13cm) ceramic quiche dish. Distribute broccoli florets on the bottom. Pour in the egg mixture. Top with grated cheddar cheese.
- Air fry at 325F (162C) for 10 minutes.

More Air Fryer Quiche Fillings:

- Tomato and Mozzarella. Garnish with fresh basil
- Spinach and Cheese
- Cooked bacon and Cheddar
- Mushroom and Thyme
- Smoked Salmon and Dill
- Goat Cheese and Crispy Leeks (cook leeks first in a skillet with olive oil until crispy)

Nutrition Information

Calories: 656| Total Fat: 58g| Saturated Fat: 34g| Trans Fat: 2g| Unsaturated Fat: 19g| Cholesterol: 349mg| Sodium: 364mg| Carbohydrates: 18g| Fiber: 6g| Sugar: 6g| Protein: 21g

75. Vegan Air Fryer Breakfast Potatoes

Cook Time: 40 minutes

Total Time: 40 minutes

Ingredients

- 3 lb potatoes, diced
- 2 bell peppers, any color, diced
- 1 onion, diced
- 15 oz mushrooms, diced
- 1 1/2 cups or 1-14 oz can black beans, drained
- Lemon Miso Tahini Sauce, optional
- Spinach and avocado for serving, optional

Instructions

- IF AIR FRYING: Add potatoes to the air fryer basket. Cook 20 minutes at 400 degrees F (or 205 degrees C), shaking basket frequently.
- Add beans and vegetables and cook 10 - 15 more minutes until potatoes are soft or crispy, according to preference.
- IF BAKING: Spread potatoes out on a lined baking tray and bake for 25-30 minutes in a 425 degree F (218 degrees C) oven.
- Remove the tray and flip the potatoes. Add your veggies and beans and stir. Put the tray back in the oven for 15-20 more minutes, until the potatoes have started to get crispy and lightly golden brown and until all the veggies have cooked.
- Make the lemon miso tahini sauce by mixing the ingredients in a bowl and thinning the sauce with water if needed.
- Add to a bowl with spinach and whatever else you like (this would be a great complement to tofu scramble, for instance). Top with sauce mixture and enjoy!
- Refrigerate leftovers in an airtight container for up to 5 days. Recommended reheating in the oven, skillet, or air fryer to retain crispiness.

Nutritional Value

- Calories: 164
- Total Fat: 0.5g
- Sodium: 200.5g
- Total carbohydrate: 34.7g
- Sugar: 4g
- Protein: 7.2g

76. Fried Eggs For The Air Fryer

Prep Time: 1 Minute

Cook Time: 8 Minutes

Total Time: 9 Minutes

Ingredients

- 2 Large Eggs
- 2 Tablespoons Butter
- Salt And Pepper

Instructions

- Add a small aluminum pan to the basket of an air fryer.
- Add the butter and heat at 350 degrees to melt (approximately 1 minute)
- Crack both eggs into the aluminum pan.
- Return to the air fryer and cook at 325-degrees until your desired doneness.

Nutrition Information

- Calories: 363
- Total Fat: 33g
- Saturated Fat: 18g
- Cholesterol: 482mg
- Sodium: 361mg
- Carbohydrates: 1g
- Sugar: 1g
- Protein: 14g

77. Turkey Breakfast Sausage - Air Fryer Or Oven Method

Prep Time: 5 Minutes

Cook Time: 13 Minutes

Total Time: 18 Minutes

Ingredients

- 1 pound ground turkey
- 1 teaspoon kosher salt

- ½ teaspoon black pepper
- 1 teaspoon fennel seed
- ½ teaspoon ground sage
- ½ teaspoon smoked paprika
- 3/4 teaspoon garlic powder
- 1/8 teaspoon red pepper flakes (or to taste)

Instructions

- Place all the ingredients in a medium bowl and mix well to combine.
- Wet hands with water and form the ground turkey mixture into 12-13 small patties (approximately 1½ tablespoons, each).
- Place the patties on an air fryer baking sheet and cook for 12-13 minutes at 350-degrees (or until an instant-read thermometer reached 165-degrees when inserted into the center of a sausage.

Nutrition Information

- Calories: 91
- Total Fat: 6g
- Saturated Fat: 2g
- Unsaturated Fat: 4g
- Cholesterol: 37mg
- Sodium: 193mg
- Protein: 9g

78. Dry Rub Skirt Steak Sandwiches

Prep Time: 10 Minutes

Cook Time: 15 Minutes

Inactive Time: 30 Minutes

Total Time: 55 Minutes

Ingredients

For The Dry Rub

- 3 tablespoons ground coriander
- 3 tablespoons smoked paprika
- 3 tablespoons ground smoked cumin
- 1 teaspoon allspice
- 1½ tablespoons ground cinnamon
- 2 tablespoons dried oregano
- 1½ tablespoons dry mustard
- 3 tablespoons salt
- 1½ tablespoons black pepper

- 2 tablespoons garlic powder
- 4 tablespoons brown sugar
- For the sandwich
- 2 beef skirt steaks
- 1 tablespoon canola oil
- 3 green bell peppers, seeded and sliced
- 2 large sweet onions, peeled and sliced
- ½ teaspoon salt
- ¼ teaspoon pepper
- 8 crusty rolls
- 1½ cup beef broth for dipping, optional
- hot sauce, optional

Instructions

- In a large bowl with a lid, mix all the ingredients for the dry rub until well combined.
- Place the meat on the baking sheet and liberally sprinkle the dry rub on both sides of the meat and rub it in lightly.
- Allow the meat to sit for approximately 30 minutes.
- Meanwhile, heat a large skillet to medium, add the canola oil and the sliced peppers and onions.
- Sautee the green peppers and onions with ½ teaspoon salt and ¼ pepper until they softened and cooked through. Remove from heat and keep warm.
- Place the steaks on a hot grill and cook for approximately 5 minutes per side.
- Remove the cooked steaks from the grill and allow them to sit, covered with aluminum foil, for at least 10 minutes.
- Slice the meat across the grain in thin slices.
- To serve pile the sliced beef onto crusty rolls and top with the sauteed peppers and onions.
- Spoon (or dip) the beef stock over the prepared sandwiches and a few shakes of hot sauce if desired.
- Serve hot!

Nutrition Information

- Calories: 399
- Total Fat: 17g
- Saturated Fat: 5g
- Trans Fat: 0g
- Unsaturated Fat: 10g
- Cholesterol: 64mg

- Sodium: 3218mg
- Carbohydrates: 37g
- Fiber: 7g
- Sugar: 13g
- Protein: 27g

79. Air Fryer Mini Breakfast Burritos

Prep Time: 15 mins

Cook Time: 30 mins

Total Time: 45 mins

Ingredient

- ¼ cup Mexican-style chorizo
- 1 tablespoon bacon grease
- ½ cup diced potatoes
- 2 tablespoons chopped onion
- 1 serrano pepper, chopped
- 2 large eggs
- Salt and ground black pepper to taste
- 4 (8 inches) flour tortillas
- Avocado oil cooking spray

Instructions

- Cook chorizo in a large skillet over medium-high heat, stirring frequently until sausage turns a dark red, 6 to 8 minutes. Remove from the skillet and set aside.
- Melt bacon grease in the same skillet over medium-high heat. Add diced potatoes and cook, stirring occasionally, 8 to 10 minutes. Add onion and serrano pepper and continue cooking and stirring until potatoes are fork-tender, onion is translucent, and serrano pepper is soft, 2 to 6 minutes. Add eggs and chorizo; stir until cooked and completely incorporated into potato mixture, about 5 minutes. Season with salt and pepper.
- Meanwhile, heat tortillas in a large skillet or directly on the grates of a gas stove until soft and pliable. Place 1/3 cup chorizo mixture down the center of each tortilla. Fold top and bottom of tortillas over the filling, then roll each into a burrito shape. Mist with cooking spray and place in the basket of an air fryer.
- Air fry at 400 degrees F (200 degrees C) for 4 to 6 minutes. Flip each burrito over, mist with

cooking spray, and air fry until lightly browned, 2 to 4 minutes more.

Nutritional Value

- Calories: 253.8
- Protein: 8.3g
- Carbohydrates: 31.4g
- Dietary Fiber: 2.2g
- Sugars: 0.6g
- Fat: 10.4g
- Saturated Fat: 3.3g
- Cholesterol: 98.1mg
- Vitamin B6: 0.1mg
- Vitamin C: 4.9mg
- Folate: 76.5mcg
- Calcium: 36.1mg
- Iron: 2.3mg
- Magnesium: 21.4mg
- Potassium: 198.4mg
- Sodium: 298.2mg

80. Air Fryer Churros

Prep Time: 5 mins

Cook Time: 15 mins

Additional Time: 5 mins

Total Time: 25 mins

Ingredient

- ¼ cup butter
- ½ cup milk
- 1 pinch salt
- ½ cup all-purpose flour
- 2 eggs
- ¼ cup white sugar
- ½ teaspoon ground cinnamon

Instructions

- Melt butter in a saucepan over medium-high heat. Pour in milk and add salt. Lower heat to medium and bring to a boil, continuously stirring with a wooden spoon. Quickly add flour all at once. Keep stirring until the dough comes together.
- Remove from heat and let cool for 5 to 7 minutes. Mix in eggs with the wooden spoon until the pastry comes together. Spoon dough

into a pastry bag fitted with a large star tip. Pipe dough into strips straight into the air fryer basket.

- Air fry churros at 340 degrees F (175 degrees C) for 5 minutes.
- Meanwhile, combine sugar and cinnamon in a small bowl and pour onto a shallow plate.
- Remove fried churros from the air fryer and roll in the cinnamon-sugar mixture.

Nutrition Facts

- Protein: 3.9g
- Carbohydrates: 17.5g
- Dietary Fiber: 0.4g
- Sugars: 9.4g
- Fat: 9.8g
- Saturated Fat: 5.6g
- Cholesterol: 84mg
- Vitamin A Iu: 356.5IU
- Niacin Equivalents: 1.5mg
- Folate: 28.2mcg
- Calcium: 38.5mg
- Iron: 0.8mg
- Magnesium: 6.8mg
- Potassium: 67.2mg
- Sodium: 112.2mg
- Thiamin: 0.1mg
- Calories From Fat: 88.5

2. Air Fryer Main & Lunch Recipes

81. Lunch Egg Rolls

Preparation time: 10 minutes Cooking time: 15 minutes

Ingredients:

- ½ cup mushrooms, chopped
- ½ cup carrots, grated
- ½ cup zucchini, grated
- 2 green onions, chopped
- 2 tablespoons soy sauce
- 8 egg roll wrappers
- 1 eggs, whisked
- 1 tablespoon cornstarch

Instructions:

- In a bowl, mix carrots with mushrooms, zucchini, green onions and soy sauce and stir well.
- Arrange egg roll wrappers on a working surface, divide veggie mix on each and roll well.
- In a bowl, mix cornstarch with egg, whisk well and brush eggs rolls with this mix.
- Seal edges, place all rolls in your preheated air fryer and cook them at 370 degrees F for 15 minutes.
- Arrange them on a platter and serve them for lunch.

Nutrition Facts:

calories 172, fat 6, fiber 6, carbs 8, protein 7

82. Veggie Toast

Preparation time: 10 minutes Cooking time: 15 minutes

Ingredients:

- 1 red bell pepper, cut into thin strips
- 1 cup cremimi mushrooms, sliced
- 1 yellow squash, chopped
- 2 green onions, sliced
- 1 tablespoon olive oil
- 4 bread slices
- 2 tablespoons butter, soft
- ½ cup goat cheese, crumbled

Instructions:

- In a bowl, mix red bell pepper with mushrooms, squash, green onions and oil, toss, transfer to your air fryer, cook them at 350 degrees F for 10 minutes, shaking the fryer once and transfer them to a bowl.
- Spread butter on bread slices, place them in air fryer and cook them at 350 degrees F for 5 minutes.
- Divide veggie mix on each bread slice, top with crumbled cheese and serve for lunch.

Nutrition Facts:

calories 152, fat 3, fiber 4, carbs 7, protein 2

83. Stuffed Mushrooms

Preparation time: 10 minutes Cooking time: 20 minutes

Ingredients:

- 4 big Portobello mushroom caps
- 1 tablespoon olive oil
- ¼ cup ricotta cheese
- 5 tablespoons parmesan, grated
- 1 cup spinach, torn
- 1/3 cup bread crumbs
- ¼ teaspoon rosemary, chopped

Instructions:

- Rub mushrooms caps with the oil, place them in your air fryer's basket and cook them at 350 degrees F for 2 minutes.
- Meanwhile, in a bowl, mix half of the parmesan with ricotta, spinach, rosemary and bread crumbs and stir well.
- Stuff mushrooms with this mix, sprinkle the rest of the parmesan on top, place them in your air fryer's basket again and cook at 350 degrees F for 10 minutes.
- Divide them on plates and serve with a side salad for lunch.

Nutrition Facts:

calories 152, fat 4, fiber 7, carbs 9, protein 5

84. Quick Lunch Pizzas

Preparation time: 10 minutes Cooking time: 7 minutes

Ingredients:

- 4 pitas
- 1 tablespoon olive oil
- ¾ cup pizza sauce
- 4 ounces jarred mushrooms, sliced
- ½ teaspoon basil, dried
- 2 green onions, chopped
- 2 cup mozzarella, grated
- 1 cup grape tomatoes, sliced

Instructions:

- Spread pizza sauce on each pita bread, sprinkle green onions and basil, divide mushrooms and top with cheese.
- Arrange pita pizzas in your air fryer and cook them at 400 degrees F for 7 minutes.
- Top each pizza with tomato slices, divide among plates and serve.

Nutrition Facts:

calories 200, fat 4, fiber 6, carbs 7, protein 3

85. Lunch Gnocchi

Preparation time: 10 minutes Cooking time: 17 minutes

Ingredients:

- 1 yellow onion, chopped
- 1 tablespoon olive oil
- 3 garlic cloves, minced
- 16 ounces gnocchi
- ¼ cup parmesan, grated
- 8 ounces spinach pesto

Instructions:

- grease your air fryer's pan with olive oil, add gnocchi, onion and garlic, toss, put pan in your air fryer and cook at 400 degrees F for 10 minutes.
- Add pesto, toss and cook for 7 minutes more at 350 degrees F.
- Divide among plates and serve for lunch.

Nutrition Facts: calories 200, fat 4, fiber 4, carbs 12,

protein 4

86. Tuna and Zucchini Tortillas

Preparation time: 10 minutes Cooking time: 10 minutes

Ingredients:

4 corn tortillas

4 tablespoons butter, soft

6 ounces canned tuna, drained

1 cup zucchini, shredded

1/3 cup mayonnaise

2 tablespoons mustard

1 cup cheddar cheese, grated

Instructions:

- Spread butter on tortillas, place them in your air fryer's basket and cook them at 400 degrees F for 3 minutes.
- Meanwhile, in a bowl, mix tuna with zucchini, mayo and mustard and stir.
- Divide this mix on each tortilla, top with cheese, roll tortillas, place them in your air fryer's basket again and cook them at 400 degrees F for 4 minutes more.

Nutrition Facts:

calories 162, fat 4, fiber 8, carbs 9, protein 4

87. Squash Fritters

Preparation time: 10 minutes Cooking time: 7 minutes

Ingredients:

- 3 ounces cream cheese
- 1 egg, whisked
- ½ teaspoon oregano, dried

- A pinch of salt and black pepper
- 1 yellow summer squash, grated
- 1/3 cup carrot, grated
- 2/3 cup bread crumbs
- 2 tablespoons olive oil

Instructions:

- In a bowl, mix cream cheese with salt, pepper, oregano, egg, breadcrumbs, carrot and squash and stir well.
- Shape medium patties out of this mix and brush them with the oil.
- Place squash patties in your air fryer and cook them at 400 degrees F for 7 minutes.

Nutrition Facts: calories 200, fat 4, fiber 7, carbs 8, protein 6

88. Lunch Shrimp Croquettes

Preparation time: 10 minutes Cooking time: 8 minutes

Ingredients:

- 2/3 pound shrimp, cooked, peeled, deveined and chopped
- 1 and ½ cups bread crumbs
- 1 egg, whisked
- 2 tablespoons lemon juice
- 3 green onions, chopped
- ½ teaspoon basil, dried
- Salt and black pepper to the taste
- 2 tablespoons olive oil

Instructions:

- In a bowl, mix half of the bread crumbs with egg and lemon juice and stir well.
- Add green onions, basil, salt, pepper and shrimp and stir really well.
- In a separate bowl, mix the rest of the bread crumbs with the oil and toss well.
- Shape round balls out of shrimp mix, dredge them in bread crumbs, place them in preheated air fryer and cook the for 8 minutes at 400 degrees F.

Nutrition Facts:

calories 142, fat 4, fiber 6, carbs 9, protein 4

89. Lunch Special Pancake

Preparation time: 10 minutes Cooking time: 10 minutes

Ingredients:

- 1 tablespoon butter
- 3 eggs, whisked
- ½ cup flour
- ½ cup milk
- 1 cup salsa
- 1 cup small shrimp, peeled and deveined

Instructions:

- Preheat your air fryer at 400 degrees F, add fryer's pan, add 1 tablespoon butter and melt it.
- In a bowl, mix eggs with flour and milk, whisk well and pour into air fryer's pan, spread, cook at 350 degrees for 12 minutes and transfer to a plate.
- In a bowl, mix shrimp with salsa, stir and serve your pancake with this on the side.

Nutrition Facts:

calories 200, fat 6, fiber 8, carbs 12, protein 4

90. Scallops and Dill

Preparation time: 10 minutes Cooking time: 5 minutes

Ingredients:

- 1 pound sea scallops, debearded
- 1 tablespoon lemon juice
- 1 teaspoon dill, chopped
- 2 teaspoons olive oil
- Salt and black pepper to the taste

Instructions:

- In your air fryer, mix scallops with dill, oil, salt, pepper and lemon juice, cover and cook at 360 degrees F for 5 minutes.
- Discard unopened ones, divide scallops and dill sauce on plates and serve for lunch.

Nutrition Facts:

calories 152, fat 4, fiber 7, carbs 19, protein 4

91. Chicken Sandwiches

Preparation time: 10 minutes Cooking time: 10 minutes

Ingredients:

- 2 chicken breasts, skinless, boneless and cubed
- 1 red onion, chopped

- 1 red bell pepper, sliced
- ½ cup Italian seasoning
- ½ teaspoon thyme, dried
- 2 cups butter lettuce, torn
- 4 pita pockets
- 1 cup cherry tomatoes, halved
- 1 tablespoon olive oil

Instructions:

- In your air fryer, mix chicken with onion, bell pepper, Italian seasoning and oil, toss and cook at 380 degrees F for 10 minutes.
- Transfer chicken mix to a bowl, add thyme, butter lettuce and cherry tomatoes, toss well, stuff pita pockets with this mix and serve for lunch.

Nutrition Facts:

calories 126, fat 4, fiber 8, carbs 14, protein 4

92. Mac and Cheese

Prep Time: 15 minutes

Ingredients

- 1 cup cooked macaroni
- 1 cup grated cheddar cheese
- ½ cup warm milk
- 1 tbsp. Parmesan cheese
- Salt and pepper, to taste

Instructions

- Preheat the air fryer to 350 degrees F. Add the macaroni to an ovenproof baking dish. Stir in the cheddar and milk. Season with some salt and pepper, to taste. Place the dish in the air fryer and cook for 10 minutes. Sprinkle with Parmesan cheese just before serving.

Nutrition Facts

Calories 375.6, Carbohydrates 23 g, Fat 1.8 g, Protein 6.4 g

93. Air Fried Calzone

Prep Time: 20 minutes

Ingredients

- Pizza dough, preferably homemade
- 4 oz. cheddar cheese, grated
- 1 oz. mozzarella cheese
- 1 oz. bacon, diced
- 2 cups cooked and shredded turkey (leftovers are fine)1 egg, beaten
- 1 tsp. thyme4 tbsp. tomato paste1 tsp. basil
- 1 tsp. oreganoSalt and pepper, to taste

Instructions

- Preheat the air fryer to 350 degrees F. Divide the pizza dough into 4 equal pieces so you have dough for 4 small pizza crusts.
- Combine the tomato paste, basil, oregano, and thyme, in a small bowl.
- Brush the mixture onto the crusts just make sure not to go all the way and avoid brushing near the edges.
- On one half of each crust, place ½ turkey, and season the meat with some salt and pepper.
- Top the meat with some bacon.
- Combine the cheddar and mozzarella and divide it between the pizzas, making sure that you layer only one half of the dough.
- Brush the edges of the crust with the beaten egg.
- Fold the crust and seal with a fork. Cook for 10 minutes

Nutrition Facts

Calories 339, Carbohydrates 10.6 g, Fat 17.3 g, Protein 33.6 g

94. Roasted Radish and Onion Cheesy Salad

Prep Time: 35 minute

Ingredients

1 lb. radishes, green parts too

- 1 large red onion, sliced
- ½ lb. mozzarella, sliced
- 2 tbsp. olive oil, plus more for drizzling
- 2 tbsp. balsamic glaze
- 1 tsp. dried basil
- 1 tsp. dried parsley
- 1 tsp. salt

Instructions

- Preheat the air fryer to 350 degrees F. Wash the radishes well and dry them by patting with paper towels.
- Cut them in half and place in a large bowl. Add the onion slices in.
- Stir in salt, basil, parsley and olive oil. Place in the basket of the air fryer.
- Cook for 30 minutes.
- Make sure to toss them twice while cooking. Stir in the mozzarella immediately so that it begins to melt. Stir in the balsamic glaze. Drizzle with olive oil

Nutrition Facts

Calories 240.1, Carbohydrates 9.7 g, Fat 16 g, Protein 15

---

95. Mock Stir Fry

Prep Time: 25 minutes

Ingredients

- 4 boneless and skinless chicken breasts cut into cubes
- 2 carrots, sliced
- 1 red bell pepper, cut into strips
- 1 yellow bell pepper, cut into strips
- 1 cup snow peas
- 15 oz. broccoli florets
- 1 scallion, slicedSauce:
- 3 tbsp. soy sauce
- 2 tbsp. oyster sauce
- 1 tbsp. brown sugar
- 1 tsp. sesame oil1 tsp. cornstarch
- 1 tsp. sriracha
- 2 garlic cloves, minced1 tbsp. grated ginger
- 1 tbsp. rice wine vinegar

Instructions

- Preheat the air fryer to 370 degrees F.
- Place the chicken, bell peppers, and carrot, in a bowl. In a small bowl, combine the sauce **Ingredients**.
- Coat the chicken mixture with the sauce. Place on a lined baking sheet and cook for 5 minutes.
- Add snow peas and broccoli and cook for additional 8 to 10 minutes. Serve garnished with scallion

Nutrition Facts

Calories 277, Carbohydrates 15.6 g, Fat 4.4 g, Protein 43.1 g

---

96. Potato and Bacon Salad

Prep Time: 10 minutes

Ingredients

- 4 lb. boiled and cubed potatoes
- 15 bacon slices, chopped
- 2 cups shredded cheddar cheese
- 15 oz. sour cream
- 2 tbsp. mayonnaise
- 1 tsp. salt
- 1 tsp. pepper
- 1 tsp. dried herbs by choice

Instructions

- Preheat the air fryer to 350 degrees F.
- Combine the potatoes, bacon, salt, pepper, and herbs, in a large bowl.
- Transfer to a baking dish. Cook for about 7 minutes.
- Stir in sour cream and mayonnaise.

Nutrition Facts

Calories 306.5, Carbohydrates 33.9 g, Fat 14.9 g, Protein 10 g

---

97. Carbonara and Mushroom Spaghetti

Prep Time: 30 - 35 minutes

Ingredients

- ½ lb. white button mushrooms, sliced
- ½ cup of water
- 1 tsp. butter
- 2 garlic cloves, chopped
- 12 oz. spaghetti, cooked
- 14 oz. carbonara mushroom sauce (store bought)Salt and pepper, to taste

Instructions

- Preheat the air fryer to 300 degrees F.
- Add the butter and garlic and cook for 3 minutes.
- Add the mushrooms and cook for 5 more

- minutes.
- Stir in mushroom carbonara sauce and water.
- Season with salt and pepper.
- Cook for 18 minutes.Stir in the spaghetti and cook for 1 minute more.

Nutrition Facts

Calories 395.7, Carbohydrates 57.9 g, Fat 13 g, Protein 13 g

98. Ham and Mozzarella Eggplant Boats

Prep Time: 17 minutes

Ingredients

- 1 eggplant
- 4 ham slices, chopped
- 1 cup shredded mozzarella cheese, divided
- 1 tsp. dried parsley
- Salt and pepper, to taste

Instructions

- Preheat the air fryer to 330 degrees.
- Peel the eggplant and cut it lengthwise in half. Scoop some of the flash out.Season with salt and pepper.
- Divide half the mozzarella cheese between the eggplants.
- Place the ham on top of the mozzarella.
- Top with the remaining mozzarella cheese.
- Sprinkle with parsley.Cook 12 minutes

Nutrition Facts

Calories 323.1, Carbohydrates 15.7 g, Fat 16.4 g, Protein 28.3 g

99. Leftover Turkey and Mushroom Sandwich

Prep Time: 15 MInutes

Ingredients

- 1/3 cup shredded leftover turkey
- 1/3 cup sliced mushrooms
- 1 tbsp. butter, divided
- 2 tomato slices
- ½ tsp. red pepper flakes
- ¼ tsp. salt
- ¼ tsp. black pepper
- 1 hamburger bun

Instructions

- Preheat the air fryer to 350 degrees F.
- Melt half of the butter and add the mushrooms.
- Cook for about 4 minutes.
- Meanwhile, cut the bun in half and spread the remaining butter on the outside of the bun.
- Place the turkey on one half of the bun.Arrange the mushroom slices on top of the turkey.Place the tomato slices on top of the mushrooms.
- Sprinkle with salt pepper and red pepper flakes.Top with the other bun half.Cook for 5 minutes.

Nutrition Facts

Calories 318.3, Carbohydrates 25.6 g, Fat 16.4 g, Protein 18.4 g

100. Italian Sausage Patties

Prep Time: 20 Minutes

Ingredients

- 1 lb. ground Italian sausage
- ¼ cup breadcrumbs
- 1 tsp. dried parsley
- 1 tsp. red pepper Flakes
- ½ tsp. salt
- ¼ tsp. black peppe
- r¼ tsp. garlic powder
- 1 egg, beaten

Instructions

- Preheat the air fryer to 350 degrees F.
- Combine all of the **Ingredients** in a large bowl.Line a baking sheet with parchment paper.
- Make patties out of the sausage mixture and arrange them on the baking sheet.Cook for about 15 minutes.
- Serve as desired (they are amazing with tzatziki sauce)

Nutrition Facts

Calories 332.3 Carbohydrates 6.2 g, Fat 24.6 g, Protein 18.6 g

101. Air-Fried Popcorn Chicken Gizzards

Prep Time: 10 mins

Cook Time: 45 mins

Additional Time: 5 mins

Total Time: 1 hr

Ingredient

- 1 pound chicken gizzards
- ⅓ cup all-purpose flour
- 1 ½ teaspoon seasoned salt
- ½ teaspoon ground black pepper
- ½ teaspoon garlic powder
- ½ teaspoon paprika
- 1 pinch cayenne pepper (optional)
- 1 large egg, beaten
- Cooking spray

Instructions

- Bring a large pot of water to a boil. Cut gizzards into bite-sized pieces and add to the boiling water. Boil for 30 minutes. Drain.
- Combine flour, seasoned salt, pepper, garlic powder, paprika, and cayenne in a flat plastic container. Snap the lid on and shake until combined.
- Add gizzards to the seasoned flour. Snap the lid back on and shake until evenly coated.
- Place beaten egg in a separate bowl. Dip each gizzard piece into the beaten egg and then place it back in the seasoned flour. Snap the lid on and shake one last time. Let sit for 5 minutes while the air fryer preheats.
- Preheat the air fryer to 400 degrees F (200 degrees C).
- Place gizzards in the basket and spray the tops with cooking spray. Cook for 4 minutes. Shake the basket and spray any chalky spots with more cooking spray. Cook for 4 minutes more.

Nutrition Facts

- Calories: 237; Protein 23.6g; Carbohydrates 11.8g; Fat 10g; Cholesterol 330.8mg; Sodium 434.2mg

102. Air Fryer Crab Rangoon

Prep Time: 15 mins

Cook Time: 20 mins

Total Time: 35 mins

Ingredient

- 1 (8 ounces) package cream cheese, softened
- 4 ounces lump crab meat
- 2 tablespoons chopped scallions
- 1 teaspoon soy sauce
- 1 teaspoon Worcestershire sauce
- 1 serving nonstick cooking spray
- 24 each wonton wrappers
- 2 tablespoons Asian sweet chili sauce, for dipping

Instructions

- Combine cream cheese, crab meat, scallions, soy sauce, and Worcestershire sauce in a bowl; stir until evenly combined.
- Preheat an air fryer to 350 degrees F (175 degrees C). Spray the basket of the air fryer with cooking spray. Fill a small bowl with warm water.
- Place 12 wonton wrappers on a clean work surface. Spoon 1 teaspoon of cream cheese mixture into the center of each wonton wrapper. Dip index finger into the warm water and wet around the sides of each wonton wrapper. Crimp wrapper corners upwards to meet in the center to form dumplings.
- Place dumplings in the prepared basket and spray the tops with cooking spray.
- Cook dumplings until desired crispness, about 8 to 10 minutes. Transfer to a paper towel-lined plate.
- While the first batch is cooking, assemble the remaining dumplings with the remaining wrappers and filling.
- Serve with sweet chili sauce for dipping.

Nutrition Facts

- Calories: 127; Protein 5.1g; Carbohydrates 11.1g; Fat 6.9g; Cholesterol 29.1mg; Sodium 240.4mg.

103. Air Fryer Cauliflower Fried Rice

Prep Time: 5 mins

Cook Time: 10 mins

Total Time: 15 mins

Ingredient

- 1 (12 ounces) package frozen cauliflower rice
- 2 large eggs
- 2 slices deli ham
- ¼ cup chopped green onions
- 2 tablespoons soy sauce

Instructions

- Cook cauliflower rice in the microwave for 5 to 6 minutes. Let stand for 1 minute before carefully opening the bag.
- Preheat the air fryer to 400 degrees F (200 degrees C). Cover the bottom and 1/2 inch of the basket sides with aluminum foil.
- Mix cauliflower rice, eggs, ham, green onions, and soy sauce in a bowl until well combined.
- Air fry for 5 minutes. Remove the basket and stir the cauliflower mixture. Return to air fryer and cook for an additional 5 minutes.

Nutrition Facts

- Calories: 170; Protein 16.2g; Carbohydrates 11.6g; Fat 7.4g; Cholesterol 202mg; Sodium 1379mg.

---

104. Air Fryer Wiener Schnitzel

Prep Time: 10 mins

Cook Time: 20 mins

Total Time: 30 mins

Ingredient

- 1 pound veal, scallopini cut
- 2 tablespoons lemon juice
- salt and ground black pepper to taste
- ¼ cup all-purpose flour
- 1 egg
- 1 tablespoon chopped fresh parsley
- 1 cup panko bread crumbs
- nonstick cooking spray
- 1 lemon, cut into wedges

Instructions

- Preheat an air fryer to 400 degrees F (200 degrees C).

- Place veal on a clean work surface and sprinkle with lemon juice, salt, and pepper.
- Place flour in a flat dish. Beat egg and parsley together in a second dish. Place bread crumbs in a third dish. Dredge each veal cutlet first in flour, then in the egg-parsley mixture, followed by bread crumbs, pressing down so that bread crumbs adhere.
- Spray the basket of the air fryer with nonstick cooking spray. Place breaded veal cutlets into the basket, making sure not to overcrowd. Spray the tops with nonstick cooking spray.
- Cook for 5 minutes. Flip, spray any chalky spots with nonstick cooking spray and cook for 5 minutes longer. Repeat with remaining veal. Serve with lemon wedges.

Nutrition Facts

- Calories: 215; Protein 18g; Carbohydrates 28.4g; Fat 6.6g; Cholesterol 104.4mg; Sodium 239.3mg.

---

105. Air Fryer Steak And Cheese Melts

Prep Time: 10 mins

Cook Time: 25 mins

Additional Time: 4 hrs 30 mins

Total Time: 5 hrs 5 mins

Ingredient

- 1 pound beef rib-eye steak, thinly sliced
- 2 tablespoons Worcestershire sauce
- 1 tablespoon reduced-sodium soy sauce
- 1 medium onion, sliced into petals
- 4 ounces sliced baby portobello mushrooms
- ½ green bell pepper, thinly sliced
- 1 tablespoon olive oil
- ½ teaspoon salt
- ½ teaspoon ground mustard
- ¼ teaspoon ground black pepper
- 4 hoagie rolls
- 4 slices Provolone cheese

Instructions

- Place steak in a bowl and add Worcestershire and soy sauce. Cover and refrigerate 4 hours to overnight. Remove from the refrigerator and let come to room temperature, about 30 minutes.

- Preheat the air fryer to 380 degrees F (190 degrees C).
- Combine onion, mushrooms, and bell pepper in a large bowl. Add olive oil, salt, ground mustard, and pepper; stir to coat.
- Place hoagie rolls in the basket of the air fryer and cook until toasted, about 2 minutes. Transfer rolls to a plate.
- Place steak in the basket of the air fryer and cook for 3 minutes. Stir and cook for 1 more minute. Transfer to a plate.
- Add vegetable mix to the basket of the air fryer and cook for 5 minutes. Stir and cook until softened, about 5 more minutes.
- Stir steak into the vegetable mixture. Place cheese slices on top, slightly overlapping. Cook until cheese is melted and bubbly, about 3 minutes. Spoon mixture onto toasted rolls and serve immediately.

Nutrition Facts

- Calories: 679; Protein 33.4g; Carbohydrates 75.4g; Fat 26.4g; Cholesterol 81.9mg; Sodium 1540.8mg.

106. Air Fryer Salmon For One

Prep Time: 5 mins

Cook Time: 15 mins

Total Time: 20 mins

Ingredient

- 1 (6 ounces) salmon fillet
- ½ teaspoon salt
- ½ teaspoon Greek seasoning (such as Cavender's®)
- ¼ teaspoon ground black pepper
- 1 pinch dried dill weed

Instructions

- Preheat the air fryer to 370 degrees F (190 degrees C) for 5 minutes.
- Meanwhile, season salmon fillet with salt, Greek seasoning, pepper, and dill.
- Line the inner basket of the air fryer with a perforated parchment round. Place salmon onto the parchment, skin side down.
- Air fry salmon until salmon is cooked through, about 15 minutes.

Nutrition Facts

- Calories: 189; Protein 31.1g; Carbohydrates 1.5g; Fat 5.8g; Cholesterol 72mg; Sodium 1478mg.

107. Easy Air Fryer French Toast Sticks

Prep Time: 10 mins

Cook Time: 10 mins

Total Time: 20 mins

Ingredient

- 4 slices of slightly stale thick bread, such as Texas toast
- Parchment paper
- 2 eggs, lightly beaten
- ¼ cup milk
- 1 teaspoon vanilla extract
- 1 teaspoon cinnamon
- 1 pinch ground nutmeg (optional)

Instructions

- Cut each slice of bread into thirds to make sticks. Cut a piece of parchment paper to fit the bottom of the air fryer basket.
- Preheat air fryer to 360 degrees F (180 degrees C).
- Stir together eggs, milk, vanilla extract, cinnamon, and nutmeg in a bowl until well combined. Dip each piece of bread into the egg mixture, making sure each piece is well submerged. Shake each breadstick to remove excess liquid and place it in a single layer in the air fryer basket. Cook in batches, if necessary, to avoid overcrowding the fryer.
- Cook for 5 minutes, turn bread pieces and cook for an additional 5 minutes.

Nutrition Facts

- Calories: 232; Protein 11.2g; Carbohydrates 28.6g; Fat 7.4g; Cholesterol 188.4mg; Sodium 423.4mg.

108. Air Fryer Fish Sticks

Prep Time: 10 mins

Cook Time: 10 mins

Total Time: 20 mins

Ingredient

- 1 pound cod fillets
- ¼ cup all-purpose flour
- 1 egg
- ½ cup panko bread crumbs
- ¼ cup grated parmesan cheese
- 1 tablespoon parsley flakes
- 1 teaspoon paprika
- ½ teaspoon black pepper
- Cooking spray

Instructions

- Preheat an air fryer to 400 degrees F (200 degrees C).
- Pat fish dry with paper towels and cut into 1x3-inch sticks.
- Place flour in a shallow dish. Beat egg in a separate shallow dish. Combine panko, Parmesan cheese, parsley, paprika, and pepper in a third shallow dish.
- Coat each fish stick in flour, then dip in beaten egg, and finally coat in seasoned panko mixture.
- Spray the basket of the air fryer with nonstick cooking spray. Arrange 1/2 the sticks in the basket, making sure none are touching. Spray the top of each stick with cooking spray.
- Cook in the preheated air fryer for 5 minutes. Flip fish sticks and cook for an additional 5 minutes. Repeat with remaining fish sticks.

Nutrition Facts

- Calories: 200; Protein 26.3g; Carbohydrates 16.5g; Fat 4.1g; Cholesterol 92.5mg; Sodium 245mg.

109. Air Fryer Keto Chicken Wings

Prep Time: 5 mins

Cook Time: 15 mins

Total Time: 20 mins

Ingredient

- 3 pounds chicken wings
- 1 tablespoon taco seasoning mix
- 2 teaspoons olive oil

Instructions

- Combine chicken wings, taco seasoning, and oil in a resealable plastic bag. Shake to coat.
- Preheat the air fryer to 350 degrees F (175 degrees C) for 2 minutes.
- Place wings in the air fryer and cook for 12 minutes, turning after 6 minutes. Serve immediately.

Nutrition Facts

- Calories: 220; Protein 18.3g; Carbohydrates 1.2g; Fat 15.1g; Cholesterol 57.1mg; Sodium 187mg.

110. Sexy Air-Fried Meatloaf

Prep Time: 10 mins

Cook Time: 45 mins

Additional Time: 1 day

Total Time: 1 day

Ingredient

- ½ pound ground pork
- ½ pound ground veal
- 1 large egg
- ¼ cup chopped fresh cilantro
- ¼ cup gluten-free bread crumbs
- 2 medium spring onions, diced
- ½ teaspoon ground black pepper
- ½ teaspoon Sriracha salt
- ½ cup ketchup
- 2 teaspoons gluten-free chipotle chili sauce
- 1 teaspoon olive oil
- 1 teaspoon blackstrap molasses

Instructions

- Preheat the air fryer to 400 degrees F (200 degrees C).
- Combine pork and veal in a nonstick baking dish that fits inside the air fryer basket. Make a well and add egg, cilantro, bread crumbs, spring

onions, black pepper, and 1/2 teaspoon of Sriracha salt. Mix well using your hands. Form a loaf inside the baking dish.

- Combine ketchup, chipotle chili sauce, olive oil, and molasses in a small bowl and whisk well. Set aside, but do not refrigerate.
- Cook meatloaf in the air fryer for 25 minutes without opening the basket. Remove meatloaf and top with ketchup mixture, covering the top completely. Return meatloaf to air fryer and bake until internal temperature reaches 160 degrees F (71 degrees C), about 7 minutes more.
- Turn off the air fryer and let the meatloaf rest inside for 5 minutes. Take the meatloaf out and let rest 5 minutes more before slicing and serving.

Nutrition Facts

- Calories: 272; Protein 22.1g; Carbohydrates 13.3g; Fat 14.4g; Cholesterol 123.5mg; Sodium 536.1mg.

111. Air-Fried Crumbed Fish

Prep Time: 10 mins

Cook Time: 12 mins

Total Time: 22 mins

Ingredient

- 1 cup dry bread crumbs
- ¼ cup vegetable oil
- 4 flounder fillets
- 1 egg, beaten
- 1 lemon, sliced

Instructions

- Preheat an air fryer to 350 degrees F (180 degrees C).
- Mix bread crumbs and oil in a bowl. Stir until the mixture becomes loose and crumbly.
- Dip fish fillets into the egg; shake off any excess. Dip fillets into the bread crumb mixture; coat evenly and fully.
- Lay coated fillets gently in the preheated air fryer. Cook until fish flakes easily with a fork, about 12 minutes. Garnish with lemon slices.

Nutrition Facts

- Calories: 354; Protein 26.9g; Carbohydrates 22.5g; Fat 17.7g; Cholesterol 106.7mg; Sodium 308.9mg

112. Air Fryer Ranch Pork Chops

Prep Time: 5 mins

Cook Time: 10 mins

Additional Time: 10 mins

Total Time: 25 mins

Ingredient

- 4 boneless, center-cut pork chops, 1-inch thick
- cooking spray
- 2 teaspoons dry ranch salad dressing mix
- Aluminum foil

Instructions

- Place pork chops on a plate and lightly spray both sides with cooking spray. Sprinkle both sides with ranch seasoning mix and let sit at room temperature for 10 minutes.
- Spray the basket of an air fryer with cooking spray and preheat the air fryer to 390 degrees F (200 degrees C).
- Place chops in the preheated air fryer, working in batches if necessary, to ensure the fryer is not overcrowded.
- Cook for 5 minutes. Flip chops and cook 5 minutes more. Let rest on a foil-covered plate for 5 minutes before serving.

Nutrition Facts

- Calories: 260; Protein 40.8g; Carbohydrates 0.6g; Fat 9.1g; Cholesterol 106.6mg; Sodium 148.2mg.

113. Air Fryer Rib-Eye Steak

Prep Time: 5 mins

Cook Time: 15 mins

Additional Time: 2 hrs 5 mins

Total Time: 2 hrs 25 mins

Ingredient

- 2 rib-eye steaks, cut 1 1/2- inch thick
- 4 teaspoons grill seasoning (such as Montreal Steak Seasoning®)
- ¼ cup olive oil
- ½ cup reduced-sodium soy sauce

Instructions

- Combine steaks, soy sauce, olive oil, and seasoning in a large resealable bag. Marinate meat for at least 2 hours.
- Remove steaks from bag and discard the marinade. Pat excess oil off the steaks.
- Add about 1 tablespoon water to the bottom of the air fryer pan to prevent it from smoking during the cooking process.
- Preheat the air fryer to 400 degrees F (200 degrees C).
- Add steaks to air fryer and cook for 7 minutes. Turn steaks and cook for another 7 minutes until steak is medium-rare. For a medium steak, increase the total cook time to 16 minutes, flipping steak after 8 minutes.
- Remove steaks, keep warm, and let sit for about 4 minutes before serving.

Nutrition Facts

- Calories: 652; Protein 44g; Carbohydrates 7.5g; Fat 49.1g; Cholesterol 164.8mg; Sodium 4043.7mg.

114. Air-Fried Sesame-Crusted Cod With Snap Peas

Prep Time: 10 mins

Cook Time: 20 mins

Total Time: 30 mins

Ingredient

- 4 (5 ounces) cod fillets
- salt and ground black pepper to taste
- 3 tablespoons butter, melted
- 2 tablespoons sesame seeds
- Vegetable oil
- 2 (6 ounce) packages sugar snap peas
- 3 cloves garlic, thinly sliced
- 1 medium orange, cut into wedges

Instructions

- Brush the air fryer basket with vegetable oil and preheat to 400 degrees F (200 degrees C).
- Thaw fish if frozen; blot dry with paper towels, and sprinkle lightly with salt and pepper.
- Stir together butter and sesame seeds in a small bowl. Set aside 2 tablespoons of the butter mixture for the fish. Toss peas and garlic with the remaining butter mixture and place in the air fryer basket.
- Cook peas in the preheated air fryer in batches, if needed, until just tender, tossing once, about 10 minutes. Remove and keep warm while cooking fish.
- Brush fish with 1/2 of the remaining butter mixture. Place fillets in an air fryer basket. Cook 4 minutes; turn fish. Brush with the remaining butter mixture. Cook 5 to 6 minutes more or until fish begins to flake when tested with a fork. Serve with snap peas and orange wedges.

Nutrition Facts

- Calories: 364; Protein 31.4g; Carbohydrates 22.9g; Fat 15.2g; Cholesterol 74.8mg; Sodium 201.5mg.

115. Breaded Air Fryer Pork Chops

Prep Time: 10 mins

Cook Time: 10 mins

Total Time: 20 mins

Ingredient

- 4 boneless, center-cut pork chops, 1-inch thick
- 1 teaspoon cajun seasoning
- 1 ½ cups cheese and garlic-flavored croutons
- 2 eggs
- Cooking spray

Instructions

- Preheat the air fryer to 390 degrees F (200 degrees C).
- Place pork chops on a plate and season both sides with Cajun seasoning.
- Pulse croutons in a small food processor until they have a fine consistency; transfer to a shallow dish. Lightly beat eggs in a separate

shallow dish. Dip pork chops into eggs, letting excess drip off. Coat chops in crouton breading and set on a plate. Mist chops with cooking spray.

- Spray basket of the air fryer with cooking spray and place chops inside, making sure to not overcrowd the fryer. You may have to do two batches depending on the size of your air fryer.
- Cook for 5 minutes. Flip chops and mist again with cooking spray if there are dry or powdery areas. Cook 5 minutes more. Repeat with remaining chops.

Nutrition Facts

- Calories: 394; Protein 44.7g; Carbohydrates 10g; Fat 18.1g; Cholesterol 218mg; Sodium 428.9mg.

116. Air Fryer Meatballs

Prep Time: 10 mins

Cook Time: 20 mins

Additional Time: 5 mins

Total Time: 35 mins

Servings: 16

Ingredient

- 16 ounces lean ground beef
- 4 ounces ground pork
- 1 teaspoon Italian seasoning
- ½ teaspoon salt
- 2 cloves garlic, minced
- 1 egg
- ½ cup grated Parmesan cheese
- ⅓ cup Italian seasoned bread crumbs

Instructions

- Preheat the air fryer to 350 degrees F (175 degrees C).
- Combine beef, pork, Italian seasoning, salt, garlic, egg, Parmesan cheese, and bread crumbs in a large bowl. Mix well until evenly combined. Form into 16 equally-sized meatballs using an ice cream scoop and place on a baking sheet.
- Place 1/2 of the meatballs in the basket of the air fryer and cook for 8 minutes. Shake the basket and cook 2 minutes more. Transfer to a serving plate and let rest for 5 minutes. Repeat with

remaining meatballs.

Nutrition Facts

- Calories: 96; Protein 7.9g; Carbohydrates 2g; Fat 6.1g; Cholesterol 35.5mg; Sodium 170.4mg.

117. Basic Air Fryer Hot Dogs

Prep Time: 5 mins

Cook Time: 5 mins

Total Time: 10 mins

Servings: 4

Ingredient

- 4 hot dog buns
- 4 hot dogs

Instructions

- Preheat air fryer to 390 degrees F (200 degrees C).
- Place buns in the basket of the air fryer and cook for 2 minutes. Remove buns to a plate.
- Place hot dogs in the basket of the air fryer and cook for 3 minutes. Transfer hot dogs to buns.

118. Air Fryer Baked Potatoes

Prep Time: 5 mins

Cook Time: 1 hr

Total Time: 1 hr 5 mins

Servings: 2

Ingredient

- 2 large russet potatoes, scrubbed
- 1 tablespoon peanut oil
- ½ teaspoon coarse sea salt

Instructions

- Preheat air fryer to 400 degrees F (200 degrees C).
- Brush potatoes with peanut oil and sprinkle with salt. Place them in the air fryer basket and place the basket in the air fryer.
- Cook potatoes until done, about 1 hour. Test for doneness by piercing them with a fork.

Nutrition Facts

- Calories: 344; Protein 7.5g; Carbohydrates 64.5g; Fat 7.1g; Sodium 462.1mg.

119. Air Fryer Baked Potatoes

Prep Time: 5 mins

Cook Time: 1 hr

Total Time: 1 hr 5 mins

Servings: 2

Ingredient

- 2 large russet potatoes, scrubbed
- 1 tablespoon peanut oil
- ½ teaspoon coarse sea salt

Instructions

- Preheat air fryer to 400 degrees F (200 degrees C).
- Brush potatoes with peanut oil and sprinkle with salt. Place them in the air fryer basket and place the basket in the air fryer.
- Cook potatoes until done, about 1 hour. Test for doneness by piercing them with a fork.

Nutrition Facts

- Calories: 344; Protein 7.5g; Carbohydrates 64.5g; Fat 7.1g; Sodium 462.1mg.

120. Air Fryer Meatloaf

Prep Time: 10 mins

Cook Time: 25 mins

Additional Time: 10 mins

Total: 45 mins

Servings: 4

Ingredient

- 1 pound lean ground beef
- 1 egg, lightly beaten
- 3 tablespoons dry bread crumbs
- 1 small onion, finely chopped
- 1 tablespoon chopped fresh thyme
- 1 teaspoon salt
- Ground black pepper to taste
- 2 mushrooms, thickly sliced
- 1 tablespoon olive oil, or as needed

Instructions

Preheat an air fryer to 392 degrees F (200 degrees C).

Combine ground beef, egg, bread crumbs, onion, thyme, salt, and pepper in a bowl. Knead and mix thoroughly.

Transfer beef mixture to a baking pan and smooth the top. Press mushrooms into the top and coat with olive oil. Place the pan into the air fryer basket and slide it into the air fryer.

Set air fryer timer for 25 minutes and roast meatloaf until nicely browned.

Let meatloaf rest at least 10 minutes before slicing into wedges and serving.

Nutrition Facts Facts

Per Serving: 297 calories; protein 24.8g; carbohydrates 5.9g; fat 18.8g; cholesterol 125.5mg; sodium 706.5mg.

22. Crumbed Chicken Tenderloins (Air Fried)

Prep: 15 mins

Cook: 12 mins

Total: 27 mins

Servings: 4

Ingredient

- 1 egg
- ½ cup dry bread crumbs
- 2 tablespoons vegetable oil
- 8 chicken tenderloins

Instructions

- Preheat an air fryer to 350 degrees F (175 degrees C).
- Whisk egg in a small bowl.
- Mix bread crumbs and oil in a second bowl until the mixture becomes loose and crumbly.
- Dip each chicken tenderloin into the bowl of an egg; shake off any residual egg. Dip chicken into the crumb mixture, making sure it is evenly and fully covered. Lay chicken tenderloins into the basket of the air fryer. Cook until no longer pink in the center, about 12 minutes. An instant-read thermometer inserted into the center should read at least 165 degrees F (74 degrees C).

Nutrition Facts

- Calories: 253; Protein 26.2g; Carbohydrates 9.8g; Fat 11.4g; Cholesterol 109mg; Sodium 170.7mg.

---

121. Air Fryer Chicken Taquitos

Prep Time: 15 mins

Cook Time: 20 mins

Total Time: 35 mins

Servings: 6

Ingredient

- 1 teaspoon vegetable oil
- 2 tablespoons diced onion
- 1 clove garlic, minced
- 2 tablespoons chopped green chiles (such as Ortega®)
- 2 tablespoons Mexican-style hot tomato sauce (such as El Pato®)
- 1 cup shredded rotisserie chicken
- 2 tablespoons Neufchatel cheese
- ½ cup shredded Mexican cheese blend
- 1 pinch salt and ground black pepper to taste
- 6 each corn tortillas
- 1 serving avocado oil cooking spray

Instructions

- Heat oil in a skillet. Add onion and cook until soft and translucent, 3 to 5 minutes. Add garlic and cook until fragrant, about 1 minute. Add green chiles and Mexican tomato sauce; stir to combine. Add chicken, Neufchatel cheese, and Mexican cheese blend. Cook and stir until cheeses have melted and the mixture is completely warmed for about 3 minutes. Season with salt and pepper.
- Heat tortillas in a skillet or directly on the grates of a gas stove until soft and pliable. Place 3 tablespoons of chicken mixture down the center of each tortilla. Fold over and roll into taquitos.
- Preheat an air fryer to 400 degrees F (200 degrees C).
- Place taquitos in the air fryer basket, making sure they are not touching, and mist with avocado oil. Cook in batches if necessary. Cook until golden brown and crispy, 6 to 9 minutes. Turn taquitos over, mist with avocado oil, and air fry for an

additional 3 to 5 minutes.

Nutrition Facts

- Calories: 174; Protein 10.3g; Carbohydrates 12.9g; Fat 9.2g; Cholesterol 32.6mg; Sodium 216.6mg.

---

122. Air Fryer Chicken Katsu With Homemade Katsu Sauce

Prep Time: 20 mins

Cook Time: 20 mins

Total Time: 40 mins

Servings: 4

Ingredients

Katsu Sauce:

- ½ cup ketchup
- 2 tablespoons soy sauce
- 1 tablespoon brown sugar
- 1 tablespoon sherry
- 2 teaspoons Worcestershire sauce
- 1 teaspoon minced garlic

Chicken:

- 1 pound boneless skinless chicken breast, sliced in half horizontally
- 1 pinch salt and ground black pepper to taste
- 2 large eggs, beaten
- 1 ½ cups panko bread crumbs
- 1 serving cooking spray

Instructions

- Whisk ketchup, soy sauce, brown sugar, sherry, Worcestershire sauce, and garlic together in a bowl until sugar has dissolved. Set katsu sauce aside.
- Preheat an air fryer to 350 degrees F (175 degrees C).
- Meanwhile, lay chicken pieces on a clean work surface. Season with salt and pepper.
- Place beaten eggs in a flat dish. Pour bread crumbs into a second flat dish. Dredge chicken pieces in egg and then in bread crumbs. Repeat by dredging the chicken in egg and then bread crumbs again, pressing down so that the bread crumbs stick to the chicken.

- Place chicken pieces in the basket of the preheated air fryer. Spray the tops with nonstick cooking spray.
- Air fry for 10 minutes. Flip chicken pieces over using a spatula and spray the tops with nonstick cooking spray. Cook for 8 minutes more. Transfer chicken to a cutting board and slice. Serve with katsu sauce.

Nutrition Facts

- Calories: 318; Protein 32g; Carbohydrates 41.2g; Fat 6.7g; Cholesterol 157.6mg; Sodium 1164.4mg.

123. Air Fryer Lemon Pepper Shrimp

Prep Time: 5 mins

Cook Time: 10 mins

Total Time: 15 mins

Servings: 2

Ingredient

- 1 tablespoon olive oil
- 1 lemon, juiced
- 1 teaspoon lemon pepper
- ¼ teaspoon paprika
- ¼ teaspoon garlic powder
- 12 ounces uncooked medium shrimp, peeled and deveined
- 1 lemon, sliced

Instructions

- Preheat an air fryer to 400 degrees F (200 degrees C).
- Combine olive oil, lemon juice, lemon pepper, paprika, and garlic powder in a bowl. Add shrimp and toss until coated.
- Place shrimp in the air fryer and cook until pink and firm, 6 to 8 minutes. Serve with lemon slices.

Nutrition Facts

- Calories: 215; Protein 28.9g; Carbohydrates 12.6g; Fat 8.6g; Cholesterol 255.4mg; Sodium 528mg.

124. Dry-Rub Air-Fried Chicken Wings

Prep Time: 10 mins

Cook Time: 35 mins

Total Time: 45 mins

Servings: 2

Ingredient

- 1 tablespoon dark brown sugar
- 1 tablespoon sweet paprika
- ½ tablespoon kosher salt
- 1 teaspoon garlic powder
- 1 teaspoon onion powder
- 1 teaspoon poultry seasoning
- ½ teaspoon mustard powder
- ½ teaspoon freshly ground black pepper
- 8 chicken wings, or more as needed

Instructions

- Preheat air fryer to 350 degrees F (175 degrees C).
- Whisk together brown sugar, paprika, salt, garlic powder, onion powder, poultry seasoning, mustard powder, and pepper in a large bowl. Toss in chicken wings and rub the seasonings into them with your hands until fully coated.
- Arrange wings in the basket of the preheated air fryer, standing up on their ends and leaning against each other and the wall of the basket.
- Cook until wings are tender inside and golden brown and crisp on the outside, about 35 minutes. Transfer wings to a plate and serve hot.

Nutrition Facts

- Calories: 318; Protein 25.9g; Carbohydrates 11.3g; Fat 18.7g; Cholesterol 77.3mg; Sodium 1519.9mg.

125. Air Fryer Chicken Cordon Bleu

Prep Time: 15 mins

Cook Time: 20 mins

Additional Time: 5 mins

Total Time: 40 mins

Servings: 2

Ingredient

- 2 boneless, skinless chicken breasts

- Salt and ground black pepper to taste
- 1 tablespoon dijon mustard
- 4 slices deli swiss cheese
- 4 slices of deli ham
- 2 toothpicks
- ¼ cup all-purpose flour
- 1 egg, beaten
- 1 cup panko bread crumbs
- ⅓ cup grated parmesan cheese
- Cooking spray

Instructions

- Set 1 chicken breast on a cutting board. Hold a sharp knife parallel to the cutting board and along one long side of the breast; cut chicken breast almost in half, leaving breast attached at one side. Open breast so it lies flat like a book and covers with plastic wrap. Lightly pound with the flat side of a meat mallet to 1/4-inch thickness. Repeat with the remaining chicken breast.
- Season each chicken breast with salt and pepper. Spread Dijon mustard on top. Place 1 slice of cheese on each breast. Top each with 2 slices of ham and 1 slice of cheese. Roll each breast up and secure it with a toothpick.
- Place flour in a shallow bowl. Place egg in a second bowl. Mix panko bread crumbs and grated Parmesan in a third bowl.
- Preheat an air fryer to 350 degrees F (175 degrees C).
- Dip chicken first in flour, followed by the egg, and finally, roll in the bread crumb mixture. Spray chicken rolls with nonstick spray and let sit for 5 minutes while the air fryer preheats.
- Place chicken in the basket of the preheated air fryer and cook for 10 minutes. Spray any chalky spots with nonstick spray again. Cook until chicken is no longer pink in the center, 8 minutes more.

Nutrition Facts

- Calories: 728; Protein 63.7g; Carbohydrates 56.9g; Fat 31.6g; Cholesterol 253.4mg; Sodium 1663.5mg.

---

126. Cajun Air Fryer Salmon

Prep Time: 10 mins

Cook Time: 10 mins

Total Time: 20 mins

Servings: 2

Ingredient

- 2 (6 ounces) skin-on salmon fillets
- Cooking spray
- 1 tablespoon cajun seasoning
- 1 teaspoon brown sugar

Instructions

- Preheat the air fryer to 390 degrees F (200 degrees C).
- Rinse and dry salmon fillets with a paper towel. Mist fillets with cooking spray. Combine Cajun seasoning and brown sugar in a small bowl. Sprinkle onto a plate. Press the flesh sides of fillets into the seasoning mixture.
- Spray the basket of the air fryer with cooking spray and place salmon fillets skin-side down. Mist salmon again lightly with cooking spray.
- Cook for 8 minutes. Remove from air fryer and let rest for 2 minutes before serving.

Nutrition Facts

- Calories: 327; Protein 33.7g; Carbohydrates 4g; Fat 18.5g; Cholesterol 99.1mg; Sodium 810.8mg.

---

127. Easy Air Fryer Pork Chops

Prep Time: 10 mins

Cook Time: 20 mins

Additional Time: 5 mins

Total Time: 35 mins

Servings: 4

Ingredient

- ½ cup grated Parmesan cheese
- 1 teaspoon paprika
- 1 teaspoon garlic powder
- 1 teaspoon kosher salt
- 1 teaspoon dried parsley
- ½ teaspoon ground black pepper
- 4 (5 ounces) center-cut pork chops
- 2 tablespoons extra virgin olive oil

Instructions

- Preheat the air fryer to 380 degrees F (190 degrees C).
- Combine Parmesan cheese, paprika, garlic powder, salt, parsley, and pepper in a flat shallow dish; mix well.
- Coat each pork chop with olive oil. Dredge both sides of each chop in the Parmesan mixture and set on a plate.
- Place 2 chops in the basket of the air fryer and cook for 10 minutes; flipping halfway through cook time.
- Transfer to a cutting board and let rest for 5 minutes. Repeat with remaining chops.

Nutrition Facts

- Calories: 305; Protein 35.3g; Carbohydrates 1.5g; Fat 16.6g; Cholesterol 90.3mg; Sodium 684.9mg

128. Lumpia In The Air Fryer

Prep Time: 15 mins

Cook Time: 20 mins

Total: 35 mins

Servings: 16

Ingredient

- 1 pound Italian hot sausage links
- ½ cup finely sliced green onions
- ¼ cup diced onions
- ½ cup finely chopped carrots
- ½ cup finely chopped water chestnuts
- 2 cloves garlic, minced
- 2 tablespoons soy sauce
- ½ teaspoon salt
- ¼ teaspoon ground ginger
- 16 spring roll wrappers
- Avocado oil cooking spray

Instructions

- Remove casing from sausage and cook in a skillet over medium heat until slightly browned 4 to 5 minutes. Add green onions, onions, carrots, and water chestnuts. Cook and stir until onions are soft and translucent, 5 to 7 minutes. Add garlic and cook for 1 to 2 minutes. Season with soy sauce, salt, and ginger. Stir until filling is well combined and remove from heat.
- Lay a spring roll wrapper at an angle. Place a scant 1/4 cup filling in the center of the wrapper. Fold bottom corner over filling and tuck in the sides to form a roll. Use your finger to lightly moisten edges with water. Repeat with remaining wrappers and filling. Mist each roll with avocado oil spray.
- Preheat an air fryer to 390 degrees F (198 degrees C). Place lumpia rolls in the basket, making sure they are not touching; cook in batches if necessary. Fry for 4 minutes; flip and cook until skins are crispy, about 4 minutes more.

Nutrition Facts

- Calories: 98; Protein 4.8g; Carbohydrates 7.2g; Fat 5.5g; Cholesterol 11.9mg; Sodium 471.1mg.

129. Air Fryer Buttermilk Fried Chicken

Prep Time: 5 mins

Cook Time: 30 mins

Additional Time: 4 hrs

Total Time: 4 hrs 35 mins

Servings: 6

Ingredient

- 1 ½ pound boneless, skinless chicken thighs
- 2 cups buttermilk
- 1 cup all-purpose flour
- 1 tablespoon seasoned salt
- ½ tablespoon ground black pepper
- 1 cup panko bread crumbs
- 1 serving cooking spray

Instructions

- Place chicken thighs in a shallow casserole dish. Pour buttermilk over chicken and refrigerate for 4 hours, or overnight.
- Preheat an air fryer to 380 degrees F (190 degrees C).
- Mix flour, seasoned salt, and pepper in a large gallon-sized resealable bag. Dredge chicken thighs in seasoned flour. Dip back into the buttermilk, then coat with panko bread crumbs.
- Spray the basket of the air fryer with nonstick

cooking spray. Arrange 1/2 of the chicken thighs in the basket, making sure none are touching. Spray the top of each chicken thigh with cooking spray.

- Cook in the preheated air fryer for 15 minutes. Flip. Spray tops of chicken again. Cook until chicken is no longer pink in the center and the juices run clear for about 10 more minutes. An instant-read thermometer inserted into the center should read at least 165 degrees F (74 degrees C). Repeat with the remaining chicken.

Nutrition Facts

- Calories: 335; Protein 24.5g; Carbohydrates 33.2g; Fat 12.8g; Cholesterol 67.1mg; Sodium 687.2mg.

130. Air Fryer Potstickers

Prep Time: 10 mins

Cook Time: 25 mins

Total Time: 35 mins

Servings: 24

Ingredient

- ½ pound ground pork
- 1 (4 ounces) can water chestnuts, drained and chopped
- 1 (4 ounces) can shiitake mushrooms, drained and chopped
- 2 tablespoons soy sauce
- 2 tablespoons sesame oil
- 1 tablespoon Sriracha sauce
- 1 (12 ounces) package round dumpling wrappers

Instructions

- Preheat an air fryer to 400 degrees F (200 degrees C).
- Combine ground pork, water chestnuts, shiitake mushrooms, sesame oil, soy sauce, and Sriracha in a large skillet over medium-high heat. Cook until pork is no longer pink, about 6 minutes. Remove from heat and let sit until cool enough to handle.
- Layout 8 dumpling wrappers on a clean work surface. Place a heaping teaspoonful of pork mixture in the middle of each wrapper. Pull both

sides up like a taco and pinch the tops until sealed.

- Cook in batches in the preheated air fryer for 3 minutes. Use tongs to flip the potstickers and cook 3 minutes more. Transfer to a paper-towel-lined plate. Repeat with remaining dumpling wrappers and filling.

Nutrition Facts

- Calories: 70; Protein 2.7g; Carbohydrates 8.7g; Fat 2.6g; Cholesterol 4.7mg; Sodium 273.1mg.

131. Mexican-Style Air Fryer Stuffed Chicken Breasts

Prep Time: 20 mins

Cook Time: 10 mins

Total Time: 30 mins

Servings: 2

Ingredient

- 4 extra-long toothpicks
- 4 teaspoons chili powder, divided
- 4 teaspoons ground cumin, divided
- 1 skinless, boneless chicken breast
- 2 teaspoons chipotle flakes
- 2 teaspoons mexican oregano
- Salt and ground black pepper to taste
- ½ red bell pepper, sliced into thin strips
- ½ onion, sliced into thin strips
- 1 fresh jalapeno pepper, sliced into thin strips
- 2 teaspoons corn oil
- ½ lime, juiced

Instructions

- Place toothpicks in a small bowl and cover with water; let them soak to keep them from burning while cooking.
- Mix 2 teaspoons chili powder and 2 teaspoons cumin in a shallow dish.
- Preheat an air fryer to 400 degrees F (200 degrees C).
- Place chicken breast on a flat work surface. Slice horizontally through the middle. Pound each half using a kitchen mallet or rolling pin until about 1/4-inch thick.
- Sprinkle each breast half equally with remaining chili powder, remaining cumin, chipotle flakes,

oregano, salt, and pepper. Place 1/2 the bell pepper, onion, and jalapeno in the center of 1 breast half. Roll the chicken from the tapered end upward and use 2 toothpicks to secure it. Repeat with other breast, spices, and vegetables and secure with remaining toothpicks. Roll each roll-up in the chili-cumin mixture in the shallow dish while drizzling with olive oil until evenly covered.

- Place roll-ups in the air-fryer basket with the toothpick side facing up. Set timer for 6 minutes.
- Turn roll-ups over. Continue cooking in the air fryer until juices run clear and an instant-read thermometer inserted into the center reads at least 165 degrees F (74 degrees C), about 5 minutes more.
- Drizzle lime juice evenly on roll-ups before serving.

Nutrition Facts

- Calories: 185; Protein 14.8g; Carbohydrates 15.2g; Fat 8.5g; Cholesterol 32.3mg; Sodium 170.8mg.

---

132. Air Fryer Chimichangas

Prep Time: 15 mins

Cook Time: 20 mins

Total Time: 35 mins

Servings: 6

Ingredient

- 1 tablespoon vegetable oil
- ½ cup diced onion
- 2 cups shredded cooked chicken
- ½ (8 ounces) package Neufchatel cheese, softened
- 1 (4 ounces) can hot fire-roasted diced green chiles (such as Ortega®)
- ¼ cup chicken broth
- 1 ½ tablespoons chicken taco seasoning mix (such as McCormick®)
- ½ teaspoon salt
- ¼ teaspoon ground black pepper
- 6 (10 inches) flour tortillas
- 1 cup shredded Mexican cheese blend, or to taste

- Avocado oil cooking spray

Instructions

- Heat oil in a medium skillet. Add onion and cook until soft and translucent, 4 to 6 minutes. Add chicken, Neufchatel cheese, diced chiles, chicken broth, taco seasoning, salt, and pepper. Cook and stir until mixture is well combined and Neufchatel has softened been incorporated.
- Heat tortillas in a large skillet or directly on the grates of a gas stove until soft and pliable. Place 1/3 cup chicken mixture down the center of each tortilla and top with a heaping tablespoon of Mexican cheese. Fold top and bottom of tortillas over the filling, then roll each into a burrito shape. Mist with cooking spray and place in the basket of an air fryer.
- Air fry at 400 degrees F (200 degrees C) for 4 to 6 minutes. Flip each chimichanga over, mist with cooking spray, and air fry until lightly browned, 2 to 4 minutes more.

Nutrition Facts

- Calories: 455; Protein 24.8g; Carbohydrates 41g; Fat 20.6g; Cholesterol 69.8mg; Sodium 1291.5mg.

---

133. Breaded Air Fryer Pork Chops

Prep Time: 10 mins

Cook Time: 10 mins

Total Time: 20 mins

Servings: 4

Ingredient

- 4 boneless, center-cut pork chops, 1-inch thick
- 1 teaspoon Cajun seasoning
- 1 ½ cups cheese and garlic-flavored croutons
- 2 eggs

Instructions

- Preheat the air fryer to 390 degrees F (200 degrees C).
- Place pork chops on a plate and season both sides with Cajun seasoning.
- Pulse croutons in a small food processor until they have a fine consistency; transfer to a

shallow dish. Lightly beat eggs in a separate shallow dish. Dip pork chops into eggs, letting excess drip off. Coat chops in crouton breading and set on a plate. Mist chops with cooking spray.

- Spray basket of the air fryer with cooking spray and place chops inside, making sure to not overcrowd the fryer. You may have to do two batches depending on the size of your air fryer.
- Cook for 5 minutes. Flip chops and mist again with cooking spray if there are dry or powdery areas. Cook 5 minutes more. Repeat with remaining chops.

Nutrition Facts

- Calories: 394; Protein 44.7g; Carbohydrates 10g; Fat 18.1g; Cholesterol 218mg; Sodium 428.9mg.

134. Air Fryer Crab Rangoon

Prep Time: 15 mins

Cook Time: 20 mins

Total Time: 35 mins

Servings: 12

Ingredient

- 1 (8 ounces) package cream cheese, softened
- 4 ounces lump crab meat
- 2 tablespoons chopped scallions
- 1 teaspoon soy sauce
- 1 teaspoon Worcestershire sauce
- 1 serving nonstick cooking spray
- 24 each wonton wrappers
- 2 tablespoons Asian sweet chili sauce, for dipping

Instructions

- Combine cream cheese, crab meat, scallions, soy sauce, and Worcestershire sauce in a bowl; stir until evenly combined.
- Preheat an air fryer to 350 degrees F (175 degrees C). Spray the basket of the air fryer with cooking spray. Fill a small bowl with warm water.
- Place 12 wonton wrappers on a clean work surface. Spoon 1 teaspoon of cream cheese mixture into the center of each wonton wrapper. Dip index finger into the warm water and wet

around the sides of each wonton wrapper. Crimp wrapper corners upwards to meet in the center to form dumplings.

- Place dumplings in the prepared basket and spray the tops with cooking spray.
- Cook dumplings until desired crispness, about 8 to 10 minutes. Transfer to a paper towel-lined plate.
- While the first batch is cooking, assemble the remaining dumplings with the remaining wrappers and filling.
- Serve with sweet chili sauce for dipping.

Nutrition Facts

- Calories: 234; Protein 5.1g; Carbohydrates 11.1g; Fat 6.9g; Cholesterol 29.1mg; Sodium 240.4mg.

135. Lemon-Garlic Air Fryer Salmon

Prep Time: 10 mins

Cook Time: 10 mins

Additional Time: 5 mins

Total Time: 25 mins

Ingredient

- 1 tablespoon melted butter
- ½ teaspoon minced garlic
- 2 (6 ounce) fillets center-cut salmon fillets with skin
- ¼ teaspoon lemon-pepper seasoning
- ⅛ teaspoon dried parsley
- Cooking spray
- 3 thin slices lemon, cut in half

Instructions

- Preheat the air fryer to 390 degrees F (200 degrees C).
- Combine melted butter and minced garlic in a small bowl.
- Rinse salmon fillets and dry with a paper towel. Brush with butter mixture and sprinkle with lemon-pepper seasoning and parsley.
- Spray the basket of the air fryer with cooking spray. Place salmon fillets in the basket, skin-side down, and top each with 3 lemon halves.
- Cook in the preheated air fryer for 8 to 10 minutes. Remove from the air fryer and let rest

for 2 minutes before serving.

Nutrition Facts

- Calories: 293; Protein 33.6g; Carbohydrates 1.4g; Fat 16.4g; Cholesterol 108.3mg; Sodium 174.4mg.

136. Air Fryer Ranch Pork Chops

Prep Time: 5 mins

Cook Time: 10 mins

Additional Time: 10 mins

Total Time: 25 mins

Ingredient

- 4 boneless, center-cut pork chops, 1-inch thick
- Cooking spray
- 2 teaspoons dry ranch salad dressing mix
- Aluminum foil

Instructions

- Place pork chops on a plate and lightly spray both sides with cooking spray. Sprinkle both sides with ranch seasoning mix and let sit at room temperature for 10 minutes.
- Spray the basket of an air fryer with cooking spray and preheat the air fryer to 390 degrees F (200 degrees C).
- Place chops in the preheated air fryer, working in batches if necessary, to ensure the fryer is not overcrowded.
- Cook for 5 minutes. Flip chops and cook 5 minutes more. Let rest on a foil-covered plate for 5 minutes before serving.

Nutrition Facts

- Calories: 260; Protein 40.8g; Carbohydrates 0.6g; Fat 9.1g; Cholesterol 106.6mg; Sodium 148.2mg.

137. Air Fryer Tacos De Papa

Cook Time: 25 mins

Additional Time: 5 mins

Total Time: 30 mins

Ingredient

- 2 cups water
- 1 (4 ounces) package instant mashed potatoes
- ½ cup shredded cheddar cheese
- 1 green onion, chopped
- ½ teaspoon ground cumin
- 10 corn tortillas
- 1 serving nonstick cooking spray
- ½ cup salsa verde
- ¼ cup crumbled cotija cheese

Instructions

- Heat water in a medium saucepan to boiling. Remove from the heat and stir in instant mashed potatoes. Mix thoroughly with a fork to moisten all potatoes and let stand 5 minutes. Stir in Cheddar cheese, green onion, and cumin.
- Preheat an air fryer to 400 degrees F (200 degrees C).
- Wrap tortillas in a damp paper towel and microwave on high until warm, about 20 seconds.
- Spread 1 tablespoon potato mixture in the center of a tortilla and fold over to make a taco. Repeat with remaining tortillas.
- Working in batches, place tacos in the basket of an air fryer. Spray the tops with cooking spray and cook until crispy, about 5 minutes. Transfer to a serving platter and repeat to cook remaining tacos.
- Drizzle salsa verde over tacos and top with cotija cheese.

Nutrition Facts

- Calories: 137; Protein 4.6g; Carbohydrates 22g; Fat 3.7g; Cholesterol 9.4mg; Sodium 138.1mg.

3. Air Fryer Side Dishes & Dinner Recipes

138. Fried Shrimp Po' Boy Sandwich Recipe

Prep Time: 20 minutes

Cook Time: 10 minutes

Total Time: 30 minutes

Ingredients

- 1 pound shrimp, deveined
- 1 teaspoon creole seasoning i used tony chachere
- 1/4 cup buttermilk
- 1/2 cup louisiana fish fry coating
- Cooking oil spray (if air frying) i use olive oil
- Canola or vegetable oil (if pan-frying) you will need enough oil to fill 2 inches of height in your frying pan.
- 4 french bread hoagie rolls i used 2 loaves, cut each in half
- 2 cups shredded iceberg lettuce
- 8 tomato slices

Remoulade Sauce

- 1/2 cup mayo I used reduced-fat
- 1 tsp minced garlic
- 1/2 lemon juice of
- 1 tsp Worcestershire
- 1/2 tsp Creole Seasoning I used Tony Chachere
- 1 tsp Dijon mustard
- 1 tsp hot sauce
- 1 green onion chopped

Instructions

Remoulade Sauce

- Combine all of the ingredients in a small bowl. Refrigerate before serving while the shrimp cooks.

Shrimp And Breading

- Marinate the shrimp in the Creole seasoning and buttermilk for 30 minutes. I like to use a sealable plastic bag to do this.
- Add the fish fry to a bowl. Remove the shrimp from the bags and dip each into the fish fry. Add the shrimp to the air fryer basket.

Pan Fry

- Heat a frying pan with 2 inches of oil to 350 degrees. Use a thermometer to test the heat.
- Fry the shrimp on both sides for 3-4 minutes until crisp.
- Remove the shrimp from the pan and drain the excess grease using paper towels.

Air Fryer

- Spray the air fryer basket with cooking oil. Add the shrimp to the air fryer basket.
- Spritz the shrimp with cooking oil.
- Cook the shrimp for 5 minutes at 400 degrees. Open the basket and flip the shrimp to the other side. Cook for an additional 3-5 minutes or until crisp.
- Assemble the Po Boy
- Spread the remoulade sauce on the French bread.
- Add the sliced tomato and lettuce, and then the shrimp.

Nutritional Facts

- Serving: 1serving | Calories: 437kcal | Carbohydrates: 55g | Protein: 24g | Fat: 12g

139. Easy Air Fryer Rotisserie Roasted Whole Chicken

Prep Time: 15 minutes

Cook Time: 55 minutes

Resting: 15 minutes

Total Time: 1 hour 25 minutes

Ingredients

- 1 4.5-5 pounds whole chicken
- 1/2 fresh lemon
- 1/4 whole onion
- 4 sprigs of fresh thyme
- 4 sprigs of fresh rosemary
- Olive oil spray
- 1 teaspoon ground thyme i like to use ground thyme in addition to fresh thyme for optimal flavor.
- 1 teaspoon onion powder

- 1 teaspoon garlic powder
- Kosher salt to taste be sure to use kosher salt.

Instructions

- I purchased my whole chicken ready with the contents of the cavity removed. If your chicken still has the giblets inside of it, you will need to remove them before cooking.
- Stuff 1/2 of fresh-cut lemon and 1/4 of a chopped onion inside the cavity of the chicken along with the fresh rosemary and thyme.
- Make sure the chicken is completely dry on the outside. Pat dry with paper towels if necessary. A dry chicken will help it crisp in the air fryer with the olive oil.
- Spray olive oil onto both sides of the chicken using an oil sprayer.
- Sprinkle the seasonings throughout and onto both sides of the chicken. You may elect to only season the bottom side of the chicken at this step. Because you will need to flip the chicken during the air frying process, you will likely lose some of the seasonings at this stage. My preference is to season both sides initially, and then re-assess if more seasoning (usually salt is needed later).
- Line the air fryer with parchment paper. This makes for easy cleanup. Load the chicken into the air fryer basket with the breast side down.
- Air fry the chicken for 30 minutes at 330 degrees.
- Open the air fryer and flip the chicken. I gripped the chicken cavity with tongs to flip.
- Re-assess if more seasoning is needed on the breasts, legs, and wings. Add additional if necessary.
- Air fry for an additional 20-25 minutes until the chicken reaches an internal temperature of 165 degrees. Use a meat thermometer.
- This step is important. Place the meat thermometer in the thickest part of the chicken, which is typically the chicken thigh area. I like to test the breast too, just to ensure the entire chicken is fully cooked.
- Remove the chicken from the air fryer basket and place it on a plate to rest for at least 15 minutes before cutting into the chicken. This will allow the moisture to redistribute throughout the chicken before you cut into it.

Nutrition Facts

- Calories: 340kcal | Carbohydrates: 2g | Protein: 33g | Fat: 22g

140. Air Fryer Beef Taco Fried Egg Rolls

Prep Time: 15 minutes

Cook Time: 25 minutes

Total Time: 40 minutes

Servings: 8

Ingredients

- 1 pound ground beef
- 16 egg roll wrappers i used wing hing brand
- 1/2 cup chopped onion i used red onion.
- 2 garlic cloves minced
- 16 oz can diced tomatoes and chilies i used mexican rotel.
- 8 oz refried black beans i used fat-free and 1/2 of a 16oz can.
- 1 cup shredded mexican cheese
- 1/2 cup whole kernel corn i used frozen
- Cooking oil spray
- Homemade taco seasoning
- 1 tablespoon chili powder
- 1 teaspoon cumin
- 1 teaspoon smoked paprika
- Salt and pepper to taste

Instructions

- Add the ground beef to a skillet on medium-high heat along with the salt, pepper, and taco seasoning. Cook until browned while breaking the beef into smaller chunks.
- Once the meat has started to brown add the chopped onions and garlic. Cook until the onions become fragrant.
- Add the diced tomatoes and chilis, Mexican cheese, beans, and corn. Stir to ensure the mixture is combined.
- Lay the egg roll wrappers on a flat surface. Dip a cooking brush in water. Glaze each of the egg roll wrappers with the wet brush along the edges. This will soften the crust and make it easier to roll.
- Load 2 tablespoons of the mixture into each of the wrappers. Do not overstuff. Depending on

the brand of egg roll wrappers you use, you may need to double wrap the egg rolls.

- Fold the wrappers diagonally to close. Press firmly on the area with the filling, cup it to secure it in place. Fold in the left and right sides as triangles. Fold the final layer over the top to close. Use the cooking brush to wet the area and secure it in place.
- Spray the air fryer basket with cooking oil.
- Load the egg rolls into the basket of the Air Fryer. Spray each egg roll with cooking oil.
- Cook for 8 minutes at 400 degrees. Flip the egg rolls. Cook for an additional 4 minutes or until browned and crisp.

Nutrition Facts

- Calories: 348kcal | Carbohydrates: 38g | Protein: 24g | Fat: 11g

141. Air Fryer Beef Taco Fried Egg Rolls

Prep Time: 15 minutes

Cook Time: 25 minutes

Total Time: 40 minutes

Servings: 8

Ingredients

- 1 pound ground beef
- 16 egg roll wrappers i used wing hing brand
- 1/2 cup chopped onion i used red onion.
- 2 garlic cloves minced
- 16 oz can diced tomatoes and chilies i used mexican rotel.
- 8 oz refried black beans i used fat-free and 1/2 of a 16oz can.
- 1 cup shredded mexican cheese
- 1/2 cup whole kernel corn i used frozen
- Cooking oil spray

Homemade Taco Seasoning

- 1 tablespoon chili powder
- 1 teaspoon cumin
- 1 teaspoon smoked paprika
- Salt and pepper to taste

Instructions

- Add the ground beef to a skillet on medium-high

heat along with the salt, pepper, and taco seasoning. Cook until browned while breaking the beef into smaller chunks.

- Once the meat has started to brown add the chopped onions and garlic. Cook until the onions become fragrant.
- Add the diced tomatoes and chilis, Mexican cheese, beans, and corn. Stir to ensure the mixture is combined.
- Lay the egg roll wrappers on a flat surface. Dip a cooking brush in water. Glaze each of the egg roll wrappers with the wet brush along the edges. This will soften the crust and make it easier to roll.
- Load 2 tablespoons of the mixture into each of the wrappers. Do not overstuff. Depending on the brand of egg roll wrappers you use, you may need to double wrap the egg rolls.
- Fold the wrappers diagonally to close. Press firmly on the area with the filling, cup it to secure it in place. Fold in the left and right sides as triangles. Fold the final layer over the top to close. Use the cooking brush to wet the area and secure it in place.
- Spray the air fryer basket with cooking oil.
- Load the egg rolls into the basket of the Air Fryer. Spray each egg roll with cooking oil.
- Cook for 8 minutes at 400 degrees. Flip the egg rolls. Cook for an additional 4 minutes or until browned and crisp.

Nutrition Facts

- Calories: 348kcal | Carbohydrates: 38g | Protein: 24g | Fat: 11g

142. Easy Crispy Garlic Parmesan Chicken Wings

Prep Time: 15 minutes

Cook Time: 45 minutes

Total Time: 1 hour

Servings: 4

Ingredients

- 1 pound chicken wings (drummettes)
- 1/2 cup flour see recipe notes for low carb substitute.
- 1/2 cup grated parmesan divided into two 1/4

cup servings

- 1/2 tablespoon mccormicks grill mates chicken seasoning you can use your favorite chicken rub.
- Salt and pepper to taste
- Cooking oil i use olive oil.
- 3 garlic cloves minced
- 1 tablespoon butter
- 1 tablespoon olive oil

Instructions

- Oven and Baking Instructions
- Preheat the oven to 375 degrees.
- Pat the chicken dry and place it on a large bowl or plastic bag.
- Add the flour, 1/4 cup of grated parmesan, chicken seasoning, salt, and pepper to the chicken. Ensure the chicken is fully coated.
- Line a sheet pan with parchment paper and add the wings. Spritz the chicken wings with cooking oil.
- Bake the wings for 20 minutes and then open and flip the wings. Spritz with cooking oil. Bake for an additional 10 minutes.
- Heat a saucepan on medium-high heat. Add the butter, 1 tablespoon of olive oil, garlic, and 1/4 cup of grated parmesan.
- Cook for 2-3 minutes until the butter and cheese have melted.
- Remove the chicken from the oven and drizzle the wings in the garlic parmesan sauce.
- Return the chicken to the oven. Bake for an additional 10-15 minutes.
- Garnish with parsley and parmesan if you wish.

Air Fryer Instructions

- Pat the chicken dry and place it on a large bowl or plastic bag.
- Add the flour, 1/4 cup of grated parmesan, chicken seasoning, salt, and pepper to the chicken. Ensure the chicken is fully coated.
- Line the air fryer basket with air fryer parchment paper. Place the chicken on the parchment paper. Spritz the chicken with olive oil.
- Air fry for 15 minutes at 400 degrees.
- Open the air fryer and flip the chicken. Spritz the chicken with cooking oil. Cook for an additional 5 minutes.
- Heat a saucepan on medium-high heat. Add the

butter, 1 tablespoon of olive oil, garlic, and 1/4 cup of grated parmesan.
- Cook for 2-3 minutes until the butter and cheese have melted.
- Remove the chicken from the air fryer and drizzle it with the garlic parmesan butter.
- Return the chicken to the air fryer. Air fryer for an additional 3-4 minutes on 400 degrees.
- Garnish with parsley and parmesan if you wish.

Nutrition Facts

- Calories: 374kcal | Carbohydrates: 11g | Protein: 26g | Fat: 24g

---

143. Air Fryer Crispy Crab Rangoon

Prep Time: 15 minutes

Cook Time: 15 minutes

Total Time: 30 minutes

Ingredients

- 4 or 6 oz cream cheese, softened If you prefer creamy crab rangoon use 6 oz
- 4 or 6 oz lump crab meat If you prefer your crab rangoon to have more cream cheese and less crab, use 4 oz. Seafood lovers may want to go for 6 oz
- 2 green onions, chopped
- 21 wonton wrappers
- 2 garlic cloves, minced
- 1 teaspoon Worcestershire sauce
- Salt and pepper to taste
- Cooking oil I use olive oil.

Instructions

- You can soften your cream cheese by heating it in the microwave for 20 seconds.
- Combine the cream cheese, green onions, crab meat, Worcestershire sauce, salt, pepper, and garlic in a small bowl. Stir to mix well.
- Layout the wonton wrappers on a working surface. I used a large, bamboo cutting board. Moisten each of the wrappers with water. I use a cooking brush, and brush it along all of the edges.
- Load about a teaspoon and a half of filling onto each wrapper. Be careful not to overfill.

- Fold each wrapper diagonally across to form a triangle. From there bring up the two opposite corners toward each other. Don't close the wrapper yet. Bring up the other two opposite sides, pushing out any air. Squeeze each of the edges together. Be sure to check out the recipe video above for illustration.
- Spritz the air fryer basket with cooking oil.
- Load the crab rangoon into the air fryer basket. Do not stack or overfill. Cook in batches if needed.
- Spritz with oil.
- Place the Air Fryer at 370 degrees. Cook for 10 minutes.
- Open and flip the crab rangoon. Cook for an additional 2-5 minutes until they have reached your desired level of golden brown and crisp.
- Remove the crab rangoon from the air fryer and serve with your desired dipping sauce.

Nutrition Facts

- Calories: 98kcal | Carbohydrates: 12g | Protein: 7g | Fat: 3g

144. Air Fryer 3 Ingredient Fried Catfish

Prep Time5 minutes

Cook Time: 20 minutes

Total Time: 25 minutes

Ingredients

- 4 catfish fillets
- 1/4 cup Louisiana Fish Fry Coating
- 1 tbsp olive oil
- 1 tbsp chopped parsley optional

Instructions

- Pat the catfish dry.
- Sprinkle the fish fry onto both sides of each fillet. Ensure the entire filet is coated with seasoning.
- Spritz olive oil on the top of each filet.
- Place the filet in the Air Fryer basket. Do not stack the fish and do not overcrowd the basket. Cook in batches if needed. Close and cook for 10 minutes at 400 degrees.
- Open the air fryer and flip the fish. Cook for an additional 10 minutes.

- Open and flip the fish.
- Cook for an additional 2-3 minutes or until desired crispness.
- Top with optional parsley.

Nutrition Facts

- Calories: 208kcal | Carbohydrates: 8g | Protein: 17g | Fat: 9g

145. Air Fryer Bang Bang Fried Shrimp

Prep Time: 10 minutes

Cook Time: 20 minutes

Total Time: 30 minutes

Ingredients

- 1 pound raw shrimp peeled and deveined
- 1 egg white 3 tbsp
- 1/2 cup all-purpose flour
- 3/4 cup panko bread crumbs
- 1 tsp paprika
- Mccormick's grill mates montreal chicken seasoning to taste
- Salt and pepper to taste
- Cooking oil

Bang Bang Sauce

- 1/3 cup plain, non-fat Greek yogurt
- 2 tbsp Sriracha
- 1/4 cup sweet chili sauce

Instructions

- Preheat Air Fryer to 400 degrees.
- Season the shrimp with the seasonings.
- Place the flour, egg whites, and panko bread crumbs in three separate bowls.
- Create a cooking station. Dip the shrimp in the flour, then the egg whites, and the panko bread crumbs last.
- When dipping the shrimp in the egg whites, you do not need to submerge the shrimp. Do a light dab so that most of the flour stays on the shrimp. You want the egg white to adhere to the panko crumbs.
- Spray the shrimp with cooking oil.
- Add the shrimp to the Air Fryer basket. Cook for 4 minutes. Open the basket and flip the shrimp

to the other side. Cook for an additional 4 minutes or until crisp.

Bang Bang Sauce

- Combine all of the ingredients in a small bowl. Mix thoroughly to combine.

Nutrition Facts

- Calories: 242kcal | Carbohydrates: 32g | Protein: 37g | Fat: 1g

146. Air Fryer Parmesan Truffle Oil Fries

Prep Time10 minutes

Cook Time40 minutes

Total Time50 minutes

Ingredients

- 3 large russet potatoes peeled and cut lengthwise
- 2 tbsp white truffle oil
- 2 tbsp parmesan shredded
- 1 tsp paprika
- salt and pepper to taste
- 1 tbsp parsley chopped

Instructions

- Place the sliced potatoes in a large bowl with cold water.
- Allow the potatoes to soak in the water for at least 30 minutes, preferably an hour.
- Spread the fries onto a flat surface and dry them completely with paper towels. Coat them with 1 tbsp of the white truffle oil and seasonings.
- Add half of the fries to the Air Fryer basket. Adjust the temperature to 380 degrees and cook for 15-20 minutes. Set a timer for 10 minutes and stop and shake the basket at the 10-minute mark (once).
- Use your judgment. If the fries need to be crisper, allow them to cook for additional time. If the fries look crisp before 15 minutes, remove them. I cooked both of my batches for almost 20 minutes.
- When the first half finishes, cook the remaining half.
- Add the remaining truffle oil and parmesan to

the fries immediately upon removing them from the Air Fryer.
- Top with shredded parsley. Serve!

Nutrition Facts

- Calories: 233kcal

147. Air Fryer Low-Fat Weight Watchers Mozzarella Cheese Sticks

Prep Time: 10 minutes

Cook Time: 16 minutes

Total Time: 26 minutes

Ingredients

- 10 pieces mozzarella string cheese I used Weight Watchers Smoked Flavor
- 1 cup Italian breadcrumbs
- 1 egg
- 1/2 cup flour
- 1 cup marinara sauce
- Salt and pepper to taste

Instructions

- Season the breadcrumbs with salt and pepper.
- Create a workstation by adding the flour, bread crumbs, and eggs to separate bowls.
- Dip each string of cheese in flour, then egg, and last the breadcrumbs.
- Freeze the sticks for one hour so that they harden. This will help the cheese maintain the stick shape while frying.
- Season your Air Fryer basket before each use so that items do not stick. I like to glaze the basket with coconut oil using a cooking brush.
- Turn the Air Fryer on 400 degrees. Add the sticks to the fryer.
- Cook for 8 minutes. Remove the basket. Flip each stick. You can use tongs, but be careful not to manipulate the shape. I used my hands to flip them. They weren't too hot. Cook for an additional 8 minutes.
- Allow the sticks to cool for 5 minutes before removing them from the pan. Some of the sticks may leak cheese on the outside. Allow the sticks to cool, and then use your hands to correct the shape.

Nutrition Facts

- Calories: 224kcal | Carbohydrates: 19g | Protein: 17g | Fat: 7g

---

148. Air Fryer Carrots (Three Ways)

Prep Time: 5 minutes

Cook Time: 20 minutes

Total Time: 25 minutes

Ingredients

- 4 cups sliced carrots (1/4-inch thick), washed and patted dry
- 2 tablespoons extra virgin olive oil

Savory Version

- 1/2 teaspoon garlic powder
- 1/2 teaspoon dried basil
- 1/2 teaspoon dried oregano
- 1/2 teaspoon dried parsley
- 1/2 teaspoon kosher salt
- 1/4 teaspoon ground black pepper

Sweet Version

- 1 tablespoon coconut sugar
- 1/2 tablespoon maple syrup
- 1/4 teaspoon kosher salt
- 1/8 teaspoon crushed red pepper flakes

Spicy Version

- 1 teaspoon ground cumin
- 1 teaspoon smoked paprika
- 1/2 teaspoon kosher salt
- 1/8 teaspoon cayenne pepper
- 1/8 teaspoon ground black pepper

Instructions

- Add the sliced carrots to a large bowl and evenly coat with oil. Add your choice of seasonings and toss to coat.
- Place carrots in the air fryer basket and air fry on 400F for 18-20 minutes, or until fork-tender. Shake or stir the carrots after about 10 minutes. Serve immediately.

Nutritional Facts

- Total Fat: 7.3g
- Total Carbohydrate: 12.2g
- Sugar: 5.8g
- Calcium: 45.9mg
- Sat Fat: 1.1g
- Sodium: 239.8mg
- Fiber: 3.6g
- Protein: 1.3g
- Vitamin C: 7.3mg
- Iron: 0.5g

---

149. Air Fryer Butternut Squash (Home Fries)

Prep Time: 10 minutes

Cook Time: 20 minutes

Total Time: 30 minutes

Ingredients

- 4 cups chopped butternut squash, 1-inch cubes (see cutting tips above)
- 2 tablespoons extra virgin olive oil
- 1 tablespoon maple syrup
- 1 teaspoon dried oregano
- 1/2 teaspoon garlic powder
- 1/2 teaspoon smoked paprika
- 1/2 teaspoon kosher salt
- 1/4 teaspoon ground chipotle chili pepper

Instructions

- In a large bowl, add the squash cubes along with the other ingredients. Toss until the cubes are well coated.
- Arrange the cubes in a single layer in the air fryer basket and air fry on 400F for 15-20 minutes, or until the squash is fork-tender and a little crispy on the outside. Shake or stir the cubes at the mid-way point.
- Carefully remove from the air fryer and serve immediately.

Nutritional Facts

- Calories: 140
- Total Fat: 7.2g
- Total Carbohydrate: 20.5g
- Sugar: 6.2g
- Calcium: 81.2mg
- Sat Fat: 1g

- Sodium: 302.3mg
- Fiber: 3.2g
- Protein: 1.6g
- Vitamin C: 29.4mg
- Iron: 1.3g

150. Air Fryer Mushrooms

Prep Time: 5 minutes

Cook Time: 15 minutes

Ingredients

- 7 oz 200 grams chestnut mushrooms
- 2 tsp vegetable oil
- 2 tsp low sodium soy sauce or tamari sauce
- 1 sprig rosemary
- ½ tsp salt and pepper

Instructions

- Cut the mushrooms into thick slices, I usually cut each into 2 halves but if it's too big then I cut into smaller pieces. Try to make the size of the slices even so everything cooks evenly.
- In a white bowl, toss the mushrooms with the rest of the ingredients so everything is well coated in soy, oil, and seasonings.
- No need to preheat the Air Fryer. Place the mushrooms directly into the Air Fryer basket, and cook at 356f (180) for about 15 minutes flipping halfway through.
- Open the Air Fryer basket and check every 5 minutes, shake the basket and decide how much longer you would like to cook the mushrooms for.
- The mushrooms should be cooked well, but not dried out or burnt. So make sure not to overcook them.
- Serve with some extra sea salt flakes, and red chili flakes if desired.

Nutrition

- Calories: 30kcal | Carbohydrates: 2g | Protein: 1g | Fat: 2g | Saturated Fat: 1g | Sodium: 377mg | Potassium: 222mg | Fiber: 1g | Sugar: 1g | Calcium: 9mg | Iron: 1mg

151. Easy Air Fryer Baked Potatoes

Prep Time: 5 minutes

Cook Time: 35 minutes

Total Time: 40 minutes

Ingredients

- 4 medium russet potatoes scrubbed and dried
- 4 teaspoons olive oil
- 1 teaspoon kosher sea salt plus more for serving if desired

Instructions

- Preheat the air fryer to 375°F for about 10 minutes.
- Wash, dry, and prick each potato
- Drizzle each potato with oil and sprinkle with salt.
- Place 2 to 4 potatoes in your air fryer, depending on size.
- Set air fryer to cook at 375° for 35 minutes, or until potatoes are fork-tender.
- Use tongs to remove potatoes from the air fryer basket then carefully cut a slit in the top of each one.
- Add desired toppings & enjoy!

Nutrition

- Serving: 1g | Calories: 204kcal | Carbohydrates: 38g | Protein: 5g | Fat: 4g | Saturated Fat: 1g | Sodium: 592mg | Potassium: 888mg | Fiber: 3g | Sugar: 1g | Vitamin C: 12mg | Calcium: 28mg | Iron: 2mg

152. Crispy Spicy Air Fryer Okra

Prep Time: 10 Minutes

Cook Time: 10 Minutes

Total Time: 20 Minutes

Ingredients

- 1 1/4 lb fresh okra
- For the egg wash:
- 1 egg
- 1/2 tsp coriander
- 1/2 tsp smoked paprika
- 1/2 tsp chili powder (optional)
- Pinch of salt
- For the panko breading:

- 1 cup gluten-free flaked panko breading
- 1 tsp coriander
- 1 tsp smoked paprika
- 1/2 tsp chili powder (optional)
- 1/2 tsp garlic powder
- 2 tbsp parsley
- 1/4 tsp each salt and pepper

Instructions

- Rinse okra and dry thoroughly - I used paper towels to do so.
- Prepare egg wash by mixing the egg with coriander, smoked paprika, chili powder (if using), and salt in a bowl.
- Prepare to bread by mixing panko bread flakes with coriander, smoked paprika, chili powder (if using), garlic powder, parsley, salt, and pepper.
- Then, using one hand, dip the dried okra in the spiced egg wash and drop it onto the plate with the breading.
- Then, using the other hand, coat the okra well with the spiced panko breading. Repeat this with all the okra.
- When the okra is all breaded, place them in a single layer at the bottom of your air fryer basket and spray them with your favorite cooking spray.
- For best results, preheat the air fryer to 400 degrees for 2-3 minutes.
- Set the air fryer to air fry the okra at 400 degrees for 4-5 minutes. Then open the air fryer, and using tongs, flip the okra over and air fry for 4-5 minutes at 400 degrees. Repeat if you have any more breaded okra (depending on the size of your air fryer, this might take 2- 3 batches to cook - but the result works it.
- Enjoy with your favorite sauces!

Nutrition Information

- Calories: 150
- Total Fat: 3g
- Saturated Fat: 1g
- Trans Fat: 0g
- Unsaturated Fat: 2g
- Cholesterol: 66mg
- Sodium: 302mg
- Carbohydrates: 23g
- Fiber: 4g
- Sugar: 4g

- Protein: 8g

153. Air Fryer Radishes (Healthy Side Dish)

Prep Time: 10 minutes

Cook Time: 15 minutes

Total Time: 25 minutes

Ingredients

- 1 pound (or 454 gram packages) fresh radishes or about 3 cups halved
- 1 tablespoon extra virgin olive oil
- 1/2 teaspoon dried oregano
- 1/2 teaspoon kosher salt
- 1/4 teaspoon garlic powder
- 1/4 teaspoon onion powder
- Dash of ground black pepper

Instructions

- Wash and trim the radishes, scrubbing off any dirt and cutting off any dark spots. Pat dry with a paper towel.
- Slice the radishes in half so they are roughly 1-inch pieces (it doesn't need to be exact), or quarter them if they are larger.
- Place the radishes in a large bowl and evenly coat with oil. Add the seasonings and toss to combine.
- Place radishes in the air fryer basket and air fry on 400F for 15-17 minutes, or until fork-tender. Shake or stir the radishes after about 10 minutes. Serve immediately.

Nutritional Facts

- Calories: 48
- Total Fat: 3.6g
- Total Carbohydrate: 3.4g
- Sugar: 0g
- Calcium: 33.7mg
- Sat Fat: 0.5g
- Sodium: 373.4mg
- Fiber: 1.7g
- Protein: 1.3g
- Vitamin C: 32.9mg
- Iron: 1mg

17. Air Fryer Zucchini And Onions

Total Time: 30 mins

Ingredients

- 2-3 zucchini small-medium sized
- 1 red onion
- 2 tbsp olive oil or avocado oil
- 1/2 tsp dried basil
- 1/2 tsp salt
- 1/2 tsp dried oregano
- 1/2 tsp garlic powder
- 1/4 tsp black pepper

Instructions

- Do the Prep Work
- Preheat your Air Fryer to 400F.
- Meanwhile, wash and dice the zucchini and onions, at least twice the size of the holes in your air fryer basket.
- In a bowl, toss the vegetables, oil, and all the Italian seasonings together.
- Cook the Dish
- Pour the vegetable mixture into the heated air fryer, then shake or spread the vegetables so they're evenly spaced out in the basket. Close and set the timer for 20 minutes.
- Halfway through cook time, open the air fryer and shake the basket or turn the vegetables with a spoon or spatula. Close and allow to finish cooking, then season to taste if needed and serve. Note: Sometime in the final two to three minutes, open the air fryer to make sure the vegetables aren't beginning to burn.

Nutrition

- Calories: 91kcal | Carbohydrates: 6g | Protein: 2g | Fat: 7g | Saturated Fat: 1g | Sodium: 300mg | Potassium: 296mg | Fiber: 1g | Sugar: 4g | Vitamin A: 196IU | Vitamin C: 20mg | Calcium: 25mg | Iron: 1mg

154. Air Fryer Baby Potatoes (Easy Side Dish)

Prep Time: 5 minutes

Cook Time: 18 minutes

Total Time: 23 minutes

Ingredients

- 4 cups baby potatoes, skin on, pre-washed, and halved

- 1 lime, juiced
- 1 tablespoon extra virgin olive oil
- 1 tablespoon chili powder
- 1/2 teaspoon sea salt

Instructions

- Place potatoes in a large bowl and coat them with lime juice. Drain any excess juice.
- Add the oil, chili powder, and sea salt and stir until potatoes are well coated.
- Arrange the potatoes in a single layer in the air fryer basket. Roast on 400F for 15-18 minutes, or until the potatoes are tender with crispy edges. You can check on them after 7-8 minutes and give them a shake or stir.
- Serve immediately (while hot and crispy).

Nutritional Facts

- Calories: 95
- Total Fat: 2.6g
- Total Carbohydrate: 17g
- Sugar: 1.4g
- Calcium: 14.6mg
- Sat Fat: 0.4g
- Sodium: 248.6mg
- Fiber: 1.7g
- Protein: 1.9g
- Vitamin C: 11.3mg
- Iron: 0.8mg

155. Air Fryer Broccoli Cheese Bites

Prep Time: 50 mins

Active Time: 20 mins

Total Time: 1 hr 10 mins

Ingredients

- 10 oz. fresh broccoli florets
- 1/4 cup water
- 1 large egg
- 1 1/2 cups shredded cheddar cheese
- 3/4 cup bread crumbs (panko or traditional)
- 1/2 tsp. kosher salt
- 1/2 tsp. black pepper

Instructions

- Place broccoli and water in a microwave-safe

container with a microwave-safe lid (if you don't have a lid you can use plastic wrap). Place lid lightly on top or cover tightly with plastic wrap. Microwave for 4 minutes.

- Remove from microwave and allow to cool enough to handle. Chop very finely then place in a bowl. Add egg, cheese, bread crumbs, salt, and pepper to the broccoli and mix well. Grab a rimmed baking sheet.
- Scoop out 1 1/2 tablespoons of the broccoli mixture and squeeze and form into a ball. Set on a baking sheet. Continue until you've used all the mixture. Place in the freezer for 30 minutes.
- Place broccoli bites in an air fryer in a single layer and cook at 350 degrees F for 5-10 minutes depending on your air fryer. You may need to do this in batches (I did). Cover lightly with foil to keep warm while others are baking.

Nutritional Facts

- Calories: 91kcal | Carbohydrates: 6g | Protein: 2g | Fat: 7g | Saturated Fat: 1g | Sodium: 300mg | Potassium: 296mg | Fiber: 1g | Sugar: 4g | Vitamin A: 196IU | Vitamin C: 20mg | Calcium: 25mg | Iron: 1mg

156. Healthy Air Fryer Eggplant [Oil Free]

Prep Time: 35 minutes

Cook Time: 15 minutes

Total Time: 50 minutes

Ingredients

- 1.5 lb eggplant cut into half-inch pieces (approx 1 medium-sized)
- 2 tbsp low sodium vegetable broth
- 1 tsp garlic powder
- 1 tsp paprika
- 1/2 tsp dried oregano
- 1/4 tsp dried thyme
- 1/4 tsp black pepper optional

Instructions

- Wash and dice your eggplant into half-inch pieces. (See step by step photos above if needed.)

- Now place your cut up eggplant in a large colander and place the colander inside a bowl. Generously sprinkle with salt and let it sit for 30 minutes. Then transfer to a clean, dry dishtowel, and using another dish towel, or paper towels, press and pat them dry.
- Now, wipe out the bowl that was sitting under your colander and place the dry eggplant inside. Add the broth and all the seasoning to the bowl and mix well to evenly coat the pieces.
- Place in your air fryer basket, set to 380 degrees, and cook for 15-20 minutes, tossing once at the halfway point. Cook until nicely golden, and fork-tender, then serve warm with a sprinkle of fresh parsley or chives and sriracha mayo for dipping.

Nutrition Facts

- Calories: 48kcal | Carbohydrates: 11g | Protein: 2g | Fat: 1g | Saturated Fat: 1g | Sodium: 161mg | Potassium: 413mg | Fiber: 5g | Sugar: 6g | Vitamin A: 322IU | Vitamin C: 4mg | Calcium: 15mg | Iron: 1mg

157. How To Make Air Fryer Tortilla Chips (With Five Flavour Options!)

Prep Time: 10 minutes

Cook Time: 9 minutes

Total Time: 19 minutes

Ingredients

Salt And Vinegar

- 6 corn tortillas
- 1 tablespoon extra virgin olive oil
- 1/2 tablespoon white vinegar
- 1 teaspoon kosher salt

Zesty Cheese

- 6 corn tortillas
- 2 tablespoons extra virgin olive oil
- 2 teaspoons **Nutrition Facts**al yeast
- 1/2 teaspoon smoked paprika
- 1/4 teaspoon kosher salt

Spicy Chipotle

- 6 corn tortillas
- 1 tablespoon extra virgin olive oil

- 1/2 teaspoon ground chipotle chili pepper
- 1/4 teaspoon kosher salt

Chili Lime

- 6 corn tortillas
- 1 tablespoon extra virgin olive oil
- 1/2 tablespoon lime juice
- 1 teaspoon chili powder
- 1/4 teaspoon kosher salt

Maple Cinnamon

- 6 corn tortillas
- 1 tablespoon extra virgin olive oil
- 1/2 tablespoon maple syrup
- 1/2 teaspoon ground cinnamon
- 1/2 teaspoon coconut sugar

Instructions

- In a small bowl, whisk together the oil with the ingredients for your flavor choice. Brush a light coating of the mixture on both sides of the tortillas.
- Cut each tortilla into quarters to form triangles.
- Arrange the tortilla triangles in a single layer in your air fryer basket. (You will need to do this in batches).
- Air fry on 350F for about 7-9 minutes, or until they start to brown around the edges. (Note: the maple cinnamon chips will take 5-7 minutes).
- Let the chips cool enough to handle and then transfer them to a wire rack to cool completely. They will get crunchier as they cool.
- Store in an airtight container at room temperature and enjoy within 5 days.

Nutritional Facts

- Calories: 156
- Total Fat: 6g
- Total Carbohydrate: 24g
- Sugar: 0g
- Calcium: 91.6mg
- Sat Fat: 0.8g
- Sodium: 780.9mg
- Fiber: 2.7g
- Protein: 3g
- Vitamin C: 0mg
- Iron: 0.7mg

158. Air Fryer Asparagus

Prep Time: 5 minutes

Cook Time: 6 minutes

Total Time: 11 minutes

Ingredients

- 1 lb fresh asparagus (16 oz.)
- 2 tsp extra virgin olive oil
- Sea salt to taste

Instructions

- Wash the asparagus spears and pat them dry. Trim the ends enough so that they fit in the air fryer basket (about 1 to 1 ½ inches up from the bottom).
- Add the asparagus to a rectangular container with a tight-fitting lid or a zip-top bag along with the olive oil and salt. Shake until asparagus is well-coated.
- If your air fryer has a separate elevated crisping tray or plate, be sure to insert it. Add the asparagus to the air fryer basket and air fry at 400° F for 6-9 minutes, shaking the basket every few minutes. Thinner spears will take less time to cook while thicker spears will take longer. Asparagus should be tender with a slight crisp. Add more sea salt to taste before serving, if desired.

Nutrition

- Calories: 43kcal | Carbohydrates: 4g | Protein: 2g | Fat: 2g | Saturated Fat: 1g | Fiber: 2g

159. Air Fryer Pumpkin Fries

Prep Time: 15 minutes

Cook Time: 15 minutes

Total Time: 30 minutes

Ingredients

- 2 mini pumpkins, peeled, seeded, and cut into 1/2-inch slices (see cutting tips above)
- 2 teaspoons extra virgin olive oil
- 1/2 teaspoon garlic powder
- 1/2 teaspoon smoked paprika
- 1/2 teaspoon kosher salt

Instructions

- Quicker version – air fry in one large batch:
- Add the pumpkin slices to a large bowl and toss with oil and seasonings.
- Place all the pumpkin in the air fryer basket and air fry on 400F for about 15 minutes, or until fork-tender. Shake or stir them at the mid-way point.

Nutritional Facts

- Calories: 60
- Total Fat: 2.5g
- Total Carbohydrate: 10g
- Sugar: 4g
- Calcium: 31.4mg
- Sat Fat: 0.4g
- Sodium: 156.9mg
- Fiber: 0.9g
- Protein: 1.6g
- Vitamin C: 13.1mg
- Iron: 1.2mg

160. Lemon Garlic Air Fryer Roasted Potatoes

Prep Time: 10 Mins

Cook Time: 30 Mins

Air Fryer Preheating Time: 5 Mins

Total Time: 45 Mins

Ingredients

- 900 g / 2 lb potatoes (about 4 large ones)
- 2 tablespoons oil of choice, avocado, olive, vegetable, sunflower are all fine
- 1 teaspoon salt
- 1 teaspoon freshly ground black pepper
- 2 lemons
- 1 entire head of garlic
- 4 big (approx 4 inches long) fresh rosemary stems
- Peel the potatoes and cut them into large pieces. With a large potato, I generally get 5 pieces.
- Put the cut potatoes in a bowl and cover with cold water. Leave to soak for 15 minutes, then drain and pour the potatoes onto a clean dish towel. Bundle it up around them and rub them dry.

- Dry the bowl you had them in and return them, then pour in the oil and sprinkle in the salt and pepper. Stir to coat them all evenly.
- Preheat your Air Fryer if it has a preheat function, then add the potatoes carefully to the hot basket and cook on 350°F (175 °C) for 15 minutes.
- While they are cooking, break up the head of garlic into individual cloves and remove any skin that is loose and papery. Leave the rest of the skin intact.
- Cut the 2 lemons in half lengthways. Save one half for juicing, then cut the other halves into 3 wedges each.
- Once the 15 minutes is up, open the Air Fryer and squeeze the juice from the half of lemon over the potatoes. Throw in the garlic cloves and the lemon wedges and give it all a really good toss together. Tuck in the rosemary stalks amongst the potatoes.
- Return the basket to the Air Fryer and cook for a further 15 minutes. Check. They should be done, but if you prefer them a little more golden, put them back on for 5 minutes.
- Pick out the woody rosemary sticks and serve the potatoes with the garlic cloves and the lemon wedges. Guests can squeeze the soft, sweet cloves of garlic out of their skins and eat it with the potatoes and the caramelized lemon.

To serve

- When serving be sure to get some of the roasted garlic cloves and lemon wedges in each portion, then while eating, smush the caramelized lemon against the potatoes, squeeze that sweet roasted garlic out of its papery skin and eat it all together. And that's your potato game changed FOREVER!

Nutrition

- Calories: 172kcal
- Carbohydrates: 28g
- Protein: 5g
- Fat: 6g
- Saturated Fat: 1g
- Sodium: 485mg

- Potassium: 817mg
- Fiber: 6g
- Sugar: 1g
- Vitamin A: 23IU
- Vitamin C: 44mg
- Calcium: 72mg
- Iron: 6mg

161. Air Fryer Broccoli

Prep Time: 5 minutes

Cook Time: 15 minutes

Total Time: 20 minutes

Ingredients

- 1 pound (450 grams) broccoli cut into florets
- 1 tablespoon olive oil
- ½ teaspoon salt
- ¼ teaspoon ground black pepper
- ¼ teaspoon chili flakes optional

Instructions

- Wash the broccoli head, and cut it into florets.
- In a mixing bowl, toss the broccoli florets with olive oil, salt, pepper, and chili flakes.
- Add to the Air Fryer basket, and cook at 390°F (200°C) for 15 minutes flipping at least twice while cooking.
- Serve with lemon wedges.

Nutrition

- Calories: 70kcal | Carbohydrates: 8g | Protein: 3g | Fat: 4g | Saturated Fat: 1g | Sodium: 330mg | Potassium: 358mg | Fiber: 3g | Sugar: 2g | Vitamin A: 744IU | Vitamin C: 101mg | Calcium: 53mg | Iron: 1mg

162. Air Fryer Green Beans

Prep Time: 5 minutes

Cook Time: 10 minutes

Total Time: 15 minutes

Ingredients

- 12 ounces (or 340 grams) fresh green beans, washed, trimmed, and dried
- 1 tablespoon extra virgin olive oil
- 1/2 teaspoon dried basil
- 1/2 teaspoon dried oregano
- 1/4 teaspoon garlic powder
- 1/4 teaspoon kosher salt
- Fresh lemon wedges (optional)

Instructions

- Place the green beans in a large bowl and add the oil and seasoning. Toss until well coated.
- Arrange the beans in the air fryer basket and air fry on 400F for 7-10 minutes (see note).
- Squeeze some fresh lemon juice over top (optional) and serve immediately.

Nutritional Facts

- Calories: 58
- Total Fat: 3.7g
- Total Carbohydrate: 6.2g
- Sugar: 2.8g
- Calcium: 35.6mg
- Sat Fat: 0.5g
- Sodium: 82.8mg
- Fiber: 2.4g
- Protein: 1.6g
- Vitamin C: 10.4mg
- Iron: 1mg

163. Air Fryer Cauliflower

Prep Time: 8 mins

Cook Time: 12 mins

Total Time: 20 mins

Ingredients

- 1 head cauliflower
- 2 tbsp olive oil
- 1 tsp salt
- 2 tsp onion powder
- **To Top:** lime wedge and parmesan

Instructions

- Cut your cauliflower into florets.

- Toss the cauliflower in olive oil, salt, and onion salt.
- Add the cauliflower into the air fryer basket (try to have it in a single layer if possible, cook in two batches if too many overlap).
- Cook for 12-15 minutes on 375F.
- When done, serve with parmesan shaved on top and some lime squeezed on top.

Nutrition

- Serving: 4servings | Calories: 102kcal | Carbohydrates: 8g | Protein: 3g | Fat: 7g | Saturated Fat: 1g | Sodium: 626mg | Potassium: 442mg | Fiber: 3g | Sugar: 3g | Vitamin C: 70mg | Calcium: 36mg | Iron: 1mg

164. Air Fryer Tater Tots

Prep Time: 15 mins

Cook Time: 20 mins

Total Time: 35 mins

Ingredients

- 6 large potatoes or 8 medium, peeled
- 2 tbsp corn starch (cornflour)
- 1 1/2 tsp dried oregano
- 1 tsp garlic powder
- Salt

Instructions

- Preheat the air fryer to 350 F / 180C.
- Boil the potatoes till they are about half cooked and then plunge them into a cold water bath to stop the cooking process and cool them down.
- Using a box shredder, shred the cooled potatoes into a large bowl, then squeeze out any excess water.
- Add in the rest of the ingredients and combine. Then form the mixture into individual tater tots (I was able to make about 20).
- Place half of the homemade tater tots into the air fryer basket (making sure they don't touch) and cook for 18-20 minutes till golden brown. Turn the tots twice during cooking so that they brown evenly.
- Remove the tater tots and keep warm, then repeat steps to make the remaining air fryer

tater tots.
- Serve your air fryer tater tots with a side of vegan ranch dressing or tomato sauce for dipping.

Nutrition

- Calories: 204kcal | Carbohydrates: 44g | Protein: 8g | Sodium: 32mg | Potassium: 1328mg | Fiber: 8g | Vitamin C: 36.4mg | Calcium: 102mg | Iron: 10.5mg

165. Air Fryer Beets (Easy Roasted Beets)

Prep Time: 10 minutes

Cook Time: 20 minutes

Total Time: 30 minutes

Ingredients

- 3 cups fresh beets, peeled and cut into 1-inch pieces (see note)
- 1 tablespoon extra virgin olive oil
- 1/2 teaspoon kosher salt
- Pinch of ground black pepper

Instructions

- Add the beets, oil, salt, and pepper to a large bowl and toss to combine.
- Place the beets in the air fryer basket and air fry on 400F for 18-20 minutes, or until fork-tender. Stir or shake them a few times while air frying.

Nutritional Facts

- Calories: 74
- Total Fat: 3.7g
- Total Carbohydrate: 9.8g
- Sugar: 6.9g
- Calcium: 16.6mg
- Sat Fat: 0.5g
- Sodium: 234.mg
- Fiber: 2.9g
- Protein: 1.6g
- Vitamin C: 5mg
- Iron: 0.8mg

166. Crispy Air Fryer Brussels Sprouts

Prep Time: 5 mins

Cook Time: 10 mins

Total Time: 15 mins

Ingredients

- 340 grams Brussels sprouts
- 1-2 tbsp olive oil
- Salt, to taste
- Pepper, to taste
- Garlic powder, to taste

Instructions

- Trim and half your Brussels sprouts and lightly coat them with olive oil.
- Coat with a mixture of salt, pepper, and garlic powder.
- Place the Brussels sprouts in the air fryer at 350F for 10 minutes. Shaking the basket once or twice during the cooking time.
- Serve immediately or warm.

Nutritional Value

- Calories: 91kcal | Carbohydrates: 6g | Protein: 2g | Fat: 7g | Saturated Fat: 1g | Sodium: 300mg | Potassium: 296mg | Fiber: 1g | Sugar: 4g | Vitamin A: 196IU | Vitamin C: 20mg | Calcium: 25mg | Iron: 1mg

167. Air-Fried Cauliflower With Almonds And Parmesan

Prep: 10 mins

Cook: 15 mins

Total: 25 mins

Servings: 4

Ingredient

- 3 cups cauliflower florets
- 3 teaspoons vegetable oil, divided
- 1 clove garlic, minced
- ⅓ cup finely shredded Parmesan cheese
- ¼ cup chopped almonds
- ¼ cup panko bread crumbs
- ½ teaspoon dried thyme, crushed

Instructions

- Place cauliflower florets, 2 teaspoons oil, and garlic in a medium bowl; toss to coat. Place in a single layer in an air fryer basket.

- Cook in the air fryer at 360 degrees F (180 degrees C), for 10 minutes, shaking the basket halfway through.
- Return cauliflower to the bowl and toss with the remaining 1 teaspoon oil. Add Parmesan cheese, almonds, bread crumbs, and thyme; toss to coat. Return cauliflower mixture to the air fryer basket and cook until mixture is crisp and browned about 5 minutes.

Nutrition Facts

- Calories: 148; Protein 6.7g; Carbohydrates 11g; Fat 10.1g; Cholesterol 5.9mg; Sodium 157.7mg.

168. Air Fryer Falafel

Prep Time: 20 mins

Cook: 20 mins

Additional: 1 day

Total: 1 day

Ingredient

- 1 cup dry garbanzo beans
- 1 ½ cups fresh cilantro, stems removed
- ¾ cup fresh flat-leafed parsley stems removed
- 1 small red onion, quartered
- 1 clove garlic
- 2 tablespoons chickpea flour
- 1 tablespoon ground coriander
- 1 tablespoon ground cumin
- 1 tablespoon sriracha sauce
- salt and ground black pepper to taste
- ½ teaspoon baking powder
- ¼ teaspoon baking soda
- cooking spray

Instructions

- Soak chickpeas in a large amount of cool water for 24 hours. Rub the soaked chickpeas with your fingers to help loosen and remove skins. Rinse and drain well. Spread chickpeas on a large clean dish towel to dry.
- Blend chickpeas, cilantro, parsley, onion, and garlic in a food processor until rough paste forms. Transfer mixture to a large bowl. Add chickpea flour, coriander, cumin, sriracha, salt, and pepper and mix well. Cover bowl and let the

mixture rest for 1 hour.

- Preheat an air fryer to 375 degrees F (190 degrees C).
- Add baking powder and baking soda to the chickpea mixture. Mix using your hands until just combined. Form 15 equal-sized balls and press slightly to form patties. Spray falafel patties with cooking spray.
- Place 7 falafel patties in the preheated air fryer and cook for 10 minutes. Transfer cooked falafel to a plate and repeat with the remaining 8 falafel, cooking for 10 to 12 minutes.

Nutrition Facts

- Calories: 60; Protein 3.1g; Carbohydrates 9.9g; Fat 1.1g; Sodium 97.9mg.

169. Air-Fried Carrots With Balsamic Glaze

Prep Time: 10 mins

Cook Time: 10 mins

Total Time: 20 mins

Ingredient

- Olive oil for brushing
- 1 tablespoon olive oil
- 1 teaspoon honey
- ¼ teaspoon kosher salt
- ¼ teaspoon ground black pepper
- 1 pound tri-colored baby carrots
- 1 tablespoon balsamic glaze
- 1 tablespoon butter
- 2 teaspoons chopped fresh chives

Instructions

- Brush an air fryer basket with olive oil.
- Whisk together 1 tablespoon olive oil, honey, salt, and pepper in a large bowl. Add carrots and toss to coat. Place carrots in the air fryer basket in a single layer, in batches, if needed.
- Cook in the air fryer at 390 degrees F (200 degrees C), stirring once, until tender, about 10 minutes. Transfer warm cooked carrots to a large bowl, add balsamic glaze and butter and toss to coat. Sprinkle with chives and serve.

Nutrition Facts Facts

- Calories: 117; Protein 0.8g; Carbohydrates 11.9g; Fat 7.7g; Cholesterol 7.6mg; Sodium 228mg.

170. Simple Air Fryer Brussels Sprouts

Prep Time: 5 mins

Cook Time: 30 mins

Total Time: 35 mins

Ingredient

- 1 ½ pound Brussels sprouts
- 2 tablespoons olive oil
- 1 teaspoon garlic powder
- 1 teaspoon salt
- ½ teaspoon ground black pepper

Instructions

- Preheat the air fryer to 390 degrees F (200 degrees C) for 15 minutes.
- Place Brussels sprouts, olive oil, garlic powder, salt, and pepper in a bowl and mix well. Spread evenly in the air fryer basket. Cook for 15 minutes, shaking the basket halfway through the cycle.

Nutrition Facts

- Calories: 91; Protein 3.9g; Carbohydrates 10.6g; Fat 4.8g; Sodium 416.2mg.

171. Air Fryer Potato Wedges

Prep Time: 5 mins

Cook Time: 30 mins

Total Time: 35 mins

Ingredient

- 2 medium Russet potatoes, cut into wedges
- 1 ½ tablespoon olive oil
- ½ teaspoon paprika
- ½ teaspoon parsley flakes
- ½ teaspoon chili powder
- ½ teaspoon sea salt
- ⅛ teaspoon ground black pepper

Instructions

- Preheat air fryer to 400 degrees F (200 degrees

C).

- Place potato wedges in a large bowl. Add olive oil, paprika, parsley, chili, salt, and pepper, and mix well to combine.
- Place 8 wedges in the basket of the air fryer and cook for 10 minutes.
- Flip wedges with tongs and cook for an additional 5 minutes. Repeat with the remaining 8 wedges.

Nutrition Facts

- Calories: 129; Protein 2.3g; Carbohydrates 19g; Fat 5.3g; Sodium 230.2mg.

---

172. Air-Fryer Roasted Veggies

Prep Time: 20 mins

Cook Time: 10 mins

Total Time: 30 mins

Ingredient

- ½ cup diced zucchini
- ½ cup diced summer squash
- ½ cup diced mushrooms
- ½ cup diced cauliflower
- ½ cup diced asparagus
- ½ cup diced sweet red pepper
- 2 teaspoons vegetable oil
- ¼ teaspoon salt
- ¼ teaspoon ground black pepper
- 1/4 teaspoon seasoning, or more to taste

Instructions

- Preheat the air fryer to 360 degrees F (180 degrees C).
- Add vegetables, oil, salt, pepper, and desired seasoning to a bowl. Toss to coat; arrange in the fryer basket.
- Cook vegetables for 10 minutes, stirring after 5 minutes.

Nutrition Facts Facts

- Calories:37; Protein 1.4g; Carbohydrates 3.4g; Fat 2.4g; Sodium 152.2mg.

---

173. Air Fryer Roasted Asparagus

Prep Time: 10 mins

Cook Time: 10 mins

Total Time: 20 mins

Ingredient

- 1 bunch fresh asparagus, trimmed
- Avocado oil cooking spray
- ½ teaspoon garlic powder
- ½ teaspoon himalayan pink salt
- ¼ teaspoon ground multi-colored peppercorns
- ¼ teaspoon red pepper flakes
- ¼ cup freshly grated parmesan cheese

Instructions

- Preheat the air fryer to 375 degrees F (190 degrees C). Line the basket with parchment paper.
- Place asparagus spears in the air fryer basket and mist with avocado oil. Sprinkle with garlic powder, pink Himalayan salt, pepper, and red pepper flakes. Top with Parmesan cheese.
- Air fry until asparagus spears start to char, 7 to 9 minutes.

Nutrition Facts

- Calories: 94; Protein 9g; Carbohydrates 10.1g; Fat 3.3g; Cholesterol 8.8mg; Sodium 739.2mg.

---

174. Air Fryer Sweet And Spicy Roasted Carrots

Prep Time: 5 mins

Cook Time: 20 mins

Total: 25 mins

Ingredient

- 1 serving cooking spray
- 1 tablespoon butter, melted
- 1 tablespoon hot honey (such as Mike's Hot Honey®)
- 1 teaspoon grated orange zest
- ½ teaspoon ground cardamom
- ½ pound baby carrots
- 1 tablespoon freshly squeezed orange juice
- 1 pinch salt and ground black pepper to taste

Instructions

- Preheat an air fryer to 400 degrees F (200

degrees C). Spray the basket with nonstick cooking spray.

- Combine butter, honey, orange zest, and cardamom in a bowl. Remove 1 tablespoon of the sauce to a separate bowl and set aside. Add carrots to the remaining sauce and toss until all are well coated. Transfer carrots to the air fryer basket.
- Air fry until carrots are roasted and fork-tender, tossing every 7 minutes, for 15 to 22 minutes. Mix orange juice with reserved honey-butter sauce. Toss with carrots until well combined. Season with salt and pepper.

Nutrition Facts

Calories: 129; Protein 0.9g; Carbohydrates 19.3g; Fat 6.1g; Cholesterol 15.3mg; Sodium 206.4mg.

175. Air Fryer One-Bite Roasted Potatoes

Prep Time: 5 mins

Cook Time: 10 mins

Total Time: 15 mins

Ingredient

- ½ Pound mini potatoes
- 2 teaspoons extra-virgin olive oil
- 2 teaspoons dry italian-style salad dressing mix
- Salt and ground black pepper to taste

Instructions

- Preheat the air fryer to 400 degrees F (200 degrees C).
- Wash and dry potatoes. Trim edges to make a flat surface on both ends.
- Combine extra-virgin olive oil and salad dressing mix in a large bowl. Add potatoes and toss until potatoes are well coated. Place in a single layer into the air fryer basket. Cook in batches if necessary.
- Air fry until potatoes are golden brown, 5 to 7 minutes. Flip potatoes and air fry for an additional 2 to 3 minutes. Season with salt and pepper.

Nutrition Facts

- Calories: 132; Protein 2.3g; Carbohydrates 20.3g;

Fat 4.8g; Sodium 166.8mg.

176. Air Fryer Cauliflower Tots

Prep Time: 5 mins

Cook Time: 10 mins

Total Time: 15 mins

Ingredient

- 1 serving nonstick cooking spray
- 1 (16 ounces) package frozen cauliflower tots (such as Green Giant® Cauliflower Veggie Tots)

Instructions

- Preheat air fryer to 400 degrees F (200 degrees C). Spray the air fryer basket with nonstick cooking spray.
- Place as many cauliflower tots in the basket as you can, making sure they do not touch, cooking in batches if necessary.
- Cook in the preheated air fryer for 6 minutes. Pull the basket out, turn tots over, and cook until browned and cooked through, about 3 minutes more.

Nutrition Facts Facts

- Calories: 147; Protein 2.7g; Carbohydrates 20g; Fat 6.1g; Sodium 493.6mg.

177. Air Fryer Sweet Potato Tots

Prep Time: 15 mins

Cook Time: 35 mins

Additional Time: 10 mins

Total Time: 1 hr

Ingredient

- 2 sweet potatoes, peeled
- ½ teaspoon cajun seasoning
- Olive oil cooking spray
- Sea salt to taste

Instructions

- Bring a pot of water to a boil and add sweet potatoes. Boil until sweet potatoes can be pierced with a fork but are still firm for about 15 minutes. Do not over-boil, or they will be messy to grate. Drain and let cool.

- Grate sweet potatoes into a bowl using a box grater. Carefully mix in Cajun seasoning. Form mixture into tot-shaped cylinders.
- Spray the air fryer basket with olive oil spray. Place tots in the basket in a single row without touching each other or the sides of the basket. Spray tots with olive oil spray and sprinkle with sea salt.
- Heat air fryer to 400 degrees F (200 degrees C) and cook tots for 8 minutes. Turn, spray with more olive oil spray, and sprinkle with more sea salt. Cook for 8 minutes more.

Nutrition Facts

- Calories: 21; Protein 0.4g; Carbohydrates 4.8g; Sodium 36.2mg.

178. Air Fryer Fried Green Tomatoes

Prep Time: 15 mins

Cook Time: 20 mins

Total Time: 35 mins

Ingredient

- 2 green tomatoes, cut into 1/4-inch slices
- Salt and freshly ground black pepper to taste
- ⅓ cup all-purpose flour
- ½ cup buttermilk
- 2 eggs, lightly beaten
- 1 cup plain panko bread crumbs
- 1 cup yellow cornmeal
- 1 teaspoon garlic powder
- ½ teaspoon paprika
- 1 tablespoon olive oil, or as needed

Instructions

- Season tomato slices with salt and pepper.
- Set up a breading station in 3 shallow dishes: pour flour into the first dish; stir together buttermilk and eggs in the second dish; and mix breadcrumbs, cornmeal, garlic powder, and paprika in the third dish.
- Dredge tomato slices in flour, shaking off the excess. Dip tomatoes into the egg mixture, and then into the bread crumb mixture, making sure

to coat both sides.

- Preheat the air fryer to 400 degrees F (200 degrees C). Brush the fryer basket with olive oil. Place breaded tomato slices in the fryer basket, making sure they do not touch each other; cook in batches if necessary. Brush the tops of tomatoes with olive oil.
- Cook for 12 minutes, then flip the tomatoes and brush again with olive oil. Cook until crisp and golden brown, 3 to 5 minutes more. Remove tomatoes to a paper towel-lined rack to keep crisp. Repeat with the remaining tomatoes.

Nutrition Facts

- Calories: 219; Protein 7.6g; Carbohydrates 39.6g; Fat 5.3g; Cholesterol 62.8mg; Sodium 165.9mg.

179. Air Fryer Latkes

Prep Time: 20 mins

Cook Time: 20 mins

Total Time: 40 mins

Ingredient

- 1 (16 ounces) package frozen shredded hash brown potatoes, thawed
- ½ cup shredded onion
- 1 egg
- Kosher salt and ground black pepper to taste
- 2 tablespoons matzo meal
- Avocado oil cooking spray

Instructions

- Preheat an air fryer to 375 degrees F (190 degrees C) according to the manufacturer's instructions. Layout a sheet of parchment or waxed paper.
- Place thawed potatoes and shredded onion on several layers of paper towels. Cover with more paper towels and press to squeeze out most of the liquid.
- Whisk together egg, salt, and pepper in a large bowl. Stir in potatoes and onion with a fork. Sprinkle matzo meal on top and stir until ingredients are evenly distributed. Use your hands to form the mixture into ten 3- to 4-inch wide patties. Place patties on the parchment or waxed paper.

- Spray the air fryer basket with cooking spray. Carefully place half of the patties in the basket and spray generously with cooking spray.
- Air-fry until crispy and dark golden brown on the outside, 10 to 12 minutes. (Check for doneness at 8 minutes if you prefer a softer latke.) Remove latkes to a plate. Repeat with remaining patties, spraying them with cooking spray before cooking.

Nutrition Facts

- Calories: 97; Protein 3.3g; Carbohydrates 18.6g; Fat 6.5g; Cholesterol 32.7mg; Sodium 121.3mg.

180. Air Fryer Truffle Fries

Prep Time: 10 mins

Cook Time: 20 mins

Additional Time: 30 mins

Total Time: 1 hr

Ingredient

- 1 ¾ pounds russet potatoes, peeled and cut into fries
- 2 tablespoons truffle-infused olive oil
- ½ teaspoon paprika
- 1 tablespoon grated Parmesan cheese
- 2 teaspoons chopped fresh parsley
- 1 teaspoon black truffle sea salt

Instructions

- Place fries in a bowl. Cover with water and let soak for 30 minutes. Drain and pat dry.
- Preheat the air fryer to 400 degrees F (200 degrees C) according to the manufacturer's **Instructions**.
- Place drained fries into a large bowl. Add truffle olive oil and paprika; stir until evenly combined. Transfer fries to the air fryer basket.
- Air fry for 20 minutes, shaking every 5 minutes. Transfer fries to a bowl. Add Parmesan cheese, parsley, and truffle salt. Toss to coat.

Nutrition Facts

- Calories: 226; Protein 4.8g; Carbohydrates 36.1g; Fat 7.6g; Cholesterol 1.1mg; Sodium 552mg.

181. Air Fryer Spaghetti Squash

Prep Time: 5 mins

Cook Time: 25 mins

Total Time: 30 mins

Ingredient

- 1 (3 pounds) spaghetti squash
- 1 teaspoon olive oil
- ¼ teaspoon sea salt
- ⅛ teaspoon ground black pepper
- ⅛ teaspoon smoked paprika

Instructions

- Using a sharp knife, make a dotted line lengthwise around the entire squash. Place whole squash in the microwave and cook on full power for 5 minutes. Transfer to a cutting board and cut the squash in half lengthwise, using the dotted line as a guide. Wrap one half in plastic wrap and refrigerate for another use.
- Spoon pulp and seeds out of the remaining half and discard. Brush olive oil over all of the flesh and sprinkle with salt, pepper, and paprika.
- Preheat an air fryer to 360 degrees F (180 degrees C). Place spaghetti squash half skin-side-down in the basket. Cook for 20 minutes.
- Transfer to a dish and fluff with a fork to create 'noodles'.

Nutrition Facts

Calories: 223; Protein 4.4g; Carbohydrates 47.2g; Fat 6.3g; Sodium 335.9mg.

182. Air Fryer Roasted Brussels Sprouts With Maple-Mustard Mayo

Prep Time: 5 mins

Cook Time: 10 mins

Total Time: 15 mins

Ingredient

- 2 tablespoons maple syrup, divided
- 1 tablespoon olive oil
- ¼ teaspoon kosher salt
- ¼ teaspoon ground black pepper
- 1 pound Brussels sprouts, trimmed and halved
- ⅓ cup mayonnaise
- 1 tablespoon stone-ground mustard

Instructions

- Preheat the air fryer to 400 degrees F (200 degrees C).
- Whisk together 1 tablespoon maple syrup, olive oil, salt, and pepper in a large bowl. Add Brussels sprouts and toss to coat. Arrange Brussels sprouts in a single layer in an air fryer basket without overcrowding; work in batches, if necessary. Cook for 4 minutes. Shake basket and cook until sprouts are deep golden brown and tender, 4 to 6 minutes more.
- Meanwhile, whisk together mayonnaise, remaining 1 tablespoon maple syrup, and mustard in a small bowl. Toss sprouts in some of the sauce mixtures and/or serve as a dipping sauce.

Nutrition Facts

Calories: 240; Protein 4g; Carbohydrates 18.3g; Fat 18.3g; Cholesterol 7mg; Sodium 298mg.

183. Air Fryer Peri Peri Fries

Prep Time: 10 mins

Cook Time: 25 mins

Additional Time: 15 mins

Total Time: 50 mins

Ingredient

- 2 pounds russet potatoes
- ¼ teaspoon smoked paprika
- ¼ teaspoon chile powder
- ¼ teaspoon garlic granules
- ⅛ teaspoon ground white pepper
- ½ teaspoon salt
- 2 tablespoons grapeseed oil

Instructions

- Peel and cut potatoes into 3/8-inch slices. Place into a bowl of water for 15 minutes to remove most of the starch. Transfer onto a clean kitchen towel and dry.
- Preheat the air fryer to 350 degrees F (180 degrees C) for 5 minutes.
- Mix paprika, chile powder, garlic. white pepper, and salt together in a small bowl.
- Place the potatoes into a medium bowl and add grapeseed oil; mix well. Pour into the air fryer basket.
- Air fry for 10 minutes, shaking occasionally. Increase the temperature to 400 degrees F (200 degrees C) and air fry until golden brown, 12 to 15 more minutes.
- Pour fries into a bowl, sprinkle with the seasoning mix, and shake the bowl to ensure fries are evenly covered. Taste and adjust salt, if necessary. Serve immediately.

Nutrition Facts

- Calories: 237; Protein 4.7g; Carbohydrates 40g; Fat 7.1g; Sodium 304.4mg.

184. Air Fryer Fish And Chips

Prep Time: 20 mins

Cook Time: 30 mins

Additional Time: 1 hr 10 mins

Total Time: 2 hrs

Ingredients

Chips:

- 1 russet potato
- 2 teaspoons vegetable oil
- 1 pinch salt and ground black pepper to taste

Fish:

- ¾ cup all-purpose flour
- 2 tablespoons cornstarch
- ½ teaspoon salt
- ½ teaspoon garlic powder
- ¼ teaspoon baking soda
- ¼ teaspoon baking powder
- ¾ cup malt beer

- 4 (3 ounces) fillets cod fillets

Instructions

- Peel the russet potato and cut it into 12 wedges. Pour 3 cups water into a medium bowl and submerge potato wedges for 15 minutes. Drain off water and replace it with fresh water. Soak wedges for 15 more minutes.
- Meanwhile, mix flour, cornstarch, salt, garlic powder, baking soda, and baking powder in a bowl. Pour in 1/2 cup malt beer and stir to combine. If batter seems too thick, add remaining beer 1 tablespoon at a time.
- Place cod fillets on a rimmed baking sheet lined with a drip rack. Spoon 1/2 of the batter over the fillets. Place rack in the freezer to allow the batter to solidify, about 35 minutes. Flip fillets over and coat the remaining side with the batter. Return to the freezer for an additional 35 minutes.
- Preheat the air fryer to 400 degrees F (200 degrees C) for 8 minutes.
- Cook frozen fish fillets for 15 minutes, flipping at the halfway point.
- Meanwhile, drain off water from potato wedges and blot dry with a paper towel. Toss with oil, salt, and pepper. Air fry for 15 minutes.

Nutrition Facts

- Calories: 465; Protein 37.5g; Carbohydrates 62.3g; Fat 6.2g; Cholesterol 62.3mg; Sodium 1006mg.

185. "Everything" Seasoning Air Fryer Asparagus

Prep Time: 5 mins

Cook Time: 5 mins

Total Time: 10 mins

Ingredient

- 1 pound thin asparagus
- 1 tablespoon olive oil
- 1 tablespoon everything bagel seasoning
- 1 pinch salt to taste
- 4 wedge (blank)s lemon wedges

Instructions

- Rinse and trim asparagus, cutting off any woody ends. Place asparagus on a plate and drizzle with olive oil. Toss with bagel seasoning until evenly combined. Place asparagus in the air fryer basket in a single layer. Work in batches if needed.
- Heat the air fryer to 390 degrees F (200 degrees C).
- Air fry until slightly soft, tossing with tongs halfway through, 5 to 6 minutes. Taste and season with salt if needed. Serve with lemon wedges.

Nutrition Facts

- Calories: 70; Protein 2.7g; Carbohydrates 5.8g; Fat 3.6g; Sodium 281.5mg.

186. Air Fryer Tajin Sweet Potato Fries

Prep Time: 10 mins

Cook Time: 10 mins

Total Time: 20 mins

Ingredient

- Cooking spray
- 2 medium sweet potatoes, cut into 1/2-inch-thick fries
- 3 teaspoons avocado oil
- 1 ½ teaspoon chili-lime seasoning (such as tajin)

Dipping Sauce:

- ¼ cup mayonnaise
- 1 tablespoon freshly squeezed lime juice
- 1 teaspoon chili-lime seasoning (such as Tajin®)
- 4 lime wedges

Instructions

- Preheat the air fryer to 400 degrees F (200 degrees C) for 5 minutes. Lightly spray the fryer basket with cooking spray.
- Place sweet potato fries in a large bowl, drizzle with avocado oil, and stir. Sprinkle with 1 1/2 teaspoons chili-lime seasoning and toss well. Transfer to the air fryer basket, working in batches if necessary.
- Cook sweet potato fries until brown and crispy, 8 to 9 minutes, shaking and turning the fries after 4 minutes.

- While sweet potatoes are cooking, whisk together mayonnaise, lime juice, and chili-lime seasoning for the dipping sauce in a small bowl. Serve sweet potato fries with dipping sauce and lime wedges.

Nutrition Facts

- Calories: 233; Protein 2g; Carbohydrates 24.1g; Fat 14.8g; Cholesterol 5.2mg; Sodium 390.1mg.

187. Air Fryer Fingerling Potatoes

Prep Time: 10 mins

Cook Time: 15 mins

Total Time: 25 mins

Ingredient

- 1 pound fingerling potatoes, halved lengthwise
- 1 tablespoon olive oil
- ½ teaspoon ground paprika
- ½ teaspoon parsley flakes
- ½ teaspoon garlic powder
- Salt and ground black pepper to taste

Instructions

- Preheat an air fryer to 400 degrees F (200 degrees C).
- Place potato halves in a large bowl. Add olive oil, paprika, parsley, garlic powder, salt, and pepper and stir until evenly coated.
- Place potatoes in the basket of the preheated air fryer and cook for 10 minutes. Stir and cook until desired crispness is reached, about 5 more minutes.

Nutrition Facts

- Calories: 120; Protein 2.4g; Carbohydrates 20.3g; Fat 3.5g; Sodium 46.5mg.

188. Sweet and Spicy Air Fried Sweet Potatoes

Prep Time: 10 mins

Cook Time: 15 mins

Total Time: 25 mins

Ingredient

- 1 large sweet potato, cut into 1/2-inch pieces
- 1 tablespoon olive oil
- 1 tablespoon packed light brown sugar
- ¼ teaspoon sea salt
- ¼ teaspoon chili powder
- ¼ teaspoon ground paprika
- ¼ teaspoon cayenne pepper
- ⅛ teaspoon onion powder
- Ground black pepper to taste

Instructions

- Preheat an air fryer to 400 degrees F (200 degrees C) according to the manufacturer's **Instructions**.
- Place sweet potato in a large bowl. Drizzle with olive oil, then add brown sugar, salt, chili powder, paprika, cayenne pepper, onion powder, and pepper. Stir until potatoes are evenly coated and spread out onto the air fryer rack.
- Cook on the upper rack of the preheated air fryer until browned and crispy, 15 to 20 minutes.

Nutrition Facts

- Calories: 189; Protein 2.5g; Carbohydrates 35.3g; Fat 4.7g; Sodium 233.6mg.

189. Rosemary Potato Wedges For The Air Fryer

Prep Time: 10 mins

Cook Time: 20 mins

Total Time: 30 mins

Ingredient

- 2 russet potatoes, sliced into 12 wedges each with skin on
- 1 tablespoon extra-virgin olive oil
- 2 teaspoons seasoned salt
- 1 tablespoon finely chopped fresh rosemary

Instructions

- Preheat an air fryer to 380 degrees F (190 degrees C).
- Place potatoes in a large bowl and toss with olive oil. Sprinkle with seasoned salt and rosemary and toss to combine.
- Place potatoes in an even layer in a fryer basket once the air fryer is hot; you may need to cook

them in batches.

- Air fry potatoes for 10 minutes, then flip wedges with tongs. Continue air frying until potato wedges reach the desired doneness, about 10 minutes more.

Nutrition Facts

- Calories: 115; Protein 2.2g; Carbohydrates 19.2g; Fat 3.5g; Sodium 465.3mg.

190. Air Fryer Roasted Cauliflower

Prep Time: 10 mins

Cook Time: 15 mins

Total Time: 25 mins

Ingredient

- 3 cloves garlic
- 1 tablespoon peanut oil
- ½ teaspoon salt
- ½ teaspoon smoked paprika
- 4 cups cauliflower florets

Instructions

- Preheat an air fryer to 400 degrees F (200 degrees C).
- Cut garlic in half and smash with the blade of a knife. Place in a bowl with oil, salt, and paprika. Add cauliflower and turn to coat.
- Place the coated cauliflower in the bowl of the air fryer and cook to desired crispiness, shaking every 5 minutes, about 15 minutes total.

Nutrition Facts

- Calories: 118; Protein 4.3g; Carbohydrates 12.4g; Fat 7g; Sodium 642.3mg.

191. Air-Fried Ratatouille, Italian-Style

Prep Time: 25 mins

Cook Time: 25 mins

Additional Time: 5 mins

Total Time: 55 mins

Ingredient

- ½ small eggplant, cut into cubes
- 1 zucchini, cut into cubes
- 1 medium tomato, cut into cubes
- ½ large yellow bell pepper, cut into cubes
- ½ large red bell pepper, cut into cubes
- ½ onion, cut into cubes
- 1 fresh cayenne pepper, diced
- 5 sprigs fresh basil, stemmed and chopped
- 2 sprigs of fresh oregano, stemmed and chopped
- 1 clove garlic, crushed
- salt and ground black pepper to taste
- 1 tablespoon olive oil
- 1 tablespoon white wine
- 1 teaspoon vinegar

Instructions

- Preheat an air fryer to 400 degrees F (200 degrees C).
- Place eggplant, zucchini, tomato, bell peppers, and onion in a bowl. Add cayenne pepper, basil, oregano, garlic, salt, and pepper. Mix well to distribute everything evenly. Drizzle in oil, wine, and vinegar, mixing to coat all the vegetables.
- Pour vegetable mixture into a baking dish and insert it into the basket of the air fryer. Cook for 8 minutes. Stir; cook for another 8 minutes. Stir again and continue cooking until tender, stirring every 5 minutes, 10 to 15 minutes more. Turn off the air fryer, leaving the dish inside. Let rest for 5 minutes before serving.

Nutritional Value

- Calories: 79; Protein 2.1g; Carbohydrates 10.2g; Fat 3.8g; Sodium 47.6mg.

192. Air Fryer Spicy Green Beans

Prep Time: 10 mins

Cook Time: 25 mins

Additional Time: 5 mins

Total Time: 40 mins

Ingredient

- 12 ounces fresh green beans, trimmed
- 1 tablespoon sesame oil
- 1 teaspoon soy sauce
- 1 teaspoon rice wine vinegar
- 1 clove garlic, minced
- ½ teaspoon red pepper flakes

Instructions

- Preheat an air fryer to 400 degrees F (200 degrees C).
- Place green beans in a bowl. Whisk together sesame oil, soy sauce, rice wine vinegar, garlic, and red pepper flakes in a separate bowl and pour over green beans. Toss to coat and let marinate for 5 minutes.
- Place half the green beans in the air fryer basket. Cook 12 minutes, shaking the basket halfway through cooking time. Repeat with remaining green beans.

Nutrition Facts

- Calories: 60; Protein 1.7g; Carbohydrates 6.6g; Fat 3.6g; Sodium 80mg.

193. Chinese Five-Spice Air Fryer Butternut Squash Fries

Prep Time: 15 mins

Cook Time: 15 mins

Total Time: 30 mins

Ingredient

- 1 large butternut squash, peeled and cut into "fries"
- 2 tablespoons olive oil
- 1 tablespoon Chinese five-spice powder
- 1 tablespoon minced garlic
- 2 teaspoons sea salt
- 2 teaspoons black pepper

Instructions

- Preheat the air fryer to 400 degrees F (200 degrees C).
- Place cut the squash in a large bowl. Add oil, five-spice powder, garlic, salt, and black pepper, and toss to coat.
- Cook butternut squash fries in the preheated air fryer, shaking every 5 minutes, until crisp, 15 to

20 minutes total. Remove fries and season with additional sea salt.

Nutrition Facts

- Calories: 150; Protein 2.5g; Carbohydrates 28.5g; Fat 4.9g; Sodium 596.4mg.

194. Air Fryer Brussels Sprouts

Prep Time: 5 mins

Cook Time: 10 mins

Total Time: 15 mins

Ingredient

- 1 teaspoon avocado oil
- ½ teaspoon salt
- ½ teaspoon ground black pepper
- 10 ounces Brussels sprouts, trimmed and halved lengthwise
- 1 teaspoon balsamic vinegar
- 2 teaspoons crumbled cooked bacon (optional)

Instructions

- Preheat an air fryer to 350 degrees F (175 degrees C).
- Combine oil, salt, and pepper in a bowl and mix well. Add Brussels sprouts and turn to coat.
- Air fry for 5 minutes, shake the sprouts and cook for an additional 5 minutes.
- Transfer sprouts to a serving dish and sprinkles with balsamic vinegar; turn to coat. Sprinkle with bacon.

Nutrition Facts

- Calories: 94; Protein 5.8g; Carbohydrates 13.3g; Fat 3.4g; Cholesterol 1.7mg; Sodium 690.6mg.

195. Air Fryer Root Vegetables With Vegan Aioli

Prep Time: 30 mins

Cook Time: 30 mins

Total Time: 1 hr

Ingredients

Garlic Aioli:

- ½ cup vegan mayonnaise (such as Vegenaise)
- 1 clove garlic, minced
- ½ teaspoon fresh lemon juice
- Salt and ground black pepper to taste

Root Vegetables:

- 4 tablespoons extra virgin olive oil
- 1 tablespoon minced fresh rosemary
- 3 cloves garlic, finely minced
- 1 teaspoon kosher salt, or to taste
- ½ teaspoon ground black pepper, or to taste
- 1 pound parsnips, peeled and cut vertically into uniform pieces
- 1 pound baby red potatoes, cut lengthwise into 4 or 6 pieces
- ½ pound baby carrots split lengthwise
- ½ red onion cut lengthwise into 1/2-inch slices
- ½ teaspoon grated lemon zest, or to taste (Optional)

Instructions

- Combine mayonnaise, garlic, lemon juice, salt, and pepper in a small bowl for the garlic aioli; place in the refrigerator until ready to serve.
- Preheat the air fryer to 400 degrees F (200 degrees C) if your air fryer manufacturer recommends preheating.
- Combine olive oil, rosemary, garlic, salt, and pepper in a small bowl; set aside to allow the flavors to mingle. Combine parsnips, potatoes, carrots, and onion in a large bowl. Add olive oil-rosemary mixture and stir until vegetables are evenly coated. Place a portion of vegetables in a single layer in the basket of the air fryer, then add a rack and another layer of vegetables.
- Air fry for 15 minutes.
- When the timer sounds, you may plate the veggies and keep warm, or continue cooking in 5-minute intervals until the vegetables reach desired doneness and browning.
- Place remaining vegetables in the bottom of the air fryer basket and air fry for 15 minutes, checking for doneness, as needed. Use the rack again, if you have more vegetables then fit in a single layer. When all the vegetables have cooked, serve with garlic aioli and garnish with lemon zest.

Nutrition Facts

calories; protein 2.2g; carbohydrates 25.5g; fat 13.8g; sodium 338.3mg.

196. Air Fryer Roasted Broccoli And Cauliflower

Prep Time: 10 mins

Cook Time: 15 mins

Total Time: 25 mins

Ingredient

- 3 cups broccoli florets
- 3 cups cauliflower florets
- 2 tablespoons olive oil
- ½ teaspoon garlic powder
- ¼ teaspoon sea salt
- ¼ teaspoon paprika
- ⅛ teaspoon ground black pepper

Instructions

- Heat an air fryer to 400 degrees F (200 degrees C) following the manufacturer's instructions.
- Place broccoli florets in a large, microwave-safe bowl. Cook in the microwave on high power for 3 minutes. Drain any accumulated liquid.
- Add cauliflower, olive oil, garlic powder, sea salt, paprika, and black pepper to the bowl with the broccoli. Mix well to combine. Pour mixture into the air fryer basket. Cook for 12 minutes, tossing vegetables halfway through cooking time for even browning.

Nutrition Facts

- Calories: 68; Protein 2.3g; Carbohydrates 5.8g; Fat 4.7g; Sodium 103.1mg.

4. Air Fryer Seafoods Recipes

197. Frozen sesame Fish Fillets

Prep Time: 20 minutes

Ingredients:

5 frozen fish fillets

5 biscuits, crumbled

3 tbsp. flour

1 egg, beaten

Pinch of salt

Pinch of black pepper

¼ tsp. rosemary

3 tbsp. olive oil divided

A handful of sesame seeds

Instructions:

Preheat the air fryer to 390 degrees F. Combine the flour, pepper and salt, in a shallow bowl. In another shallow bowl, combine the sesame seeds, crumbled biscuits, oil, and rosemary. Dip the fish fillets into the flour mixture first, then into the beaten egg, and finally, coat them with the sesame mixture. Arrange them inside the air fryer on a sheet of aluminum foil. Cook the fish for 8 minutes. Flip the fillets over and cook for additional 4 minutes.

Nutrition Facts

Calories 257.6, Carbohydrates 16.4 g, Fat 14 g, Protein 19.1 g

198. Fish Tacos

Prep Time: 15 minutes

Ingredients:

4 corn tortillas

1 halibut fillet

2 tbsp. olive oil1

½ cup flour, divided

1 can of beer

1 tsp. salt

4 tbsp. peach salsa

4 tsp. chopped cilantro1 tsp. baking powder

Instructions:

Preheat the air fryer to 390 degrees F. Combine 1 cup of flour, baking, powder and salt. Pour in some of the beer, enough to form a batter-like consistency. Save the rest of the beer to gulp with the taco. Slice the fillet into

4 strips and toss them in half cup of flour. Dip them into the beer batter and arrange on a lined baking sheet. Place in the air fryer and cook for 8 minutes. Meanwhile, spread the peach salsa on the tortillas. Top each tortilla with one fish strip and 1 tsp. chopped cilantro.

Nutrition Facts

Calories 369, Carbohydrates 52 g, Fat 8.8 g, Protein 14.2 g

199. Peppery and Lemony Haddock

Prep Time: 15 minutes

Ingredients:

4 haddock fillets

1 cup breadcrumbs

2 tbsp. lemon juice

½ tsp. black pepper

¼ cup dry instant potato flakes1 egg, beaten¼ cup Parmesan cheese

3 tbsp. flour

¼ tsp. salt

Instructions:

Combine the flour, pepper and salt, in a small shallow bowl. In another bowl, combine the lemon, breadcrumbs, Parmesan, and potato flakes. Dip the fillets in the flour first, then in the beaten egg, and coat them with the lemony crumbs. Arrange on a lined sheet and place in the air fryer. Air fry for about 8 to 10 minutes at 370 degrees F.

Nutrition Facts

Calories 310.6, Carbohydrates 26.9 g, Fat 6.3 g, Protein 34.8 g

200. Soy Sauce Glazed Cod

Prep Time: 15 minutes

Ingredients:

1 cod fillet1 tsp. olive oil

Pinch of sea salt

Pinch of pepper

1 tbsp. soy sauce

Dash of sesame oil

¼ tsp. ginger powder

¼ tsp. honey

Instructions:

Preheat the air fryer to 370 degrees F. Combine the olive oil, salt and pepper, and brush that mixture over the cod. Place the cod onto an aluminum sheet and into the air fryer. Cook for about 6 minutes. Meanwhile, combine the soy sauce, ginger, honey, and sesame oil. Brush the glaze over the cod. Flip the fillet over and cook for additional 3 minutes.

Nutrition Facts

Calories 148, Carbohydrates 2.9 g, Fat 5.8 g, Protein 21 g

---

201. Salmon Cakes

Prep Time: 1 hour and 15 minutes

Ingredients:

10 oz. cooked salmon

14 oz. boiled and mashed potatoes

2 oz. flour

Handful capers

Handful chopped parsley

1 tsp. olive oil

Zest of 1 lemon

Instructions:

Place the mashed potatoes in a large bowl and flake the salmon over. Stir in capers, parsley, and lemon zest. Shape small cakes out of the mixture. Dust them with flour and place in the fridge to set, for about 1 hour. Preheat the air fryer to 350 degrees F. Brush the olive oil over the basket's bottom and add the cakes. Cook for about 7 minutes.

Nutrition Facts

Calories 240.8, Carbohydrates 28.6 g, Fat 6.4 g, Protein 17.7 g

---

202. Rosemary Garlicky Prawns

Prep Time:

1 h 15 minutes

Ingredients:

8 large prawns

3 garlic cloves, minced

1 rosemary sprig, chopped

½ tbsp. melted butter

Salt and pepper, to taste

Instructions:

Combine the garlic, butter, rosemary, and some salt and pepper, in a bowl. Add the prawns to the bowl and mix to coat them well. Cover the bowl and refrigerate for about an hour. Preheat the air fryer to 350 degrees F. Cook for about 6 minutes. Increase the temperature to 390 degrees, and cook for one more minute.

Nutrition Facts

Calories 152.2, Carbohydrates 1.5 g, Fat 2.9 g, Protein 0.3 g

---

203. Parmesan Tilapia

Prep Time: 15 minutes

Ingredients:

¾ cup grated Parmesan cheese

1 tbsp. olive oil

2 tsp. paprika

1 tbsp. chopped parsley

¼ tsp. garlic powder¼ tsp. salt4 tilapia fillets

Instructions:

Preheat the air fryer to 350 degrees F. Mix parsley, Parmesan, garlic, salt, and paprika in a shallow bowl. Brush the olive oil over the fillets, and then coat them with the Parmesan mixture. Place the tilapia onto a lined baking sheet, and then into the air fryer. Cook for about 4 to 5 minutes on all sides.

Nutrition Facts

Calories 228.4, Carbohydrates 1.3 g, Fat 11.1 g, Protein 31.9 g

---

204. Fish Finger Sandwich

Prep Time: 20 minutes

Ingredients:

- 4 cod fillets
- 2 tbsp. flour10 capers
- 4 bread rolls
- 2 oz. breadcrumbs
- 4 tbsp. pesto sauce
- 4 lettuce leaves
- Salt and pepper, to taste

Instructions:

Preheat the air fryer to 370 degrees F. Season the fillets with some salt and pepper, and coat them with the flour, and then dip in the breadcrumbs. You should get a really thin layer of breadcrumbs, that's why we don't use eggs for this recipe. Arrange the fillets onto a baking mat. Air fry for about 10 to 15 minutes. Cut the bread rolls in half. Place a lettuce leaf on top of the bottom halves. Place the fillets over. Spread a tablespoon of pesto sauce on top of each fillet. Top with the remaining halves.

Nutrition Facts

Calories 360.7, Carbohydrates 39.2 g, Fat 10.4 g, Protein 29.3 g

205. Quick and Easy Air Fried Salmon

Prep Time: 13 minutes

Ingredients:

- 1 salmon fillet
- 1 tbsp. soy sauce
- ¼ tsp. garlic powder
- Salt and pepper

Instructions:

Preheat the air fryer to 350 degrees F. Combine the soy sauce with the garlic powder and some salt and pepper. Brush the mixture over the salmon. Place the salmon onto a sheet of parchment paper and into the air fryer. Cook for 10 minutes.

Nutrition Facts

Calories 172, Carbohydrates 1.7 g, Fat 7.2 g, Protein 23.7 g

206. Delicious Coconut Shrimp

Prep Time: 30 minutes

Ingredients:

- 8 large shrimp
- ½ cup breadcrumbs
- 8 oz. coconut milk
- ½ cup shredded coconut
- ¼ tsp. salt¼ tsp. pepper
- ½ cup orange jam
- 1 tsp. mustard1 tbsp. honey
- ½ tsp. cayenne pepper
- ¼ tsp. hot sauce

Instructions:

Preheat the air fryer to 350 degrees F. Combine the breadcrumbs, cayenne pepper, shredded coconut, salt, and pepper in a small bowl. Dip the shrimp in the coconut milk, first, and then in the coconut crumbs. Arrange on a lined sheet, and air fry for 20 minutes. Meanwhile whisk the jam, honey, hot sauce, and mustard. Serve the shrimp with the sauce.

Nutrition Facts

Calories 436, Carbohydrates 69.9 g, Fat 16.4 g, Protein 7.6 g

207. Crab Cakes

Prep Time: 55 minutes

Ingredients:

- ½ cup cooked crab meat
- ¼ cup chopped red onion
- 1 tbsp. chopped basil¼ cup chopped celery
- ¼ cup chopped red pepper
- 3 tbsp. mayonnaise
- Zest of half a lemon
- ¼ cup breadcrumbs
- 2 tbsp. chopped parsley
- Old Bay seasoning, as desired
- Cooking spray

Instructions:

Preheat the air fryer to 390 degrees F. Place all of the **Ingredients** in a large bowl and mix well until completely incorporated. Make 4 large crab cakes from the mixture and place them on a lined sheet. Refrigerate for about 30 minutes, to set. Spay the air basket with cooking spray and arrange the crab cakes in it. Cook for about 7 minutes on each side.

Nutrition Facts

Calories 159.6, Carbohydrates 5.1 g, Fat 10.4 g, Protein 11.3 g

208. Cajun Lemony Salmon

Prep Time: 10 minutes

Ingredients:

- 1 salmon fillet
- ¼ tsp. brown sugar
- Juice of ½ lemon
- 1 tbsp. Cajun seasoning
- 2 lemon wedges, for serving
- 1 tbsp. chopped parsley, for garnishing

Instructions:

Preheat the air fryer to 350 degrees F. Meanwhile, Combine the sugar and lemon and coat the salmon with this mixture completely. Coat the salmon with the Cajun seasoning as well. Place a parchment paper into your air fryer and cook the salmon for 7 minutes. Remember if using a thicker fillet, cook no more than 6 minutes. Serve with lemon wedges and chopped parsley.

Nutrition Facts

Calories 170, Carbohydrates 9 g, Fat 7.2 g, Protein 22.6 g

209. Cod Cornflakes Nuggets

Prep Time: 25 minutes

Ingredients:

- 1-¼ lb. cod fillets, cut into 4 to 6 chunks each
- ½ cup flour
- 1 egg
- 1 tbsp. water
- 1 cup (use more if needed) cornflakes
- 1 tbsp. olive oil salt and pepper, to taste

Instructions:

Place the oil and cornflakes in a food processor and process until crumbed. Season the fish chunks with some salt and pepper. Beat the egg along with 1 tbsp. water. Dredge the chunks in flour first, then dip in the egg, and coat with cornflakes. Arrange on a lined

sheet. Air fry at 350 degrees for about 15 minutes.

Nutrition Facts

Calories 267.7, Carbohydrates 15.9 g, Fat 5.8 g, Protein 35.1 g

210. Tuna Patties Servings:

Time: 50 minutes

Ingredients:

- 5 oz. of canned tuna
- 1 tsp. lime juice
- 1 tsp. paprika
- ¼ cup flour
- ½ cup milk
- 1 small onion, diced
- 2 eggs
- 1 tsp. chili powder, optional
- ½ tsp. salt

Instructions:

Place all of the **Ingredients** in a bowl and mix well to combine. Make two large patties, or a few smaller ones, out of the mixture. Place them on a lined sheet and refrigerate for 30 minutes. Preheat the air fryer to 350 degrees F. Air fry the patties for about 6 minutes on each side.

Nutrition Facts

Calories 235.5, Carbohydrates 20.5 g, Fat 6.6 g, Protein 24.6 g

211. Pistachio Crusted Salmon

Prep Time: 15 - 20 minutes

Ingredients:

- 1 salmon fillet
- 1 tsp. mustard
- 3 tbsp. pistachios
- Pinch of sea salt
- Pinch of garlic powder
- Pinch of black pepper
- 1 tsp. lemon juice1 tsp. grated Parmesan cheese1 tsp. olive oil

Instructions:

Preheat the air fryer to 350 degrees F. Whisk the

mustard and lemon juice together. Season the salmon with salt, pepper, and garlic powder. Brush the olive oil on all sides. Brush the mustard/lemon mixture on top of the salmon. Chop the pistachios finely and combine them with the Parmesan cheese. Sprinkle them on top of the salmon. Place the salmon in the air fryer basket with the skin side down. Cook for about 10 minutes, or to your liking.

Nutrition Facts

Calories 357, Carbohydrates 8.2 g, Fat 23.8 g, Protein 28.8 g

5. Snacks And Appetizers

212. Pita Pizza

Preparation Time: 5 minutes

Ingredients:

- ¼ cup pizza sauce
- 1 large thin pita bread
- ¼ cup sliced mushrooms
- 10 black olives
- ¼ cup green pepper
- ½ cup fat free mozzarella
- Pinch of pizza seasoning
- 2 teaspoon parmesan

Instructions:

Preheat oven to broil.

Spread the pita with pizza sauce.

Layer on the vegetables and the top with the cheese and seasoning.

Spray with cooking spray.

Broil for 2 minutes.

Nutritional Value

Calories 317

Fat 11g

Protein 15g

Carbohydrates 39g

213. Vegan Bacon Wrapped Mini Breakfast Burritos

Preparation time: 20 mins

Ingredients

- 2 tablespoons cashew butter
- 6-8 stalks fresh asparagus
- handful spinach, kale, other greens
- 2 – 3 tablespoons tamari
- 2 servings Vegan Egg scramble or Tofu Scramble
- veggie add-ins:
- ⅓ cup roasted sweet potato cubes
- 1 – 2 tablespoons liquid smoke

- 1-2 tablespoons water
- 4 pieces of rice paper
- 8 strips roasted red pepper
- 1 small tree broccoli, sautéed

Instructions

Preheat Air Fryer to 350 °F. In a small shallow bowl, whisk together cashew butter, tamari, liquid smoke, and water. Set aside.

Prepare all fillings to assemble rolls.

Rice Paper Hydrating Technique: have a large plate/surface ready to fill/roll wrapper. Hold one rice paper under water faucet running cool water, getting both sides of wrapper wet, for just a few seconds. Remove from water and while still firm, place on a plate to fill – rice paper will soften as it sits, but will not be so soft that it sticks to the surface or rips when handling.

Fill by placing **Ingredients** just off from the middle, leaving sides of rice paper free. Fold two sides in like a burrito, roll from ingredient side to other side, and seal. Dip each roll into cashew - liquid smoke mixture, coating completely. Arrange rolls on parchment Air fryer.

Cook at 350 °F for 8-10 minutes, or until crisp.

Serve warm

Nutrition facts:

Calorie 394.9

Fats 25.1g

Fiber 11g

Carbs 19.5g

Protein 21g

214. Air fryer Baked Thai Peanut Chicken Egg Rolls

Preparation time: 18 mins

Ingredients

- 1 medium carrot, very thinly sliced or ribboned
- 3 green onions, chopped
- 4 egg roll wrappers
- 2 c. rotisserie chicken, shredded
- ¼ c. Thai peanut sauce
- ¼ red bell pepper, julienned

- non-stick cooking spray or sesame oil

Instructions

Preheat Air fryer to 390° or oven to 425°.

In a small bowl, toss the chicken with the Thai peanut sauce.

Lay the egg roll wrappers out on a clean dry surface. Over the bottom third of an egg roll wrapper, arrange ¼ the carrot, bell pepper, and onions. Spoon ½ cup of the chicken mixture over the vegetables.

Moisten the outside edges of the wrapper with water. Fold the sides of the wrapper toward the center and roll tightly.

Repeat with remaining wrappers. (Keep remaining wrappers covered with a damp paper towel until ready to use.)

Spray the assembled egg rolls with non-stick cooking spray. Turn them over and spray the backsides as well.

Place the egg rolls in the Air fryer and bake at 390° for 6-8 minutes or until they are crispy and golden brown.

(If you are baking the egg rolls in an oven, place the seam side down on a baking sheet coated with cooking spray. Bake at 425° for 45-20 minutes.)

Slice in half and serve with additional Thai Peanut Sauce for dipping.

Nutrition facts:

Calorie 235

Fats 7g

Fiber 1g

Carbs 17g

Protein 21g

215. Air Fryer Cheese Sticks Recipe

Preparation time: 22 mins

Ingredients

- 1/4 cup grated parmesan cheese
- 1 tsp. Italian Seasoning
- 1 tsp. garlic powder
- 6 snack-size cheese sticks (the individual ones you buy for kids)
- 2 large eggs
- 1/4 cup whole wheat flour (any type - pastry or

white whole wheat work well)
- 1/4 tsp. ground rosemary

Instructions

Unwrap your cheese sticks and set aside.

Crack and beat your eggs with a fork a shallow bowl that is wide enough to fit the length of the cheese sticks.

In another bowl (or plate), mix the flour, cheese, and seasonings.

Roll the cheese sticks in the egg, then in the batter. Repeat until the cheese sticks are well coated.

Place them in the basket of your air fryer, ensuring they don't touch.

Cook to your air fryer's **Instructions**. On mine, the temperature was 370 F. for 6-7 minutes.

Serve with a clean marinara or ketchup (or ranch dressing!)

Nutrition facts:

Calorie 50

Fats 2g

Fiber 0g

Carbs 3g

Protein 3g

216. Healthy Air Fried Chicken Meatballs

Prep Time: 20 mins

Total Time: 25 mins

Ingredients

- 1 Pound of ground chicken
- 2 Finely chopped green onions
- ½ Cup of chopped cilantro
- 1 Tbsp of Hoisin Sauce
- 1 Tbsp of soy sauce
- 1 tsp of Sriracha
- 1 tsp of sesame oil
- ¼ Cup of unsweetened shredded coconut
- 1 Pinch of salt
- 1 Pinch of ground black pepper

Instructions:

Heat your Air Fryer to a temperature of about 350°F.

Mix all your **Ingredients** in a large bowl. Line your Air Fryer baking pan with a paper sheet. With spoon, scoop the mixture into small rounds.

Place the baking pan in your Air Fryer; then lock the lid of your Air Fryer. Set the timer to about 10 to 12 minutes and the temperature to about 380° F

When the timer beeps; turn off your Air Fryer; then remove the pan from the air fryer and set it aside to cool for about 5 minutes.

Serve and enjoy your appetizing chicken balls!

Nutrition facts:

Calories 279

Total Fats 13 g

Carbs: 9.8 g

Protein 28.8 g

Sugar 1.5 g

Fiber 0.5 g

217. Mexican Empanada

Preparation time: 40 mins

Ingredients

- 1 shallot, chopped
- 7 ounces store-bought pizza dough
- ¼ red bell pepper, diced
- 4 ½ ounces chorizo, cubed
- 2 tbsp. parsley

Instructions:

In a pan over medium heat, sauté the pepper, shallots, and chorizo together for 3-5 minutes.

Turn the heat off before adding in the parsley.

Take 20 small rounds from the dough. You may use a cookie cutter if you want.

Scoop out some of the chorizo mixture and place it on the center of each round of dough. Fold and secure the edges. Do the same for the rest of the **Ingredients**.

Cook the empanadas in the air fryer at 390°F for 10-12 minutes.

Nutrition facts:

Calorie 283

Fats 22g

Fiber 1g

Carbs 5g

Protein 17g

218. Mushroom-Salami Pizza

Preparation time: 30mins

Ingredients

- 1 tsp. butter, melted
- ¼ cup tomato sauce
- 1 small, store-bought
- 8-in pizza dough
- ½ ball of mozzarella sliced thinly
- ½ tbsp. olive oil
- 3 mushrooms, sliced
- 1 ½ ounces salami, cut into strips
- Pepper to taste
- 2 tsp. dried oregano
- 2 tbsp. Parmesan cheese, grated

Instructions:

Press and pat the dough on a well-greased pizza pan. Use the butter to grease the pan.

Spread the sauce all over the dough then top it all with cheese.

Now, sprinkle the mushrooms and salami over the pizza base.

Season it with oregano, pepper, and cheese.

Cook it in a preheated air-fryer at 390°F for 12 minutes.

Nutrition facts:

Calorie 233.9

Fats 9g

Fiber 1.3g

Carbs 26.3g

Protein 11.3g

219. Lemony Roasted Bell Peppers

Preparation time: 10mins

Ingredients

- 4 Bell Peppers
- 1 tsp. chopped Parsley
- ¼ tsp. minced garlic
- 1 tsp. Olive Oil
- Pinch of Sea Salt
- 1 tbsp. Lemon Juice
- Pinch of Pepper

Instructions

Preheat your Air Fryer to 390 degrees F.

Arrange the bell peppers in the Air Fryer and drizzle with the olive oil.

Air Fry for 5 minutes. Transfer to a serving plate.

In a small bowl, combine the lemon juice, garlic, parsley, salt, and pepper. Drizzle this mixture over the peppers.

Serve and enjoy!

Nutrition facts:

Calorie 59.0

Fats 3.5g

Fiber 2g

Carbs 6.6g

Protein 1.4g

220. Crunchy Onion Rings

Preparation time: 10mins

Ingredients

- ¾ cup Breadcrumbs
- ¼ tsp. Salt
- ¾ Cup Milk
- 1 Large Onion 1 cup Flour
- 1 tbsp. Baking Powder
- 1 Egg
- ¼ tsp. Paprika

Instructions:

Preheat your Air Fryer to 340 degrees F.

Whisk together the milk, eggs, flour, salt, and paprika in a bowl. Peel and slice the onion. Separate into rings.

grease the Air Fryer with some cooking spray. Dip each onion ring into the batter and then coat with breadcrumbs.

Arrange in the Air Fryer. Cook for 10 minutes.

Serve and enjoy!

Nutrition facts:

Calorie 497

Fats 13g

Fiber 4g

Carbs 59g

Protein 30g

221. Crispy Kale

Preparation time: 10 mins

Ingredients

- 1 tsp. soy sauce
- 1 tbsp. olive oil
- 4 cups kale leaves, torn into 1 ½ pieces

Instructions:

Preheat the air fryer to 390°F.

Season the kale with soy sauce and some olive oil.

Cook it for 3-5 minutes.

Nutrition facts:

Calorie 104.0

Fats 4.5g

Fiber 5.2g

Carbs 14.6g

Protein 4.9g

222. Roasted Mushrooms

Preparation time: 40 mins

Ingredients

- 2 teaspoons of herbes de Provence
- 2 tbsp. of white (French) vermouth
- 2 pounds of mushrooms
- 1 tbsp. of duck fat

- ½ tsp. of garlic powder

Instructions

Wash mushrooms and spin dry in a salad spinner, quarter them and set aside.

Put duck fat, garlic and the herbes de Provence in the pan of your paddle type air fryer.

Heat for 2 minutes. Stir with a wooden spoon if it clumped.

Include mushrooms, cook for 25 minutes Include vermouth and cook for an additional 5 minutes.

Nutrition facts:

Calorie 94.4

Fats 8.9g

Fiber 0.7g

Carbs 3.2g

Protein 1.9g

223. Crispy Kale Chips

Preparation time: 10 mins

Ingredients

- 1 head of kale
- 1 tbsp. of Olive oil
- 1 tsp. of soya sauce

Instructions

Remove the center stem of the kale

Tear the kale up into 1½" pieces.

Wash clean and dry thoroughly.

Toss with the olive oil and soya sauce.

Fry in the air fryer at 200oC for 2 to 3 minutes, tossing the leaves halfway through.

Nutrition facts:

Calorie 66.2

Fats 3.9g

Fiber 2.6g

Carbs 7.3g

Protein 2.5g

224. Air Fried Vegetable Spring Rolls

Preparation time: 40 mins

Ingredients

- 10 spring roll sheets
- 5-6 mushrooms, sliced
- 1 clove garlic, smashed
- 1/4 yellow bell pepper, thinly sliced
- 1/4 red bell pepper, thinly sliced
- 1 tsp. galangal/ginger, minced
- 1 green onion, finely chopped
- 1/2 cup carrot, thinly sliced
- 1/2 cup cabbage, thinly sliced
- 2 birds eye chilies, finely chopped
- 1 tbsp. soya sauce
- 1 tbsp. vegetarian oyster sauce (optional)

To serve

- 2 tbsp. sweet chili sauce
- 2 tbsp. soya sauce

Instructions

In a small saucepan, sauté the green onion, ginger, and garlic until soft and fragrant.

Mix in the carrot and after a few minutes the rest of the vegetables (except the chilies). The pan may seem overcrowded but in a few minutes the vegetables will release their juices and it will cook down noticeably.

Add the soy sauce and the oyster sauce and cook for 10-12 minutes, stirring occasionally. Once the pan seems dry (no liquid is visible when you move the vegetables around), take off the heat, add the chilies to taste, and leave to cool completely.

Remove the spring roll sheets from the freezer and cover with a cloth, for approx. 30 minutes until the vegetables cool.

Preheat the air fryer to 200*.

Place a single sheet on a clean surface/plate in a diamond shape (as pictured above). Place a tablespoon full on the mixture once inch from the triangle closest to you.

Roll tightly halfway, tuck on the left and right corners and continue rolling. It's actually really easy.

Place on the rack of the air fryer and brush with a little bit of vegetable oil. Air fry, shaking every few minutes and brushing with oil if it looks very dry. Your perfect golden brown and super crisp spring rolls will be ready in under 10 minutes.

Enjoy served with 2 dipping sauces - soy and sweet chili.

Nutrition facts:

Calorie 90

Fats 6g

Fiber 2g

Carbs 3g

Protein 5g

225. Parsley Flakes Onion Chips

Prep Time: 9 mins

Total Time: 10 mins

Ingredients

- 1 Onion
- 1 Large egg
- 2 Tbsp of coconut flour
- 2 Tbsp of grated parmesan cheese
- 1/8 tsp of garlic powder
- ¼ tsp of parsley flakes
- 1/8 tsp of cayenne pepper
- 1 Pinch of salt
- 1 Tbsp of olive oil

Instructions:

Preheat your Air Fryer to a temperature of 360° F

Crack the egg and beat it a shallow bowl

Mix the parmesan with the coconut flour, the garlic powder, the parsley flakes, the cayenne and the salt in a shallow bowl

Slice the onion into rings of about ½ inch of thickness

Add the onion rings to the egg wash for about 1 minute; then coat very well

Remove the onion rings from the egg wash; then coat it in the shallow dish of the flour

Arrange the onion rings in the Air Fryer basket; then drizzle with 1 tbsp of oil

Lock the lid of your Air Fryer

Set the timer for about 9 to 10 minutes and set the temperature to about 200°C/ 390° F

When the timer beeps; turn off your Air Fryer

Serve and enjoy your delicious appetizer!

Nutrition facts:

Calories 170

Total Fats 8.1 g

Carbs: 12 g

Protein 3 g

Sugar 1.8 g

Fiber 25 g

226. Air Fried Shrimp Tails

Prep Time: 15 mins

Total Time: 20 mins

Ingredients

1 lb of peeled and deveined raw Shrimp

1 Cup of almond flour

1 tbsp of pepper to taste

1 tbsp of salt

1 tsp of cayenne pepper

1 tsp of cumin

1 tsp of garlic powder

1 tbsp of paprika

1 tbsp of onion powder

Instructions:

Preheat your Air Fryer to a temperature of 390° F

Peel the shrimp and devein it

Dip in the shrimp into the heavy cream

Dredge the shrimp into the mixture of the almond flour

Shake off any excess of flour

Put the shrimp in the Air Fryer basket and

Lock the lid of your Air Fryer and set the timer to about 15 minutes and the temperature to 200° C/400° F

You can check your appetizer after about 6 minutes and you can flip the shrimp if needed

When the timer beeps; turn off your Air Fryer

Serve and enjoy your shrimps!

Nutrition facts:

Calories 335

Total Fats 15.8 g

Carbs: 2.2 g

Protein 46 g

Sugar 0.2 g

Fiber 0.5 g

227. Air fried Radish with Coconut Oil

Prep Time: 12 mins

Total Time: 15 mins

Ingredients

- 16 Ounces of fresh radishes
- 2 tbsp of melted coconut oil
- ½ tsp of sea salt
- ½ tsp of pepper

Instructions:

Preheat your Air Fryer to a temperature of about 400 degrees F.

Slice the radishes into thin slices

Place the radish slices in a bowl and toss it with oil

Lay the radishes in the Air Fryer basket

Whisk the pepper and the salt together; then sprinkle it over the radishes

Lock the lid of your Air Fryer and set the timer for about 12 minutes

Set the temperature to about 200° C/400° F

When the timer beeps; turn off your Air Fryer

Remove the pan from the air fryer

Serve and enjoy your air fried radishes!

Nutritional info per serving:

Calories 148

Total Fats 14 g

Carbs: 6 g

Protein 3 g

Sugar 1 g

Fiber 3 g

228. Air fried Okra with Parmesan Cheese

Prep Time: 25 mins

Total Time: 10 mins

Ingredients

- 1 Pound of fresh okra
- 1 tsp of sea salt
- 2 tbsp of almond flour
- ¼ Cup of finely grated Parmesan cheese
- ½ tsp of pepper
- 1 Pinch of sea salt

Instructions:

Preheat your Air Fryer to a temperature of about 390° F

Wash the okra; then chop it into small pieces

Toss the chopped okra with the salt and a little bit of ground pepper; then set it aside for about 3 minutes

In a bowl; mix the almond flour with Parmesan cheese, the pepper, and the salt

Coat the okra pieces into the mixture and place it in your Air Fryer basket

Lock the lid and set the timer to about 25 minutes and the temperature to 390° F

When the timer beeps; turn off your Air Fryer

Remove the pan; then serve and enjoy your okras!

Nutrition facts:

Calories 42

Total Fats 1 g

Carbs: 4 g

Protein 2 g

Sugar 0.1 g

Fiber 2 g

229. Chicken Nuggets with Almond Flour

Prep Time: 15 mins

Total Time: 18 mins

Ingredients

- 1 Whisked egg
- 4 tbsp of oil
- 2 lbs of chicken breast
- 1 Cup of almond flour

- ½ tsp of salt
- ½ tsp of garlic powder
- 1 tsp of onion flakes

Instructions

Combine the egg and the oil and whisk very well

In a separate bowl; combine the almond flour, the salt, the garlic and the onion

Cut the chicken breast meat into thin strips; then dip each of the strips into the egg mixture and coat very well

Arrange the chicken nuggets in the Air Fryer basket and spray with a little bit of oil

Lock the lid of the Air Fryer and set the timer for about 15 minutes and set the temperature for about 180° C/350° F

When the timer beeps; turn off your Air Fryer

Serve and enjoy the chicken nuggets!

Nutrition facts:

Calories 170.1

Total Fats 9.2 g

Carbs: 13 g

Protein 11 g

Sugar 5 g

Fiber 1 g

230. Easy Crab Sticks

Preparation time: 15 mins

Ingredients

- 20 ounces crabsticks, sliced into thin strips
- 2 tsps. sesame oil
- 1 tsp. Cajun seasoning

Instructions:

Season the crabsticks with some Cajun seasoning and sesame oil.

Cook it in the air fryer at 320°F for 10-12 minutes

Nutrition facts:

Calorie 104.0

Fats 4.5g

Fiber 5.2g

Carbs 14.6g

Protein 4.9g

231. Sausage Balls

Preparation time: 30 mins

Ingredients

- 1 tsp. sage
- 3 tbsp. breadcrumbs
- ¼ tsp. salt
- 3 ½ ounces sausage meat
- 1 onion, diced
- ½ tsp. garlic powder
- 1/8 tsp. black pepper

Instructions:

Mix all the **Ingredients** in the bowl.

Take about 2-3 tbsp. of the mixture and roll it into a ball in between your palms.

Do the same for the rest of the mixture.

Cook the meatballs in a preheated air fryer at 350°F for 15-20 minutes.

Nutrition facts:

Calorie 65.8

Fats 2.5g

Fiber 0g

Carbs 6.3g

Protein 4.5g

232. Cajun Salmon

Preparation time: 10 mins

Ingredients

- 0.44lbs/1 piece of fresh salmon fillet
- Cajun seasoning
- Juice from ¼ of lemon to serve

Direction

Preheat Air Fryer to 180oC for 5 minutes.

Clean the salmon and pat dry.

In a plate, sprinkle Cajun seasoning all over and ensure all sides are coated.

Air fry for a salmon fillet about ¾ of an inch thick, air fry for 7 minutes, skin side upon the grill pan.

Serve hot or immediately with a squeeze of lemon.

Nutrition facts:

Calorie 113.4

Fats 12g

Fiber 0g

Carbs 0g

Protein 22g

6. AIR FRYER SEAFOODS

233. Cheesy Bacon Wrapped Shrimp

Preparation time: 20mins

Ingredients

- 16 extra-large raw shrimp, peeled, deveined, and butterflied
- 16 (1 in) cubes cheddar jack cheese
- 16 slices of bacon, cooked half way
- ¼ cup BBQ sauce

Instructions

- Preheat the air fryer to 350 degrees F.
- Stuff each shrimp with a cheese cube and wrap with a slice of bacon.
- Secure the bacon to the shrimp with a toothpick.
- Brush the wrapped shrimp with BBQ sauce and place in the air fryer.
- Cook for 6 minutes.
- Remove and brush with additional BBQ sauce.

Nutrition facts:

Calorie 110

Fats 0g

Fiber 0g

Carbs 0g

Protein 11g

234. Salmon Quiche

Preparation time: 60mins

Ingredients

- 2 cups salmon, skinless and cubed
- 1 tsp. salt
- ¼ tsp. ground black pepper
- 1 (9 in) premade pie crust
- 3 large eggs
- 1 tbsp. Dijon mustard
- ¼ cup green onion, chopped
- ½ cup shredded mozzarella cheese
- 4 tbsp. heavy cream

Instructions

- Preheat the air fryer to a temperature of 350 degrees F
- Then, Season the salmon with salt and pepper to your taste. Set aside. Place the pre-made pie crust into individual quiche pans and press into the sides of the pans.
- Trim off any overhanging crust. Trim the dough onto the edges of the pan you intend to use or just let it stick out.
- Place the cubed salmon into the crust and top with the green onion and mozzarella. In a mixing bowl, combine the heavy cream, eggs, and mustard.
- Carefully pour over the salmon, being careful not cause the mixture to overflow.
- Carefully slide the quiche into the fryer basket and cook for 20 minutes.
- Let rest for 10 minutes before serving.

Nutrition facts:

Calorie 287.2

Fats 13g

Fiber 0.4g

Carbs 11.4g

Protein 29.5g

235. Cedar Plank Salmon

Preparation time: 30mins

Ingredients

- 4 untreated cedar planks
- 1½ tbsp. of rice vinegar
- 2 tbsp. sesame oil
- ½ cup soy sauce
- ¼ cup green onions, chopped
- 3 cloves garlic, minced
- 1 tbsp. fresh ginger grated
- 2 lb. of salmon fillets, skin removed

Instructions

Submerge the cedar planks in water and soak for 2 hours.

- In a shallow dish, combine all **Ingredients** except salmon and mix well.
- Add the salmon to the marinade and coat each side.
- Marinate, refrigerated, for 30minutes.
- Preheat fryer to 350 degrees F.
- Remove the cedar planks from the water and pat dry.
- Place on the fryer basket and place the salmon on top
- Cook for 15 minutes. Serve and enjoy

Nutrition facts:

Calorie 540

Fats 32g

Fiber 3g

Carbs 28g

Protein 38g

236. Chinese Mushroom Tilapia

Preparation time: 20mins

Ingredients

- ½ cup yellow onion, sliced thin
- 2 cloves garlic, minced
- 4 (8oz) fillets tilapia
- 2½ tsps. of salt
- 2 tbsp. olive oil
- 2 cups sliced mushrooms
- 4 tbsp. soy sauce
- 1 tsp. red chili flakes
- 1 tbsp. honey 2 tbsp. rice vinegar

Instructions

- Preheat the fryer to 350 degrees F.
- Season the fish with half the salt and drizzle with half the oil. Cook for 15 minutes.
- Meanwhile, heat the remaining oil in a large skillet.
- Once hot add the mushroom onion and garlic.
- Cook until onions are soft. Stir in the soy sauce, chili flakes, honey, and vinegar. Simmer for 1 minute.
- Remove fish from the fryer and top with mushroom sauce.

Serve and enjoy!

Nutrition facts:

Calorie 57

Fats 3.5g

Fiber 1.8g

Carbs 1.7g

Protein 1.8g

237. Air Fried Spinach Fish

Preparation time: 20mins

Ingredients

- 1 cup spinach leaves, wilted
- 2 cups flour
- 1 tsp. salt
- ½ tsp. ground black pepper
- 2 tbsp. olive oil
- 1 large egg
- 4 (6oz) filets perch
- 1 tbsp. lemon juice

Instructions

- Preheat the fryer to 370 degrees F.
- In a bowl, combine the spinach, flour, salt, pepper, and egg.
- Dip each filet in the batter and place on the fryer tray.
- Drizzle with olive oil. Cook for 12 minutes.
- Remove and drizzle with lemon juice.

Nutrition facts:

Calorie 227.8

Fats 5.1g

Fiber 1.8g

Carbs 14.2g

Protein 1.8g

238. Air Fryer Fried Louisiana Shrimp Po Boy with Remoulade Sauce

Preparation time: 30mins

Ingredients

- 4 French bread hoagie rolls I used 2 loaves, cut each in half
- 2 cups shredded lettuce
- 1 pound shrimp, deveined I usually go for the biggest shrimp I can find because they shrink a little when you cook them
- 1/2 cup Louisiana Fish Fry
- 1/4 cup buttermilk
- 8 tomato slices
- 1 tsps. Creole Seasoning I used Cony Chachere
- 1 tsps. butter optional

Remoulade Sauce

- 1/2 cup mayo I used reduced-fat
- 1 tsp. minced garlic
- 1/2 lemon juice of
- 1 tsp. Worcestershire
- 1/2 tsp. Creole Seasoning I used Cony Chachere
- 1 tsp. Dijon mustard
- 1 tsp. hot sauce
- 1 green onion chopped

Instructions

- Remoulade Sauce
- Combine all of the **Ingredients** in a small bowl. Refrigerate prior to serving while the shrimp cooks.
- Shrimp Po Boy
- Season the shrimp with the seasonings.
- Pour the buttermilk in a bowl. Dip each of the shrimp in the buttermilk. Place the shrimp in a Ziploc bag and in the fridge to marinate. Marinate for at least 30 minutes. I prefer overnight.
- Add the fish fry to a bowl. Remove the shrimp from the bags and dip each into the fish fry. Add the shrimp to Air Fryer basket.
- Preheat Air Fryer to 400 degrees.
- Spray the shrimp with olive oil. Do not spray directly on the shrimp. The fish fry will go flying. Keep a nice distance.
- Cook the shrimp for 5 minutes. Open the basket and flip the shrimp to the other side. Cook for an additional 5 minutes or until crisp.
- Preheat oven to 325 degrees. Place the sliced bread on a sheet pan.

- Allow the bread to toast for a couple of minutes.
- Optional step if you prefer butter: Melt the butter in the microwave. Using a cooking brush, spread the butter over the bottom of the French bread.
- Assemble the po boy. Spread the remoulade sauce on the French bread. Add the sliced tomato and lettuce, and then the shrimp.

Nutrition facts:

Calorie 437

Fats 12g

Fiber 1.8g

Carbs 32g

Protein 28g

---

239. Air Fryer 3 Ingredient Fried Catfish

Preparation time: 65mins

Ingredients

- 4 catfish fillets
- 1/4 cup seasoned fish fry I used Louisiana
- 1 tbsp. olive oil
- 1 tbsp. chopped parsley optional

Instructions

- Preheat Air Fryer to 400 degrees.
- Rinse the catfish and pat dry.
- Pour the fish fry seasoning in a large Ziploc bag.
- Add the catfish to the bag, one at a time. Seal the bag and shake. Ensure the entire filet is coated with seasoning.
- Spray olive oil on the top of each filet.
- Place the filet in the Air Fryer basket. (Due to the size of my fillets, I cooked each one at a time). Close and cook for 10 minutes.
- Flip the fish. Cook for an additional 10 minutes.
- Flip the fish.
- Cook for an additional 2-3 minutes or until desired crispness.
- Top with parsley

Nutrition facts:

Calorie 208

Fats 11.2g

Fiber 0.5g

Carbs 15.4g

Protein 13.3g

240. Air Fried Dragon Shrimp

Preparation time: 15mins

Ingredients

- 1 lb. raw shrimp, peeled and deveined
- 2 eggs 2 tbsp. olive oil
- ½ cup soy sauce
- 1 cup yellow onion, diced
- ½ tsps. ground ginger
- ½ tsps. salt
- ¼ cup flour
- ½ tsps. ground red pepper

Instructions

- Preheat air fryer to 350 degrees F.
- Combine all **Ingredients**, except for the shrimp, and create a batter. Let sit for 10 minutes.
- Dip the shrimp into the batter to coat all sides and place in the fryer basket.
- Cook for 10 minutes and serve.

Nutrition facts:

Calorie 221

Fats 13g

Fiber 0.06g

Carbs 1g

Protein 23g

241. Air Fryer Keto Shrimp Scampi

Preparation time: 15mins

Ingredients

- 1 tablespoon chopped chives or 1 teaspoon dried chives
- 1 tablespoon minced basil leaves plus more for sprinkling or 1 teaspoon dried basil
- 2 tablespoons chicken stock (or white wine)
- 4 tablespoons butter

- 1 tablespoon lemon juice
- 1 tablespoon minced garlic
- 2 teaspoons red pepper flakes
- 1 lb. defrosted shrimp (21-25 count)

Instructions

- Turn your air fryer to 330F. Place a 6 x 3 metal pan in it and allow the oven to start heating while you gather your **Ingredients**.
- Place the butter, garlic, and red pepper flakes into the hot 6-inch pan.
- Allow it to cook for 2 minutes, stirring once, until the butter has melted. Do not skip this step. This is what infuses garlic into the butter, which is what makes it all taste so good.
- Open the air fryer, add all **Ingredients** to the pan in the order listed, stirring gently.
- Allow shrimp to cook for 5 minutes, stirring once. At this point, the butter should be well-melted and liquid, bathing the shrimp in spiced goodness.
- Mix very well, remove the 6-inch pan using silicone mitts, and let it rest for 1 minute on the counter. You're doing this so that you let the shrimp cook in the residual heat, rather than letting it accidentally overcook and get rubbery.
- Stir at the end of the minute. The shrimp should be well-cooked at this point.
- Sprinkle additional fresh basil leaves and enjoy.

Nutrition facts:

Calorie 219

Fats 14g

Fiber 0.4g

Carbs 1g

Protein 26g

242. Fish Lettuce Wraps

Preparation time: 20mins

Ingredients

- 6 iceberg lettuce leaves
- 6 small filets of tilapia
- 1 tsp. salt
- ½ tsp. ground black pepper
- 2 tsp. Cajun seasoning

- 1 tbsp. olive oil
- ½ cup shredded purple cabbage
- ½ cup shredded carrot
- 1 tbsp. lemon juice

Instructions

- Preheat the air fryer to 390 degrees F.
- Season tilapia with salt, pepper and Cajun seasoning.
- Drizzle with olive oil and place in the air fryer.
- Cook for 10 minutes.
- Remove fish from the fryer and place the fish on each lettuce leaf.
- Top with carrots and cabbage.
- Drizzle lemon juice on top

Nutrition facts:

Calorie 180

Fats 7g

Fiber 0g

Carbs 0g

Protein 14g

243. Tuna Risotto

Preparation time: 35mins

Serves: 6

Ingredients

- 4 cups chicken broth, warm
- ¼ cup grated parmesan cheese
- 1 tbsp. olive oil
- 2 cups Arborio rice
- ½ cup yellow onion, minced
- 1 cup peas 2 (4oz) cans tuna, drained
- 1 tsp. ground black pepper

Instructions

- Preheat air fryer to 320.
- Season the tuna and peas with black pepper.
- Place in the air fryer and cook for 10 minutes.
- Meanwhile, heat the oil and add the onion and rice. Cook until lightly browned.
- Add 1 cup of the warm broth, and cook until absorbed.

- Repeat until all the broth is used. Stir in the parmesan, tuna, and peas.

Nutrition facts:

Calorie 553

Fats 40g

Fiber 4g

Carbs 23g

Protein 52g

244. Tandoori Fish

Preparation time: 25mins

Ingredients

- 1 whole fish, such as trout
- 1 tbsp. garam Masala seasoning
- 3 tbsp. olive oil
- 8 cloves garlic, minced
- 1 cup papaya, mashed
- 1 tsp. ground turmeric
- ½ tsp. ground cumin
- 1 tbsp. chili powder
- 1 tsp. salt ½ tsp. ground black pepper

Instructions

- Preheat the air fryer to 340 degrees F.
- Slash slits into the sides of the fish.
- Combine all remaining **Ingredients** and coat all sides of the fish with the mixture.
- Place the coated fish into the fryer basket and cook for 20 minutes.

Nutrition facts:

Calorie 294.2

Fats 11g

Fiber 7.4g

Carbs 21.4g

245. Pecan Crusted Salmon

Preparation time: 20mins

Ingredients

- ½ cup pecans

- 3 tbsp. fresh chopped parsley
- 1 tsp. salt
- ½ tsp. ground black pepper
- 3 tbsp. Dijon mustard
- 3 tbsp. olive oil
- 1 tbsp. honey
- ½ cup Panko breadcrumbs
- 4 salmon filets 1 tbsp. lemon juice

Instructions

- Preheat air fryer to 390 degrees F.
- In a small bowl combine the mustard, oil, and honey. Combine the Panko, pecans, parsley, salt, and pepper in a food processor and process until crumbs are fine.
- Dip the salmon in the mustard mixture then dip the salmon into the pecan mixture, pressing the pecans into all sides of the fish.
- Place the coated salmon in the fryer basket and cook for 10 minutes.
- Drizzle with lemon juice.

Nutrition facts:

Calorie 353.2

Fats 24.8g

Fiber 1.1g

Carbs 1.7g

Protein 30.5g

246. Broiled Tilapia Done

Preparation time: 9mins

Ingredients

- 1 to 1 1/2 lb. tilapia fillets
- molly mcbutter or butter buds
- light spritz of canola oil from an oil spritzer
- Old Bay seasoning,
- lemon pepper
- salt

Instructions

- Thaw fillets, if frozen. Spray the basket of your air fryer with cooking spray.
- Place fillets in the basket (do not stack them) and season to taste with the spices. Spray lightly with oil.

- Set temperature at 400 degrees and set timer for 7 minutes.
- When the timer goes off, check for doneness. Fish should flake easily with a fork.
- Serve and enjoy with your favorite veggies.

Nutrition facts:

Calorie 110

Fats 3g

Fiber 0g

Carbs 23g

247. Prawn Curry

Preparation time: 15mins

Ingredients

- 2 tbsp. curry powder
- 1 medium finely chopped onion
- 1½ cup chicken broth
- ½ tsp. of coriander
- 6 king prawns
- 1 tsp. salt
- ½ tsp. ground black pepper
- 1 tbsp. olive oil
- 1 tbsp. tomato paste

Instructions

Preheat the air fryer to 370 degrees F. Season the prawns with salt and pepper.

Cook for 7 minutes. Meanwhile, heat the olive oil in a large skillet. Once hot add the onion.

Cook until soft. Sit in the curry, tomato paste, and coriander.

Cook, stirring, for 1 minute.

Add the chicken broth and stir until smooth.

Remove prawns from the fryer and add to the sauce.

Serve and enjoy!

Nutrition facts:

Calorie 294.2

Fats 11g

Fiber 7.4g

Carbs 21.4g

248. Crusted Halibut

Preparation time: 30mins

Ingredients

- 2 tsp. lemon zest
- 1 tsp. salt
- ½ tsp. ground black pepper
- ¾ cup Panko bread crumbs
- ½ cup fresh parsley, chopped
- ¼ cup fresh dill, chopped
- 4 halibut filets
- 1 tbsp. olive oil

Instructions

- Preheat the air fryer to 390 degrees F.
- Combine all **Ingredients** except halibut and olive oil in a food processor and pulse until the mixture is a fine crumb.
- gently coat the halibut in the mixture and place inside the fryer basket.
- Drizzle with olive oil and cook for 25 minutes.

Nutrition facts:

Calorie 454

Fats 15g

Fiber 5g

Carbs 38g

Protein 4g

249. Shrimp and Mushroom Risotto

Preparation time: 30mins

Ingredients

- 4 Chicken Legs
- 2 tbsp. Olive Oil
- 4 tsp. dried Basil
- 2 tsp. minced garlic
- Pinch of Pepper
- Pinch of Salt
- 1 Lemon, sliced

Instructions

- Preheat your Air Fryer to 350 degrees F.
- Brush the chicken with the oil and sprinkle with the remaining **Ingredients**.

- Place in the Air Fryer and arrange the lemon slices around the chicken legs.
- Close the lid and cook for 20 minutes.

Nutrition facts:

Calorie 328.3

Fats 14.5g

Fiber 2.3g

Carbs 24.1g

Protein 24.4g

250. Halibut Sitka

Preparation time: 20mins

Ingredients

- ½ cup green onion, chopped
- ½ cup mayonnaise
- ½ cup sour cream
- 6 (8 oz.) skinless halibut filets
- 1 tsp. salt
- ½ tsp. ground black pepper
- 1 tsp. dry dill

Instructions

- Preheat the air fryer to 390 degrees F
- Season the halibut with salt and pepper, place on the fryer plate.
- In a small bowl, combine the remaining **Ingredients**.
- Mix well then spread over the top of the halibut. Cook for 15 minutes.

!

Nutrition facts:

Calorie 333.26

Fats 37.03g

Fiber 0.06g

Carbs 1.74g

Protein 22.17g

251. Air Fried Calamari and Tomato Pasta

Preparation time: 25mins

Ingredients

- 2 cloves garlic, minced
- 1 lb. sliced calamari, cut into rings
- 1 egg 1 cup Italian bread crumbs
- 1 tbsp. of olive oil
- ½ cup diced onion
- 2 tsps. Italian seasoning
- 2 (15 oz.) cans diced tomatoes, drained
- 1 lb. dry angel hair pasta
- ½ cup grated parmesan

Instructions

- Preheat fryer to 360 degrees.
- Dip the calamari into the egg and then into the breadcrumbs. Coating all sides. Place in the air fryer basket and drizzle with olive oil. Cook for 15 minutes. Meanwhile, bring a large pot of water to a boil.
- Add the pasta and cook for 10 minutes or until tender. Drain. Combine the pasta, garlic, onion, Italian seasoning, and diced tomatoes. Heat just until hot. Spoon on to a serving plate. Remove calamari from air fryer and place on top of pasta. Sprinkle with Parmesan

Nutrition facts:

Calorie 303.6

Fats 14.2g

Fiber 0.06g

Carbs 28.3g

Protein 18.7g

252. Pork Chop Perfection

Preparation time: 35mins

Ingredients

- ½ cup Dijon mustard
- ½ cup bread crumbs, seasoned
- ½ tsp. cayenne pepper
- 4 pork chops, lean, bone-in or boneless
- 1 tsp. salt
- 1 tsp. pepper
- 1 tbsp. canola or sunflower oil

Instructions

- Coat each pork chop with Dijon mustard.

- In a shallow bowl, combine bread crumbs, salt, pepper, and cayenne pepper.
- Dredge pork chops in breadcrumb mixture, coating evenly.
- Brush or spray thin coating of oil on each pork chop.
- Air fry at 400°F for 10 minutes.
- Remove air fryer basket, flip chops.
- Air fry at 400°F for an additional 10 minutes.
- Allow to cool five minutes before serving.

Nutrition facts:

Calorie 175.5

Fats 8g

Fiber 0.1g

Carbs 1.4g

Protein 0g

253. Almond, and Poppy Seed Cabbage Salad

Preparation time: 15mins

Ingredients

- ½ cup diced green Pepper
- 1 cup of Mayonnaise
- 2 tbsp. minced Chives
- 1 tbsp. Poppy Seeds
- ½ cup Slivered Almonds
- 5 cups Shredded Cabbage
- ½ cup chopped Celery
- 2 tbsp. Mustard
- 1 tbsp. Honey
- ¼ tsp. Salt Pinch of Black Pepper
- 1 tbsp. Lemon Juice

Instructions

- Preheat your Air Fryer to 340 degrees F. Place the cabbage and almonds, in the air dryer. Drizzle with olive oil and cook for 5 minutes. ransfer to a bowl.
- Add the green peppers, chives, and celery, and toss to combine. In a small bowl, whisk together

the rest of the **Ingredients**. Pour the mixture over the salad.
- Toss to coat well.

Nutrition facts:

Calorie 364.4

Fats 20.5g

Fiber 1.4g

Carbs 38.4g

Protein 6.5g

254. Easy Eggplant Parmesan

Preparation time: 140mins

Ingredients

- 1 lb. fresh mozzarella cheese, sliced into rounds
- 1 medium eggplant
- 1 tsp. salt
- ½ cup all-purpose flour
- 2 eggs, beaten
- 1 cup seasoned breadcrumbs
- ¼ cup olive oil
- 16 oz. jar marinara sauce

Instructions

- Peel and slice eggplant into ½" slices.
- Place the eggplant rounds in a colander and toss them with 1 teaspoon of salt. Let them drain in the colander over a bowl in the sink for 45 minutes to remove excess moisture. Mix breadcrumbs and olive oil in a medium bowl. Bread the eggplant rounds in batches by coating them in the flour, then the eggs and then the breadcrumbs. Preheat air fryer to 390 F.
- Place 4-5 slices of breaded eggplant into the fryer and air fry for 8 minutes. Transfer fried eggplant to a non-stick cookie sheet and top with one tablespoon of marinara sauce and one slice of mozzarella cheese.
- Broil eggplant until cheese bubbles and browns lightly.
- Allow five minutes to cool before serving.

Nutrition facts:

Calorie 210

Fats 8.6g

Fiber 4g

Carbs 12.4g

Protein 12.8g

255. Rib Eye Steak

Preparation time: 35mins

Ingredients

- 1 tbsp. onion powder
- 1 tbsp. garlic powder
- 1 tbsp. oregano
- 2 tsp. ground cumin
- 2 lb. ribeye steak
- 4 ½ tsp. salt
- 2 tbsp. ground black pepper
- 2 tbsp. paprika
- 1 tbsp. high-heat cooking

Instructions

- In a small bowl, mix all the seasonings to create a dry rub. Rub seasoning into the surface of the entire ribeye.
- Brush oil over the seasoned ribeye. Preheat air fryer to 400°F . Place rib eye into fryer basket and air fry at 400°F for 7 minutes. gently flip rib eye with tongs.
- Air fry at 400°F for an additional 7 to 10 minutes.
- Allow to cool at least five minutes.

Nutrition facts:

Calorie 290

Fats 23g

Fiber 0g

Carbs 0g

Protein 21g

256. Philly Cheese Steak Stromboli

Preparation time: 45mins

Ingredients

- 1½ cup grated Cheddar cheese
- ½ onion, sliced
- ½ cup jarred cheese sauce
- ¼ tsp. salt
- ¼ tsp. ground black pepper
- 1 lb. strip loin steak, trimmed and thinly sliced
- 14 ounces pizza dough store-bought or homemade
- 1 tbsp. Worcestershire sauce
- 2 tsp. high-heat cooking oil
- 1 cup marinara sauce

Instructions

- Mix 1 tsp. oil and onion in air fry basket and air fry for 8 minutes, stirring once at 4 minutes. Add the sliced beef, Worcestershire sauce, salt and pepper, and mix well. Air fry for 8 minutes at 400ºF, stirring occasionally.
- Remove the chicken and onion from the air fryer and allow to cool. On a lightly floured surface, roll the pizza dough into a 13x11" rectangle.
- Sprinkle half of the Cheddar cheese over the dough leaving an empty 1" border on one side. Evenly top the cheese with the beef mixture. Warm the jarred cheese sauce and drizzle over the meat.
- Sprinkle the remaining Cheddar cheese on top. Roll the Stromboli toward the empty border, keeping the filling tightly tucked inside the roll. Tuck the ends of the dough in and pinch the seam shut.
- Cut 4 small slits evenly in the top of the dough and brush with remaining oil.
- Place the seam side down and shape the Stromboli into a U-shape to fit in the air fry basket.
- Air fry at 370°F 6 minutes. gently flip the Stromboli, apply additional oil, and air fry for an additional 6 to 8 minutes until the dough becomes golden brown.

- Allow to cool 10 minutes before serving. Service with marinara sauce.

Nutrition facts:

Calorie 421

Fats 21g

Fiber 2g

Carbs 45g

Protein 14g

257. Baked Marinarah Eggs

Preparation time: 25mins

Ingredients

- 2 tsps. parmesan cheese
- 1 tsp. salt
- 1 tsp. pepper
- 4 eggs
- ½ cup whole milk or heavy cream
- 1 cup spinach
- 2 tsps. marinara sauce

Instructions

- In a medium saucepan, stir spinach with ¼ cup of milk or cream over medium heat for 3 minutes or until spinach wilts and absorbs milk. Divide spinach equally between four small baking dishes Crack an egg into each ramekin. Add one tablespoon of milk to each egg to the side of the yolk. prinkle salt and pepper on each egg.
- Add an equal dollop of marinara to each ramekin.
- Sprinkle parmesan cheese over each ramekin. Air fry at 350°F for seven minutes.
- Remove from air fryer and check yoke consistency. If too runny, air fry for an additional 3-5 minutes until desired yoke consistency.
- Allow to cool for 2-3 minutes before serving.

Nutrition facts:

Calorie 90.2

Fats 7g

Fiber 0g

Carbs 4g

Protein 0g

258. Beefalo Burgers

Preparation time: 25mins

Ingredients

- 1 tsp. garlic powder
- ½ tsp. celery salt
- ½ tsp. oregano
- 1 lb. lean ground beef
- 3 tbsp. buffalo wing sauce
- 4 slices blue cheese

Instructions

- In a medium bowl, gently mix together ground beef and seasonings.
- Shape ground beef into four ¼ lb. patties. Preheat air fryer to 350°F
- Air fry at 350°F for 10 minutes.
- Remove and place a single blue cheese slice on each patty. Return patties to hot air fryer and allow the cheese to melt slightly without additional frying.
- Allow to cool five minutes before serving.

Nutrition facts:

Calorie 180

Fats 5g

Fiber 0g

Carbs 4g

Protein 0g

Total Time: 40mins

Ingredients

- 2 tbsp of Olive oil
- 1 and ½ pounds of chopped stewing steak
- ½ Cup of almond flour
- 1 Large, thinly sliced onion
- 2 Finely chopped garlic clove
- 1 Deseeded and thinly sliced green pepper
- 1 Thinly sliced red pepper
- 2 tbsp of tomato puree
- 2 tbsp of Paprika
- 2 large diced Tomatoes
- 3 tbsp of beef stock
- 2 tbsp of chopped leaf parsley
- 1 Pinch of black pepper
- 1 cup of low fat sour cream

Instructions:

- Preheat your air fryer to 390° F . Place 1 tablespoon oil in your air fryer pan .
- Sprinkle the beef steak with the almond flour and add it to the pan .
- Add the onion, the garlic, the green pepper and the red pepper .
- Add the tomato puree and the paprika.
- Place the pan in your air fryer and lock the lid .
- Set your timer to 35 minutes and the temperature to 35 minutes .When the timer beeps; turn off your air fryer .

Nutrition facts:

Calories 280

Total Fats 20.7 g

Carbs: 8 g

Protein 18.9 g

Sugar 1g

Fiber 3.0 g

259. Beef Goulash with Sour Cream

260. Chicken Kebobs with Cilantro

Total Time: 15mins

Ingredients

- 1 and ¼ pounds of cubed beef sirloin
- 1 Pinch of fresh ground pepper
- 1 and ¼ tsp of kosher salt
- 1 large; diced red onion
- 17 to 18 cherry tomatoes
- Soaked bamboo skewers

To make the Chimichurri sauce:

- 2 tbsp of finely chopped parsley
- 2 tbsp of chopped cilantro
- 2 tbsp of finely chopped red onion
- 1 Minced garlic clove
- 2 tbsp of extra virgin olive oil
- 2 tbsp of apple cider vinegar
- 1 tbsp of water
- ¼ tsp of kosher salt
- 1/8 tsp of fresh black pepper
- 1/8 tsp of crushed red pepper flakes

Instructions

- Season your meat with 1 pinch of salt and 1 pinch of pepper.
- To make the chimichurri, combine the vinegar, the red onion, the salt and the olive oil and set it aside for about 5 minutes. Put the onions, the beef and the tomatoes into the skewers.
- Place the skewers in the air fryer basket and lock the lid.
- Set the timer to about 10 minutes and the temperature to about 375 degrees.
- When the timer beeps, turn off your air fryer.
- Serve and enjoy your kabobs with the chimichurri sauce!

Nutrition facts:

Calories 220

Total fats 14g

Carbs 5.9g

Protein 38g

Sugar 1.5g

Fiber 3g

---

261. Juicy Sweet Chili Chicken Fillets

Preparation Time: 35 minutes

Ingredients

- 2 Chicken Fillets
- Salt and Pepper to taste
- 1 cup Almond Flour
- 3 Eggs
- ½ cup Apple Cider Vinegar
- ½ tsp ginger Paste
- ½ tsp garlic Paste
- 1 tbsp Swerve Sweetener
- 2 Red Chilies, minced
- 2 tsp Tomato Puree
- 1 Red Pepper
- 1 green Pepper
- 1 tsp Paprika
- 4 tbsp Water Cooking Spray

Instructions

- Preheat the Air Fryer to 350 F.
- Put the chicken breasts on a clean flat surface.
- Cut them in cubes. Pour the almond flour in a bowl, crack the eggs into it, add the salt and pepper.
- Whisk it using a fork or whisk.
- Put the chicken in the flour mixture.
- Mix to coat the chicken with it using a wooden spatula. Place the chicken in the fryer basket, spray them with cooking spray, and fry them for 8 minutes.
- Pull out the fryer basket, shake it to toss the chicken, and spray again with cooking spray.
- Keeping cooking for 7 minutes or until golden and crispy.
- Remove the chicken into a plate and set aside. Put the red, yellow, and green peppers on a chopping board. Using a knife, cut them open and deseed them.
- Cut the flesh in long strips.
- In a bowl, add the water, apple cider vinegar, swerve sweetener, ginger and garlic puree, red chili, tomato puree, and smoked paprika. Mix with a fork.

- Place a skillet over medium heat on a stove top and spray it with cooking spray.
- Add the chicken to it and the pepper strips. Stir and cook until the peppers are sweaty but still crunchy.
- Pour the chili mixture on the chicken, stir, and bring it to simmer for 10 minutes. Turn off the heat.
- Dish the chicken chili sauce into a serving bowl and serve with a side of steamed cauli rice.

Nutrition facts:

Calories: 226

Total Fat: 8g

Sodium: 486mg

Total Carbs: 2g

Net Carbs: 2g

Protein: 18.27g

---

262. Chicken Lollipop

Preparation Time: 20 minutes

Ingredients

- 1 lb mini Chicken Drumsticks
- ½ tsp Soy Sauce
- 1 tsp Lime Juice Salt and Pepper to taste
- 1 tsp Arrowroot Starch
- ½ tsp Minced garlic
- ½ tsp Chili Powder
- ½ tsp chopped Coriander
- ½ tsp garlic ginger Paste
- 1 tsp Plain Vinegar
- 1 tsp Chili Paste
- ½ tsp Beaten Egg
- 1 tsp Paprika
- 1 tsp Almond Flour
- 2 tsp Monk Fruit Syrup

Instructions

- Mix the garlic ginger paste, chili powder, monk fruit syrup, paprika powder, chopped coriander, plain vinegar, egg, garlic, and salt in a bowl.
- Add the chicken drumsticks and toss to coat completely.
- Stir in the arrowroot starch, almond flour, and lime juice.
- Preheat the Air Fryer to 350 F.
- Remove each drumstick, shake off the excess marinade, and place them in a single layer in the fryer basket.
- Cook them for 5 minutes. Slide out the fryer basket, spray the chicken with cooking spray and continue cooking for 5 minutes.
- Remove them onto a serving platter and serve with a tomato dip and a side of steamed asparagus.

Nutrition facts:

Calories: 17

Total Fat: 0.94g

Sodium: 28mg

Total Carbs: 0g

Net Carbs: 0g

Protein: 4.89g

---

263. Chicken Cheesy Divan Casserole

Preparation Time: 53 minutes

Ingredients

- 3 Chicken Breasts
- Salt and Pepper to taste
- 1 cup shredded Cheddar Cheese
- 1 Broccoli Head
- ½ cup Mushroom Soup Cream
- ½ cup Keto Croutons
- Cooking Spray

Instructions

- Preheat the Air Fryer to 390 F.

- Place the chicken breasts on a clean flat surface and season with salt and pepper. grease with cooking spray and place them in the fryer basket.
- Close the Air Fryer and cook for 13 minutes. Meanwhile, place the broccoli on the chopping board and use a knife to chop.
- Remove them onto the chopping board, let cool, and cut into bite-size pieces. In a bowl, add the chicken, broccoli, cheddar cheese, and mushroom soup cream and mix well.
- Scoop the mixture into a 3 X 3cm casserole dish, add the keto croutons on top and spray with cooking spray.
- Put the dish in the fryer basket and cook for 10 minutes. Serve with a side of steamed greens.

Nutrition facts:

Calories: 321

Total Fat: 13.74g

Sodium: 387mg

Total Carbs: 0g

Net Carbs: 0g

Protein: 35g

264. Chipotle Steak with Avocado-Lime Salsa

Preparation Time: 32 minutes

Ingredients:

- 1 ½ lb Rib Eye Steak
- 2 tsp Olive Oil
- 1 tbsp Chipotle Chili Pepper
- Salt and Black pepper to taste
- 1 Avocado, diced
- Juice from ½ Lime

Instructions:

- Place the steak on a chopping board.
- Pour the olive oil over it and sprinkle with the chipotle pepper, salt, and black pepper. Use your hands to rub the spices on the meat. Leave

it to sit and marinate for 10 minutes. Preheat the Air Fryer to 400 F.
- Pull out the fryer basket and place the meat in it. Slide it back into the Air Fryer and cook for 14 minutes.
- Turn the steak and continue cooking for 6 minutes.
- Remove the steak, cover with foil, and let it sit for 5 minutes before slicing. Meanwhile, prepare the avocado salsa by mashing the avocado with potato mash.
- Add in the lime juice and mix until smooth. Taste, adjust the seasoning.
- Slice and serve the steak with salsa.

Nutrition facts:

Calories 523

Total Fat 45g

Sodium 102mg

Total Carbs 6.5g

Net Carbs 2.3g

Protein 32g

265. Air Fried Stuffed Pizza Pastries

Preparation time: 25mins

Ingredients

- 1 (13.5-ounce) readymade pizza crust
- 6-ounces of sliced pepperoni
- 1 tbsp. of melted butter
- 1 tsp. of black pepper
- 1 tsp. of garlic powder
- 3 tbsp. of Parmesan cheese, grated
- 1 tsp. of salt
- 1 tsp. of Italian seasoning
- 12-ounces of mozzarella cheese, shredded

Instructions

- Preheat the air fryer to 390 degrees Fahrenheit. In a bowl combine the butter, salt, garlic powder, Italian seasoning, and black pepper.

- Cut the pizza crust into 4-inch squares. Fill the middle of each square using the pepperoni.
- Add cheese on top. Take one edge of each square and bring it to another end. Seal using a fork.
- Brush the pastries using the butter mixture. Air fry for about 15 minutes.
- Serve hot.

Nutrition facts:

Calorie 500

Fats 25g

Fiber 4g

Carbs 57g

Protein 25g

266. Royal Meatball Sub

Preparation time: 30mins

Ingredients

- 3 baguettes
- 1 onion, peeled and chopped
- 1 (15-ounce) can of tomato sauce
- ½ cup of cheddar cheese, shredded
- 1 pound of ground beef
- ¼ cup of panko breadcrumbs
- 1 egg
- 4 slices of provolone cheese
- 1 tbsp. of olive oil
- 1 tsp. of black pepper
- 1 tbsp. of dried parsley
- 1 tbsp. of dried oregano
- 1 tsp. of salt

Instructions

- Preheat the air fryer to 360 degrees Fahrenheit. Combine the ground beef, egg, seasonings, breadcrumbs, and onion in a bowl.
- Mix well and create meatballs using the hands.
- Fry them in the air fryer for 15 minutes.

- Put egg and stir until it is properly mixed Cut the baguettes into small pieces and drizzle some olive oil.
- Toast them in the air fryer for a minute or two.
- In a pan add the tomato sauce and add to the air fryer.
- Cook for about 5 minutes. Brush the baguettes with the tomato sauce, add the meatballs and cheese.
- Add to the air fryer one more time and wait for the cheese to melt.
- Serve hot.

Nutrition facts:

Calorie 530

Fats 40g

Fiber 2g

Carbs 52g

Protein 38g

267. Spinach Stuffed Cannelloni

Preparation time: 25mins

Ingredients

- 2 tbsp. Parmesan cheese
- 1 egg 1 cup spinach, cooked
- 9 cannelloni shells, cooked
- 3 cups Tomato Sauce
- 2 cups alfredo sauce
- 1 cup ricotta cheese
- 1 cup shredded mozzarella

Instructions

- Preheat the fryer to 380 degrees F .Combine the spinach, ricotta, parmesan, garlic, and egg. Mix well.
- Place the spinach mixture into a piping bag and fill the cannelloni shells. Place the filled shells on to the fryer try. Top with the alfredo and tomato sauce. Sprinkle mozzarella on top. Bake for 15 minutes.

Nutrition facts:

Calorie 207.4

Fats 9.9g

Fiber 1.5g

Carbs 13.5g

Protein 16.3g

---

268. Cheesy Stuffed Manicotti

Preparation time: 25mins

Ingredients

- 1 tbsp. dried parsley
- 8 Manicotti Shells, cooked
- 1 large egg
- 1 cups ricotta cheese
- 2 cups shredded mozzarella
- 1 cup grated Parmesan cheese
- 3 cups alfredo sauce

Instructions

- Preheat the air fryer to 350 degrees F.
- Combine the egg, ricotta, one cup of the mozzarella, and parmesan cheese. Mix well. Place the filling into a piping bag and fill the manicotti shells with the mixture. Place the filled shells on the fryer tray. Top with Alfredo sauce and sprinkle the last cup of mozzarella on top.
- Bake for 15 minutes. Remove and sprinkle parsley on top.

Nutrition Facts

Calories: 216; Protein 15.8g; Carbohydrates 27.6g; Fat 9.1g; Cholesterol 147.1mg; Sodium 316.4mg.

269. Air Fryer Coconut Shrimp

Prep Time: 30 mins

Cook Time: 15 mins

Total Time: 45 mins

Ingredient

- ½ cup all-purpose flour
- 1 ½ teaspoon ground black pepper
- 2 large eggs
- ⅔ cup unsweetened flaked coconut
- ⅓ cup panko bread crumbs
- 12 ounces uncooked medium shrimp, peeled and deveined
- cooking spray
- ½ teaspoon kosher salt, divided
- ¼ cup honey
- ¼ cup lime juice
- 1 serrano chile, thinly sliced
- 2 teaspoons chopped fresh cilantro

Instructions

- Stir together flour and pepper in a shallow dish. Lightly beat eggs in a second shallow dish. Stir together coconut and panko in a third shallow dish. Hold each shrimp by the tail, dredge in flour mixture, and shake off excess. Then dip floured shrimp in egg, and allow any excess to drip off. Finally, dredge in coconut mixture, pressing to adhere. Place on a plate. Coat shrimp well with cooking spray.
- Preheat air fryer to 400 degrees F (200 degrees C). Place 1/2 the shrimp in the air fryer and cook for about 3 minutes. Turn shrimp over and continue cooking until golden, about 3 minutes more. Season with 1/4 teaspoon salt. Repeat with remaining shrimp.
- Meanwhile, whisk together honey, lime juice, and serrano chile in a small bowl for the dip.
- Sprinkle fried shrimp with cilantro and serve with dip.

Nutrition Facts

Calories: 236; Protein 13.8g; Carbohydrates 27.6g; Fat 9.1g; Cholesterol 147.1mg; Sodium 316.4mg.

270. Air-Fried Shrimp

Prep Time: 5 mins

Cook Time: 10 mins

Total Time: 15 mins

Servings: 4

Ingredient

- 1 tablespoon butter, melted
- 1 teaspoon lemon juice
- ½ teaspoon garlic granules
- ⅛ teaspoon salt
- 1 pound large shrimp - peeled, deveined, and tails removed
- Perforated parchment paper
- ⅛ cup freshly grated parmesan cheese

Instructions

- Place melted butter in a medium bowl. Mix in lemon juice, garlic granules, and salt. Add shrimp and toss to coat.
- Line air fryer basket with perforated parchment paper. Place shrimp in the air fryer basket and sprinkle with Parmesan cheese.
- Cook shrimp in the air fryer at 400 degrees F (200 degrees C) until shrimp are bright pink on the outside and the meat is opaque for about 8 minutes.

Nutrition Facts

- Calories: 125; Protein 19.6g; Carbohydrates 0.5g; Fat 4.6g; Cholesterol 182.4mg; Sodium 329.7mg.

---

271. Chef John's Salmon Cakes

Prep Time: 15 mins

Cook Time: 10 mins

Additional Time: 30 mins

Total Time: 55 mins

Servings: 4

Ingredient

- 1 (14.75 ounces) can red salmon, skin, and bone removed, drained, and flaked
- 2 eggs
- ½ lemon, juiced
- 1 tablespoon chopped capers
- ½ teaspoon salt
- ½ teaspoon ground black pepper

- ½ teaspoon cayenne pepper
- 12 saltine crackers
- 1 tablespoon bread crumbs, or as needed
- 1 tablespoon butter
- 1 tablespoon olive oil

Instructions

- Stir salmon, eggs, lemon juice, capers, salt, black pepper, and cayenne pepper together in a bowl until well-combined.
- Crush saltine crackers with your hands into the salmon mixture and mix well. Wrap the bowl with plastic wrap and refrigerate, 30 minutes to overnight.
- Dust a plate with half the bread crumbs. Divide salmon mixture into 4 portions and shape into patties; place onto a prepared plate and sprinkle remaining bread crumbs atop the salmon patties.
- Melt butter and oil in a large skillet over medium heat. Cook patties in hot oil until cooked and heated through, about 5 minutes per side.

Nutrition Facts

- Calories: 305; Protein 30.9g; Carbohydrates 14.6g; Fat 14.6g; Cholesterol 174.2mg; Sodium 1019.9mg.

---

272. Garlicky Appetizer Shrimp Scampi

Prep Time: 15 mins

Cook Time: 6 mins

Total Time: 21 mins

Servings: 6

Ingredient

- 6 tablespoons unsalted butter, softened
- ¼ cup olive oil
- 1 tablespoon minced garlic
- 1 tablespoon minced shallots
- 2 tablespoons minced fresh chives
- Salt and freshly ground black pepper to taste
- ½ teaspoon paprika
- 2 pounds large shrimp - peeled and deveined

Instructions

- Preheat grill for high heat.

- In a large bowl, mix softened butter, olive oil, garlic, shallots, chives, salt, pepper, and paprika; add the shrimp, and toss to coat.
- Lightly oil grill grate. Cook the shrimp as close to the flame as possible for 2 to 3 minutes per side, or until opaque.

Nutrition Facts

- Calories: 303; Protein 25g; Carbohydrates 0.9g; Fat 21.8g; Cholesterol 261mg; Sodium 460.8mg.

273. Grilled Fish Steaks

Prep Time: 10 mins

Cook Time: 10 mins

Additional Time: 1 hr 10 mins

Total: 1 hr 30 mins

Servings: 2

Ingredient

- 1 clove garlic, minced
- 6 tablespoons olive oil
- 1 teaspoon dried basil
- 1 teaspoon salt
- 1 teaspoon ground black pepper
- 1 tablespoon fresh lemon juice
- 1 tablespoon chopped fresh parsley
- 2 (6 ounces) fillets of halibut

Instructions

- In a stainless steel or glass bowl, combine garlic, olive oil, basil, salt, pepper, lemon juice, and parsley.
- Place the halibut fillets in a shallow glass dish or a resealable plastic bag, and pour the marinade over the fish. Cover or seal and place in the refrigerator for 1 hour, turning occasionally.
- Preheat an outdoor grill for high heat and lightly oil grate. Set grate 4 inches from the heat.
- Remove halibut fillets from marinade and drain off the excess. Grill filets 5 minutes per side or until fish is done when easily flaked with a fork.

Nutrition Facts

- Calories: 554; Protein 36.3g; Carbohydrates 2.2g; Fat 43.7g; Cholesterol 62.5mg; Sodium 1259.3mg.

274. Mussels Mariniere

Prep Time: 35 mins

Cook Time: 15 mins

Total Time: 50 mins

Servings: 4

Ingredient

- 4 quarts mussels, cleaned and debearded
- 2 cloves garlic, minced
- 1 onion, chopped
- 6 tablespoons chopped fresh parsley
- 1 bay leaf
- ¼ teaspoon dried thyme
- 2 cups white wine
- 3 tablespoons butter, divided

Instructions

- Scrub mussels. Pull off beards, the tuft of fibers that attach each mussel to its shell, cutting them at the base with a paring knife. Discard those that do not close when you handle them and any with broken shells. Set aside.
- Combine onion, garlic, 4 tablespoons parsley, bay leaf, thyme, wine, and 2 tablespoons butter in a large pot. Bring to boil. Lower heat, and cook for 2 minutes. Add mussels, and cover. Cook just until shells open, 3 to 4 minutes. Do not overcook. Remove mussels from the sauce, and place in bowls.
- Strain liquid, and return to pot. Add remaining butter and parsley. Heat until butter melts. Pour over mussels.

Nutrition Facts

- Calories: 298; Protein 18.6g; Carbohydrates 10.3g; Fat 10.1g; Cholesterol 69.6mg; Sodium 329.6mg.

275. Chef John's Baked Lemon Pepper Salmon

Prep Time: 10 mins

Cook Time: 15 mins

Additional Time: 30 mins

Total Time: 55 mins

Servings: 2

Ingredient

- 2 tablespoons lemon juice
- 1 tablespoon ground black pepper
- 1 ½ tablespoons mayonnaise
- 1 tablespoon yellow miso paste
- 2 teaspoons dijon mustard
- 1 pinch cayenne pepper, or to taste
- 2 (8 ounces) center-cut salmon fillets, boned, skin on
- Sea salt to taste

Instructions

- Whisk together lemon juice and black pepper in a small bowl. Add mayonnaise, miso paste, Dijon mustard, and cayenne pepper to lemon-pepper mixture; whisk together.
- Spread the lemon-pepper mixture over salmon fillets. Reserve about a tablespoon for later use.
- Cover salmon with plastic wrap and refrigerate for 30 minutes.
- Preheat oven to 450 degrees F (230 degrees C). Line a baking sheet with parchment paper or a silicone baking mat.
- Place fillets on the prepared baking sheet. Spread the remaining lemon-pepper mixture on fillets without letting it pool around the base. Sprinkle with a pinch more black pepper and a generous amount of sea salt.
- Bake in the preheated oven until the fish flakes easily with a fork, 10 to 15 minutes.

Nutrition Facts

- Calories: 488; Protein 49.5g; Carbohydrates 7.1g; Fat 28.1g; Cholesterol 156.6mg; Sodium 784.3mg.

---

276. Rockin' Oysters Rockefeller

Prep Time: 30 mins

Cook Time: 30 mins

Total Time: 1 hr

Servings: 16

Ingredient

- 48 fresh, unopened oysters
- 1 ½ cups beer
- 2 cloves garlic
- seasoned salt to taste
- 7 black peppercorns
- ½ cup butter
- 1 onion, chopped
- 1 clove garlic, crushed
- 1 (10 ounces) package frozen chopped spinach, thawed and drained
- 8 ounces Monterey Jack cheese, shredded
- 8 ounces fontina cheese, shredded
- 8 ounces mozzarella cheese, shredded
- ½ cup milk
- 2 teaspoons salt, or to taste
- 1 teaspoon ground black pepper
- 2 tablespoons fine bread crumbs

Instructions

- Clean oysters, and place them in a large stockpot. Pour in beer and enough water to cover oysters; add 2 cloves garlic, seasoned salt, and peppercorns. Bring to a boil. Remove from heat, drain, and cool.
- Once oysters are cooled, break off and discard the top shell. Arrange the oysters on a baking sheet. Preheat oven to 425 degrees F (220 degrees C.)
- Melt butter in a saucepan over medium heat. Cook onion and garlic in butter until soft. Reduce heat to low, and stir in spinach, Monterey Jack, fontina, and mozzarella. Cook until cheese melts, stirring frequently. Stir in the milk, and season with salt and pepper. Spoon sauce over each oyster, just filling the shell. Sprinkle with bread crumbs.
- Bake until golden and bubbly, approximately 8 to 10 minutes.

Nutrition Facts

- Calories: 248; Protein 16.4g; Carbohydrates 5.3g;

Fat 17.4g; Cholesterol 65.7mg; Sodium 652.2mg.

277. Sesame Seared Tuna

Prep Time: 10 mins

Cook Time: 10 mins

Total Time: 20 mins

Servings: 4

Ingredient

- ¼ Cup soy sauce
- 1 tablespoon mirin (japanese sweet wine)
- 1 tablespoon honey
- 2 tablespoons sesame oil
- 1 tablespoon rice wine vinegar
- 4 (6 ounces) tuna steaks
- ½ cup sesame seeds
- Wasabi paste
- 1 tablespoon olive oil

Instructions

- In a small bowl, stir together the soy sauce, mirin, honey, and sesame oil. Divide into two equal parts. Stir the rice vinegar into one part and set aside as a dipping sauce.
- Spread the sesame seeds out on a plate. Coat the tuna steaks with the remaining soy sauce mixture, then press into the sesame seeds to coat.
- Heat olive oil in a cast-iron skillet over high heat until very hot. Place steaks in the pan, and sear for about 30 seconds on each side. Serve with the dipping sauce and wasabi paste.

Nutrition Facts

Calories: 422; Protein 44.1g; Carbohydrates 13.2g; Fat 20.7g; Cholesterol 77.2mg; Sodium 1045.5mg.

278. Dinah's Baked Scallops

Prep Time: 20 mins

Cook Time: 15 mins

Total Time: 35 mins

Servings: 4

Ingredient

- 20 buttery round crackers, crushed
- black pepper to taste
- 1 teaspoon garlic powder
- 1 pound sea scallops, rinsed and drained
- ½ cup butter, melted
- ¼ cup dry white wine
- ½ lemon, juiced
- 1 tablespoon chopped fresh parsley, for garnish

Instructions

- Preheat oven to 350 degrees F (175 degrees C). Lightly grease an 8x8 inch baking dish.
- Combine crushed crackers, black pepper, and garlic powder in a small bowl. Press scallops into the mixture so that they are evenly coated, and place them in the greased baking dish.
- In a separate bowl, mix melted butter, wine, and lemon juice; drizzle mixture over scallops.
- Bake in the preheated oven until scallops are lightly browned, about 15 minutes. Garnish with chopped parsley.

Nutrition Facts

- Calories: 431; Protein 19.7g; Carbohydrates 15.3g; Fat 31.5g; Cholesterol 96.5mg; Sodium 530.1mg.

279. Easy-Bake Fish

Prep Time: 15 mins

Cook Time: 20 mins

Total Time: 35 mins

Servings: 4

Ingredient

- 3 tablespoons honey
- 3 tablespoons Dijon mustard
- 1 teaspoon lemon juice
- 4 (6 ounces) salmon steaks
- ½ teaspoon pepper

Instructions

- Preheat oven to 325 degrees F (165 degrees C).
- In a small bowl, mix honey, mustard, and lemon juice. Spread the mixture over the salmon steaks. Season with pepper. Arrange in a medium baking dish.

- Bake 20 minutes in the preheated oven, or until fish easily flakes with a fork.

Nutrition Facts

- Calories: 368; Protein 33.5g; Carbohydrates 15.6g; Fat 18.2g; Cholesterol 99.1mg; Sodium 381.1mg.

---

280. Seared Scallops With Jalapeno Vinaigrette

Prep Time: 5 mins

Cook Time: 10 mins

Total Time: 15 mins

Servings: 4

Ingredient

- 1 large jalapeno pepper, seeded and membranes removed
- ¼ cup rice vinegar
- ¼ cup olive oil
- ¼ teaspoon dijon mustard
- Salt and freshly ground black pepper to taste
- 1 tablespoon vegetable oil
- 12 large fresh sea scallops
- 1 pinch sea salt
- 1 pinch cayenne pepper
- 2 oranges, peeled and cut in between sections as segments

Instructions

- Place jalapeno, rice vinegar, olive oil, and Dijon mustard in a blender. Puree on high until mixture is completely liquefied, 1 to 2 minutes. Season with salt and black pepper to taste.
- Season scallops with sea salt and cayenne pepper. Heat vegetable oil in a skillet over high heat. Place scallops in skillet and cook until browned, 2 to 3 minutes per side. Transfer to a plate. Garnish scallops with orange segments and drizzle jalapeno vinaigrette over the top.

Nutrition Facts

- Calories: 307; Protein 30.1g; Carbohydrates 5.9g; Fat 18g; Cholesterol 72.4mg; Sodium 472mg.

---

281. Hudson's Baked Tilapia With Dill Sauce

Prep Time: 10 mins

Cook Time: 20 mins

Total Time: 30 mins

Servings: 4

Ingredient

- 4 (4 ounce) fillets tilapia
- Salt and pepper to taste
- 1 tablespoon cajun seasoning, or to taste
- 1 lemon, thinly sliced
- ¼ cup mayonnaise
- ½ cup sour cream
- ⅛ teaspoon garlic powder
- 1 teaspoon fresh lemon juice
- 2 tablespoons chopped fresh dill

Instructions

- Preheat the oven to 350 degrees F (175 degrees C). Lightly grease a 9x13 inch baking dish.
- Season the tilapia fillets with salt, pepper, and Cajun seasoning on both sides. Arrange the seasoned fillets in a single layer in the baking dish. Place a layer of lemon slices over the fish fillets. I usually use about 2 slices on each piece so that it covers most of the surface of the fish.
- Bake uncovered for 15 to 20 minutes in the preheated oven, or until fish flakes easily with a fork.
- While the fish is baking, mix the mayonnaise, sour cream, garlic powder, lemon juice, and dill in a small bowl. Serve with tilapia.

Nutrition Facts

- Calories: 284; Protein 24.5g; Carbohydrates 5.7g; Fat 18.6g; Cholesterol 58.9mg; Sodium 500.5mg.

---

282. Angy Lemon-Garlic Shrimp

Prep Time: 10 mins

Cook Time: 10 mins

Total Time: 20 mins

Servings: 4

Ingredient

- 16 large shrimp - peeled, deveined, and tails on, or more to taste

- 3 large cloves garlic, smashed, or more to taste
- 1 teaspoon crushed red pepper, or to taste
- 2 teaspoons seafood seasoning (such as old bay®), or to taste
- Salt and ground black pepper to taste
- 2 tablespoons lemon juice
- 3 tablespoons chopped fresh parsley
- 3 teaspoons lemon zest

Instructions

- Heat a large skillet over medium-low heat until warm, about 3 minutes. Add shrimp, garlic, and crushed red pepper all at once and stir together. Add seafood seasoning, salt, and black pepper. Mix everything.
- Cook over medium heat until shrimp are fully cooked, 3 to 5 minutes. Pour lemon juice into skillet and stir again. Reduce heat to low; add parsley and lemon zest. Transfer only shrimp to a serving platter.

Nutrition Facts

- Calories: 76; Protein 14.2g; Carbohydrates 2.4g; Fat 0.9g; Cholesterol 127.7mg; Sodium 460.3mg.

283. Parmesan-Crusted Shrimp Scampi With Pasta

Prep Time: 25 mins

Cook Time: 20 mins

Total Time: 45 mins

Servings: 6

Ingredient

- 2 cups angel hair pasta
- ½ cup butter, divided
- 4 cloves garlic, minced
- 1 pound uncooked medium shrimp, peeled and deveined
- ½ cup white cooking wine
- 1 lemon, juiced
- 1 teaspoon red pepper flakes
- ¾ cup seasoned bread crumbs
- ¾ cup freshly grated Parmesan cheese, divided
- 2 tablespoons finely chopped fresh parsley

Instructions

- Bring a large pot of lightly salted water to a boil.

Cook angel hair pasta in the boiling water, stirring occasionally, until tender yet firm to the bite, 4 to 5 minutes. Drain and set aside.
- Set an oven rack about 6 inches from the heat source and preheat the oven's broiler.
- Heat 1/4 cup butter over medium heat in a large, deep skillet. Add garlic; cook and stir until fragrant. Add shrimp, white wine, and lemon juice; continue to cook and stir until shrimp is bright pink on the outside and the meat is opaque about 5 minutes. Stir in red pepper flakes until well combined. Remove from heat and set aside.
- Place remaining 1/4 cup butter, bread crumbs, 1/2 the Parmesan cheese, and parsley in a bowl. Stir until well combined. Set aside.
- Place cooked pasta into shrimp scampi mixture; toss until fully coated in sauce. Add remaining Parmesan cheese and toss well. Top with bread crumb mixture.
- Broil in the preheated oven until golden brown, 3 to 4 minutes. Serve immediately.

Nutrition Facts

- Calories: 419; Protein 22.6g; Carbohydrates 33.4g; Fat 20.8g; Cholesterol 164.7mg; Sodium 731.6mg.

284. Chef John's Fresh Salmon Cakes

Prep Time: 20 mins

Cook Time: 15 mins

Additional Time: 1 hr

Total Time: 1 hr 35 mins

Servings: 4

Ingredient

- 1 tablespoon extra-virgin olive oil
- ¼ cup minced onion
- 2 tablespoons minced red bell pepper
- 2 tablespoons minced celery
- Salt and pepper to taste
- 1 tablespoon capers
- 1 ¼ pound fresh wild salmon, coarsely chopped
- ¼ cup mayonnaise
- ¼ cup panko bread crumbs
- 2 cloves garlic, minced

- 1 teaspoon dijon mustard
- 1 pinch cayenne pepper
- 1 pinch seafood seasoning (such as old bay®)
- 1 tablespoon panko bread crumbs, or to taste
- 2 tablespoons olive oil, or as needed

Instructions

- Heat extra virgin olive oil in a skillet over medium heat. Cook and stir onion, red pepper, celery, and a pinch of salt in hot oil until onion is soft and translucent about 5 minutes. Add capers; cook and stir until fragrant, about 2 minutes. Remove from heat and cool to room temperature.
- Stir salmon, onion mixture, mayonnaise, 1/4 cup bread crumbs, garlic, mustard, cayenne, seafood seasoning, salt, and ground black pepper together in a bowl until well-mixed. Cover the bowl with plastic wrap and refrigerate until firmed and chilled, 1 to 2 hours.
- Form salmon mixture into four 1-inch thick patties; sprinkle remaining panko bread crumbs over each patty.
- Heat olive oil in a skillet over medium heat. Cook patties in hot oil until golden and cooked through, 3 to 4 minutes per side.

Nutrition Facts

- Calories: 460; Protein 31.6g; Carbohydrates 8.5g; Fat 33.5g; Cholesterol 101.6mg; Sodium 337.3mg.

285. Best Tuna Casserole

Prep Time: 15 mins

Cook Time: 20 mins

Total Time: 35 mins

Servings: 6

Ingredient

- 1 (12 ounces) package egg noodles
- ¼ cup chopped onion
- 2 cups shredded Cheddar cheese
- 1 cup frozen green peas
- 2 (5 ounce) cans tuna, drained
- 2 (10.75 ounces) cans condensed cream of mushroom soup
- ½ (4.5 ounces) can sliced mushrooms
- 1 cup crushed potato chips

Instructions

- Bring a large pot of lightly salted water to a boil. Cook pasta in boiling water for 8 to 10 minutes, or until al dente; drain.
- Preheat oven to 425 degrees F (220 degrees C).
- In a large bowl, thoroughly mix noodles, onion, 1 cup cheese, peas, tuna, soup, and mushrooms. Transfer to a 9x13 inch baking dish, and top with potato chip crumbs and remaining 1 cup cheese.
- Bake for 15 to 20 minutes in the preheated oven, or until cheese is bubbly.

Nutrition Facts

- Calories: 595; Protein 32.1g; Carbohydrates 58.1g; Fat 26.1g; Cholesterol 99.2mg; Sodium 1061.1mg

286. Good New Orleans Creole Gumbo

Prep Time: 1 hr

Cook Time: 2 hrs 40 mins

Total Time: 3 hrs 40 mins

Servings: 20

Ingredient

- 1 cup all-purpose flour
- ¾ cup bacon drippings
- 1 cup coarsely chopped celery
- 1 large onion, coarsely chopped
- 1 large green bell pepper, coarsely chopped
- 2 cloves garlic, minced
- 1 pound andouille sausage, sliced
- 3 quarts water
- 6 cubes beef bouillon
- 1 tablespoon white sugar
- Salt to taste
- 2 tablespoons hot pepper sauce (such as tabasco®), or to taste
- ½ teaspoon cajun seasoning blend (such as tony chachere's), or to taste
- 4 bay leaves
- ½ teaspoon dried thyme leaves
- 1 (14.5 ounces) can stewed tomatoes
- 1 (6 ounces) can tomato sauce
- 4 teaspoons file powder, divided

- 2 tablespoons bacon drippings
- 2 (10 ounces) packages frozen cut okra, thawed
- 2 tablespoons distilled white vinegar
- 1 pound lump crabmeat
- 3 pounds uncooked medium shrimp, peeled and deveined
- 2 tablespoons worcestershire sauce

Instructions

- Make a roux by whisking the flour and 3/4 cup bacon drippings together in a large, heavy saucepan over medium-low heat to form a smooth mixture. Cook the roux, whisking constantly until it turns a rich mahogany brown color. This can take 20 to 30 minutes; watch heat carefully and whisk constantly or roux will burn. Remove from heat; continue whisking until the mixture stops cooking.
- Place the celery, onion, green bell pepper, and garlic into the work bowl of a food processor, and pulse until the vegetables are very finely chopped. Stir the vegetables into the roux, and mix in the sausage. Bring the mixture to a simmer over medium-low heat, and cook until vegetables are tender, 10 to 15 minutes. Remove from heat, and set aside.
- Bring the water and beef bouillon cubes to a boil in a large Dutch oven or soup pot. Stir until the bouillon cubes dissolve, and whisk the roux mixture into the boiling water. Reduce heat to a simmer, and mix in the sugar, salt, hot pepper sauce, Cajun seasoning, bay leaves, thyme, stewed tomatoes, and tomato sauce. Simmer the soup over low heat for 1 hour; mix in 2 teaspoons of file gumbo powder at the 45-minute mark.
- Meanwhile, melt 2 tablespoons of bacon drippings in a skillet, and cook the okra with vinegar over medium heat for 15 minutes; remove okra with a slotted spoon, and stir into the simmering gumbo. Mix in crabmeat, shrimp, and Worcestershire sauce, and simmer until flavors have blended, 45 more minutes. Just before serving, stir in 2 more teaspoons of file gumbo powder.

Nutrition Facts

- Calories: 283; Protein 20.9g; Carbohydrates

12.1g; Fat 16.6g; Cholesterol 142.6mg; Sodium 853.1mg.

---

287. Shrimp Scampi With Pasta

Prep Time: 20 mins

Cook Time: 20 mins

Total Time: 40 mins

Servings: 6

Ingredient

- 1 (16 ounces) package linguine pasta
- 2 tablespoons butter
- 2 tablespoons extra-virgin olive oil
- 2 shallots, finely diced
- 2 cloves garlic, minced
- 1 pinch red pepper flakes (optional)
- 1 pound shrimp, peeled and deveined
- 1 pinch kosher salt and freshly ground pepper
- ½ cup dry white wine
- 1 lemon, juiced
- 2 tablespoons butter
- 2 tablespoons extra-virgin olive oil
- ¼ cup finely chopped fresh parsley leaves
- 1 teaspoon extra-virgin olive oil, or to taste

Instruction

- Bring a large pot of salted water to a boil; cook linguine in boiling water until nearly tender, 6 to 8 minutes. Drain.
- Melt 2 tablespoons butter with 2 tablespoons olive oil in a large skillet over medium heat. Cook and stir shallots, garlic, and red pepper flakes in the hot butter and oil until shallots are translucent, 3 to 4 minutes. Season shrimp with kosher salt and black pepper; add to the skillet and cook until pink, stirring occasionally, 2 to 3 minutes. Remove shrimp from skillet and keep warm.
- Pour white wine and lemon juice into skillet and bring to a boil while scraping the browned bits of food off of the bottom of the skillet with a wooden spoon. Melt 2 tablespoons butter in a skillet, stir 2 tablespoons olive oil into butter mixture, and bring to a simmer. Toss linguine, shrimp, and parsley in the butter mixture until coated; season with salt and black pepper.

Drizzle with 1 teaspoon olive oil to serve.

Nutrition Facts

- Calories: 511; Protein 21.9g; Carbohydrates 57.5g; Fat 19.4g; Cholesterol 135.4mg; Sodium 260mg.

288. Easy Garlic-Lemon Scallops

Prep Time: 10 mins

Cook Time: 10 mins

Total Time: 20 mins

Servings: 6

Ingredient

- ¾ cup butter
- 3 tablespoons minced garlic
- 2 pounds large sea scallops
- 1 teaspoon salt
- ⅛ teaspoon pepper
- 2 tablespoons fresh lemon juice

Instructions

- Melt butter in a large skillet over medium-high heat. Stir in garlic, and cook for a few seconds until fragrant. Add scallops, and cook for several minutes on one side, then turn over, and continue cooking until firm and opaque.
- Remove scallops to a platter, then whisk salt, pepper, and lemon juice into butter. Pour sauce over scallops to serve.

Nutrition Facts

- Calories: 408; Protein 38.5g; Carbohydrates 8.9g; Fat 24.4g; Cholesterol 152.4mg; Sodium 987.9mg.

289. Perfect Ten Baked Cod

Prep Time: 10 mins

Cook Time: 25 mins

Total Time: 35 mins

Servings: 4

Ingredient

- 2 tablespoons butter

- ½ sleeve buttery round crackers (such as Ritz®), crushed
- 2 tablespoons butter
- 1 pound thick-cut cod loin
- ½ lemon, juiced
- ¼ cup dry white wine
- 1 tablespoon chopped fresh parsley
- 1 tablespoon chopped green onion
- 1 lemon, cut into wedges

Instructions

- Preheat oven to 400 degrees F (200 degrees C).
- Place 2 tablespoons butter in a microwave-safe bowl; melt in the microwave on high, about 30 seconds. Stir buttery round crackers into melted butter.
- Place remaining 2 tablespoons butter in a 7x11-inch baking dish. Melt in the preheated oven, 1 to 3 minutes. Remove dish from oven.
- Coat both sides of cod in melted butter in the baking dish.
- Bake cod in the preheated oven for 10 minutes. Remove from oven; top with lemon juice, wine, and cracker mixture. Place back in the oven and bake until fish is opaque and flakes easily with a fork, about 10 more minutes.
- Garnish baked cod with parsley and green onion. Serve with lemon wedges.

Nutrition Facts

- Calories: 280; Protein 20.9g; Carbohydrates 9.3g; Fat 16.1g; Cholesterol 71.5mg; Sodium 282.3mg.

290. Marinated Tuna Steak

Prep Time: 10 mins

Cook Time: 11 mins

Additional Time: 30 mins

Total Time: 51 mins

Servings: 4

Ingredient

- ¼ cup orange juice
- ¼ cup soy sauce
- 2 tablespoons olive oil
- 1 tablespoon lemon juice

- 2 tablespoons chopped fresh parsley
- 1 clove garlic, minced
- ½ teaspoon chopped fresh oregano
- ½ teaspoon ground black pepper
- 4 (4 ounces) tuna steaks

Instructions

- In a large non-reactive dish, mix the orange juice, soy sauce, olive oil, lemon juice, parsley, garlic, oregano, and pepper. Place the tuna steaks in the marinade and turn to coat. Cover, and refrigerate for at least 30 minutes.
- Preheat grill for high heat.
- Lightly oil grill grate. Cook the tuna steaks for 5 to 6 minutes, then turn and baste with the marinade. Cook for an additional 5 minutes, or to the desired doneness. Discard any remaining marinade.

Nutrition Facts

- Calories: 200; Protein 27.4g; Carbohydrates 3.7g; Fat 7.9g; Cholesterol 50.6mg; Sodium 944.6mg.

291. Seared Ahi Tuna Steaks

Prep Time: 5 mins

Cook Time: 12 mins

Total Time: 17 mins

Servings: 2

Ingredient

- 2 (5 ounces) ahi tuna steaks
- 1 teaspoon kosher salt
- ¼ teaspoon cayenne pepper
- ½ tablespoon butter
- 2 tablespoons olive oil
- 1 teaspoon whole peppercorns

Instructions

Season the tuna steaks with salt and cayenne pepper.

Melt the butter with the olive oil in a skillet over medium-high heat. Cook the peppercorns in the mixture until they soften and pop about 5 minutes. Gently place the seasoned tuna in the skillet and cook to desired doneness, 1 1/2 minutes per side for rare.

Nutrition Facts

- Calories: 301; protein 33.3g; carbohydrates 0.7g; fat 17.8g; cholesterol 71.4mg; sodium 1033.6mg.

292. Easy Paella

Prep Time: 30 mins

Cook Time: 30 mins

Total Time: 1 hr

Servings: 8

Ingredient

- 2 tablespoons olive oil
- 1 tablespoon paprika
- 2 teaspoons dried oregano
- Salt and black pepper to taste
- 2 pounds skinless, boneless chicken breasts, cut into 2-inch pieces
- 2 tablespoons olive oil, divided
- 3 cloves garlic, crushed
- 1 teaspoon crushed red pepper flakes
- 2 cups uncooked short-grain white rice
- 1 pinch saffron threads
- 1 bay leaf
- ½ bunch italian flat-leaf parsley, chopped
- 1-quart chicken stock
- 2 lemons, zested
- 2 tablespoons olive oil
- 1 spanish onion, chopped
- 1 red bell pepper, coarsely chopped
- 1 pound chorizo sausage, casings removed and crumbled
- 1 pound shrimp, peeled and deveined

Instructions

- In a medium bowl, mix 2 tablespoons of olive oil, paprika, oregano, and salt and pepper. Stir in chicken pieces to coat. Cover, and refrigerate.
- Heat 2 tablespoons olive oil in a large skillet or paella pan over medium heat. Stir in garlic, red pepper flakes, and rice. Cook, stirring, to coat the rice with oil, about 3 minutes. Stir in saffron threads, bay leaf, parsley, chicken stock, and lemon zest. Bring to a boil, cover, and reduce heat to medium-low. Simmer 20 minutes.
- Meanwhile, heat 2 tablespoons olive oil in a separate skillet over medium heat. Stir in marinated chicken and onion; cook 5 minutes.

Stir in bell pepper and sausage; cook 5 minutes. Stir in shrimp; cook, turning the shrimp until both sides are pink.

- Spread rice mixture onto a serving tray. Top with meat and seafood mixture.

Nutrition Facts

- Calories: 736; Protein 55.7g; Carbohydrates 45.7g; Fat 35.1g; Cholesterol 202.5mg; Sodium 1204.2mg.

293. Simple Garlic Shrimp

Prep Time: 15 mins

Cook Time: 10 mins

Total Time: 25 mins

Servings: 4

Ingredient

- 1 ½ tablespoon olive oil
- 1 pound shrimp, peeled and deveined
- Salt to taste
- 6 cloves garlic, finely minced
- ¼ teaspoon red pepper flakes
- 3 tablespoons lemon juice
- 1 tablespoon caper brine
- 1 ½ teaspoon cold butter
- ⅓ cup chopped italian flat-leaf parsley, divided
- 1 ½ tablespoon cold butter
- Water, as needed

Instructions

- Heat olive oil in a heavy skillet over high heat until it just begins to smoke. Place shrimp in an even layer on the bottom of the pan and cook for 1 minute without stirring.
- Season shrimp with salt; cook and stir until shrimp begin to turn pink about 1 minute.
- Stir in garlic and red pepper flakes; cook and stir for 1 minute. Stir in lemon juice, caper brine, 1 1/2 teaspoon cold butter, and half the parsley.
- Cook until the butter has melted, about 1 minute, then turn heat to low and stir in 1 1/2 tablespoon cold butter. Cook and stir until all butter has melted to form a thick sauce and shrimp are pink and opaque about 2 to 3 minutes.

- Remove shrimp with a slotted spoon and transfer to a bowl; continue to cook butter sauce, adding water 1 teaspoon at a time if too thick, about 2 minutes. Season with salt to taste.
- Serve shrimp topped with the pan sauce. Garnish with remaining flat-leaf parsley.

Nutrition Facts

- Calories: 196; Protein 19.1g; Carbohydrates 2.9g; Fat 12g; Cholesterol 188.1mg; Sodium 243.7mg.

294. Baked Haddock

Prep Time: 10 mins

Cook Time: 15 mins

Total Time: 25 mins

Servings: 4

Ingredient

- ¾ cup milk
- 2 teaspoons salt
- ¾ cup bread crumbs
- ¼ cup grated Parmesan cheese
- ¼ teaspoon ground dried thyme
- 4 haddock fillets
- ¼ cup butter, melted

Instructions

- Preheat oven to 500 degrees F (260 degrees C).
- In a small bowl, combine the milk and salt. In a separate bowl, mix the bread crumbs, Parmesan cheese, and thyme. Dip the haddock fillets in the milk, then press into the crumb mixture to coat. Place haddock fillets in a glass baking dish, and drizzle with melted butter.
- Bake on the top rack of the preheated oven until the fish flakes easily, about 15 minutes.

Nutrition Facts

- Calories: 325; Protein 27.7g; Carbohydrates 17g; Fat 15.7g; Cholesterol 103.3mg; Sodium 1565.2mg.

295. Pan-Seared Tilapia

Prep Time: 10 mins

Cook Time: 8 mins

Total Time: 18 mins

Servings: 4

Ingredient

- 4 (4 ounce) fillets tilapia
- Salt and pepper to taste
- ½ cup all-purpose flour
- 1 tablespoon olive oil
- 2 tablespoons unsalted butter, melted

Instructions

- Rinse tilapia fillets in cold water and pat dry with paper towels. Season both sides of each fillet with salt and pepper. Place the flour in a shallow dish; gently press each fillet into the flour to coat and shake off the excess flour.
- Heat the olive oil in a skillet over medium-high heat; cook the tilapia in the hot oil until the fish flakes easily with a fork, about 4 minutes per side. Brush the melted butter onto the tilapia at the last minute before removing it from the skillet. Serve immediately.

Nutrition Facts

- Calories: 249; Protein 24.6g; Carbohydrates 11.9g; Fat 10.8g; Cholesterol 56.3mg; Sodium 50.9mg.

296. Classic Fish And Chips

Prep Time: 10 mins

Cook Time: 25 mins

Additional Time: 10 mins

Total Time: 45 mins

Servings: 4

Ingredient

- 4 large potatoes, peeled and cut into strips
- 1 cup all-purpose flour
- 1 teaspoon baking powder
- 1 teaspoon salt
- 1 teaspoon ground black pepper
- 1 cup milk
- 1 egg
- 1-quart vegetable oil for frying

- 1 ½ pounds cod fillets

Instructions

- Place potatoes in a medium-size bowl of cold water. In a separate medium-size mixing bowl, mix flour, baking powder, salt, and pepper. Stir in the milk and egg; stir until the mixture is smooth. Let mixture stand for 20 minutes.
- Preheat the oil in a large pot or electric skillet to 350 degrees F (175 degrees C).
- Fry the potatoes in the hot oil until they are tender. Drain them on paper towels.
- Dredge the fish in the batter, one piece at a time, and place them in the hot oil. Fry until the fish is golden brown. If necessary, increase the heat to maintain the 350 degrees F (175 degrees C) temperature. Drain well on paper towels.
- Fry the potatoes again for 1 to 2 minutes for added crispness.

Nutrition Facts

- 782 Calories: 787; Protein 44.6g; Carbohydrates 91.9g; Fat 26.2g; Cholesterol 124.6mg; Sodium 860.7mg.

297. Linguine With Clam Sauce

Prep Time: 20 mins

Cook Time: 12 mins

Total Time: 32 mins

Servings: 4

Ingredient

- 2 (6.5 ounces) cans minced clams, with juice
- ¼ cup butter
- ½ cup vegetable oil
- ½ teaspoon minced garlic
- 1 tablespoon dried parsley
- Ground black pepper to taste
- ¼ tablespoon dried basil
- 1 (16 ounces) package linguini pasta

Instructions

- Bring a large pot of salted water to boil. Cook pasta according to package directions.
- Combine clams with juice, butter, oil, minced garlic, parsley, basil, and pepper in a large

saucepan. Place over medium heat until boiling. Serve warm over pasta.

Nutrition Facts

Calories: 88; Protein 37.2g; Carbohydrates 84.6g; Fat 42.7g; Cholesterol 92.3mg; Sodium 189.6mg.

298. Pan Seared Salmon I

Prep Time: 10 mins

Cook Time: 10 mins

Total Time: 20 mins

Servings: 4

Ingredient

- 4 (6 ounces) fillets of salmon
- 2 tablespoons olive oil
- 2 tablespoons capers
- ⅛ teaspoon salt
- ⅛ teaspoon ground black pepper
- 4 slices lemon

Instructions

- Preheat a large heavy skillet over medium heat for 3 minutes.
- Coat salmon with olive oil. Place in skillet, and increase heat to high. Cook for 3 minutes. Sprinkle with capers, and salt and pepper. Turn salmon over, and cook for 5 minutes, or until browned. Salmon is done when it flakes easily with a fork.
- Transfer salmon to individual plates, and garnish with lemon slices.

Nutrition Facts

- Per Serving: 371 Calories; Protein 33.7g; Carbohydrates 1.7g; Fat 25.1g; Cholesterol 99.1mg; Sodium 299.8mg.

299. Easy Extremely Garlic Shrimp

Prep Time: 10 mins

Cook Time: 10 mins

Total Time: 20 mins

Servings: 4

Ingredient

- ⅓ cup butter
- 2 teaspoons minced garlic
- 1 pound large shrimp, peeled and deveined
- 3 tablespoons garlic salt, or to taste
- 3 tablespoons garlic powder, or to taste
- ½ lemon, juiced, or to taste

Instructions

- Melt butter in a large skillet over medium heat; cook and stir minced garlic until lightly browned. Add shrimp; season with garlic salt and garlic powder. Pour lemon juice over shrimp. Continue to cook and stir until shrimp are bright pink on the outside and the meat is no longer transparent in the center, 5 to 10 minutes.

Nutrition Facts

- Calories: 254; Protein 20.1g; Carbohydrates 6.9g; Fat 16.4g; Cholesterol 213.2mg; Sodium 4386.4mg.

300. Spicy Grilled Shrimp

Prep Time: 15 mins

Cook Time: 6 mins

Total Time: 21 mins

Servings: 6

Ingredient

- 1 large clove garlic
- 1 teaspoon coarse salt
- ½ teaspoon cayenne pepper
- 1 teaspoon paprika
- 2 tablespoons olive oil
- 2 teaspoons lemon juice
- 2 pounds large shrimp, peeled and deveined
- 8 wedges lemon, for garnish

Instructions

- Preheat grill for medium heat.
- In a small bowl, crush the garlic with the salt. Mix in cayenne pepper and paprika, and then stir in olive oil and lemon juice to form a paste. In a large bowl, toss shrimp with garlic paste until evenly coated.

- Lightly oil grill grate. Cook shrimp for 2 to 3 minutes per side, or until opaque. Transfer to a serving dish, garnish with lemon wedges and serve.

Nutrition Facts

- Calories: 164; Protein 25.1g; Carbohydrates 2.7g; Fat 5.9g; Cholesterol 230.4mg; Sodium 585.7mg.

---

301. Sheet Pan Salmon and Bell Pepper Dinner

Prep Time: 20 mins

Cook Time: 10 mins

Total Time: 30 mins

Servings: 4

Ingredient

- 2 tablespoons olive oil
- 4 (3 ounce) fillets salmon fillets
- 2 red bell peppers, chopped
- 1 yellow bell pepper, chopped
- 1 onion, sliced

Sauce:

- 6 tablespoons lemon juice
- 3 tablespoons olive oil
- 2 tablespoons water
- 1 tablespoon maple syrup
- 5 cloves garlic
- 1 ½ teaspoons salt
- 1 ½ teaspoon red pepper flakes
- 1 teaspoon ground cumin
- ½ bunch fresh parsley, chopped
- 1 lemon, sliced

Instructions

- Preheat oven to 400 degrees F (200 degrees C). Grease a sheet pan with 2 tablespoons olive oil.
- Place salmon fillets, red and yellow bell peppers, and onion on the prepared sheet pan.
- Combine lemon juice, 3 tablespoons olive oil, water, maple syrup, garlic, salt, red pepper flakes, cumin, and parsley in a small bowl. Drizzle 2/3 of the sauce over the ingredients on the sheet pan.
- Bake in the preheated oven until salmon is cooked through and flakes easily with a fork, 10

to 15 minutes.
- Serve with lemon slices and remaining sauce.

Nutrition Facts

- Calories: 337; Protein 18.8g; Carbohydrates 16.9g; Fat 22.9g; Cholesterol 47mg; Sodium 920.7mg.

---

302. Maple Sriracha Salmon

Prep Time: 30 Min

Cook Time: 15 Min

Total Time: 45 Min

Servings: 15

Ingredients

- 1 Tbsp. brown sugar
- 2 green onions, thinly sliced
- 2 Tbsp. lime juice
- 1 tsp. finely grated lime zest
- 1 Tbsp. maple syrup
- 3 lb. salmon fillet
- ½ tsp. salt
- 2 Tbsp. sriracha sauce

Directions

- Preheat your grill on setting #4. Whisk together sriracha, lime juice, maple syrup, brown sugar, lime zest, and salt. Brush over top of salmon and let stand for 20 minutes.
- Grill, covered and without turning, for 15 to 18 minutes or until grill-marked and fish flakes easily when tested with a fork. Sprinkle with green onions before serving.

Nutrition Facts

- Calories: 327; Protein 33.7g; Carbohydrates 4g; Fat 18.5g; Cholesterol 99.1mg; Sodium 810.8mg.

33. Lemon Garlic Tilapia

Prep Time: 10 mins

Cook Time: 30 mins

Total Time: 40 mins

Servings: 4

Ingredient

- 4 each tilapia fillets
- 3 tablespoons fresh lemon juice
- 1 tablespoon butter, melted
- 1 clove garlic, finely chopped
- 1 teaspoon dried parsley flakes
- 1 dash pepper to taste

Instructions

- Preheat oven to 375 degrees F (190 degrees C). Spray a baking dish with non-stick cooking spray.
- Rinse tilapia fillets under cool water, and pat dry with paper towels.
- Place fillets in baking dish. Pour lemon juice over fillets, then drizzle butter on top. Sprinkle with garlic, parsley, and pepper.
- Bake in the preheated oven until the fish is white and flakes when pulled apart with a fork, about 30 minutes.

Nutrition Facts

- calories: 142; protein 23.1g; carbohydrates 1.4g; fat 4.4g; cholesterol 49.1mg; sodium 93mg.

303. Szechwan Shrimp

Prep Time: 10 mins

Cook Time: 10 mins

Total Time: 20 mins

Servings: 4

Ingredient

- 4 tablespoons water
- 2 tablespoons ketchup
- 1 tablespoon soy sauce
- 2 teaspoons cornstarch
- 1 teaspoon honey
- ½ teaspoon crushed red pepper
- ¼ teaspoon ground ginger
- 1 tablespoon vegetable oil
- ¼ cup sliced green onions
- 4 cloves garlic, minced
- 12 ounces cooked shrimp, tails removed

Instructions

- In a bowl, stir together water, ketchup, soy sauce, cornstarch, honey, crushed red pepper, and ground ginger. Set aside.

- Heat oil in a large skillet over medium-high heat. Stir in green onions and garlic; cook for 30 seconds. Stir in shrimp, and toss to coat with oil. Stir in sauce. Cook and stir until sauce are bubbly and thickened.

Nutrition Facts

- Calories: 142; Protein 18.3g; Carbohydrates 6.7g; Fat 4.4g; Cholesterol 163.8mg; Sodium 499.5mg.

304. Lemony Steamed Fish

Prep Time: 15 mins

Cook Time: 30 mins

Total Time: 45 mins

Servings: 6

Ingredient

- 6 (6 ounces) halibut fillets
- 1 tablespoon dried dill weed
- 1 tablespoon onion powder
- 2 teaspoons dried parsley
- ¼ teaspoon paprika
- 1 pinch seasoned salt, or more to taste
- 1 pinch lemon pepper
- 1 pinch garlic powder
- 2 tablespoons lemon juice

Instructions

- Preheat oven to 375 degrees F (190 degrees C).
- Cut 6 foil squares large enough for each fillet.
- Center fillets on the foil squares and sprinkle each with dill weed, onion powder, parsley, paprika, seasoned salt, lemon pepper, and garlic powder. Sprinkle lemon juice over each fillet. Fold foil over fillets to make a pocket and fold the edges to seal. Place sealed packets on a baking sheet.
- Bake in the preheated oven until fish flakes easily with a fork, about 30 minutes.

Nutrition Facts

- Calories: 142; protein 29.7g; carbohydrates 1.9g; fat 1.1g; cholesterol 60.7mg; sodium 183.9mg.

305. Salmon With Fruit Salsa

Prep Time: 15 mins

Cook Time: 40 mins

Total Time: 55 mins

Servings: 4

Ingredient

- 1 pound salmon steaks
- 1 lemon, juiced
- 1 tablespoon chopped fresh rosemary
- Salt and pepper to taste
- 1 lemon, sliced
- ⅓ cup water
- ¼ cup diced fresh pineapple
- ¼ cup minced onion
- 3 cloves garlic, minced
- 2 fresh jalapeno peppers, diced
- 1 tomato, diced
- ½ cup pineapple juice
- ¼ cup diced red bell pepper
- ¼ cup diced yellow bell pepper

Instructions

- Preheat oven to 350 degrees F (175 degrees C).
- Arrange salmon steaks in a shallow baking dish, and coat with lemon juice. Season with rosemary, salt, and pepper. Top with lemon slices. Pour water into the dish.
- Bake for 30 to 40 minutes in the preheated oven, or until easily flaked with a fork.
- In a medium bowl, mix pineapple, onion, garlic, jalapeno, tomato, pineapple juice, red bell pepper, and yellow bell pepper. Cover, and refrigerate while fish is baking. Top fish with salsa to serve.

Nutritional Value

- Calories: 217; Protein 25.9g; Carbohydrates 15.7g; Fat 7g; Cholesterol 50.4mg; Sodium 198.3mg.

---

306. Mainely Fish

Prep Time: 30 mins

Cook Time: 20 mins

Total Time: 50 mins

Servings: 6

Ingredient

- 6 (3 ounce) fillets haddock
- salt and pepper to taste
- 4 Roma (plum) tomatoes, thinly sliced
- 1 red bell pepper, thinly sliced
- 1 yellow bell pepper, thinly sliced
- 1 small onion, thinly sliced
- 5 tablespoons capers
- 8 tablespoons chopped fresh parsley
- 6 tablespoons fresh lemon juice
- 6 tablespoons extra virgin olive oil

Instructions

- Preheat oven to 400 degrees F (200 degrees C).
- Center each piece of fish on an individual piece of aluminum foil (large enough to enclose the fish when folded). Sprinkle each piece of fish with salt and pepper. Divide the sliced tomatoes, onion, and red and yellow peppers between the 6 pieces of fish, and place them on top of the fillets. Sprinkle evenly with the capers and parsley. Drizzle each fillet with 1 tablespoon of olive oil and 1 tablespoon of lemon juice.
- Fold and seal the foil into a packet and place on a baking sheet. Leave 2 inches between each packet for even cooking.
- Bake in preheated oven for 20 minutes.
- Let rest for 5 minutes and unwrap. One packet per person.

Nutrition Facts

- Calories;: 226 Protein 17.3g; Carbohydrates 7.1g; Fat 14.4g; Cholesterol 48.4mg; Sodium 276.9mg.

---

307. Grilled Tuna Teriyaki

Prep Time: 15 mins

Cook Time: 10 mins

Additional Time: 30 mins

Total Time: 55 mins

Servings: 4

Ingredient

- 2 tablespoons light soy sauce
- 1 tablespoon Chinese rice wine
- 1 tablespoon minced fresh ginger root

- 1 large clove garlic, minced
- 4 (6 ounces) tuna steaks (about 3/4 inch thick)
- 1 tablespoon vegetable oil

Instructions

- Stir soy sauce, rice wine, ginger, and garlic together in a shallow dish. Place tuna in the marinade, and turn to coat. Cover the dish and refrigerate for at least 30 minutes.
- Preheat grill for medium-high heat.
- Remove tuna from marinade and discard remaining liquid. Brush both sides of steaks with oil.
- Cook tuna on the preheated grill until cooked through, 3 to 6 minutes per side.

Nutrition Facts

- Calories: 227; Protein 40.4g; Carbohydrates 1.5g; Fat 5.1g; Cholesterol 77.1mg; Sodium 328.6mg.

308. Anaheim Fish Tacos

Prep Time: 15 mins

Cook Time: 30 mins

Total Time: 45 mins

Servings: 6

Ingredient

- 1 teaspoon vegetable oil
- 1 anaheim chile pepper, chopped
- 1 leek, chopped
- 2 cloves garlic, crushed
- Salt and pepper to taste
- 1 cup chicken broth
- 2 large tomatoes, diced
- ½ teaspoon ground cumin
- 1 ½ pound halibut fillets
- 1 lime
- 12 corn tortillas

Instructions

- Heat the oil in a large skillet over medium heat, and saute the chile, leek, and garlic until tender and lightly browned. Season with salt and pepper.
- Mix the chicken broth and tomatoes into the skillet, and season with cumin. Bring to a boil.

Reduce heat to low. Place the halibut into the mixture. Sprinkle with lime juice. Cook 15 to 20 minutes until the halibut is easily flaked with a fork. Wrap in warmed corn tortillas to serve.

Nutrition Facts

- Calories: 273; Protein 27.7g; Carbohydrates 29.9g; Fat 5.1g; Cholesterol 36.3mg; Sodium 285.8mg.

309. Batter Fried Basa Fish

Prep Time: 15 mins

Cook Time: 20 mins

Total Time: 35 mins

Ingredients

- Boneless Basa fillet – 2
- All-purpose flour (Maida) – 1 cup
- Egg – 2
- Milk – 1 cup
- Salt to taste
- Vegetable oil – 1 tsp + more for shallow frying
- Freshly crushed black pepper – ½ tsp or more as per taste

Instructions

- Wash the fish fillet well. I used frozen fillets, so I had to thaw them completely before starting. Season the fillet with a pinch of salt on both sides.
- In a big bowl, combine the flour, eggs, milk, salt [approximately a little less than ½ teaspoon will do], and 1 teaspoon of oil.
- Whisk them well to make a thick and smooth batter. The batter must be very smooth without any lumps. Consistency should be such that it should adhere to the fish fillet covering all sides and does not drip off completely. [See notes below for more details.]
- Heat oil in a non-stick frying pan. I didn't deep fry my fish; I did shallow frying which worked quite well.
- Dip a fillet into the batter. Take it out, let the excess batter drip off and when the oil is quite hot, tip in the batter-coated fish on the pan. If you find that the batter is flowing out of the fillet,

take a little amount of batter from the bowl using a spoon and smear it on the top of the fillet. Do not move the fish for 2 minutes and let it cook on medium-low flame.

- When the bottom side of the fillet turns golden brown after about 5 minutes on medium flame, carefully flip the fillet and fry the other side till it turns golden brown. It will take around 5 to 6 minutes on each side but it also depends on the thickness of the fillets you are using. Mine took about 6 minutes on each side. To check the doneness, take a toothpick and prick the fish in the middle. If it goes in very easily without any resistance, your fish is done. Else give it two more minutes.
- Once done, take out the batter-fried basa fillets on a plate lined with an absorbent kitchen towel to soak the excess oil.
- Serve the batter-fried basa warm with tartar sauce on the side. Enjoy!

Nutrition Facts

- Calories: 142; Protein 18.3g; Carbohydrates 6.7g; Fat 4.4g; Cholesterol 163.8mg; Sodium 499.5mg.

310. Lemon-Garlic Marinated Shrimp

Total Time: 10 mins

Servings: 12

Ingredient

- 3 tablespoons minced garlic
- 2 tablespoons extra-virgin olive oil
- ¼ cup lemon juice
- ¼ cup minced fresh parsley
- ½ teaspoon kosher salt
- ½ teaspoon pepper
- 1 ¼ pounds cooked shrimp

Instructions

Place garlic and oil in a small skillet and cook over medium heat until fragrant, about 1 minute. Add lemon juice, parsley, salt, and pepper. Toss with shrimp in a large bowl. Chill until ready to serve.

Nutrition Facts

- Calories: 82; Protein 11g; Carbohydrates 1.9g;

Dietary Fiber 0.1g; Sugars 0.2g; Fat 3.2g;; Calcium 49.3mg; Iron 0.3mg; Magnesium 19.1mg; Potassium 102.3mg; Sodium 495.3mg.

311. Shrimp Poke

Active Time: 30 mins

Total Time: 30 mins

Servings: 4

Ingredient

- ¾ cup thinly sliced scallion greens
- ¼ cup reduced-sodium tamari
- 1 ½ tablespoons mirin
- 1 ½ tablespoon toasted (dark) sesame oil
- 1 tablespoon white sesame seeds
- 2 teaspoons grated fresh ginger
- ½ teaspoon crushed red pepper (Optional)
- 12 ounces cooked shrimp, cut into 1/2-inch pieces
- 2 cups cooked brown rice
- 2 tablespoons rice vinegar
- 2 cups sliced cherry tomatoes
- 2 cups diced avocado
- ¼ cup chopped cilantro
- ¼ cup toasted black sesame seeds

Instructions

- Whisk scallion greens, tamari, mirin, oil, white sesame seeds, ginger, and crushed red pepper, if using, in a medium bowl. Set aside 2 tablespoons of the sauce in a small bowl. Add shrimp to the sauce in the medium bowl and gently toss to coat.
- Combine rice and vinegar in a large bowl. Divide among 4 bowls and top each with 3/4 cup shrimp, 1/2 cup each tomato and avocado, and 1 tablespoon each cilantro and black sesame seeds. Drizzle with the reserved sauce and serve.

Nutrition Facts

- Calories: 460; Protein 28.9g; Carbohydrates 40.2g; Dietary Fiber 9.9g; Sugars 4.5g; Fat 22.1g; Saturated Fat 3.2g;; Calcium 113.2mg; Iron 3.2mg; Magnesium 145.1mg; Potassium 939.3mg; Sodium 860.6mg.

312. Creamy Lemon Pasta With Shrimp

Active Time: 20 mins

Total Time: 20 mins

Servings: 4

Ingredients

- 8 ounces whole-wheat fettuccine
- 1 tablespoon extra-virgin olive oil
- 12 ounces sustainably sourced peeled and deveined raw shrimp (26-30 per pound)
- 2 tablespoons unsalted butter
- 1 tablespoon finely chopped garlic
- ¼ teaspoon crushed red pepper
- 4 cups loosely packed arugula
- ¼ cup whole-milk plain yogurt
- 1 teaspoon lemon zest
- 2 tablespoons lemon juice
- ¼ teaspoon salt
- ⅓ cup grated Parmesan cheese, plus more for garnish
- ¼ cup thinly sliced fresh basil

Instructions

- Bring 7 cups of water to a boil. Add fettuccine, stirring to separate the noodles. Cook until just tender, 7 to 9 minutes. Reserve 1/2 cup of the cooking water and drain.
- Meanwhile, heat oil in a large nonstick skillet over medium-high heat. Add shrimp and cook, stirring occasionally, until pink and curled, 2 to 3 minutes. Transfer the shrimp to a bowl.
- Add butter to the pan and reduce heat to medium. Add garlic and crushed red pepper; cook, stirring often, until the garlic is fragrant, about 1 minute. Add arugula and cook, stirring, until wilted, about 1 minute. Reduce heat to low. Add the fettuccine, yogurt, lemon zest, and the reserved cooking water, 1/4 cup at a time, tossing well, until the fettuccine is fully coated and creamy. Add the shrimp, lemon juice, and salt, tossing to coat the fettuccine. Remove from the heat and toss with Parmesan.
- Serve the fettuccine topped with basil and more Parmesan, if desired.

Nutrition Facts

- Calories: 403; Protein 28.3g; Carbohydrates 45.5g; Dietary Fiber 5.8g; Sugars 3g; Fat 13.9g;; Calcium 207.5mg; Iron 3mg; Magnesium 124.7mg; Potassium 626.4mg; Sodium 396.3mg.

313. Grilled Blackened Shrimp Tacos

Active Time: 20 mins

Total Time: 20 mins

Servings: 4

Ingredient

- 1 ripe avocado
- 1 tablespoon lime juice
- 1 small clove garlic, grated
- ¼ teaspoon salt
- 1 pound large raw shrimp (16-20 count), peeled and deveined
- 2 tablespoons salt-free Cajun spice blend
- 8 corn tortillas, warmed
- 2 cups iceberg lettuce, chopped
- ½ cup fresh cilantro leaves
- ½ cup prepared pico de gallo

Instructions

- Preheat grill to medium-high.
- Mash avocado with a fork in a small bowl. Add lime juice, garlic, and salt and stir to combine.
- Pat shrimp dry. Toss the shrimp with Cajun seasoning in a medium bowl. Thread onto four 10- to 12-inch metal skewers. Grill, turning once until the shrimp are just cooked through, about 4 minutes total.
- Serve the shrimp in tortillas, topped with guacamole, lettuce, cilantro, and pico de gallo.

Nutrition Facts

- Calories: 286; Protein 24g; Carbohydrates 30.4g; Dietary Fiber 6.9g; Sugars 3.5g; Fat 9.3g; Calcium 117.8mg; Iron 1.6mg; Magnesium 87.2mg; Potassium 662.1mg; Sodium 442.7mg;

314. Moqueca (Seafood & Coconut Chowder)

Active Time: 30 mins

Total Time: 30 mins

Servings: 8

Ingredient

- 1 pound fresh crabmeat (preferably claw meat), cleaned and picked over
- 1 pound raw shrimp (16-20 per pound), peeled and deveined if desired
- ¼ cup lemon juice
- 1 ½ tablespoons dendê (red palm oil; see Tip) or canola oil
- 3 cups sliced red bell peppers
- 2 ½ cups sliced green bell peppers
- 2 ½ cups sliced red onions
- ½ cup minced fresh cilantro, plus more for garnish
- 4 large cloves garlic, minced
- ¼ cup tomato paste
- ¾ teaspoon salt
- ¾ teaspoon ground pepper
- 2 14-ounce cans of coconut milk
- 2 cups clam juice or fish stock
- 4 cups cooked brown rice

Instructions

- Combine crab, shrimp, and lemon juice in a medium bowl.
- Heat oil in a large pot over medium-high heat. Add red peppers, green peppers, and onions; cook, stirring occasionally, until beginning to soften, about 4 minutes. Add cilantro, garlic, tomato paste, salt, and pepper; cook, stirring, for 1 minute. Add coconut milk and clam juice (or fish stock) and bring to a simmer. Reduce heat to maintain a simmer, cover, and cook until the peppers are softened, 8 to 10 minutes.
- Add the crab and shrimp and return to a simmer over medium heat. Cover and cook until the shrimp is cooked through, 3 to 4 minutes more. Serve the chowder over rice. Garnish with cilantro, if desired.

Nutrition Facts

- Calories: 485 Fat 26g; Cholesterol 112mg; Sodium 686mg; Carbohydrates 39g; Dietary Fiber 5g; Protein 28g; Sugars 5g; Saturated Fat 20g.

---

315. Brodetto Di Pesce (Adriatic-Style Seafood Stew)

Active Time: 45 mins

Total Time: 1 hr 15 mins

Servings: 8

Ingredient

- ¼ Cup extra-virgin olive oil, plus more for serving
- 1 medium yellow or red onion, finely diced
- ⅓ cup finely diced celery
- ⅓ cup finely chopped flat-leaf parsley, plus more for serving
- 4 cloves garlic, lightly crushed, divided
- ½ teaspoon crushed red pepper
- ¾ cup dry white wine
- 3 sprigs of fresh oregano
- 3 fresh bay leaves
- 2 1/2 cups clam juice or seafood stock, divided
- 2 cups petite diced or crushed canned tomatoes
- 2 pounds littleneck clams, scrubbed
- 1 pound mussels, scrubbed
- 1 pound cleaned squid tubes or tentacles, tubes cut into rings
- 1 pound meaty white fish, such as cod, monkfish, rockfish, snapper, or a combination, cut into 2-inch pieces
- 2 tablespoons lemon juice
- 8 diagonal slices whole-grain baguette (1/2 inch thick), plus more for serving

Instructions

- Cook oil, onion, celery, parsley, 3 cloves garlic, and crushed red pepper in a large pot over medium-low heat, stirring occasionally, until the vegetables are very tender, about 15 minutes.
- Increase heat to medium-high and add wine; cook for 1 minute. Add oregano and bay leaves; cook for 30 seconds. Add 2 cups clam juice (or stock) and tomatoes and bring to a boil over high heat. Reduce heat to a simmer and cook until slightly thickened, 20 to 25 minutes.
- Add clams and mussels; cover and cook for 5 minutes. Add squid, fish, and the remaining 1/2 cup clam juice (or stock). Cover and cook until the fish is just cooked through, 8 to 12 minutes. Remove from heat and gently stir in lemon juice.
- Meanwhile, preheat the broiler to high.
- Place bread on a rimmed baking sheet and broil until lightly browned for 1 to 2 minutes.

Immediately rub with the remaining garlic clove.

- Place one slice of bread in each of 8 shallow bowls and top with the stew. Serve with more oil, parsley, and bread, if desired.

Nutrition Facts

- Calories: 334; Protein 31g; Carbohydrates 25.7g; Dietary Fiber 2.1g; Sugars 4.2g; Fat 10.2g; Saturated Fat 1.5g; Calcium 97.2mg; Iron 5.3mg; Magnesium 77.1mg; Potassium 902.6mg; Sodium 770.3mg.

48. Seafood Linguine

Total Time: 35 mins

Servings: 4

Ingredient

- 8 ounces whole-wheat linguine, or spaghetti
- 2 tablespoons extra-virgin olive oil
- 4 cloves garlic, chopped
- 1 tablespoon chopped shallot
- 1 28-ounce can diced tomatoes, drained
- ½ cup white wine
- ½ teaspoon salt
- ¼ teaspoon freshly ground pepper
- 12 littleneck or small cherrystone clams, (about 1 pound), scrubbed
- 8 ounces dry sea scallops
- 8 ounces tilapia, or other flaky white fish, cut into 1-inch strips
- 1 tablespoon chopped fresh marjoram or 1 teaspoon dried, plus more for garnish
- 1/4 cup grated Parmesan cheese, (optional)

Instructions

- Bring a large pot of water to a boil. Add pasta and cook until just tender, 8 to 10 minutes, or according to package directions. Drain and rinse.
- Meanwhile, heat oil in a large skillet over medium heat. Add garlic and shallot and cook, stirring, until beginning to soften, about 1 minute.
- Increase the heat to medium-high. Add tomatoes, wine, salt, and pepper. Bring to a simmer and cook for 1 minute. Add clams, cover, and cook for 2 minutes. Stir in scallops, fish, and

marjoram. Cover and cook until the scallops and fish are cooked through and the clams have opened, 3 to 5 minutes more. (Discard any clams that don't open.)

- Spoon the sauce and clams over the pasta and sprinkle with additional marjoram and Parmesan (if using).

Nutrition Facts

- Calories: 460; Protein 34.5g; Carbohydrates 55.8g; Dietary Fiber 8.2g; Sugars 7.5g; Fat 9.5g; Saturated Fat 1.6g; Calcium 86.5mg; Iron 4.5mg; Magnesium 122.1mg; Potassium 474.9mg; Sodium 1173.3mg.

316. Seafood Paella With Spring Vegetables

Active Time: 1 hr 15 mins

Total Time: 1 hr 35 mins

Servings: 6

Ingredient

- 6 tablespoons extra-virgin olive oil, divided
- 2 cups diced onion
- 1 cup diced fennel
- 3 medium tomatoes, grated on the large holes of a box grater (skins discarded)
- 4 cloves garlic, thinly sliced
- 2 tablespoons white-wine vinegar
- 1 teaspoon sea salt, divided
- ½ teaspoon ground pepper
- ½ teaspoon crushed red pepper
- Pinch of saffron
- 1 large fresh artichoke
- 1 cup Calasparra rice or other paella rice
- 2 cups seafood stock
- 1 cup green beans, trimmed and cut into 2-inch pieces
- 4 ounces squid bodies, sliced into rings
- 6-12 clams and/or mussels, scrubbed
- 8 ounces skinned monkfish or cod, cut into 1-inch-thick pieces

Instructions

- Heat 3 tablespoons oil in a 13- to 14-inch paella pan over medium-high heat. Add onion and fennel; cook, stirring often, until the onion is translucent, about 5 minutes. Add tomatoes, garlic, vinegar, 1/2 teaspoon salt, pepper, crushed red pepper, and saffron. Reduce heat to maintain a simmer and cook, stirring occasionally, until the tomato liquid has evaporated, 20 to 25 minutes.

- Meanwhile, clean artichoke. Cut lengthwise into 6 wedges. Heat 2 tablespoons oil in a large skillet over medium heat until very hot but not smoking. Add the artichoke wedges; sprinkle with 1/8 teaspoon salt and cook until browned, about 2 minutes per side. Transfer to a plate.
- Preheat oven to 375 degrees F.
- When the tomato liquid has evaporated, add rice to the paella pan, increase heat to medium, and cook, stirring, for 2 minutes. Add stock. Turn on a second burner so both the front and rear burner on one side of the stove are on; bring to a boil over high heat.
- Spread the rice evenly in the pan and nestle the artichokes and beans into it. Reduce heat to maintain a low simmer and cook for 10 minutes, rotating and shifting the pan around the burners periodically to help the rice cook evenly. Season squid with 1/8 teaspoon salt and place on the rice. Cook, without stirring but continuing to rotate the pan, for 5 minutes more.
- Nestle clams and/or mussels into the rice with the open edges facing up. Season fish with the remaining 1/4 teaspoon salt and place on top of the rice. Remove the paella from the heat and very carefully cover the pan with foil.
- Transfer the pan to the oven and bake for 10 minutes. Let stand, covered, for 10 minutes before serving.

To Prep A Fresh Artichoke:

1. Trim 1/2 to 1 inch from the stem end. Peel the stem with a vegetable peeler.

2. Trim 1/2 inch off the top.

3. Remove the small, tough outer leaves from the stem end and snip all spiky tips from the remaining outer leaves using kitchen shears.

4. Cut in half lengthwise and scoop out the fuzzy choke with a melon baller or grapefruit spoon.

Keep artichokes from browning by rubbing the cut edges with a lemon half or putting them in a large bowl of ice water with lemon juice.

Nutrition Facts

354 calories; protein 16.1g; carbohydrates 38.2g; dietary fiber 4.7g; sugars 5.2g; fat 15.3g; saturated fat 2.3g; calcium 65.6mg; iron 1.7mg; magnesium 51.4mg; potassium 695.1mg; sodium 695.3mg;

317. Spaghetti With Garlic & Clam Sauce

Total Time: 45 mins

Servings: 8

Ingredient

- 2 heads garlic
- 28 fresh littleneck clams, scrubbed and rinsed well
- ¾ cup cold water
- 5 tablespoons extra-virgin olive oil, divided
- 2 tablespoons all-purpose flour
- 1 cup dry white wine, such as Pinot Grigio
- 1 cup chopped fresh parsley plus 2 tablespoons, divided
- 1 tablespoon chopped fresh tarragon
- ¾ teaspoon freshly ground pepper, divided
- 1/8 teaspoon crushed red pepper (optional)
- 1 pound whole-wheat spaghetti or linguine

Instructions

- Put a large pot of water on to boil.
- Peel 1 head of garlic, separate cloves, and halve any large ones. Peel the second head and chop all the cloves.
- Place clams in a Dutch oven or large saucepan with cold water. Cover and cook over high heat, stirring frequently, until the shells just open, 6 to 10 minutes. Transfer to a bowl as they open, making sure to keep all the juice in the pan. Discard any unopened clams. Reserve 16 whole clams in their shells. Then, working over the pot so you don't lose any of the juice, remove the meat from the remaining clams. Coarsely chop the meat; set aside separately from the whole clams. Pour the clam juice from the pan into a medium bowl, being careful not to include any of the sediment. Rinse and dry the pan.
- Heat 4 tablespoons of oil in the pan over medium heat. Add all the garlic and cook, stirring, for 1

minute. Stir in the chopped clams and cook for 15 seconds. Add flour and cook, stirring, for 15 seconds. Increase heat to high, stir in wine and the reserved clam juice. Bring the sauce to a simmer, stirring constantly to prevent the flour from clumping. Once it's simmering, reduce the heat to medium and stir in 1 cup parsley, tarragon, and 1/2 teaspoon pepper. Cook, stirring often, until slightly thickened, 6 to 8 minutes. Add crushed red pepper, if using. Add the reserved clams in shells and stir to coat with the sauce.

- Meanwhile, cook pasta in boiling water until al dente, 10 to 13 minutes, or according to package directions. Stir 2 tablespoons of the pasta-cooking water into the clam sauce, then drain the pasta and transfer to a large serving dish. Stir the remaining 1 tablespoon oil and 1/4 teaspoon pepper into the pasta. Spoon the clams and sauce over the pasta. Sprinkle with the remaining 2 tablespoons parsley.

Nutrition Facts

- Calories: 371; Protein 17.8g; Carbohydrates 49.6g; Dietary Fiber 7.3g; Sugars 2.5g; Fat 10.3g; Saturated Fat 1.5g;; Calcium 83mg; Iron 3.8mg; Magnesium 97mg; Potassium 431.8mg; Sodium 412mg;

7. Air Fryer Meat Recipes

318. Air Fryer Steak

Prep Time: 5 mins

Cook Time: 25 mins

Total Time: 30 mins

Ingredients

- 2 (6 oz.) ((170g)) steaks, 3/4" thick rinsed and patted dry
- 1 teaspoon (5 ml) olive oil, to coat
- 1/2 teaspoon (0.5) garlic powder (optional)
- Salt, to taste
- Pepper, to taste
- Butter

Instructions

- Lightly coat steaks with olive oil. Season both sides of steaks with garlic powder (optional), salt, and pepper (we'll usually season liberally with salt & pepper).
- Preheat the Air Fryer at 400°F for 4 minutes.
- Air Fry for 400°F for 10-18 minutes, flipping halfway through (cooking time depends on how thick and cold the steaks are plus how do you prefer your steaks).
- If you want steaks to be cooked more, add additional 3-6 minutes of cooking time.
- Add a pat of butter on top of the steak, cover with foil, and allow the steak to rest for 5 minutes.
- Season with additional salt and pepper, if needed. Serve immediately.

Nutrition Facts

- Calories: 373kcal | Protein: 34g | Fat: 26g | Saturated Fat: 10g | Cholesterol: 103mg | Sodium: 88mg | Potassium: 455mg | Vitamin A: 25IU | Calcium: 12mg | Iron: 2.9mg

Air Fryer Steak Bites & Mushrooms

Prep Time: 10 mins

Cook Time: 18 mins

Total Time: 28 mins

Ingredients

- 1 lb. (454 g) steaks, cut into 1/2" cubes (ribeye, sirloin, tri-tip, or what you prefer)
- 8 oz. (227 g) mushrooms (cleaned, washed, and halved)
- 2 tablespoons (30 ml) butter, melted (or olive oil)
- 1 teaspoon (5 ml) worcestershire sauce
- 1/2 teaspoon (2.5 ml) garlic powder, optional
- Flakey salt, to taste
- Fresh cracked black pepper, to taste
- Minced parsley, garnish
- Melted butter, for finishing - optional
- Chili flakes, for finishing - optional
- **Instructions**
- Rinse and thoroughly pat dry the steak cubes. Combine the steak cubes and mushrooms. Coat with the melted butter and then season with Worcestershire sauce, optional garlic powder, and a generous seasoning of salt and pepper.
- Preheat the Air Fryer at 400°F for 4 minutes.
- Spread the steak and mushrooms in an even layer in the air fryer basket. Air fry at 400°F for 10-18 minutes, shaking and flipping and the steak and mushrooms 2 times through the cooking process (time depends on your preferred doneness, the thickness of the steak, size of air fryer).
- Check the steak to see how well done it is cooked. If you want the steak more done, add an extra 2-5 minutes of cooking time.
- Garnish with parsley and drizzle with optional melted butter and/or optional chili flakes. Season with additional salt & pepper if desired. Serve warm.

Nutrition Facts

Calories: 401kcal | Carbohydrates: 3g | Protein: 32g | Fat: 29g | Saturated Fat: 14g | Cholesterol: 112mg | Sodium: 168mg | Potassium: 661mg | Sugar: 1g | Vitamin A: 25 IU | Vitamin C: 1.6mg | Calcium: 11mg | Iron: 3.1mg

319. Air fryer Steak Tips

Prep Time: 5 minutes

Cook Time: 9 minutes

Total Time: 14 minutes

Servings: 3

Ingredients

- 1.5 lb steak or beef chuck for a cheaper version cut to 3/4 inch cubes
- Air Fryer Steak Marinade
- 1 tsp oil
- 1/4 tsp salt
- 1/2 tsp black pepper, freshly ground
- 1/2 tsp dried garlic powder
- 1/2 tsp dried onion powder
- 1 tsp Montreal Steak Seasoning
- 1/8 tsp cayenne pepper
- Air Fryer Asparagus
- 1 lb Asparagus, tough ends trimmed (could replace with spears of zucchini)
- 1/4 tsp salt
- 1/2 tsp oil (optional)

Instructions

- Preheat the air fryer at 400F for about 5 minutes.
- Meanwhile, trim the steak of any fat and cut it into cubes. Then, toss with the ingredients for the marinade (oil, salt, black pepper, Montreal seasoning, onion and garlic powder & the cayenne pepper) and massage the spices into the meat to coat evenly. Do this in a ziplock bag for easier cleanup.
- Spray the bottom of the air fryer basket with nonstick spray if you have any and spread the prepared meat along the bottom of it. Cook the beef steak tips for about 4-6 minutes and check for doneness.
- Toss the asparagus with 1/2 tsp oil and 1/4 tsp salt until evenly coated.
- Once the steak bites are browned to your liking, toss them around and move to one side. Add the asparagus to the other side of the air fryer basket and cook for another 3 minutes.
- Remove the steak tips and the asparagus to a serving plate and serve while hot.

Nutrition Facts

- Calories: 526| |Fat: 34g|Saturated Fat: 14g|Cholesterol:138mg|Sodium: 703mg|Potassium:913mg|Carbohydrates:6g|Fiber:3g|Sugar:2g|Protein: 49g|Calcium: 52mg|Iron:7.1mg

320. Easy Air Fryer Steak Bites

Prep Time: 5 minutes

Cook Time: 9 minutes

Total Time: 14 minutes

Yield: 2-4 servings

Ingredients

- Sirloin Steak Bites or a 1lb. sirloin steak cut into bite-size pieces
- Steak seasoning or salt and pepper
- Olive oil

Instructions

- Start by preheating your air fryer to 390° or 400°.
- Place the steak bites in a bowl and add about a tablespoon of steak seasoning or season with salt and pepper.
- Pour in a tablespoon of olive oil and toss to coat all of the steak bites.
- Place the steak bites in a single layer in your air fryer basket and cook for 5 minutes.
- Turn the steak bites over and cook for an additional 4 minutes for a medium steak. Cook for an additional 2-3 minutes for medium-well and a couple of minutes less for medium-rare.
- Remove from the air fryer and allow them to rest for 5-10 minutes so the meat will retain its juices.
- Enjoy a salad or with your favorite veggies for lunch or dinner!

Nutritional Value

- Calories: 572kcal | Carbohydrates: 1g | Protein: 46g | Fat: 43g | Saturated Fat: 22g | Cholesterol: 168mg | Sodium: 219mg | Potassium: 606mg | Sugar: 1g | Calcium: 16mg | Iron: 4mg

321. Air Fryer Steak Bites (With Or Without Potatoes)

Prep Time: 10 mins

Cook Time: 20 mins

Total Time: 30 mins

Servings: 4 Servings

Ingredients

- 1 lb. (454 g) steaks, cut into 1/2" cubes & patted dry
- 1/2 lb. (227 g) potatoes (optional), cut into 1/2" pieces
- 2 tablespoons (30 ml) butter, melted (or oil)
- 1 teaspoon (5 ml) worcestershire sauce
- 1/2 teaspoon (2.5 ml) garlic powder
- Salt, to taste
- Black pepper, to taste
- Minced parsley, garnish
- Melted butter for finishing, optional
- Chili flakes, for finishing, optional

Instructions

- Heat a large pot of water to a boil and then add the potatoes. Cook for about 5 minutes, or until nearly tender, and then drain.
- Combine the steak cubes and blanched potatoes. Coat with the melted butter and then season with Worcestershire sauce, garlic powder, salt, and pepper.
- Preheat the Air Fryer at 400°F for 4 minutes.
- Spread the steak and potatoes in an even layer in an air fryer basket. Air fry at 400°F for 10-18 minutes, shaking and flipping and the steak and potatoes about 3 times through the cooking process (time depends on your preferred doneness, the thickness of the steak, and size of air fryer).
- Check the steak to see how well done it is cooked. If you want the steak more done, add an extra 2-5 minutes of cooking time.
- Garnish with parsley and drizzle with optional melted butter and/or optional chili flakes. Season with additional salt & pepper if desired. Serve warm

Nutrition

- Calories: 321kcal | Carbohydrates: 8g | Protein:

24g | Fat: 22g | Saturated Fat: 11g | Cholesterol: 84mg | Sodium: 130mg | Potassium: 550mg | Fiber: 1g | Sugar: 1g | Vitamin A: 192IU | Vitamin C: 6mg | Calcium: 25mg | Iron: 4mg

---

322. Perfect Air Fryer Steak

Prep Time: 20 minutes

Cook Time: 12 minutes

Resting Time: 5 minutes

Total Time: 32 minutes

Servings: 2

Ingredients

- 2 8 oz Ribeye steak
- Salt
- Freshly cracked black pepper
- Olive oil
- Garlic Butter
- 1 stick unsalted butter softened
- 2 tbsp fresh parsley chopped
- 2 tsp garlic minced
- 1 tsp Worcestershire Sauce
- 1/2 tsp salt

Instructions

- Prepare Garlic Butter by mixing butter, parsley garlic, Worcestershire sauce, and salt until thoroughly combined.
- Place in parchment paper and roll into a log. Refrigerate until ready to use.
- Remove steak from the fridge and allow to sit at room temperature for 20 minutes. Rub a little bit of olive oil on both sides of the steak and season with salt and freshly cracked black pepper.
- Grease your Air Fryer basket by rubbing a little bit of oil on the basket. Preheat Air Fryer to 400 degrees Fahrenheit. Once preheated, place steaks in the air fryer and cook for 12 minutes, flipping halfway through.
- Remove from air fryer and allow to rest for 5 minutes. Top with garlic butter.

Nutrition

- Calories: 683kcal

323. Air Fryer Steak

Prep Time: 5 min

Cook Time: 12 min

Total Time: 12 min

Yield: 2

Ingredients

- 2 (1 in thick) Steaks Rib Eye, or Tri-Tip), 4 to 6 oz each
- Salt and Pepper to taste
- 2 tablespoons of butter (optional)

Instructions

- If your air fryer requires preheating, preheat your air fryer.
- Set the temperature to 400 degrees Fahrenheit.
- Season your steak with salt and pepper on each side.
- Place the steak in your air fryer basket. Do not overlap the steaks.
- **Medium Steak**: Set the time to 12 minutes and flip the steak at 6.
- **Medium Rare**: For a medium-rare steak, cook the steak for 10 minutes and flip it at 5 minutes.

Nutrition

- Calories: 250|Sodium: 60|Fat: 17|Saturated Fat: 7|Carbohydrates: 0|Fiber: 0|Protein: 23

324. Air Fryer Steak

Prep Time: 5 Minutes

Cook Time: 8 Minutes

Rest Time: 5 Minutes

Total Time: 18 Minutes

Servings: 2 Steaks

Ingredients

- 2 steaks 1" thick, ribeye, sirloin, or striploin
- 1 tablespoon olive oil
- 1 tablespoon salted butter melted
- Steak seasoning to taste

Instructions

- Remove steaks from the fridge at least 30 minutes before cooking.
- Preheat air fryer to 400°F.
- Rub the steaks with olive oil and melted butter. Generously season on each side.
- Add the steaks to the air fryer basket and cook for 8-12 minutes (flipping after 4 minutes) or until steaks reach desired doneness.
- Remove steaks from the air fryer and transfer them to a plate. Rest at least 5 minutes before serving.
- Top with additional butter if desired and serve.

Nutrition Information

- Calories: 582, Carbohydrates: 1g, Protein: 46g, Fat: 45g, Saturated Fat: 19g, Cholesterol: 153mg, Sodium: 168mg, Potassium: 606mg, Sugar: 1g, Vitamin A: 209IU, Calcium: 16mg, Iron: 4mg

325. Air Fryer Roast Beef With Herb Crust

Prep Time: 5 minutes

Cook Time: 1 hour

Resting Time: 10 minutes

Total Time: 1 hour 15 minutes

Servings: 6 people

Ingredients

- 2- 2-pound beef roast
- 2 teaspoons garlic powder
- 2 teaspoons onion salt
- 2 teaspoons parsley
- 2 teaspoons thyme
- 2 teaspoons basil
- 1/2 tablespoon salt
- 1 teaspoon pepper
- 1 tablespoon olive oil

Instructions

- Preheat the air fryer for 15 minutes at 390 degrees.
- Combine the garlic powder, onion salt, parsley, thyme, and basil, salt, and pepper.
- Rub the roast with olive oil then rub the herb mixture over the entire roast.
- Place the roast in the preheated air fryer. Set

- timer for 15 minutes.
- After 15 minutes, remove the basket and turn the roast over.
- Reduce the temperature to 360 degrees on the air fryer and return the roast. Cook for another 60 minutes, or until the thermometer reaches desired degree of doneness.
- Let roast rest for 15 minutes before slicing.

Nutrition

- Calories: 336kcal | Carbohydrates: 1g | Protein: 69g | Fat: 16g | Saturated Fat: 5.5g | Cholesterol: 136mg

---

326. Air Fryer Garlic Steak Bites

Prep Time: 10 Minutes

Cook Time: 15 Minutes

Total Time: 25 Minutes

Servings: 4 People

Ingredients

- 1 pound New York steak or sirloin steak cut into one inch cubes
- 2 Tablespoons olive oil
- 1/2 teaspoon salt
- 1/4 teaspoon pepper
- 1 teaspoon Italian seasoning
- 3 cloves garlic minced

Herb Butter:

- 1/4 cup butter melted
- 1/2 teaspoon thyme
- 1/2 teaspoon rosemary minced
- 1 teaspoon parsley minced

Instructions

- In a medium-sized bowl add the steak bites, olive oil, salt, pepper, Italian seasoning, and garlic. Add to the basket of the air fryer.
- Cook at 400 degrees for 10-12 minutes. Once cooked toss to coat with the garlic herb butter.

Nutrition Facts

- Calories: 169kcal
- Carbohydrates: 1g
- Protein: 1g

- Fat: 19g
- Saturated Fat: 8g
- Cholesterol: 31mg
- Sodium: 393mg
- Potassium: 9mg
- Fiber: 1g
- Sugar: 1g
- Calcium: 15mg
- Iron: 1mg

---

327. Best Air Fryer Steak Recipe

Prep Time: 15 minutes

Cook Time: 10 minutes

Total Time: 25 minutes

Servings: 2

Ingredients

- 2 Steak Ribeye, New York, Sirloin, or any steak of choice.
- 1 teaspoon Paprika
- 1/2 teaspoon Oregano
- 1/2 teaspoon Black pepper or to taste
- Salt
- For the Garlic Herb Butter
- 2 tablespoons Butter
- 1 teaspoon garlic granules
- 1 tablespoon freshly chopped Parsley

Instructions

- Add the paprika, oregano, black pepper, salt to a bowl and mix.
- Add the garlic granules and freshly chopped parsley in the butter, mix well and store in the fridge till it's time to use.
- Garlic herb butter displayed.
- Pat steak dry and season both sides with the seasoning mix. Leave to marinate for 10-15 minutes.
- Seasoned steaks.
- Arrange the side of the steak by side in the air fryer basket and air fry at a temperature of 195C for 10 minutes (well done). After half of the time, bring the air fryer basket out and turn the steak to the other side.
- Steaks displayed in the air fryer basket.
- After the 5 minutes cycle is done, bring the

steaks out, serve and immediately add the garlic butter to the steaks.
- Enjoy air fryer garlic butter steak.
- Air fryer steak topped with garlic butter.

Nutrition Information

- Calories: 581kcal | Carbohydrates: 2g | Protein: 46g | Fat: 43g | Saturated Fat: 21g | Cholesterol: 168mg | Sodium: 219mg | Potassium: 646mg | Fiber: 1g | Sugar: 1g | Vitamin A: 876IU | Calcium: 24mg | Iron: 4mg

328. Perfect Air Fryer Steak: Paleo, Whole30, Keto, Easy!

Prep Time: 5 Mins

Cook Time: 12 Mins

Total Time: 17 Mins

Ingredients

- 2 sirloin steaks
- 2–3 tbsp steak seasoning
- Spray oil or cooking fat of choice (I prefer avocado oil)

Instructions

- First, pat the steak dry and let come to room temperature
- Spray (or brush) oil lightly on the steak and season liberally
- Spray or coat the bottom of the air fryer basket with oil and place the steaks into the air fryer. The steaks can be touching or sort of "smooshed" in the basket.
- Cook at 400 degrees F. for 6 minutes, flip the steaks, and cook for another 6 minutes. If you want your steak more well-done, add 2-3 minutes. Let rest before serving.

Nutritional Value

- Calories: 195kcal | Carbohydrates: 5g | Protein: 12g | Saturated Fat: 6g | Cholesterol:44mg | Sodium: 43mg | Potassium: 321mg | Fiber: 2g | Sugar: 1g | Calcium: 15mg | Iron: 3mg

329. How To Make Steak In The Air Fryer

Prep Time: 5 Minutes

Cook Time: 15 Minutes

Total Time: 20 Minutes

Ingredients

- 2 Pounds Steak (I Used Delmonico)
- Salt
- Pepper
- Garlic Powder
- 2 Tbs Butter

Instructions

- Preheat your air fryer to 400 for about 5 minutes
- Salt and pepper both sides of the steak
- Place a pad of butter on top of each steak
- Place on the top rack of your air fryer
- Cook on-air fry for 15 minutes for medium-well
- Flip over after 7 minutes
- For Medium-rare cook for 10 minutes flipping after 5
- For well-done cook for 20 minutes flipping after 10 minutes
- Remove steak and let rest for 5 minutes and serve

Nutrition Information:

Calories: 1371| Total Fat: 95g| Saturated Fat: 40g| Trans Fat: 0g| Unsaturated Fat: 41g| Cholesterol: 471mg| Sodium: 619mg| Carbohydrates: 2g| Fiber: 0g| Sugar: 0g| Protein: 119g

330. Air Fryer Steak Bites With Mushrooms

Prep Time: 10 mins

Cook Time: 15 mins

Total Time: 25 mins

Ingredients

- 2 lb beef
- 2 lb mushrooms
- 2 tbsp Worcester sauce
- 1 tbsp salt
- 1 tbsp pepper

Instructions

- Preheat an Air Fryer for 3 minutes at 400 °F. Cut beef into bite-size pieces and mushrooms into halves.

- Mushrooms and steak in a bowl
- Add Worchester sauce, salt, and pepper to the mixture. Let it sit for a few minutes.
- Steak and mushrooms withs seasoning
- Add beef and mushrooms to the air fryer basket. Air-dry it for 5 minutes.
- Uncooked steak and mushrooms in a basket
- Remove the basket and toss the steak bites to ensure all the sides are getting nice and crispy.
- Basket with steak and mushrooms
- Air fry for another 5-7 minutes. Once complete, check to make sure the temperature of the beef reached 145F.
- Steak bites with mushrooms in an air fryer basket

Nutrition Facts

- Fat: 31g
- Saturated Fat: 12g
- Cholesterol: 107mg
- Sodium: 1327mg
- Potassium: 948mg
- Carbohydrates: 7g
- Fiber: 2g
- Sugar: 4g
- Protein: 31g
- Vitamin C: 4mg
- Calcium: 42mg
- Iron: 4mg

331. Air Fryer Steak

Ready In: 49min

Prep Time: 15min

Cook Time: 9min

Ingredients

- 2 boneless ribeye steaks
- 1 tablespoon steak rub
- 1 teaspoon kosher salt
- 1 tablespoon unsalted butter

Directions

- Rub steaks with steak rub and salt. Allow resting at room temperature for 15 to 30 minutes. The longer you allow them to rest with the rub on, the more flavorful they will be!

- Preheat air fryer for 5 minutes at 400°F (200°C).
- Arrange steaks in a single layer in an air fryer basket, work in batches as needed and cook about 9 minutes for medium-rare. The internal temperature should read at least 145°F (63°C).
- Transfer steak to a cutting board and put half the butter on each steak. Allow resting for at least 5 minutes before slicing into 1/2-inch thick slices.

Nutrition Facts

- Calories: 301; 23g Fat; 0.0g Carbohydrates; 23g Protein; 88mg Cholesterol; 1111mg Sodium.

332. Air Fryer Italian-Style Meatballs

Active Time: 10 Mins

Total Time: 45 Mins

Yield: Serves 12 (2 meatballs)

Ingredients

- 2 tablespoons olive oil 1 medium shallot, minced (about 2 Tbsp.) 3 cloves garlic, minced (about 1 Tbsp.) 1/4 cup whole-wheat panko crumbs 2 tablespoons whole milk 2/3 pound lean ground beef 1/3 pound bulk turkey sausage 1 large egg, lightly beaten 1/4 cup finely chopped fresh flat-leaf parsley 1 tablespoon chopped fresh rosemary 1 tablespoon finely chopped fresh thyme 1 tablespoon Dijon mustard 1/2 teaspoon kosher salt

How To Make It

- Preheat air-fryer to 400°F. Heat oil in a medium nonstick pan over medium-high heat. Add shallot and cook until softened, 1 to 2 minutes. Add garlic and cook just until fragrant, 1 minute. Remove from heat.
- In a large bowl, combine panko and milk. Let stand 5 minutes.
- Add cooked shallot and garlic to the panko mixture, along with beef, turkey sausage egg, parsley, rosemary, thyme, mustard, and salt. Stir to gently combine.
- Gently shape mixture into 1 1/2-inch ball. Place shaped balls in a single-layer in the air-fryer basket. Cook half the meatballs at 400°F until lightly browned and cooked for 10 to 11 minutes. Remove and keep warm. Repeat with remaining

meatballs.

- Serve warm meatballs with toothpicks as an appetizer or serve over pasta, rice, or spiralized zoodles for a main dish.

Nutritional Information

- Calories: 122 | Fat: 8g | Sat fat: 2g | Unsatfat: 5g | Protein: 10g | Carbohydrate | 0g Fiber 0g | Sugars 0g | Added sugars: 0g | Sodium: 254mg

333. Air Fryer Marinated Steak

Prep Time: 5 minutes

Cook Time: 10 minutes

Total Time: 15 minutes

Servings: 2

Ingredients

- 2 New York Strip Steaks (mine were about 6-8 oz each) You can use any cut of steak
- 1 tablespoon low-sodium soy sauce This is used to provide liquid to marinate the meat and make it juicy.
- 1 teaspoon liquid smoke or a cap full
- 1 tablespoon mccormick's Grill Mates Montreal Steak Seasoning or Steak Rub (or season to taste) See recipe notes for instructions on how to create your steak rub
- 1/2 tablespoon unsweetened cocoa powder
- Salt and pepper to taste
- Melted butter (optional)

Instructions

- Drizzle the steak with soy sauce and liquid smoke. You can do this inside Ziploc bags if you wish.
- Season the steak with the seasonings.
- Refrigerate for at least a couple of hours, preferably overnight.
- Place the steak in the air fryer. I did not use any oil. Cook two steaks at a time (if the air fryer is the standard size). You can use an accessory grill pan, a layer rack, or the standard air fryer basket.
- Cook for 5 minutes at 370 degrees. After 5 minutes, open the air fryer and examine your steak. Cook time will vary depending on your desired doneness. Use a meat thermometer and

cook to 125° F for rare, 135° F for medium-rare, 145° F for medium, 155° F for medium-well, and 160° F for well done.

- I cooked the steak for an additional 2 minutes for medium-done steak.
- Remove the steak from the air fryer and drizzle with melted butter.

Nutrition

- Serving: 0.5steak | Calories: 476kcal | Carbohydrates: 1g | Protein: 49g | Fat: 28g

334. Air Fryer Steak Bites And Mushrooms

Prep Time: 1 hour 5 minutes

Cook Time: 15 minutes

Total Time: 1 hour 20 minutes

Servings: 2

Ingredients

- 1 teaspoon kosher salt
- 1/2 teaspoon garlic powder
- 1/4 teaspoon black pepper
- 2 Tablespoons Worcestershire Sauce
- 2 Tablespoons avocado oil (Click here for my favorite brand on Amazon)
- 8 oz Baby Bella Mushrooms, sliced
- 1 pound Top Sirloin steak, cut into 1.5 inch cubes

Instructions

- Combine all your ingredients for the marinade into a large mixing bowl.
- Add your steak cubes and sliced mushrooms into your mixing bowl with the marinade and toss to coat.
- Let the steak and mushrooms marinate for 1 hour.
- Preheat your Air Fryer to 400F for 5 minutes.
- Make sure you spray the inside of your air fryer will a cooking spray and pour your steak and mushrooms into the air fryer basket.
- Cook the steak and mushrooms in the Air Fryer for 5 minutes at 400F. Open the basket and shake the steak and mushrooms so they cook evenly. Continue to cook for 5 minutes more.
- Check the steak using an internal meat thermometer. If the steak has not reached your

desired doneness, continue to cook in 3-minute intervals until the thermometer placed in the center of 1 steak bite reaches the desired temperature. (Rare=125F, Medium-rare=130F, Medium=140F, Medium-well=150F, well-done=160F)

- Serve

Nutritional Value

- Calories: 572kcal | Carbohydrates: 1g | Protein: 46g | Fat: 43g | Saturated Fat: 22g | Cholesterol: 168mg | Sodium: 219mg | Potassium: 606mg | Sugar: 1g | Calcium: 16mg | Iron: 4mg

335. Air Fryer Beef Tips

Prep Time 2 minutes

Cook Time 12 minutes

Marinate Time 5 minutes

Total Time 14 minutes

Servings: 4

Ingredients

- 1 pound ribeye or New York steak, cut into 1-inch cubes
- 2 tsp sea salt
- 1 tsp black pepper
- 1 tsp garlic powder
- 2 tsp onion powder
- 1 tsp paprika
- 2 tsp rosemary crushed
- 2 tbsp coconut aminos

Instructions

- Place steak cubes in a medium sized bowl.
- In a small bowl, combine the salt, pepper, garlic powder, onion powder, paprika, and rosemary. Mix well.
- Sprinkle the mixed dry seasoning on the steak cubes. Mix to evenly distribute the seasoning.
- Sprinkle the coconut aminos all over the seasoned steak. Mix well.
- Let it sit for 5 minutes.
- Place the steak in a single layer in the air fryer basket.
- Cook at 380F for 12 minutes.
- Shake the basket halfway to ensure that the

steak cooks evenly.
- Remove from the air fryer and let it cool for a few minutes before serving.

Nutritional Value

- Total fat: 3.7g
- sodium: 1820.8mg
- sugar: 11.3g
- Vitamin A: 169.2ug
- Carbohydrates: 33.6mg
- Protein: 18g
- Vitamin C: 165.5mg

336. Air Fryer Beef Kabobs

Prep Time: 30 minutes

Cook Time: 8 minutes

Servings: 4 servings

Ingredients

- 1.5 pounds sirloin steak cut into 1-inch chunks
- 1 large bell pepper color of choice
- 1 large red onion or onion of choice

For The Marinade:

- 4 tablespoons olive oil
- 2 cloves garlic minced
- 1 tablespoon lemon juice
- 1/2 teaspoon
- 1/2 teaspoon
- Salt and pepper pinch

Instructions

- In a large bowl, combine the beef and ingredients for the marinade until fully combined. Cover and marinate in the fridge for 30 minutes or up to 24 hours.
- When ready to cook, preheat the air fryer to 400F. Thread the beef, pepper, and onion onto skewers.
- Place skewers into the preheated air fryer and the air fryer for 8-10 minutes, turning halfway through until charred on the outside and tender on the inside.

Nutrition

Calories: 382kcal | Carbohydrates: 6g | Protein: 38g |

Fat: 22g | Saturated Fat: 5g | Cholesterol: 104mg | Sodium: 105mg | Potassium: 708mg | Fiber: 1g | Sugar: 3g | Vitamin A: 1358IU | Vitamin C: 56mg | Calcium: 60mg | Iron: 3mg

337. Air Fryer Corned Beef

Total Time: 2 hours

Ingredients

- Corned Beef, 3-4 pounds
- 1/2 Cup Brown Sugar
- 1/4 cup Dijon Mustard
- 1 TBSP Apple Cider Vinegar

Instructions

- Mix brown sugar, Dijon mustard, & apple cider vinegar together.
- Baste corned beef with glaze and tightly wrap it in aluminum foil.
- Air Fry at 360 degrees for 1 hour.
- Unwrap aluminum foil, baste again, and loosely wrap with aluminum foil.
- Air Fry at 360 degrees for 40 minutes.
- Remove foil, baste one last time. Air Fry at 400 degrees for 10 minutes.

Nutrition Information:

- Total Fat: 8g|Saturated Fat: 3g|Trans Fat: 0g|Unsaturated Fat: 5g|Cholesterol: 42mg|Sodium: 688mg|Carbohydrates: 16g|Fiber: 0g|Sugar: 15g|Protein: 8g

338. Air Fryer Ground Beef

Prep Time: 2 minutes

Cook Time: 10 minutes

Yield: 6 servings

Ingredients

- 1 to 1 and 1/2 lbs. ground beef
- 1 tsp. salt
- 1/2 tsp. pepper
- 1/2 tsp. garlic powder

Instructions

- Put the ground beef into the basket of the air

fryer.
- Season the beef with salt, pepper, and garlic powder. Stir it a bit with a wooden spoon.
- Cook in the air fryer at 400°F for 5 minutes. Stir it around.
- Continue to cook until cooked through and no longer pink, 3-5 more minutes.
- Crumble the beef up using a wooden spoon. Remove the basket and discard any fat and liquid left behind. Use the beef in your favorite ground beef recipe.

Nutritional Value

- Total Fat: 7.5g
- Sodium: 437.5mg
- Sugar: 0g
- Vitamin A: 3.1ug
- Carbohydrates: 0.3g
- Protein: 15.1g

339. Air Fryer Steak With Easy Herb Butter

Prep Time: 6 Mins

Cook Time: 9 Mins

Total Time: 15 Mins

Ingredients

- 2 medium steaks about 8 ounces each
- 2 teaspoon salt
- Herb butter
- 1/4 cup butter softened
- 1 clove garlic
- 1/4 teaspoon salt minced
- 1 tablespoon parsley chopped
- Pepper lots, to taste
- Wine pairings
- 2018 adelante pinot noir
- 2017 hushkeeper zinfandel
- 2018 middle jane cabernet sauvignon reserve

Instructions

- Mix butter, garlic, salt, parsley, and pepper together for herb butter.
- Shape into a log. Chill in the fridge. (See notes.)
- Preheat the air fryer for 5 minutes at 400º F. Liberally salt both sides of the steak. Add the steaks and cook for 7-9 minutes for medium-

rare.

- Immediately remove from air fryer. Rest 5 minutes.

Nutrition

- Calories: 678kcal
- Carbohydrates: 1g
- Protein: 46g
- Fat: 55g
- Saturated Fat: 29g
- Cholesterol: 199mg
- Sodium: 2938mg
- Potassium: 608mg
- Sugar: 1g
- Vitamin A: 912IU
- Vitamin C: 3mg
- Calcium: 23mg
- Iron: 4mg
- Net Carbs: 1g

340. Air Fryer Roast Beef

Prep Time: 5 Minutes

Cook Time: 45 Minutes

Inactive Time: 10 Minutes

Total Time: 1 Hour

Ingredients

- 2 lb beef roast
- 1 tbsp olive oil
- 1 medium onion, (optional)
- 1 tsp salt
- 2 tsp rosemary and thyme, (fresh or dried)

Instructions

- Preheat air fryer to 390°F (200°C).
- Mix sea salt, rosemary, and oil on a plate.
- Pat the beef roast dry with paper towels. Place beef roast on a plate and turn so that the oil-herb mix coats the outside of the beef.
- Seasoned beef roast on a white plate
- If using, peel the onion and cut it in half, place onion halves in the air fryer basket.
- Place beef roast in the air fryer basket.
- Beef roast in the air fryer basket
- Set to air fry beef for 15 minutes.

- When the time is up, change the temperature to 360°F (180°C). Some air fryers require you to turn food during cooking, so check your manual and turn the beef roast over if required (my Philips Viva air fryer doesn't need food to be turned).
- Set the beef to cook for an additional 30 minutes. This should give you medium-rare beef. Though is best to monitor the temperature with a meat thermometer to ensure that it is cooked to your liking. Cook for additional 5-minute intervals if you prefer it more well done.
- Remove roast beef from the air fryer, cover with kitchen foil and leave to rest for at least ten minutes before serving. This allows the meat to finish cooking and the juices to reabsorb into the meat.
- Carve the roast beef thinly against the grain and serve with roasted or steamed vegetables, wholegrain mustard, and gravy.

Nutrition Information:

- Calories: 212 | Total Fat: 7g | Saturated Fat: 2g | Unsaturated Fat: 0g | Cholesterol: 83mg | Sodium: 282mg | Carbohydrates: 2g | Fiber: 1g | Sugar: 1g | Protein: 33g

341. Air Fryer Chicken Fried Steak

Prep Time: 20 minutes

Cook Time: 8 minutes

Total Time: 28 minutes

Ingredients

For The Steaks

- 2 cube steaks, 5-6 ounces each
- 3/4 cup All-Purpose Flour
- 1 teaspoon Ground Black Pepper
- 1 teaspoon Kosher Salt
- 1/2 teaspoon smoked paprika
- 1/2 teaspoon Onion Powder
- 1/2 teaspoon garlic powder
- 1/4 teaspoon Cayenne Pepper
- 2 teaspoons crumbled dried sage
- 3/4 cup buttermilk
- 1 teaspoon hot pepper sauce
- 1 Egg

- Non-Stick Cooking Spray

For The Gravy

- 4 tablespoons butter
- 2 tablespoons All-Purpose Flour
- 1 teaspoon Cracked Black Pepper
- 1/2 teaspoon Kosher Salt
- 1/4 teaspoon garlic salt
- 1/2 cup Whole Milk
- 1/2 cup Heavy Cream

Instructions

Steaks

- For the flour dredge, mix together in a shallow bowl, whisk the flour, 1 teaspoon pepper, 1 teaspoon salt, paprika, onion powder, garlic powder, cayenne, and sage.
- In a separate shallow bowl, whisk the buttermilk, hot pepper sauce, and egg.
- Pat the steaks dry with a paper towel. Season to taste with salt and pepper. Allow standing for 5 minutes, then pat dry again with a paper towel.
- Dredge the steaks in the seasoned flour mixture, shaking off any excess. Then dredge in the buttermilk mixture, allowing excess to drip off. Dredge in the flour mixture again, shaking off excess. Place the breaded steaks on a sheet pan and press any remaining flour mixture onto the steaks, making sure that each steak is completely coated. Let stand for 10 minutes.
- Place steaks in the air fryer basket. Lightly coat with vegetable oil spray. Set the air fryer to 400°F for 8 minutes, carefully turning steaks and coating the other side with vegetable oil spray halfway through the cooking time.

Gravy

- Meanwhile, for the gravy: In a small saucepan, melt the butter over low heat. Whisk in the flour, pepper, salt, and garlic salt, continually whisking.
- Slowly add the milk and cream mixture, whisking constantly. Turn the heat to medium and cook, whisking occasionally, until thickened.
- Use a meat thermometer to ensure the steaks have reached an internal temperature of 145°F. Serve the steaks topped with the gravy.

Nutrition Facts

- Calories: 787kcal | Carbohydrates: 54g | Protein: 51g | Fat: 40g | Fiber: 2g | Sugar: 11g

---

342. Air Fryer Korean BBQ Beef

Prep Time: 15 Minutes

Cook Time: 30 Minutes

Total Time: 45 Minutes

Ingredients

Meat

- 1 Pound Flank Steak or Thinly Sliced Steak
- 1/4 Cup Corn Starch
- Pompeian Oils Coconut Spray

Sauce

- 1/2 Cup Soy Sauce or Gluten-Free Soy Sauce
- 1/2 Cup Brown Sugar
- 2 Tbsp Pompeian White Wine Vinegar
- 1 Clove Garlic, Crushed
- 1 Tbsp Hot Chili Sauce
- 1 Tsp Ground Ginger
- 1/2 Tsp Sesame Seeds
- 1 Tbsp Cornstarch
- 1 Tbsp Water

Instructions

- Begin by preparing the steak. Thinly slice it then toss in the cornstarch.
- Spray the basket or line it with foil in the air fryer with coconut oil spray.
- Add the steak and spray another coat of spray on top.
- Cook in the air fryer for 10 minutes at 390*, turn the steak, and cook for an additional 10 minutes.
- While the steak is cooking add the sauce ingredients EXCEPT for the cornstarch and water to a medium saucepan.
- Warm it up to a low boil, then whisk in the cornstarch and water.
- Carefully remove the steak and pour the sauce over the steak, mix well.
- Serve topped with sliced green onions, cooked rice, and green beans.

Nutrition Information

- Total Fat: 22g | Saturated Fat: 10g | Trans Fat: 0g |

Unsaturated Fat: 10g|Cholesterol: 113mg| Sodium: 1531mg| Carbohydrates: 32g| Fiber: 2g| Sugar: 21g| Protein: 39g

343. Air Fryer Mongolian Beef

Prep Time: 20 Minutes

Cook Time: 20 Minutes

Total Time: 40 Minutes

Ingredients

Meat

- 1 Lb Flank Steak
- 1/4 Cup Corn Starch

Sauce

- 2 Tsp Vegetable Oil
- 1/2 Tsp Ginger
- 1 Tbsp Minced Garlic
- 1/2 Cup Soy Sauce or Gluten Free Soy Sauce
- 1/2 Cup Water
- 3/4 Cup Brown Sugar Packed

Extras

- Cooked Rice
- Green Beans
- Green Onions

Instructions

- Thinly slice the steak into long pieces, then coat with the corn starch.
- Place in the Air Fryer and cook on 390* for 5 minutes on each side. (Start with 5 minutes and add more time if needed. I cook this for 10 minutes on each side; however, others have suggested that was too long for theirs.)
- While the steak cooks, warm up all sauce ingredients in a medium sized saucepan on medium-high heat.
- Whisk the ingredients together until it gets to a low boil.
- Once both the steak and sauce are cooked, place the steak in a bowl with the sauce and let it soak in for about 5-10 minutes.
- When ready to serve, use tongs to remove the steak and let the excess sauce drip off.
- Place steak on cooked rice and green beans, top

with additional sauce if you prefer.

Nutrition Information:

- Total Fat: 16g| Saturated Fat: 5g| Trans Fat: 0g| Unsaturated Fat: 8g| Cholesterol: 116mg| Sodium: 2211mg| Carbohydrates: 57g| Fiber: 1g| Sugar: 35g| Protein: 44g

344. Air Fryer Beef And Bean Taquitos

Prep Time: 10 Minutes

Cook Time: 15 Minutes

Total Time: 25 Minutes

Ingredients

- 1 Pound Ground Beef
- 1 Package Gluten-Free or Regular Taco Seasoning
- 1 Can of Refried Beans
- 1 Cup Shredded Sharp Cheddar
- 20 White Corn Tortillas

Instructions

- Begin by preparing the ground beef if it isn't already.
- Brown the meat on medium-high heat and add in the taco seasoning per the instructions on the package.
- Once you are done with the meat, heat up the corn tortillas for about 30 seconds.
- Spray the air fryer basket with non-stick cooking spray or add a sheet of foil and spray.
- Add ground beef, beans, and a bit of cheese to each tortilla.
- Wrap them tightly and place seam side down in the air fryer.
- Add a quick spray of cooking oil spray, such as olive oil cooking spray.
- Cook at 390 degrees for 12 minutes.
- Repeat for any additional tortillas.

Nutrition Information:

- Total Fat: 9g| Saturated Fat: 4g| Trans Fat: 0g| Unsaturated Fat: 4g| Cholesterol: 31mg| Sodium: 207mg| Carbohydrates: 14g| Fiber: 2g| Sugar: 0g| Protein: 11g

345. Air Fryer Steak Fajitas With Onions And Peppers

Prep Time: 10 Minutes

Cook Time: 15 Minutes

Total Time: 25 Minutes

Ingredients

- 1 lb Thin Cut Steak
- 1 Green Bell Pepper Sliced
- 1 Yellow Bell Pepper Sliced
- 1 Red Bell Pepper Sliced
- 1/2 Cup White Onions Sliced
- 1 Packet Gluten Free Fajita Seasoning
- Olive Oil Spray
- Gluten-Free Corn Tortillas or Flour Tortillas

Instructions

- Line the basket of the air fryer with foil and coat with spray.
- Thinly slice the steak against the grain, this should be about 1/4 inch slices.
- Mix the steak with peppers and onions.
- Add to the air fryer.
- Evenly coat with the fajita seasoning.
- Cook for 5 minutes on 390*.
- Mix up the steak mixture.
- Continue cooking for an additional 5-10 minutes until your desired doneness.
- Serve in warm tortillas.

Nutrition Information:

- Total Fat: 17g | Saturated Fat: 6g | Trans Fat: 0g | Unsaturated Fat: 9g | Cholesterol: 73mg | Sodium: 418mg | Carbohydrates: 15g | Fiber: 2g | Sugar: 4g | Protein: 22g

346. Air Fryer Meatballs (Low Carb)

Prep Time: 10 minutes

Cook Time: 14 minutes

Total Time: 24 minutes

Servings: 3 -4

Ingredients

- 1 lb Lean Ground Beef
- 1/4 Cup Marinara Sauce

- 1 Tablespoon Dried Minced Onion or Freeze Dried Shallots
- 1 teaspoon Minced Garlic I used freeze-dried
- 1 teaspoon Pizza Seasoning or Italian Seasoning
- 1/3 Cup Shredded Parmesan
- 1 Egg
- Salt and Pepper to taste
- Shredded Mozzarella Cheese optional
- 1 1/4 cups Marinara Sauce optional

Instructions

- Mix together all ingredients except reserve 1 1/4 cup of the marinara sauce and the mozzarella cheese.
- Form mixture into 12 meatballs and place in a single layer in the air fryer basket.
- Cook in the air fryer at 350 for 11 minutes.
- Optional: Place meatballs in an air fryer pan, toss in remaining marinara sauce, and top with mozzarella cheese. Place air fryer pan into the basket and cook at 350 for 3 minutes.

Nutritional Value

- Calories: 572kcal | Carbohydrates: 1g | Protein: 46g | Fat: 43g | Saturated Fat: 22g | Cholesterol: 168mg | Sodium: 219mg | Potassium: 606mg | Sugar: 1g | Vitamin A: 355IU | Calcium: 16mg | Iron: 4mg

347. Air Fryer Roast Beef

Prep Time: 5 mins

Cook Time: 35 mins

Total Time: 40 mins

Ingredients

- 2 lb beef roast top round or eye of round is best
- Oil for spraying
- Rub
- 1 tbs kosher salt
- 1 tsp black pepper
- 2 tsp garlic powder
- 1 tsp summer savory or thyme

Instructions

- Mix all rub ingredients and rub into the roast.
- Place fat side down in the basket of the air fryer

(or set up for rotisserie if your air fryer is so equipped)

- Lightly spray with oil.
- Set fryer to 400 degrees F and air fry for 20 minutes; turn fat-side up and spray lightly with oil. Continue cooking for 15 additional minutes at 400 degrees F.
- Remove the roast from the fryer, tent with foil, and let the meat rest for 10 minutes.
- The time given should produce a rare roast which should be 125 degrees F on a meat thermometer. Additional time will be needed for medium, medium-well, and well. Always use a meat thermometer to test the temperature.
- Approximate times for medium and well respectively are 40 minutes and 45 minutes. Remember to always use a meat thermometer as times are approximate and fryers differ by wattage.

Nutrition

- Calories: 238kcal | Carbohydrates: 1g | Protein: 25g | Fat: 14g | Saturated Fat: 6g | Cholesterol: 89mg | Sodium: 1102mg | Potassium: 448mg | Vitamin A: 55IU | Vitamin C: 0.3mg | Calcium: 37mg | Iron: 3mg

348. Air Fryer Stuffed Peppers

Prep Time: 15 Minutes

Cook Time: 15 Minutes

Total Time: 30 Minutes

Ingredients

- 6 Green Bell Peppers
- 1 Lb Lean Ground Beef
- 1 Tbsp Olive Oil
- 1/4 Cup Green Onion Diced
- 1/4 Cup Fresh Parsley
- 1/2 Tsp Ground Sage
- 1/2 Tsp Garlic Salt
- 1 Cup Cooked Rice
- 1 Cup Marinara Sauce More to Taste
- 1/4 Cup Shredded Mozzarella Cheese

Instructions

- Warm-up a medium-sized skillet with the ground

beef and cook until well done.

- Drain the beef and return to the pan.
- Add in the olive oil, green onion, parsley, sage, and salt. Mix this well.
- Add in the cooked rice and marinara, mix well.
- Cut the top off of each pepper and clean the seeds out.
- Scoop the mixture into each of the peppers and place it in the basket of the air fryer. (I did 4 the first round, 2 the second to make them fit.)
- Cook for 10 minutes at 355*, carefully open and add cheese.
- Cook for an additional 5 minutes or until peppers are slightly soft and cheese is melted.
- Serve.

Nutrition Information

- Total Fat: 13g | Saturated Fat: 4g | Trans Fat: 0g | Unsaturated Fat: 7g | Cholesterol: 70mg | Sodium: 419mg | Carbohydrates: 19g | Fiber: 2g | Sugar: 6g | Protein: 25g

349. Air Fryer Steak

Prep Time: 10 mins

Cook Time: 15 mins

Resting Time: 8 mins

Total Time: 30 mins

Ingredients

- 2 (10 to 12 ounces EACH) sirloin steaks, about one inch thick, and at room temperature which is important for proper and even cooking.
- ½ tablespoon olive oil OR olive oil cooking spray, for the steaks
- 1 tablespoon kosher salt
- 1 tablespoon garlic powder
- 1 tablespoon onion powder
- ½ tablespoon paprika, sweet or smoked
- ½ tablespoon freshly ground black pepper
- 2 teaspoons dried herbs of choice

Instructions

- Preheat Air Fryer to 400˚F.
- Rub both steaks with olive oil, or spray with cooking spray, and set aside.
- In a small mixing bowl combine salt, garlic

powder, onion powder, paprika, pepper, and dried herbs. This makes enough seasoning for about 4 large steaks.

- Rub preferred amount of seasoning all over the steaks. Store leftover seasoning blends in a small airtight container and keeps it in a cool, dry place.
- Place 1 steak in the Air Fryer basket and cook for 6 minutes at 400°F.
- If you have a bigger Air Fryer, both steaks can fit in at the same time, but just make sure they aren't one on top of the other. You want a little space between the two.
- Flip over the steak and continue to cook for 4 to 5 more minutes, or until cooked through.
- Please use an Instant Read Thermometer to check for doneness; for a RARE steak, the temperature should register at 125°F to 130°F. For Medium-Rare, you want an internal temperature of 135°F.
- IF the steak isn't cooked through, it may be too thick and you'll want to return the steak to the air fryer and give it a minute or two to finish cooking.
- Repeat the cooking method with the other steak.
- Remove from air fryer and let rest for 5 to 8 minutes before cutting.
- Serve with a pat of butter and garnish with chopped parsley.

Nutrition Facts

- Fat: 17g
- Saturated Fat: 5g
- Cholesterol: 173mg
- Sodium: 3656mg
- Potassium: 1112mg
- Carbohydrates: 8g
- Fiber: 2g
- Sugar: 1g
- Protein: 64g
- Calcium: 99mg
- Iron: 5mg

350. Air Fryer Steak Fajitas

Prep Time: 10 mins

Cook Time: 10 mins

Total Time: 20 mins

Ingredients

- 2 pounds flank steak strips
- 1 packet taco seasoning
- 1/2 red bell pepper, seeded, cored, and sliced
- 1/2 yellow bell pepper, seeded, cored, and sliced
- 1 onion, peeled and sliced
- 2 tablespoons freshly squeezed lime juice
- Cooking spray
- Flour tortillas
- Cilantro, chopped

Instructions

- Season steak with taco seasoning. Marinate for about 20 to 30 minutes.
- Preheat your air fryer to 400 degrees. Spray the air fryer tray with cooking spray,
- Arrange the seasoned beef on the air fryer tray, cooking in batches depending on the size of the air fryer.
- Add a layer of the sliced onions and a layer of bell peppers on top of the meat.
- Place in the air fryer for 10 minutes. Toss halfway through cooking to ensure the steak is cooked evenly.
- Remove from the air fryer and drizzle with lime juice.
- Serve in warm tortillas with fresh cilantro.

Nutrition

- Calories: 620kcal | Carbohydrates: 56g | Protein: 56g | Fat: 17g | Saturated Fat: 6g | Cholesterol: 136mg | Sodium: 1446mg | Potassium: 1014mg | Fiber: 5g | Sugar: 8g | Vitamin A: 1350IU | Vitamin C: 55mg | Calcium: 149mg | Iron: 7mg

351. Air Fryer Taco Calzones

Prep Time: 10 Minutes

Cook Time: 10 Minutes

Total Time: 20 Minutes

Ingredients

- 1 tube Pillsbury thin crust pizza dough
- 1 cup taco meat
- 1 cup shredded cheddar

Instructions

- Spread out your sheet of pizza dough on a clean surface. Using a pizza cutter, cut the dough into 4 even squares.
- Cut each square into a large circle using the pizza cutter. Set the dough scraps aside to make cinnamon sugar bites.
- Top one half of each circle of dough with 1/4 cup taco meat and 1/4 cup shredded cheese.
- Fold the empty half over the meat and cheese and press the edges of the dough together with a fork to seal it tightly. Repeat with all four calzones.
- Gently pick up each calzone and spray it with pan spray or olive oil. Arrange them in your Air Fryer basket.
- Cook the calzones at 325° for 8-10 minutes. Watch them closely at the 8-minute mark so you don't overcook them.
- Serve with salsa and sour cream.
- To make cinnamon sugar bites, cut the scraps of dough into even-sized pieces, about 2 inches long. Add them to the Air Fryer basket and cook at 325° for 5 minutes. Immediately toss with a 1:4 cinnamon-sugar mixture.

Nutrition Information

- Total Fat: 31g | Saturated Fat: 14g | Trans Fat: 1g | Unsaturated Fat: 14g | Cholesterol: 58mg | Sodium: 814mg | Carbohydrates: 38g | Fiber: 2g | Sugar: 1g | Protein: 18g

352. Jalapeno Lime Air Fryer Steak

Prep Time: 5 mins

Cook Time: 10 mins

Marinate Time: 30 mins

Total Time: 45 mins

Servings: 4

Ingredients

- 1 lb flank steak used flat iron – check keywords
- 1 lime juice and zest
- 1 jalapeno, sliced
- 3 cloves of garlic, minced
- 1/2 cup fresh cilantro, roughly chopped
- 2 tablespoons light brown sugar
- 1/2 teaspoon paprika
- 1/2 teaspoon fresh cracked pepper
- 1/4 cup avocado oil
- Salt

Instructions

- Preheat the air fryer to 400F.
- Season the steak with salt and pepper. In a large mixing bowl, combine the avocado oil, paprika, pepper, brown sugar, cilantro, garlic, jalapeño, and lime zest from 1 lime. Add the steak and toss to coat. Marinate for 30 minutes.
- Air fry for 10 minutes for medium-rare, flipping the steak halfway through. When the steak is finished cooking, squeeze lime juice from half a lime over it. Allow it to rest with the air fryer lid open for 10 minutes before slicing. Serve the steak with steamed veggies, over a salad, or in a taco.

Oven Instructions

- To make the steak in the oven, preheat the broiler on high and cook for 6 minutes for medium-rare. Squeeze lime juice from half a lime over the steak and allow it to rest for 10 minutes before slicing. Serve the steak with steamed veggies, over a salad, or in a taco.

Nutrition

- Calories: 312kcal | Carbohydrates: 10g | Protein: 25g | Fat: 19g | Saturated Fat: 4g | Cholesterol: 68mg | Sodium: 64mg | Potassium: 432mg | Fiber: 1g | Sugar: 6g | Vitamin A: 296IU | Vitamin C: 13mg | Calcium: 41mg | Iron: 2mg

353. Air Fryer Ribeye Steak (Frozen + Fresh)

Prep Time: 5 Minutes

Cook Time: 10 Minutes

Additional Time: 30 Minutes

Total Time: 45 Minutes

Ingredients

- 8-ounce ribeye steak, about 1-inch thick
- 1 tablespoon McCormick Montreal Steak

Seasoning

Instructions

- Remove the ribeye steak from the fridge and season with the Montreal Steak seasoning. Let steak rest for about 20 minutes to come to room temperature (to get a more tender juicy steak).
- Preheat your air fryer to 400 degrees.
- Place the ribeye steak in the air fryer and cook for 10-12 minutes, until it reaches 130-135 degrees for medium-rare. Cook for an additional 5 minutes for medium-well.
- Remove the steak from the air fryer and let rest at least 5 minutes before cutting to keep the juices inside the steak then enjoy!

Nutrition Information

- Total Fat: 22g | Saturated Fat: 10g | Trans Fat: 0g | Unsaturated Fat: 12g | Cholesterol: 88mg | Sodium: 789mg | Carbohydrates: 2g | Fiber: 1g | Sugar: 0g | Protein: 29g

354. Air Fryer Beef Chips

Prep Time: 1 minute

Cook Time: 1 hour

Cooling Time: 5 minutes

Total Time: 1 hour 6 minutes

Servings: 2

Ingredients

- 1/2 lb Thinly Sliced Beef we recommend leaner cuts like sirloin
- 1/4 tsp Salt
- 1/4 tsp Black Pepper
- 1/4 tsp Garlic Powder

Instructions

- Gather all the ingredients.
- In a small mixing bowl, combine salt, black pepper, garlic powder and mix well to create the seasoning.
- Lay the beef slices flat and sprinkle seasoning on both sides.
- Transfer beef into the air fryer tray single stacked (very important each slice is single stacked, otherwise they will not get crispy) and air fry for

45-60 minutes at 200F. Once done, let beef slices cool for 5 minutes before enjoying. Note - the time is going to vary greatly depending on thickness.

Nutrition

- Calories: 290kcal | Carbohydrates: 1g | Protein: 20g | Fat: 23g | Saturated Fat: 9g | Cholesterol: 81mg | Sodium: 367mg | Potassium: 306mg | Sugar: 1g | Calcium: 20mg | Iron: 2mg

355. Best Air Fryer Meatloaf With Tangy Sauce | Makes Two

Prep Time: 9 Mins

Cook Time: 20 Mins

Resting Time: 5 Mins

Total Time: 34 Mins

Ingredients

- 1 large egg
- 2 pounds ground chuck or a combination of ground beef and venison or ground sirloin
- 1/2 cup quick-cooking oats
- 3/4 teaspoon salt or garlic salt
- 1/4 teaspoon ground black pepper
- Tangy sauce
- 3/4 cup ketchup
- 2 tablespoons light brown sugar
- 1 tablespoon apple cider vinegar or white vinegar or rice vinegar
- 1 teaspoon worcestershire sauce or soy sauce or liquid amino liquid aminos are gluten-free

Instructions

- To save washing another bowl, start by beating the egg in a large bowl with a fork.
- Break up the ground meat in the bowl. There's no getting around using your hands here. I usually use a pair of nylon/rubber gloves simply for easy cleanup. Gloves may be a luxury this day, though.
- Add quick-cooking oats, salt, and pepper.
- With your hands, gently mix in the egg, oats, salt, and pepper with the ground meat. Overworking the meat will make it tough. Under mixing may leave patches of oats or eggs not evenly incorporated.

- Shape the mixture into 2 free-form loaves, roughly 3 x 5.5 inches. The size will depend on what will fit into your air fryer. (For conventional oven method, see the size in recipe notes) Carefully place the loaves side by side in the preheated air fryer basket or tray.
- Air fry or Roast for about 19 minutes or until meatloaves are done in the middle-firm when pressed in the middle of temperature on an instant-read thermometer reads 155°.
- It's a good idea to check at 17 minutes to make sure they aren't getting too brown. All air fryers are not alike.
- Prepare Tangy Sauce and Spread on Meatloaf
- Stir or whisk together ketchup, brown sugar, vinegar, and Worcestershire sauce.
- When meat waves are 155° or no pink shows in the center, evenly spread the Tangy Sauce over both meatloaves. Cook an additional 1 minute on Air Fry to set the sauce.
- Remove the meatloaves with silicone coated tongs if the air fryer basket is coated with a nonstick surface. Let the meatloaf stand on a cutting board or plate 5 minutes before slicing.

Nutritional Value

- Calories: 572kcal | Carbohydrates: 1g | Protein: 46g | Fat: 43g | Saturated Fat: 22g | Cholesterol: 168mg | Sodium: 219mg | Potassium: 606mg | Sugar: 1g | Vitamin A: 355IU | Calcium: 16mg | Iron: 4mg

---

356. Air Fryer Asian Beef & Veggies

Prep Time: 10 minutes

Cook Time: 8 minutes

Total Time: 18 minutes

Servings: 4 people

Ingredients

- 1 lb sirloin steak cut into strips
- 2 tablespoons cornstarch (or arrowroot powder)
- 1/2 medium yellow onion, sliced
- 1 medium red pepper, sliced into strips
- 3 cloves garlic, minced

- 2 tablespoons grated ginger do not sub dry ground ginger
- 1/4 teaspoon red chili flakes
- 1/2 cup low sodium soy sauce
- 1/4 cup rice vinegar
- 1 tsp sesame oil
- 1/3 cup brown sugar
- 1 teaspoon chinese 5 spice optional
- 1/4 cup water

Instructions

For Freezer Prep

- Add all ingredients to a gallon-sized zip bag. Ensure all of the ingredients are combined.
- Label and freeze for up to 4 months.

To Cook

- Thaw zip bag in the fridge overnight.
- Using tongs, remove the steak and veggies, and transfer to the Air Fryer. Discard the marinade.
- Set the Air Fryer to 400F and the timer to 8 minutes. I like to shake the basket halfway through, but I don't think it is necessary.
- Serve with rice, and garnish with sesame seeds and scallions.

Nutrition

- Calories: 289kcal | Carbohydrates: 27g | Protein: 31g | Fat: 7g | Fiber: 1g | Sugar: 19g

---

357. Kofta Kebabs

Prep Time: 45 mins

Cook Time: 5 mins

Additional Time: 30 mins

Total Time: 1 hr 20 mins

Servings: 28

Ingredient

- 4 cloves garlic, minced
- 1 teaspoon kosher salt
- 1 pound ground lamb

- 3 tablespoons grated onion
- 3 tablespoons chopped fresh parsley
- 1 tablespoon ground coriander
- 1 teaspoon ground cumin
- ½ tablespoon ground cinnamon
- ½ teaspoon ground allspice
- ¼ teaspoon cayenne pepper
- ¼ teaspoon ground ginger
- ¼ teaspoon ground black pepper
- 28 bamboo skewers, soaked in water for 30 minutes

Instructions

- Mash the garlic into a paste with the salt using a mortar and pestle or the flat side of a chef's knife on your cutting board. Mix the garlic into the lamb along with the onion, parsley, coriander, cumin, cinnamon, allspice, cayenne pepper, ginger, and pepper in a mixing bowl until well blended. Form the mixture into 28 balls. Form each ball around the tip of a skewer, flattening into a 2-inch oval; repeat with the remaining skewers. Place the kebabs onto a baking sheet, cover, and refrigerate for at least 30 minutes or up to 12 hours.
- Preheat an outdoor grill for medium heat, and lightly oil grate.
- Cook the skewers on the preheated grill, turning occasionally, until the lamb has cooked to your desired degree of doneness, about 6 minutes for medium.

Nutrition Facts

- Calories: 35; Protein 2.9g; Carbohydrates 0.6g; Fat 2.3g; Cholesterol 10.8mg; Sodium 78.2mg.

358. Simple Grilled Lamb Chops

Prep Time: 10 mins

Cook Time: 6 mins

Additional Time: 2 hrs

Total Time: 2 hrs 16 mins

Servings: 6

Ingredient

- ¼ cup distilled white vinegar
- 2 teaspoons salt

- ½ teaspoon black pepper
- 1 tablespoon minced garlic
- 1 onion, thinly sliced
- 2 tablespoons olive oil
- 2 pounds lamb chops

Instructions

- Mix together the vinegar, salt, pepper, garlic, onion, and olive oil in a large resealable bag until the salt has dissolved. Add lamb, toss until coated, and marinate in the refrigerator for 2 hours.
- Preheat an outdoor grill for medium-high heat.
- Remove lamb from the marinade and leave any onions on that stick to the meat. Discard any remaining marinade. Wrap the exposed ends of the bones with aluminum foil to keep them from burning. Grill to desired doneness, about 3 minutes per side for medium. The chops may also be broiled in the oven for about 5 minutes per side for medium.

Nutrition Facts

- Calories: 519; Protein 25g; Carbohydrates 2.3g; Fat 44.8g; Cholesterol 112mg; Sodium 861mg.

359. Roast Leg Of Lamb

Prep Time: 15 mins

Cook Time: 1 hr 45 mins

Additional Time: 10 mins

Total Time: 2 hrs 10 mins

Servings: 12

Ingredient

- 4 cloves garlic, sliced
- 2 tablespoons fresh rosemary
- Salt to taste
- Ground black pepper to taste
- 5 pounds leg of lamb

Instructions

- Preheat oven to 350 degrees F (175 degrees C).
- Cut slits in the top of the leg of lamb every 3 to 4 inches, deep enough to push slices of garlic down into the meat. Salt and pepper generously all

over the top of the lamb, place several sprigs of fresh rosemary under and on top of the lamb. Place lamb on roasting pan.

- Roast in the preheated oven until the lamb is cooked to your desired doneness, about 1 3/4 to 2 hours. Do not overcook the lamb, the flavor is best if the meat is still slightly pink. Let rest at least 10 minutes before carving.

Nutrition Facts

- Calories: 382; Protein 35.8g; Carbohydrates 0.4g; Fat 25.3g; Cholesterol 136.1mg; Sodium 136.3mg.

360. Roasted Lamb Breast

Prep Time: 30 mins

Cook Time: 2 hrs 25 mins

Total Time: 2 hrs 55 mins

Servings: 4

Ingredient

- 2 tablespoons olive oil
- 2 teaspoons salt
- 2 teaspoons ground cumin
- 1 teaspoon freshly ground black pepper
- 1 teaspoon dried Italian herb seasoning
- 1 teaspoon ground cinnamon
- 1 teaspoon ground coriander
- 1 teaspoon paprika
- 4 pounds lamb breast, separated into two pieces
- ½ cup chopped Italian flat-leaf parsley
- ⅓ cup white wine vinegar, more as needed
- 1 lemon, juiced
- 2 cloves garlic, crushed
- 1 teaspoon honey
- ½ teaspoon red pepper flakes
- 1 pinch salt

Instructions

- Preheat oven to 300 degrees F (150 degrees C).
- Combine chopped parsley, vinegar, fresh lemon juice, garlic, honey, red pepper flakes, and salt in a large bowl. Mix well and set aside.
- Whisk olive oil, salt, cumin, black pepper, dried Italian herbs, cinnamon, coriander, and paprika in a large bowl until combined.

- Coat each lamb breast in the olive oil and spice mixture and transfer to a roasting pan, fat side up.
- Tightly cover the roasting pan with aluminum foil and bake in the preheated oven until the meat is tender when pierced with a fork, about 2 hours.
- Remove lamb from the oven and cut into four pieces.
- Increase oven temperature to 450 degrees F (230 degrees C).
- Line a baking sheet with aluminum foil and place lamb pieces on it. Brush the tops of each piece with fat drippings from the roasting pan.
- Bake lamb until meat is browned and edges are crispy about 20 minutes.
- Increase the oven's broiler to high and brown lamb for 4 minutes. Remove from oven.
- Serve lamb topped with parsley and vinegar sauce.

Nutrition Facts

- Calories: 622; Protein 46.2g; Carbohydrates 7.7g; Fat 45.3g; Cholesterol 180.4mg; Sodium 1301.6mg.

361. Moroccan Lamb Stew With Apricots

Prep Time: 30 mins

Cook Time: 1 hr 55 mins

Total Time: 2 hrs 25 mins

Servings: 4

Ingredient

- 2 pounds boneless leg of lamb, cut into 1-inch cubes
- 2 teaspoons ground coriander
- 1 teaspoon ground cumin
- 1 teaspoon sweet paprika
- ½ teaspoon cayenne pepper
- ½ teaspoon ground cardamom
- ½ teaspoon ground turmeric
- 2 teaspoons kosher salt
- 2 tablespoons olive oil
- 2 cups finely chopped onion
- 4 cloves garlic, minced
- 1 tablespoon minced fresh ginger root
- 2 (3 inches) cinnamon sticks

- 2 cups low-sodium chicken stock
- 1 cup dried apricots, halved
- 2 (3 inches) orange peel strips
- 1 tablespoon honey
- ¼ cup chopped fresh cilantro
- ¼ cup toasted pine nuts

Instructions

- Combine lamb, coriander, cumin, paprika, cayenne, cardamom, turmeric, and salt in a large bowl; toss together until lamb is evenly coated.
- Heat oil in a large Dutch oven or tagine over medium heat. Add onions; cook, stirring occasionally until soft and translucent, about 5 minutes. Stir in garlic, ginger, and cinnamon; cook, stirring frequently, until fragrant, about 1 minute. Add seasoned lamb; cook, stirring frequently until light brown, being careful not to caramelize, about 2 minutes. Add chicken stock and bring to a gentle boil over medium heat. Reduce heat to low and simmer, covered, until the lamb is just tender, about 1 hour and 15 minutes.
- Stir in apricots, orange peels, and honey; continue to simmer over low heat, uncovered, until the liquid has thickened slightly and lamb is fork-tender, about 30 minutes. Remove from the heat, discard cinnamon sticks and orange peels.
- Divide evenly among 4 bowls. Garnish each bowl with a tablespoon each of cilantro and pine nuts.

Nutrition Facts

- Calories: 553; Protein 44.5g; Carbohydrates 40.9g; Fat 24.8g; Cholesterol 125.5mg; Sodium 1129.7mg.

---

362. Slow Cooker Lamb Chops

Prep Time: 15 mins

Cook Time: 4 hrs 30 mins

Additional Time: 5 mins

Total Time: 4 hrs 50 mins

Servings: 6

Ingredient

- ½ cup red wine
- ½ sweet onion, roughly chopped

- 3 tablespoons honey
- 2 tablespoons Dijon mustard
- 2 tablespoons lemon juice
- 4 garlic cloves, minced
- 1 tablespoon ground thyme
- 1 tablespoon dried rosemary
- 2 teaspoons ground basil
- 1 teaspoon salt
- 1 teaspoon coarse ground black pepper
- ¼ cup tapioca starch
- 1 ½ pound sirloin lamb chops, room temperature

Instructions

- Combine red wine and onion in a slow cooker.
- Whisk honey, mustard, lemon juice, garlic, thyme, rosemary, basil, salt, and pepper together in a small bowl until well blended. Add tapioca starch and whisk until well combined. Let sit until the mixture is thickened, at least 5 minutes.
- Dip lamb chops in the mustard mixture and massage until fully coated.
- Place chops in a single layer over the red wine and onion mixture in the slow cooker. Pour the remaining mustard mixture on top.
- Cover slow cooker and cook on Low until an instant-read thermometer inserted into the center of a chop reads at least 130 degrees F (54 degrees C), about 4 1/2 hours.

Nutrition Facts

- Calories: 209; Protein 13g; Carbohydrates 18.5g; Fat 7.7g; Cholesterol 43.6mg; Sodium 550.5mg.

---

363. Grilled Leg Of Lamb Steaks

Prep Time: 10 mins

Cook Time: 10 mins

Additional Time: 30 mins

Total: 50 mins

Servings: 4

Ingredient

- 4 bone-in lamb steaks
- ¼ cup olive oil
- 4 large cloves garlic, minced

- 1 tablespoon chopped fresh rosemary
- Salt and ground black pepper to taste

Instructions

- Place lamb steaks in a single layer in a shallow dish. Cover with olive oil, garlic, rosemary, salt, and pepper. Flip steaks to coat both sides. Let sit until steaks absorb flavors, about 30 minutes.
- Preheat an outdoor grill for high heat and lightly oil the grate. Cook steaks until browned on the outside and slightly pink in the center, about 5 minutes per side for medium. An instant-read thermometer inserted into the center should read at least 140 degrees F (60 degrees C).

Nutrition Facts

- Calories: 327; Protein 29.6g; Carbohydrates 1.7g; Fat 21.9g; Cholesterol 92.9mg; Sodium 112.1mg.

364. Easy Meatloaf

Prep Time: 10 mins

Cook Time: 1 hr

Total Time: 1 hr 10 mins

Servings: 8

Ingredient

- 1 ½ pounds ground beef
- 1 egg
- 1 onion, chopped
- 1 cup milk
- 1 cup dried bread crumbs
- Salt and pepper to taste
- 2 tablespoons brown sugar
- 2 tablespoons prepared mustard
- ⅓ cup ketchup

Instructions

- Preheat oven to 350 degrees F (175 degrees C).
- In a large bowl, combine the beef, egg, onion, milk, and bread OR cracker crumbs. Season with salt and pepper to taste and place in a lightly greased 9x5-inch loaf pan, or form into a loaf and place in a lightly greased 9x13-inch baking dish.
- In a separate small bowl, combine the brown sugar, mustard, and ketchup. Mix well and pour over the meatloaf.

- Bake at 350 degrees F (175 degrees C) for 1 hour.

Nutrition Facts

- Calories: 372; Protein 18.2g; Carbohydrates 18.5g; Fat 24.7g; Cholesterol 98mg; Sodium 334.6mg.

365. Classic Meatloaf

Prep: 30 mins

Cook: 45 mins

Total: 1 hr 15 mins

Servings: 10

Meatloaf Ingredients:

- 1 carrot, coarsely chopped
- 1 rib celery, coarsely chopped
- ½ onion, coarsely chopped
- ½ red bell pepper, coarsely chopped
- 4 white mushrooms, coarsely chopped
- 3 cloves garlic, coarsely chopped
- 2 ½ pounds ground chuck
- 1 tablespoon Worcestershire sauce
- 1 egg, beaten
- 1 teaspoon dried Italian herbs
- 2 teaspoons salt
- 1 teaspoon ground black pepper
- ½ teaspoon cayenne pepper
- 1 cup plain bread crumbs
- 1 teaspoon olive oil

Glaze Ingredients:

- 2 tablespoons brown sugar
- 2 tablespoons ketchup
- 2 tablespoons dijon mustard
- Hot pepper sauce to taste

Instructions

- Preheat the oven to 325 degrees F.
- Place the carrot, celery, onion, red bell pepper, mushrooms, and garlic in a food processor, and pulse until very finely chopped, almost to a puree. Place the minced vegetables into a large mixing bowl, and mix in ground chuck, Worcestershire sauce, and egg. Add Italian herbs, salt, black pepper, and cayenne pepper. Mix gently with a wooden spoon to incorporate

vegetables and egg into the meat. Pour in bread crumbs. With your hand, gently mix in the crumbs with your fingertips just until combined, about 1 minute.

- Form the meatloaf into a ball. Pour olive oil into a baking dish and place the ball of meat into the dish. Shape the ball into a loaf, about 4 inches high by 6 inches across.
- Bake in the preheated oven just until the meatloaf is hot, about 15 minutes.
- Meanwhile, in a small bowl, mix together brown sugar, ketchup, Dijon mustard, and hot sauce. Stir until the brown sugar has dissolved.
- Remove the meatloaf from the oven. With the back of a spoon, smooth the glaze onto the top of the meatloaf, then pull a little bit of glaze down the sides of the meatloaf with the back of the spoon.
- Return meatloaf to the oven, and bake until the loaf is no longer pink inside and the glaze has baked onto the loaf, 30 to 40 more minutes. An instant-read thermometer inserted into the thickest part of the loaf should read at least 160 degrees F (70 degrees C). Cooking time will depend on the shape and thickness of the meatloaf.

Nutrition Facts

- Calories: 284; Protein 21.6g; Carbohydrates 14.8g; Fat 14.9g; Cholesterol 85.3mg; Sodium 755.4mg.

---

366. Salisbury Steak

Prep Time: 20 mins

Cook Time: 20 mins

Total Time: 40 mins

Servings: 6

Ingredient

- 1 (10.5 ounces) can condense French onion soup
- 1 ½ pounds ground beef
- ½ cup dry bread crumbs
- 1 egg
- ¼ teaspoon salt
- ⅛ teaspoon ground black pepper
- 1 tablespoon all-purpose flour

- ¼ cup ketchup
- ¼ cup water
- 1 tablespoon Worcestershire sauce
- ½ teaspoon mustard powder

Instructions

- In a large bowl, mix together 1/3 cup condensed French onion soup with ground beef, bread crumbs, egg, salt, and black pepper. Shape into 6 oval patties.
- In a large skillet over medium-high heat, brown both sides of patties. Pour off excess fat.
- In a small bowl, blend flour and remaining soup until smooth. Mix in ketchup, water, Worcestershire sauce, and mustard powder. Pour over meat in skillet. Cover, and cook for 20 minutes, stirring occasionally.

Nutrition Facts

- Calories: 440; Protein 23g; Carbohydrates 14.1g; Fat 32.3g; Cholesterol 127.5mg; Sodium 818.3mg.

8. Air Fryer Vegetables Recipes

367. Nutty Pumpkin with Blue Cheese

Prep Time : 30 minutes

Ingredients:

- ½ small pumpkin
- 2 oz. blue cheese, cubed
- 2 tbsp. pine nuts 1 tbsp. olive oil ½ cup baby spinach, packed
- 1 spring onion, sliced
- 1 radish, thinly sliced
- 1 tsp. vinegar

Instructions:

- Preheat the air fryer to 330 degrees F.
- Place the pine nuts in a baking dish and toast them for 5 minutes. Set aside. Peel the pumpkin and chop it into small pieces.
- Place in the baking dish and toss with the olive oil. I
- ncrease the temperature to 390 degrees and cook the pumpkin for about 20 minutes.
- Make sure to toss every 5 minutes or so. Place the pumpkin in a serving bowl.
- Add baby spinach, radish and spring onion. Toss with the vinegar.
- Stir in the cubed blue cheese. Top with the toasted pine nuts.

Nutrition Facts

Calories 495, Carbohydrates 29 g, Fat 27 g, Protein 9 g

368. Eggplant Cheeseburger

Prep Time: 10 minutes

Ingredients:

- 1 hamburger bun
- 1 2-inch eggplant slice, cut along the round axis
- 1 mozzarella slice Red onion cut into 3 rings
- 1 lettuce leaf
- ½ tbsp. tomato sauce
- 1 pickle, sliced

Instructions:

- Preheat the air fryer to 330 degrees F.

- Place the eggplant slice and roast for 6 minutes.
- Place the mozzarella slice on top of the eggplant and cook for 30 more seconds.
- Spread the tomato sauce on one half of the bun.
- Place the lettuce leaf on top of the sauce.
- Place the cheesy eggplant on top of the lettuce.
- Top with onion rings and pickles.
- Top with the other bun half and enjoy.

Nutrition Facts

Calories 399, Carbohydrates 21 g, Fat 17 g, Protein 8 g

369. Veggie Meatballs

Prep Time: 30 minutes

Ingredients:

- 2 tbsp. olive oil
- 2 tbsp. soy sauce
- 1 tbsp. flax meal
- 2 cups cooked chickpeas
- ½ cup sweet onion, diced
- ½ cup grated carrots
- ½ cup roasted cashews Juice of 1 lemon
- ½ tsp. turmeric 1 tsp. cumin
- 1 tsp. garlic powder
- 1 cup rolled oats

Instructions:

- Preheat the air fryer to 350 degrees F.
- Combine the oil, onions, and carrots into a baking dish and cook them in the air fryer for 5 minutes.
- Meanwhile, ground the oats and cashews in a food processor. Place them in a large bowl. Process the chickpeas with the lemon juice and soy sauce, until smooth. Add them to the bowl as well.
- Add the onions and carrots to the bowl with the chickpeas.
- Stir in all of the remaining ingredients, and mix until fully incorporated. Make 12 meatballs out of the mixture.
- Increase the temperature to 370 degrees. Cook the meatballs for about 12 minutes..

Nutrition Facts

Calories 288, Carbohydrates 32 g, Fat 21 g, Protein 6 g

370. Crunchy Parmesan Zucchini

Prep Time: 40 minutes

Ingredients:

- 4 small zucchini cut lengthwise
- ½ cup grated Parmesan cheese
- ½ cup breadcrumbs
- ¼ cup melted butter
- ¼ cup chopped parsley
- 4 garlic cloves, minced
- Salt and pepper, to taste

Instructions:

- Preheat the air fryer to 350 degrees F. In a bowl, mix the breadcrumbs, Parmesan, garlic, and parsley. Season with some salt and pepper, to taste.
- Stir in the melted butter. Arrange the zucchinis with the cut side up. Spread the mixture onto the zucchini evenly.
- Place half of the zucchinis in your air fryer and cook for 13 minutes.
- Increase the temperature to 370 degrees F and cook for 3 more minutes for extra crunchiness. Repeat with the other batch.

Nutrition Facts

Calories 369, Carbohydrates 14 g, Fat 12 g, Protein 9.5 g

371. Chili Bean Burritos

Prep Time: 30 minutes

Ingredients:

- 6 tortillas
- 1 cup grated cheddar cheese
- 1 can (8 oz.) beans
- 1 tsp. seasoning, by choice

Instructions:

- Preheat the air fryer to 350 degrees F.
- Mix the beans with the seasoning.
- Divide the bean mixture between the tortillas. Top the beans with cheddar cheese.
- Roll the burritos and arrange them on a lined baking dish.
- Place in the air fryer and cook for 5 minutes, or to your liking. Serve as desired (I recommend

salsa dipping)

Nutrition Facts

Calories 248, Carbohydrates 25 g, Fat 8.7 g, Protein 9 g

372. Spinach and Feta Crescent Triangles

Prep Time: 20 minutes

Ingredients:

- 14 oz. store-bought crescent dough
- 1 cup steamed spinach
- 1 cup crumbled feta cheese
- ¼ tsp. garlic powder
- 1 tsp. chopped oregano
- ¼ tsp. salt

Instructions:

- Preheat the air fryer to 350 degrees F.
- Roll the dough onto a lightly floured flat surface.
- Combine the feta, spinach, oregano, salt, and garlic powder together in a bowl.
- Cut the dough into 4 equal pieces.
- Divide the spinach/feta mixture between the dough pieces.
- Make sure to place the filling in the center. Fold the dough and secure with a fork.
- Place onto a lined baking dish, and then in the air fryer.
- Cook for about 12 minutes, or until lightly browned.

Nutrition Facts

Calories 178, Carbohydrates 10.8 g, Fat 11.9 g, Protein 8g

373. Ratatouille

Prep Time: 30 minutes

Ingredients:

- 1 tbsp. olive oil
- 3 roma tomatoes, thinly sliced
- 2 garlic cloves, minced
- 1 zucchini, thinly sliced
- 2 yellow bell peppers, sliced
- 1 tbsp. vinegar
- 2 tbsp. Herbs de Provence

- Salt and pepper, to taste

Instructions:

- Preheat the air fryer to 390 degrees F.
- Place all of the ingredients in a bowl.
- Season with some salt and pepper, and stir until the veggies are well coated.
- Arrange the vegetable in a round baking dish and place in the air fryer.
- Cook for about 15 minutes, shaking occasionally.
- Let sit for 5 more minutes after the time goes off.

Nutrition Facts

Calories 171, Carbohydrates 25.8 g, Fat 7.8 g, Protein 4.2 g

---

374. Cabbage Steaks

Prep Time: 25 minutes

Ingredients:

- 1 cabbage head
- 1 tbsp. garlic stir-in paste
- 1 tsp. salt
- 2 tbsp. olive oil
- ½ tsp. black pepper
- 2 tsp. fennel seeds

Instructions:

- Preheat the air fryer to 350 degrees F.
- Slice the cabbage into 1-½ inch slices.
- In a small bowl combine all of the other ingredients.
- Brush the cabbage with the mixture.
- Arrange the cabbage steaks in your air fryer and cook for 15 minutes.

Nutrition Facts

Calories 161, Carbohydrates 17.5 g, Fat 10 g, Protein 4.6 g

---

375. Vegetable Spring Rolls

Prep Time: 15 minutes

Ingredients:

½ cabbage, grated

2 carrots, grated

1 tsp. minced ginger

1 tsp. minced garlic

1 tsp. sesame oil1 tsp. soy sauce

1 tsp. sesame seeds½ tsp. salt

1 tsp. olive oil

1 package spring roll wrappers (8 to 10 wrappers)

Instructions:

- Preheat the air fryer to 370 degrees F.
- Combine all of the ingredients in a large bowl.
- Divide the mixture between the spring roll sheets, and roll them up.
- Arrange on the baking mat. Cook in the air fryer for about 5 minutes.
- Serve with your favorite dipping sauce.

Nutrition Facts

Calories 169.1, Carbohydrates 32.3 g, Fat 2.3 g, Protein 5.5 g

---

376. Stuffed Mushrooms

Prep Time: 15 minutes

Ingredients:

- 3 Portobello mushrooms
- 1 tomato, diced
- 1 small red onion, diced
- 1 green bell pepper, diced
- ½ cup grated mozzarella cheese
- ½ tsp. garlic powder
- ¼ tsp. pepper
- ¼ tsp. salt

Instructions:

- Preheat the air fryer to 330 degrees F.
- Wash the mushrooms, remove the stems, and pat them dry.
- Coat them with the olive oil.
- Combine all of the remaining ingredients, except the mozzarella, in a small bowl.
- Divide the filling between the mushrooms. Top the mushrooms with mozzarella.

- Place in the air fryer and cook for 8 minutes.

Nutrition Facts

Calories 111, Carbohydrates 12.3 g, Fat 3.8 g, Protein 8.9 g

377. Cauliflower Rice

Prep Time: 30 minutes

Ingredients:

- Tofu: ½ block tofu
- ½ cup diced onion
- 2 tbsp. soy sauce
- 1 tsp. turmeric
- 1 cup diced carrot
- Cauliflower: 3 cups cauliflower rice (pulsed in a food processor)
- 2 tbsp. soy sauce
- ½ cup chopped broccoli
- 2 garlic cloves, minces
- 1-½ tsp. toasted sesame oil
- 1 tbsp. minced ginger
- ½ cup frozen peas
- 1 tbsp. rice vinegar

Instructions:

Preheat the air fryer to 370 degrees F. Crumble the tofu and combine it with all of the tofu ingredients .Place in a baking dish and air fry for 10 minutes. Meanwhile, place all of the cauliflower ingredients in a large bowl. Mix to combine well. Add the cauliflower mixture to the tofu and stir to combine. Cook for 12 minutes.

Nutrition Facts

Calories 137, Carbohydrates 19.7 g, Fat 4 g, Protein 10.2 g

378. Pasta with Roasted Veggies

Prep Time: 25 minutes

Ingredients:

- 1 lb. penne, cooked
- 1 zucchini, sliced
- 1 pepper, sliced
- 1 acorn squash, sliced
- 4 oz. mushrooms, sliced
- ½ cup kalamata olives, pitted and halved
- ¼ cup olive oil
- 1 tsp. Italian seasoning
- 1 cup grape tomatoes, halved
- 3 tbsp. balsamic vinegar
- 2 tbsp. chopped basil
- Salt and pepper, to taste

Instructions:

- Preheat the air fryer to 380 degrees F.
- Combine the pepper, zucchini, squash, mushrooms, and olive oil, in a large bowl. Season with some salt and pepper.
- Air fry the veggies for 15 minutes. In a large bowl, combine the penne, roasted vegetables, olives, tomatoes, Italian seasoning, and vinegar.
- Divide between 6 serving bowls and sprinkle basil.

Nutrition Facts

Calories 391, Carbohydrates 64.4 g, Fat 14.4 g, Protein 9.5 g

379. Poblano and Tomato Stuffed Squash

Prep Time: 50 minutes

Ingredients:

- ½ butternut squash
- 6 grape tomatoes, halved
- 1 poblano pepper, cut into strips
- ¼ cup grated mozzarella, optional
- 2 tsp. olive oil divided
- Salt and pepper, to taste

Instructions:

- Preheat the air fryer to 350 degrees F. Meanwhile, cut trim the ends and cut the squash lengthwise.
- You will only need one half for this recipe. Scoop the flash out, so you make room for the filling.
- Brush 1 tsp. oil over the squash. Place in the air fryer and roast for 30 minutes.
- Combine the other teaspoon of olive oil with the tomatoes and poblanos. Season with salt and pepper, to taste.
- Place the peppers and tomatoes into the squash.
- Cook for 15 more minutes.

- If using mozzarella, add it on top of the squash, two minutes before the end.

Nutrition Facts

Calories 98, Carbohydrates 8.2 g, Fat 5.3 g, Protein 4.3 g

380. Spicy Pepper, Sweet Potato Skewers

Prep Time: 20 minutes

4.9 g

Ingredients:

- 1 large sweet potato
- 1 beetroot
- 1 green bell pepper
- 1 tsp. chili flakes
- ¼ tsp. black pepper
- ½ tsp. turmeric
- ¼ tsp. garlic powder
- ¼ tsp. paprika 1 tbsp. olive oil

Instructions:

- Soak 3 to 4 skewers until ready to use.
- Preheat the air fryer to 350 degrees F.
- Peel the veggies and cut them into bite-sized chunks.
- Place the chunks in a bowl along with the remaining ingredients.
- Mix until fully coated. Thread the veggies in this order: potato, pepper, beetroot.
- Place in the air fryer and cook for 15 minutes.

Nutrition Facts

Calories 335, Carbohydrates 49.6 g, Fat 14.3 g, Protein

381. Grilled Tofu Sandwich

Prep Time: 20 minutes

Ingredients:

- 2 slices of bread
- 1 1-inch thick Tofu slice
- ¼ cup red cabbage, shredded
- 2 tsp. olive oil divided ¼ tsp. vinegar Salt and pepper, to taste

Instructions:

- Preheat the air fryer to 350 degrees F.
- Place the bread slices and toast for 3

minutes. Set aside.
- Brush the tofu with 1 tsp. oil and place in the basket of your air fryer. grill for 5 minutes on each side.
- Combine the cabbage, remaining oil, and vinegar, and season with salt and pepper.
- Place the tofu on top of one bread slice, place the cabbage over, and top with the other bread slice.

Nutrition Facts

Calories 225.8, Carbohydrates 21.5 g, Fat 30.5 g, Protein 12.3g

382. Quinoa and Veggie Stuffed Peppers

Prep Time: 16 minutes

Ingredients:

- ¼ cup cooked quinoa
- 1 bell pepper
- ½ tbsp. diced onion
- ½ diced tomato, plus one tomato slice
- ¼ tsp. smoked paprika
- Salt and pepper, to taste 1 tsp. olive oil
- ¼ tsp. dried basil

Instructions:

- Preheat the air fryer to 350 degrees F.
- Core and clean the bell pepper to prepare it for stuffing.
- Brush the pepper with half of the olive oil on the outside. In a small bowl, combine all of the other ingredients, except the tomato slice and reserved half-teaspoon olive oil.
- Stuff the pepper with the filling. Top with the tomato slice.
- Brush the tomato slice with the remaining half-teaspoon of olive oil and sprinkle with basil.
- Air fry for 10 minutes.

Nutrition Facts

Calories 190, Carbohydrates 29.6 g, Fat 6.6 g, Protein 5.7 g

383. Avocado Rolls

Prep Time: 15 minutes

Ingredients:

- 3 ripe avocados, pitted and peeled
- 10 egg roll wrappers
- 1 tomato, diced
- ¼ tsp. pepper
- ½ tsp. salt

Instructions:

- Place all of the filling ingredients in a bowl.
- Mash with a fork until somewhat smooth. There should be chunks left.
- Divide the feeling between the egg wrappers.
- Wet your finger and brush along the edges, so the wrappers can seal well. Roll and seal the wrappers.
- Arrange them on a baking sheet lined dish, and place in the air fryer.
- Air fry at 350 degrees F, for 5 minutes. Serve with favorite dipping (I recommend a chili one)

Nutrition Facts

Calories 270, Carbohydrates 24.7 g, Fat 18.7 g, Protein 5.8g

---

384. Simple Air Fried Ravioli

Prep Time: 15 minutes

Ingredients:

- 1 package cheese ravioli
- 2 cup Italian breadcrumbs
- ¼ cup Parmesan cheese
- 1 cup buttermilk
- 1 tsp. olive oil
- ¼ tsp. garlic powder

Instructions:

- Preheat the air fryer to 390 degrees F.
- In a small bowl, combine the breadcrumbs, Parmesan cheese, garlic powder, and olive oil.
- Dip the ravioli in the buttermilk and then coat them with the breadcrumb mixture.
- Line a baking sheet with parchment paper and arrange the ravioli on it.
- Place in the air fryer and cook for 5 minutes.
- Serve the air-fried ravioli with favorite sauce (I used simple marinara jar sauce)

Nutrition Facts

Calories 298.8, Carbohydrates 42.1 g, Fat 8.7 g, Protein 13.4 g

---

385. Veggie Kebab

Prep Time: 20 minutes

Ingredients:

- 2 tbsp. corn flour
- 2/3 cup canned beans
- 1/3 cup grated carrots
- 2 boiled and mashed potatoes
- ¼ cup chopped fresh mint leaves½ tsp. garam masala powder
- ½ cup paneer
- 1 green chili1-inch piece of fresh ginger
- 3 garlic clovesSalt, to taste

Instructions:

- Soak 12 skewers until ready to use.
- Preheat the air fryer to 390 degrees F.
- Place the beans, carrots, garlic, ginger, chili, paneer, and mint, in a food processor and process until smooth.
- Transfer to a bowl. Add the mashed potatoes, corn flour, some salt, and garam masala powder to the bowl.
- Mix until fully incorporate. Divide the mixture into 12 equal pieces. (Mine were lemon-sized.)Shape each of the pieces around a skewer.
- Air fry the skewers for 10 minutes.

Nutrition Facts

Calories 211, Carbohydrates 25 g, Fat 11.4 g, Protein 8 g

---

386. Roasted Vegetable Salad

Prep Time: 25 minutes

Ingredients:

- 1 potato, peeled and chopped
- ¼ onion, sliced
- 1 carrot, sliced diagonally
- ½ small beetroot, sliced
- 1 cup cherry tomatoes
- Juice of 1 lemon
- Handful of rocket salad
- Handful of baby spinach

- 3 tbsp. canned chickpeas
- ½ tsp. cumin
- ½ tsp. turmeric
- ¼ tsp. sea salt
- 2 tbsp. olive oil
- Parmesan shavings

Instructions:

- Preheat the air fryer to 370 degrees F.
- Combine the onion, potato, cherry tomatoes, carrot, beetroot, cumin, seas salt, turmeric, and 1 tbsp. olive oil, in a bowl.
- Place in the air fryer and cook for 20 minutes. Let cool for 2 minutes. Place the rocket, salad, spinach, lemon juice, and 1 tbsp. olive oil, into a serving bowl.
- Mix to combine. Stir in the roasted veggies.
- Top with chickpeas and Parmesan shavings.

Nutrition Facts

Calories 263.8, Carbohydrates 21.4 g, Fat 12 g, Protein 10.7 g

387. Stuffed Meatballs

Preparation time: 10 minutes Cooking time: 10 minutes

Ingredients:

- 1/3 cup bread crumbs
- 3 tablespoons milk
- 1 tablespoon ketchup
- 1 egg
- ½ teaspoon marjoram, dried
- Salt and black pepper to the taste
- 1 pound lean beef, ground
- 20 cheddar cheese cubes
- 1 tablespoon olive oil

Instructions:

- In a bowl, mix bread crumbs with ketchup, milk, marjoram, salt, pepper and egg and whisk well.
- Add beef, stir and shape 20 meatballs out of this mix.
- Shape each meatball around a cheese cube, drizzle the oil over them and rub.
- Place all meatballs in your preheated air fryer

and cook at 390 degrees F for 10 minutes.
- Serve them for lunch with a side salad.

Nutrition Facts:

calories 200, fat 5, fiber 8, carbs 12, protein 5

388. Steaks and Cabbage

Preparation time: 10 minutes Cooking time: 10 minutes

Ingredients:

- ½ pound sirloin steak, cut into strips
- 2 teaspoons cornstarch
- 1 tablespoon peanut oil
- 2 cups green cabbage, chopped
- 1 yellow bell pepper, chopped
- 2 green onions, chopped
- 2 garlic cloves, minced
- Salt and black pepper to the taste

Instructions:

- In a bowl, mix cabbage with salt, pepper and peanut oil, toss, transfer to air fryer's basket, cook at 370 degrees F for 4 minutes and transfer to a bowl.
- Add steak strips to your air fryer, also add green onions, bell pepper, garlic, salt and pepper, toss and cook for 5 minutes.
- Add over cabbage, toss, divide among plates and serve for lunch.

Nutrition Facts:

calories 282, fat 6, fiber 8, carbs 14, protein 6

389. Succulent Lunch Turkey Breast

Preparation time: 10 minutes Cooking time: 47 minutes

Ingredients:

- 1 big turkey breast
- 2 teaspoons olive oil
- ½ teaspoon smoked paprika
- 1 teaspoon thyme, dried
- ½ teaspoon sage, dried
- Salt and black pepper to the taste
- 2 tablespoons mustard
- ¼ cup maple syrup
- 1 tablespoon butter, soft

Instructions:

- Brush turkey breast with the olive oil, season with salt, pepper, thyme, paprika and sage, rub, place in your air fryer's basket and fry at 350 degrees F for 25 minutes.
- Flip turkey, cook for 10 minutes more, flip one more time and cook for another 10 minutes.
- Meanwhile, heat up a pan with the butter over medium heat, add mustard and maple syrup, stir well, cook for a couple of minutes and take off heat.
- Slice turkey breast, divide among plates and serve with the maple glaze drizzled on top.

Nutrition Facts:

calories 280, fat 2, fiber 7, carbs 16, protein 14

390. Italian Eggplant Sandwich

Preparation time: 10 minutes Cooking time: 16 minutes

Ingredients:

- 1 eggplant, sliced
- 2 teaspoons parsley, dried
- Salt and black pepper to the taste
- ½ cup breadcrumbs
- ½ teaspoon Italian seasoning
- ½ teaspoon garlic powder
- ½ teaspoon onion powder
- 2 tablespoons milk
- 4 bread slices
- ½ cup mayonnaise
- ¾ cup tomato sauce
- 2 cups mozzarella cheese, grated

Instructions:

- Season eggplant slices with salt and pepper, leave aside for 10 minutes and then pat dry them well.
- In a bowl, mix parsley with breadcrumbs, Italian seasoning, onion and garlic powder, salt and black pepper and stir.
- In another bowl, mix milk with mayo and whisk well.
- Brush eggplant slices with mayo mix, dip them in breadcrumbs, place them in your air fryer's basket, spray with cooking oil and cook them at

400 degrees F for 15 minutes, flipping them after 8 minutes.
- Brush each bread slice with olive oil and arrange 2 on a working surface.
- Add mozzarella and parmesan on each, add baked eggplant slices, spread tomato sauce and basil and top with the other bread slices, greased side down.
- Divide sandwiches on plates, cut them in halves and serve for lunch.

Nutrition Facts:

calories 324, fat 16, fiber 4, carbs 39, protein 12

391. Creamy Chicken Stew

Preparation time: 10 minutes Cooking time: 25 minutes

Ingredients:

1 and ½ cups canned cream of celery soup

6 chicken tenders

Salt and black pepper to the taste

2 potatoes, chopped

1 bay leaf

1 thyme spring, chopped

1 tablespoon milk

1 egg yolk

½ cup heavy cream

Instructions:

- In a bowl, mix chicken with cream of celery, potatoes, heavy cream, bay leaf, thyme, salt and pepper, toss, pour into your air fryer's pan and cook at 320 degrees F for 25 minutes.
- Leave your stew to cool down a bit, discard bay leaf, divide among plates and serve right away.

Nutrition Facts:

calories 300, fat 11, fiber 2, carbs 23, protein 14

392. Lunch Pork and Potatoes

Preparation time: 10 minutes Cooking time: 25 minutes

Ingredients:

- 2 pounds pork loin
- Salt and black pepper to the taste
- 2 red potatoes, cut into medium wedges
- ½ teaspoon garlic powder
- ½ teaspoon red pepper flakes
- 1 teaspoon parsley, dried
- A drizzle of balsamic vinegar

Instructions:

- In your air fryer's pan, mix pork with potatoes, salt, pepper, garlic powder, pepper flakes, parsley and vinegar, toss and cook at 390 degrees F for 25 minutes.
- Slice pork, divide it and potatoes on plates and serve for lunch.

Nutrition Facts:

calories 400, fat 15, fiber 7, carbs 27, protein 20

393. Turkey Cakes

Preparation time: 10 minutes Cooking time: 10 minutes

Ingredients:

- 6 mushrooms, chopped
- 1 teaspoon garlic powder
- 1 teaspoon onion powder
- Salt and black pepper to the taste
- 1 and ¼ pounds turkey meat, ground
- Cooking spray
- Tomato sauce for serving

Instructions:

- In your blender, mix mushrooms with salt and pepper, pulse well and transfer to a bowl.
- Add turkey, onion powder, garlic powder, salt and pepper, stir and shape cakes out of this mix.
- Spray them with cooking spray, transfer them to your air fryer and cook at 320 degrees F for 10 minutes.
- Serve them with tomato sauce on the side and a tasty side salad.

Nutrition Facts:

calories 202, fat 6, fiber 3, carbs 17, protein 10

394. Cheese Ravioli and Marinara Sauce

Preparation time: 10 minutes Cooking time: 8 minutes

Ingredients:

- 20 ounces cheese ravioli
- 10 ounces marinara sauce
- 1 tablespoon olive oil
- 1 cup buttermilk
- 2 cups bread crumbs
- ¼ cup parmesan, grated

Instructions:

- Put buttermilk in a bowl and breadcrumbs in another bowl.
- Dip ravioli in buttermilk, then in breadcrumbs and place them in your air fryer on a baking sheet.
- Drizzle olive oil over them, cook at 400 degrees F for 5 minutes, divide them on plates, sprinkle parmesan on top and serve for lunch

Nutrition Facts:

calories 270, fat 12, fiber 6, carbs 30, protein 15

395. Beef Stew

Preparation time: 10 minutes Cooking time: 20 minutes

Ingredients:

- 2 pounds beef meat, cut into medium chunks
- 2 carrots, chopped
- 4 potatoes, chopped
- Salt and black pepper to the taste
- 1 quart veggie stock
- ½ teaspoon smoked paprika
- A handful thyme, chopped

Instructions:

- In a dish that fits your air fryer, mix beef with carrots, potatoes, stock, salt, pepper, paprika and thyme, stir, place in air fryer's basket and cook at 375 degrees F for 20 minutes.
- Divide into bowls and serve right away for lunch.

Nutrition Facts:

calories 260, fat 5, fiber 8, carbs 20, protein 22

396. Meatballs Sandwich

Preparation time: 10 minutes Cooking time: 22 minutes

Ingredients:

- 3 baguettes, sliced more than halfway through
- 14 ounces beef, ground
- 7 ounces tomato sauce
- 1 small onion, chopped
- 1 egg, whisked
- 1 tablespoon bread crumbs
- 2 tablespoons cheddar cheese, grated
- 1 tablespoon oregano, chopped
- 1 tablespoon olive oil
- Salt and black pepper to the taste
- 1 teaspoon thyme, dried
- 1 teaspoon basil, dried

Instructions:

- In a bowl, combine meat with salt, pepper, onion, breadcrumbs, egg, cheese, oregano, thyme and basil, stir, shape medium meatballs and add them to your air fryer after you've greased it with the oil.
- Cook them at 375 degrees F for 12 minutes, flipping them halfway.
- Add tomato sauce, cook meatballs for 10 minutes more and arrange them on sliced baguettes.
- Serve them right away.

Nutrition Facts:

calories 380, fat 5, fiber 6, carbs 34, protein 20

397. Air-Fryer Roasted Veggies

Prep Time: 20 mins

Cook Time: 10 mins

Total Time: 30 mins

Servings: 4

Ingredient

- ½ cup diced zucchini
- ½ cup diced summer squash
- ½ cup diced mushrooms
- ½ cup diced cauliflower
- ½ cup diced asparagus
- ½ cup diced sweet red pepper
- 2 teaspoons vegetable oil
- ¼ teaspoon salt
- ¼ teaspoon ground black pepper
- 1/4 teaspoon seasoning, or more to taste

Instructions

- Preheat the air fryer to 360 degrees F (180 degrees C).
- Add vegetables, oil, salt, pepper, and desired seasoning to a bowl. Toss to coat; arrange in the fryer basket.
- Cook vegetables for 10 minutes, stirring after 5 minutes.

Nutrition Facts

- Calories: 37; Protein; 1.4g; Carbohydrates: 3.4g; Fat: 2.4g; Sodium: 152.2mg.

398. Marinated Air Fryer Vegetables

Prep Time: 10 minutes

Cook Time: 15 minutes

Marinading time: 20 minutes

Total Time: 25 minutes

Servings: 4 servings

Ingredients

- Vegetables
- 2 green zucchini cut into ½ inch pieces
- 1 yellow squash cut into ½ inch pieces
- 4 oz button mushrooms cut in half
- 1 red onion cut into ½ inch pieces
- 1 red bell pepper cut into ½ inch pieces
- Marinade
- 4 Tbsp Olive Oil
- 2 Tbsp Balsamic Vinegar
- 1 Tbsp Honey
- 1 ½ tsp salt
- ½ tsp dried thyme
- ½ tsp dried oregano
- ¼ tsp garlic powder
- A few drops of liquid smoke optional
- Salt to taste

Instructions

- Place marinade ingredients in a large bowl and whisk until combined. Place chopped vegetables in a bowl and stir until all vegetables are fully covered.
- Allow vegetables to marinate for 20-30 minutes.
- Place marinated vegetables in an air fryer basket and cook at 400 degrees Fahrenheit for 15-18 minutes, stirring every 5 minutes, until tender. Salt to taste.

Nutrition

- Calories: 200kcal | Carbohydrates: 16g | Protein: 3g | Fat: 15g | Saturated Fat: 2g | Sodium: 890mg | Potassium: 586mg | Fiber: 3g | Sugar: 12g | Vitamin A: 1225IU | Vitamin C: 67mg | Calcium: 34mg | Iron: 1mg

399. Air Fryer Vegetables

Prep Time: 3 mins

Cook Time: 7 mins

Total Time: 10 mins

Ingredients

- 1/2 lb broccoli fresh
- 1/2 lb cauliflower fresh
- 1 TBSP olive oil
- 1/4 tsp seasoning can use pepper, salt, garlic salt - I prefer Flavor God Garlic Everything
- 1/3 c water

Instructions

- In a medium bowl, mix vegetables, olive oil, and seasonings.
- Pour 1/3 c. water in the Air Fryer base to prevent smoking.
- Place vegetables in the air fryer basket.
- Cook at 400 degrees for 7-10 minutes.
- Shake vegetables to make sure they get evenly cooked about halfway through the 7-10 minutes.

Nutrition

- Calories: 65kcal | Carbohydrates: 7g | Protein: 3g | Fat: 4g | Saturated Fat: 1g | Sodium: 37mg | Potassium: 349mg | Fiber: 3g | Sugar: 2g | Vitamin A: 355IU | Vitamin C: 77.9mg | Calcium: 44mg | Iron: 0.8mg

400. Airfried Vegetables

Prep time: 10 min

Cook time: 20 min

Total time: 30 min

Serves: 4

Ingredients

- 1 lb / 0.5kg of vegetables (broccoli, brussels sprouts, carrots, cauliflower, parsnips, potatoes, sweet potatoes, zucchini will all work), chopped evenly
- 1 Tbsp / 30 mL of cooking oil
- Some salt and pepper

Instructions

Prep

- Preheat air fryer for about 5 minutes at 360F / 182C degrees.
- Evenly chop veggies and toss with oil and some salt and pepper. If making potato or sweet potato fries, soak them in water for ~30 minutes to draw out excess starch for crispier results, and then pat dry thoroughly with paper towels before tossing with oil.

Make

- Transfer veggies into frying compartment and fry for 15 to 20 minutes, stirring veggies every 5 to 8 minutes or so. Some veggies might need longer and some will need less – just use your judgment when you open the compartment to stir the veggies. You want the outside to be golden and crispy and the inside to be tender.
- Enjoy or toss with your favorite dipping sauce when done! If you need sauce ideas, check out 5 of our favorites.

Nutrition Information

- Calories: 172
- Total Fat: 11g
- Saturated Fat: 2g
- Unsaturated Fat: 9g
- Sodium: 577mg
- Carbohydrates: 16g

- Fiber: 6g
- Sugar: 4g
- Protein: 6g

401. Air Fryer Vegetables

Prep Time: 10 minutes

Cook Time: 15 minutes

Total Time: 25 minutes

Servings: 4

Ingredients

- 380 g Broccoli
- 250 g Carrots
- 1 Large Bell pepper
- 1 Large Onion
- 1/2 teaspoon Black pepper
- 1 tablespoon Olive oil
- 1 teaspoon Seasoning vegetable, chicken, turkey seasoning, or any of choice.
- Salt to taste

Instructions

- Wash and cut the vegetables into bite-size.
- Cut veggies on a white flat plate.
- Add them to a bowl and season with salt, black pepper, or any seasoning of choice, and olive oil. Mix so that the veggies are covered in the seasoning.
- Seasoning and olive oil added to the veggies.
- Add the seasoned veggies into the air fryer basket and air fry at a temperature of 175c for 15 minutes.
- Air fryer roasted vegetables in the air fryer basket.
- Toss the veggies in the basket halfway through cooking so that all sides are crisp.
- When done, take out the basket and serve.
- The finished dish displayed.

Nutrition Information

- Calories: 120kcal | Carbohydrates: 19g | Protein: 4g | Fat: 4g | Saturated Fat: 1g | Sodium: 78mg | Potassium: 657mg | Fiber: 6g | Sugar: 8g | Vitamin A: 12338IU | Vitamin C: 144mg | Calcium: 96mg | Iron: 2mg

402. Roasted Air Fryer Vegetables

Prep Time: 5 minutes

Cook Time: 12 minutes

Total Time: 17 minutes

Servings: 4

Ingredients

- 1 red bell pepper
- 1-2 yellow squash
- 1 zucchini
- 1/4 medium red onion
- 1 cup broccoli
- 1 tbsp olive oil
- 1/2 teaspoon salt
- 1/2 teaspoon garlic powder
- 1/8 teaspoon black pepper

Instructions

- Cut up 1 red bell pepper, 2 small yellow zucchini squash, 1 zucchini, 1/2 a medium onion, and 1 cup of broccoli into similar sized chunks.
- Add the sliced vegetables into a large bowl and toss them with 1 tablespoon of olive oil, 1/2 teaspoon salt, 1/2 teaspoon garlic powder, and 1/8 teaspoon black pepper.
- Once the veggies a coated in the oil and seasoning, place them onto the bottom of your air fryer basket and roast for 10-12 minutes at 400 degrees Fahrenheit.

Nutrition

- Calories: 65kcal | Carbohydrates: 7g | Protein: 2g | Fat: 4g | Saturated Fat: 1g | Sodium: 305mg | Potassium: 391mg | Fiber: 2g | Sugar: 4g | Vitamin A: 1269IU | Vitamin C: 75mg | Calcium: 26mg | Iron: 1mg

403. Air Fryer Roast Vegetables

Prep Time: 5 Minutes

Cook Time: 10 Minutes

Total Time: 15 Minutes

Ingredients

- 1 large sweet potato
- 1 large potato
- 1 large carrot
- ¼ small pumpkin
- ½ tsp spice or herb mix, optional

Instructions

- Wash the vegetables or peel if preferred, and cut into chunks no thicker than 1 inch (they can be as long as you like). Pat vegetables dry.
- Place vegetable pieces in an air fryer basket and spray with olive oil. Add spice if desired. Shake and spray with oil again.
- Cook in the air fryer at 360°F (180°C) for 5 minutes. Remove the basket and shake.
- Return to the air fryer and cook for a further 5-10 minutes until golden brown.

Nutrition Information

- Calories: 156| Unsaturated Fat: 0g| Sodium: 69mg| Carbohydrates: 35g| Fiber: 5g| Sugar: 6g| Protein: 4g

404. Air Fryer Veggies

Prep Time: 5 mins

Cook Time: 20 mins

Total Time: 25 mins

Ingredients

- 3 cups mixed vegetables, cut into 1-inch pieces (cauliflower, broccoli, squash, carrots, beets, etc)
- 1 tablespoon olive oil
- 1/2 teaspoon kosher salt

Preparation

- Place the vegetables in a bowl and toss to coat with the oil and salt.
- Place the vegetables in the air fryer basket and cook at 375F degrees for 15-20 minutes or until golden and fork-tender.

Nutrition Information

- Calories: 172
- Total Fat: 11g
- Sodium: 234mg
- Carbohydrates: 16g

- Fiber: 6g
- Sugar: 4g
- Protein: 6g

405. Air Fryer "Roasted" Asparagus

Prep Time: 3 mins

Cook Time: 7 mins

Total Time: 10 mins

Servings: 4 servings

Ingredients

- 1 pound fresh asparagus, ends trimmed
- Oil spray or olive oil
- Salt, to taste
- Black pepper, to taste

Instructions

- Coat the asparagus with oil spray or olive oil and season with salt and pepper. Lay the asparagus evenly in the air fryer basket. Make sure to coat the asparagus tips so they don't burn or dry out too fast. It is best to season before you put it in the air fryer basket. Too much excess salt in the air fryer baskets will often start to break down with coating.
- Air Fry at 380°F for 7-10 minutes, depending on thickness, shake, and turn asparagus halfway through cooking.
- Taste for seasoning & tenderness, then serve.

Nutritional Value

- Calories: 572kcal | Carbohydrates: 1g | Protein: 46g | Fat: 43g | Saturated Fat: 22g | Cholesterol: 168mg | Sodium: 219mg | Potassium: 606mg | Sugar: 1g | Calcium: 16mg | Iron: 4mg

406. Air Fryer Vegetables

Prep Time: 10 minutes

Cook Time: 10 minutes

Servings: 6

Ingredients

- 2 zucchini cut into dials

- 2 yellow squash cut into dials
- 1 container mushrooms cut in half
- 1/2 c olive oil
- 1/2 onion sliced
- 3/4 tsp Italian seasoning
- 1/2 tsp garlic salt
- 1/4 tsp Lawry's seasoned salt

Instructions

- Slice zucchini and yellow squash into dials. The thinner they are the softer they will get. I would recommend 3/4" thick so they all are the same consistency when done.
- Slice mushrooms in half. Put all vegetables in a bowl and toss together gently. (if you want to add 1/2-1 full precooked sausage link diced into bite-size pcs., add that now too)
- Pour olive oil on top and toss gently, then sprinkle in all seasonings in a bowl and gently toss one more time.
- Add half of your vegetables into your air fryer, close, and set to 400 degrees for 10 minutes. I did not bother shaking or tossing halfway through and they came out amazing.
- Remove, enjoy, and add another half at 400 degrees for 10 minutes to finish the cooking batch.

Nutrition Facts

- Fat: 18g
- Saturated Fat: 3g1
- Sodium: 201mg
- Potassium: 355mg
- Carbohydrates: 5g
- Fiber: 2g
- Sugar: 3g
- Protein: 2g
- Vitamin: A 261IU
- Vitamin C: 23mg
- Calcium: 26mg
- Iron: 1mg

407. Air Fryer Frozen Broccoli, Carrots, And Cauliflower – (Gluten-Free, Vegan, Keto, And Paleo)

Prep time: 5 min

Cook time: 10 min

Total time: 15 min

Serves: 3 people

Ingredients:

- 3 cups frozen mixed broccoli, carrots, and cauliflower
- 1 TBS extra virgin olive oil
- 1 tsp Italian seasoning blend (or basil, oregano, rosemary, and thyme)
- 1/2 tsp **Nutrition Facts**al yeast (optional)
- 1/2 tsp sea salt
- 1/4 tsp freshly cracked pepper

Directions:

- Preheat the air fryer to 375°F for 5 minutes.
- Place the frozen vegetables in a large mixing bowl. Pour the olive oil over the vegetables and toss to coat. Sprinkle the herbs, salt, pepper, and nutritional yeast over the vegetables and toss again.
- Add the vegetables to the crisper plate or basket of the air fryer in an even layer. Cook for 5 minutes. Shake the bucket, or rotate the vegetables. Continue to cook for an additional 4 to 6 minutes until the vegetables are tender and cooked through to a warm temperature. Taste one to test for doneness.
- Place the cooked vegetables on a serving platter. You can top with more **Nutrition Facts**al yeast before serving.

Nutritional Facts

- Total fat: 3.7g
- Sodium: 1820.8mg
- Sugar: 11.3g
- Vitamin A: 169.2ug
- Carbohydrates: 33.6mg
- Protein:18g
- Vitamin C: 165.5mg

408. Healthy Air Fryer Chicken And Veggies

Prep Time: 5 minutes

Cook Time: 15 minutes

Total Time: 20 minutes

Servings: 4 servings

Ingredients

- 1 pound chicken breast, chopped into bite-size pieces (2-3 medium chicken breasts)
- 1 cup broccoli florets (fresh or frozen)
- 1 zucchini chopped
- 1 cup bell pepper chopped (any colors you like)
- 1/2 onion chopped
- 2 cloves garlic minced or crushed
- 2 tablespoons olive oil
- 1/2 teaspoon EACH garlic powder, chili powder, salt, pepper
- 1 tablespoon Italian seasoning (or spice blend of choice)

Instructions

- Preheat air fryer to 400F.
- Chop the veggies and chicken into small bite-size pieces and transfer to a large mixing bowl.
- Add the oil and seasoning to the bowl and toss to combine.
- Add the chicken and veggies to the preheated air fryer and cook for 10 minutes, shaking halfway, or until the chicken and veggies are charred and chicken is cooked through. If your air fryer is small, you may have to cook them in 2-3 batches.

Nutrition Facts

- Calories: 230kcal | Carbohydrates: 8g | Protein: 26g | Fat: 10g | Saturated Fat: 2g | Cholesterol: 73mg | Sodium: 437mg | Potassium: 734mg | Fiber: 3g | Sugar: 4g | Vitamin A: 1584IU | Vitamin C: 79mg | Calcium: 50mg | Iron: 1mg

409. Air Fryer Vegetable "Stir-Fry"

Prep Time: 5 minutes

Cook Time: 7 minutes

Total Time: 12 minutes

Ingredients

- 50 grams extra firm tofu, cut into strips (about 1 cup)
- 4 stalks asparagus, ends trimmed and cut in half
- 4 brussels sprouts, halved
- 3 brown mushrooms, sliced

- 2 cloves garlic, minced
- 1 teaspoon italiano seasoning
- ½ teaspoon sesame oil (or olive oil)
- ¼ teaspoon soy sauce
- Salt and pepper, to taste
- Roasted white sesame seeds (for garnish)

Instructions

- Combine all ingredients into a large mixing bowl, and toss to combine.
- Transfer into air fryer basket and air fry at 350 F for 7-8 minutes, depending on how well done you would like the vegetables. Give the basket a shake halfway through.
- Remove from air fryer basket, sprinkle some roasted white sesame seeds on top, and serve with a side of rice.

Nutrition Facts

- Total fat: 3.7g
- sodium: 1820.8mg
- sugar: 11.3g
- Vitamin A: 169.2ug
- Carbohydrates: 33.6mg
- Protein: 18g
- Vitamin C: 165.5mg

410. Air Fryer Roasted Vegetables

Prep Time: 5 minutes

Cook Time: 20 minutes

Total Time: 25 minutes

Servings: 4

Ingredients

- 2 tablespoons olive oil
- 1 medium zucchini sliced
- 8 oz fresh mushrooms sliced
- 1 tablespoon minced garlic
- Garlic powder to taste
- Onion powder to taste
- Salt and pepper to taste

Instructions

- Preheat air fryer to 390.
- Combine all ingredients in a bowl and toss well

to coat in oil.

- Spread out in a single layer in your air fryer basket (in batches if needed).
- Cook for 10 minutes and stir.
- Cook for an additional 5 to 10 minutes until vegetables reach your desired texture.

Nutrition

- Calories: 84kcal | Carbohydrates: 4g | Protein: 2g | Fat: 7g | Saturated Fat: 1g | Sodium: 6mg | Potassium: 281mg | Fiber: 1g | Sugar: 2g | Vitamin A: 78IU | Vitamin C: 9mg | Calcium: 10mg | Iron: 1mg | Net Carbs: 3g

411. Air Fryer vegetables

Prep Time: 10 mins

Cook Time: 10 mins

Total Time: 20 mins

Ingredients

- 2 zucchini
- 1-2 yellow squash
- 1/2 sweet onion
- 1 8 oz container mushrooms
- 1 bell pepper
- 1/4 cup olive oil
- 1 teaspoon Italian seasoning
- 1/2 teaspoon salt
- 1/4 teaspoon ground black pepper

Instructions

- Cut squash, zucchini, pepper, onion, and mushrooms into bite-sized pieces. Place in a large bowl.
- Pour olive oil over vegetables. Sprinkle Italian seasoning, salt, and pepper over vegetables. Toss to coat.
- Pour vegetables into an air fryer basket. Spread out for one layer. (You might need to cook in 2 batches.)
- Cook at 400 degrees F for 10-12 minutes.
- Serve warm.

Nutrition

- Calories: 168kcal | Carbohydrates: 10g | Protein: 2g | Fat: 14g | Saturated Fat: 2g | Sodium:

304mg | Potassium: 496mg | Fiber: 3g | Sugar: 7g | Vitamin A: 1225IU | Vitamin C: 66mg | Calcium: 39mg | Iron: 1mg

412. Air Fryer Garlic Zucchini

Prep Time: 5 mins

Cook Time: 15 mins

Total Time: 20 mins

Servings: 2 servings

Ingredients

- 2 zucchini (1 lb. Or 455g total)
- Olive oil or cooking spray
- 1/2 teaspoon garlic powder
- Salt, to taste
- Black pepper, to taste

Instructions

- Trim the ends of the zucchini, if desired. Cut the zucchini into 1/2" thick slices (either into lengthwise slices or into coins). If cutting into lengthwise slices, cut to length to fit the width of your air fryer basket if needed.
- Lightly oil or spray the zucchini slices on both sides and then season with garlic powder, salt, and pepper.
- Air Fry at 400°F for 8-14 minutes or until browned and cooked through.

Nutrition

- Calories: 36kcal | Carbohydrates: 7g | Protein: 2g | Fat: 1g | Saturated Fat: 1g | Sodium: 16mg | Potassium: 512mg | Fiber: 2g | Sugar: 5g | Vitamin A: 390IU | Vitamin C: 35.1mg | Calcium: 31mg | Iron: 0.7mg

413. Healthy Air Fryer Chicken And Veggies

Prep Time: 5 minutes

Cook Time: 15 minutes

Total Time: 20 minutes

Servings: 4 servings

Ingredients

- 1 pound chicken breast, chopped into bite-size pieces (2-3 medium chicken breasts)
- 1 cup broccoli florets (fresh or frozen)
- 1 zucchini chopped
- 1 cup bell pepper chopped (any colors you like)
- 1/2 onion chopped
- 2 cloves garlic minced or crushed
- 2 tablespoons olive oil
- 1/2 teaspoon EACH garlic powder, chili powder, salt, pepper
- 1 tablespoon Italian seasoning (or spice blend of choice)

Instructions

- Preheat air fryer to 400F.
- Chop the veggies and chicken into small bite-size pieces and transfer to a large mixing bowl.
- Add the oil and seasoning to the bowl and toss to combine.
- Add the chicken and veggies to the preheated air fryer and cook for 10 minutes, shaking halfway, or until the chicken and veggies are charred and chicken is cooked through. If your air fryer is small, you may have to cook them in 2-3 batches.

Nutrition

- Calories: 230kcal | Carbohydrates: 8g | Protein: 26g | Fat: 10g | Saturated Fat: 2g | Cholesterol: 73mg | Sodium: 437mg | Potassium: 734mg | Fiber: 3g | Sugar: 4g | Vitamin A: 1584IU | Vitamin C: 79mg | Calcium: 50mg | Iron: 1mg

414. Air Fryer Veggie Tots

Prep Time: 10 minutes

Cook Time: 12 minutes

Servings: 20 tots

Ingredients

- 1 cup sweet potato (baked in the oven until soft and skin removed)
- 1 ½ cups kale
- 1 egg
- ½ cup rice crumbs I grab my rice crumbs at Trader Joe's. These are a great gluten-free option. Panko bread crumbs can be substituted.
- ½ tsp garlic powder

- ½ tsp paprika
- ¼ tsp salt
- ¼ tsp pepper
- 2 tsp olive oil

Instructions

- Spray or drizzle 1/2 tsp olive oil in the air fryer. Place the tots into the air fryer. Do not stack them on top of each other to ensure they become crispy. Spray or drizzle 1 tsp olive oil over the top of the tots and cook at 400 degrees for 10-15 minutes. Repeat if needed (depending on the size of your air fryer.)
- Pulse kale in a food processor into small flakes.

Air Fryer Veggie Tots

- Mash the cooked sweet potato with a fork. If you just cooked the sweet potato, allow it to cool completely. Mix in the kale, egg, and rice crumbs and spices until combined.
- Form into "tot-like" shapes with a 1 tbsp scoop or just create small round shapes. They don't have to be perfect!
- Spray or drizzle ½ tsp olive oil into the air fryer. Place the tots into the air fryer. Do not stack them on top of each other to ensure they become crispy. Spray or drizzle 1 tsp olive oil over the top of the tots and air fry at 400 degrees for 10-15 minutes. Repeat if needed, depending on the size of your air fryer.
- Serve with a dipping sauce! I made an easy 3 ingredient sauce with Wunder Creamery Quark, Primal Kitchen Dairy-Free Mayo, and Primal Kitchen Ketchup.
- Enjoy!

Nutritional Value

- Total fat: 3.7g
- Sodium: 1820.8mg
- Sugar: 11.3g
- Vitamin A: 169.2ug
- Carbohydrates: 33.6mg
- Protein: 18g
- Vitamin C: 165.5mg

415. Air Fryer Vegetables Recipe

Prep Time: 15 Minutes

Cook Time: 20 Minutes

Total Time: 35 Minutes

Ingredients

- 1 cup broccoli florets
- 1 cup cauliflower florets
- 1/2 cup baby carrots
- 1/2 cup yellow squash, sliced
- 1/2 cup baby zucchini, sliced
- 1/2 cup sliced mushrooms
- 1 onion, sliced
- 1/4 cup balsamic vinegar
- 1 tbsp olive oil
- 1 tbsp minced garlic
- 1 tsp sea salt
- 1 tsp black pepper
- 1 tsp red pepper flakes
- 1/4 cup parmesan cheese

Instructions

- Pre-heat Air Fryer at 400 for 3 minutes (you can skip this step if you'd like)
- In a large bowl, olive oil, balsamic vinegar, garlic, salt and pepper, and red pepper flakes. Whisk together.
- Add vegetables and toss to coat.
- Add vegetables to the Air Fryer basket. Cook for 8 minutes. Shake vegetables and cook for 6-8 additional minutes.
- Add cheese and bake for 1-2 minutes.

Nutrition Information:

- Total Fat: 3g|Saturated Fat: 1g|Trans Fat: 0g|Unsaturated Fat: 2g|Cholesterol: 3mg|Sodium: 366mg|Carbohydrates: 8g|Fiber: 2g|Sugar: 3g|Protein: 2g

416. Asian-Style Air Fryer Green Beans

Prep Time: 5 Minutes

Cook Time: 5 Minutes

Total Time: 10 Minutes

Ingredients

- 1 lb green beans, washed and trimmed
- 2 teaspoons sesame oil
- 1 teaspoon garlic salt

- Pepper to taste

Instructions

- Preheat your air fryer to 400 degrees.
- Place the trimmed green beans, sesame oil, garlic salt, and pepper into a bowl and mix to evenly coat green beans.
- Put green beans into your preheated air fryer for 5-7 minutes shaking the basket halfway through. You can check the tenderness with a fork to test if the green beans are done.
- Remove green beans from the air fryer and enjoy!

Nutrition Information

- Total Fat: 3g| Unsaturated Fat: 2g| |Sodium: 398mg|Carbohydrates: 10g|Fiber: 4g|Sugar: 4g|Protein: 2g

417. Air Fryer Broccoli

Prep Time: 5 min

Cook Time: 6 min

Total Time: 11 minutes

Ingredients

- 12 oz fresh broccoli florets, cut/torn into toughly even, very-small pieces
- 2 tablespoons extra virgin olive oil
- 1/4 tsp garlic powder
- 1/4 tsp onion powder
- 1/8 tsp kosher salt
- 1/8 tsp freshly ground black pepper

Instructions

- Combine all ingredients in a bowl; toss well to fully incorporate seasonings into the broccoli florets
- Pour 1 TB water into the bottom of the air fryer pan (this helps prevent contents from smoking.)
- Add broccoli mixture evenly into the air fryer basket. Set to 400F for 6 minutes. Once the timer goes off, immediately remove the basket and serve.

Nutritional Value

- Calories: 572kcal | Carbohydrates: 1g | Protein:

46g | Fat: 43g | Saturated Fat: 22g | Cholesterol: 168mg | Sodium: 219mg | Potassium: 606mg | Sugar: 1g | Calcium: 16mg | Iron: 4mg

418. Instant Pot Vortex Air Fryer Vegetables

Prep Time: 5 Minutes

Cook Time: 18 Minutes

Total Time: 23 Minutes

Ingredients

Vegetables Of Choice. Used Here Are:

- 1 cup broccoli
- 1 cup cauliflower
- 1 cup carrots
- 1 Tablespoon Olive oil or oil of choice

Instructions

- Place the vegetables in a bowl and toss with the oil
- Add seasoning and toss
- Add the vegetable to the Vortex rotisserie basket (or your air fryer basket with other brands)
- Air fry on 380 or 18 minutes or until vegetables are roasted with golden brown parts
- Carefully remove the basket using the removal tool, serve, and enjoy!

Nutrition Information:

- Total Fat: 10g| Saturated Fat: 1g| Trans Fat: 0g| Unsaturated Fat: 8g| Cholesterol: 0mg| Sodium: 68mg| Carbohydrates: 14g| Fiber: 6g| Sugar: 4g| Protein: 3g

419. "Fried" Tempura Veggies

Hands-On: 15 mins

Total Time: 25 mins

Servings: 4

Ingredients

- ½ Cup flour
- ½ teaspoon salt, plus more to taste
- ½ teaspoon black pepper
- 2 eggs

- 2 water
- 1 cup panko bread crumbs
- 2 teaspoons vegetable oil
- ¼ teaspoon seasoning, or more to taste
- 2 – 3 cups vegetable pieces (whole green beans, sweet pepper rings, zucchini slices, whole asparagus spears, red onion rings, or avocado wedges), cut 1/2 inch thick

Instructions

- Mix together flour, 1/4 tsp. salt, and the pepper in a shallow dish. Whisk together eggs and water in another shallow dish. Stir together panko and oil in a third shallow dish. Add the desired Seasoning to either panko and/or flour mixture.
- Sprinkle vegetables with remaining 1/4 tsp. salt. Dip in flour mixture, then in egg mixture, and finally in panko mixture to coat.
- Preheat air fryer to 400°F and oven to 200°F. Arrange half of the vegetables in a single layer in a fryer basket. Cook until golden brown, about 10 minutes. Sprinkle with additional salt, if desired. Transfer vegetables to the oven to keep warm. Repeat with remaining vegetables. Serve with dipping sauce.

Nutrition Facts

- Calories: 179; Total Fat: 5g; Saturated Fat: 1g; Sodium: 375mg; Carbohydrates: 25g; Fiber: 2g; Sugar: 2g; Protein: 7g.

420. Air Fryer Roasted Potatoes

Prep Time: 5 minutes

Cook Time: 22 minutes

Total Time: 27 minutes

Servings 4

Ingredients

- 1.5 pounds potatoes (diced into 1-inch pieces - gold, red, or russets)
- 1/2 teaspoon garlic powder or granulated garlic
- 1/2 teaspoon salt or more, to taste
- 1/4 teaspoon pepper
- 1/2 teaspoon oregano dried
- 1/2 teaspoon basil dried
- Cooking spray (i am using avocado oil cooking

spray)

Instructions

- Spray the air fryer cooking basket with the cooking spray.
- Add diced potatoes to the basket, and give the potatoes a spray.
- Add salt, pepper, garlic powder, oregano, and basil, and toss to combine and evenly coat the potatoes.
- Cook at 400 degrees (not preheated) until brown and crispy, about 20 to 24 minutes.
- Toss them halfway through with a flipper, and shake the basket once more to ensure even cooking.

Nutrition Facts

- Calories: 110
- Fat: 1g
- Sodium: 308mg
- Potassium: 702mg
- Carbohydrates: 21g
- Fiber: 4g
- Protein: 4g
- Vitamin C: 19.4mg
- Calcium: 51mg
- Iron: 5.6mg

421. Air Fryer Cauliflower & Broccoli Bites

Total Time: 1 hour

SERVES: 6 servings

Ingredients

- Cooking spray
- 1 cup panko bread crumbs
- ¼ cup grated Parmesan
- 1 Tbsp. Creole seasoning
- 2 cups cauliflower florets
- 2 cups broccoli florets
- ½ cup whole wheat flour
- 2 large eggs
- 1 Tbsp. Fresh parsley, finely chopped, optional
- Marinara sauce for serving, optional

Directions

- Preheat air fryer to 400°F.
- Lightly spray the fryer basket with oil.
- In a large bowl, combine panko, Parmesan, and creole seasoning. Set aside.
- Place flour in a shallow dish and set aside. In a separate dish, whisk 2 eggs and set aside.
- Working in small batches, dip cauliflower and broccoli florets into flour and gently shake off excess. Dip into egg and then press into breadcrumb mixture.
- Place florets in the basket and cook until golden and crispy, about 5-6 minutes. Remove from fryer basket and sprinkle with parsley.
- Serve immediately with marinara sauce.

Nutrition

- Calories: 130, Total Fat: 3.5g, Cholesterol: 65mg, Sodium: 420mg, Total Carbohydrate: 20g (Dietary Fiber 2g, Sugars 1g, Includes 1g Added Sugar), Protein: 8g, Calcium: 4%, Iron: 10%, Potassium: 6%

422. Air Fryer Vegetable And Cheese Quesadillas

Servings: 2

Ready In: 18min

Prep Time: 10min

Cook Time: 8min

Ingredients

- 2 (6 inches) flour tortillas
- Cooking spray
- 1/2 cup shredded cheddar cheese
- 1/2 red bell pepper, sliced
- 1/2 zucchini, sliced

Directions

- Preheat air fryer to 400°F (200°C).
- Spray 1 side of a single tortilla generously with cooking spray and place flat in an air fryer basket.
- Spread half the Cheddar cheese over tortilla. Top cheese layer with bell pepper and zucchini. Spread remaining Cheddar cheese over top.
- Place the second tortilla over fillings and spray the top with cooking spray.
- Air fry until cheese is melted and tortillas are crisp, 8 to 9 minutes.

Nutrition Facts

- Calories: 291; Fat: 13g; Carbohydrates: 31.5g;Protein: 12g ; Cholesterol: 28g ; Sodium: 421g.

423. Air Fryer Veggie Fajitas

- Yield: 2-3 Servings
- Prep Time: 10 Minutes
- Cook Time: 15 Minutes
- Total Time: 25 Minutes

Ingredients

- 4 portobello mushrooms, sliced into strips
- 2 sweet peppers (red or yellow), sliced into strips
- 1 large onion, sliced into strips
- Fajita sauce
- 3 tbsp sweet chili sauce
- 1 tbsp soy sauce
- 1 tsp smoked paprika
- 1/8 tsp chili powder (more if you want it spicy)
- 1/2 tsp cumin
- 1/4 tsp ground coriander
- To serve
- 8 tortillas
- Toppings of your choice - guacamole, salsa, sour cream or vegan cream, chopped fresh cilantro (coriander)

Instructions

- Make the fajita sauce by whisking all ingredients together.
- Place the sliced vegetables in a large bowl and coat with the fajita sauce. Allow marinating for a little while in the fridge if you have the time. If you don't, that's OK too - you can go ahead and put them in straight away.
- Heat the air fryer to 200C / 390F.
- Coat the marinated vegetables with a spray of oil and place them in the fry basket.
- Cook for 15 minutes, opening the fryer up to mix the vegetables halfway through.
- They're ready when the vegetables are juicy and a little bit charred. You may want to cook for another 5 minutes if they're not yet charred to your liking.
- Serve immediately with warmed tortillas and

your toppings of choice.

Nutrition Information:

- Total Fat: 19g| Saturated Fat: 6g| Trans Fat: 0g| Unsaturated Fat: 11g| Cholesterol: 16mg| Sodium: 1448mg| Carbohydrates: 121g| Fiber: 12g| Sugar: 26g| Protein: 21g

424. Roasted Winter Vegetables

Servings: 6 Persons

Prep Time: 5 Minutes

Cooking Time: 20 Minutes

Total Time: 25 Minutes

Ingredients

- 300 g parsnips
- 300 g celeriac
- 2 red onions
- 300 g 'butternut squash'
- 1 tbsp fresh thyme needles
- 1 tbsp olive oil
- pepper & salt

Directions

- Preheat the Airfryer to 200°C.
- Peel the parsnips, celeriac, and onions. Cut the parsnips and celeriac into 2 cm cubes and the onions into wedges. Halve the 'butternut squash', remove the seeds and cut into cubes. (There's no need to peel it.)
- Mix the cut vegetables with thyme and olive oil. Season to taste.
- Place the vegetables into the basket and slide the basket into the Airfryer. Set the timer for 20 minutes and roast the vegetables until the timer rings and the vegetables are nicely brown and done. Stir the vegetables once while roasting.

Nutritional Value

- Calories: 572kcal | Carbohydrates: 1g | Protein: 46g | Fat: 43g | Saturated Fat: 22g | Cholesterol: 168mg | Sodium: 219mg | Potassium: 606mg | Sugar: 1g | Calcium: 16mg | Iron: 4mg

425. Roast Potatoes In A Basket Air Fryer

Prep Time: 5 minutes

Cook Time: 40 minutes

Total Time: 45 minutes

Servings: 4 servings

Ingredients

- 1.25 kg potato (3 lbs)
- 1 teaspoon oil

Instructions

- Wash potato, peel, cut into large chunks, adding chunks to a large bowl.
- Add 1 teaspoon of oil to the bowl of potato chunks and just using your clean hands, toss well until all surfaces are coated. (Tip! first, have the air basket pulled out and beside you, ready to receive the potatoes because your hands will be oily.)
- Cook (no need to pre-heat) at 160 C (320 F) for 25 minutes.
- Take out the potatoes and tip them back into the bowl you have been using. Toss them in there briefly and gently using a large spoon.
- Transfer potato chunks back into fryer basket. Place back into the machine, raise the temperature on the machine to 180 C (350 F), and cook for another 7 minutes.
- Take out the potatoes and tip them back into the bowl you have been using. Toss them in there using a large spoon. (At this point, a few might look just about done, but once you toss them you'll see that there are loads that aren't quite as far along.)
- Transfer potato chunks back into fryer basket. Leave temperature unchanged. Roast for a final 7 minutes.
- Serve piping hot.

Nutrition

- Serving: 1g | Calories: 250kcal | Protein: 6.3g | Fat: 1.5g | Sodium: 19mg | Fiber: 6.9g

426. Crispy Air Fryer Broccoli

Prep Time: 5 mins

Cook Time: 8 mins

Total Time: 13 mins

Ingredients

- 4-6 cups broccoli florets
- 1 tablespoon olive oil
- 1 tablespoon balsamic vinegar
- 1/8 teaspoon salt

Instructions

- Heat air fryer to 200°C/390°F.
- Chop broccoli into equal-sized 1 to 1.5-inch florets and place in a bowl.
- Toss broccoli florets with olive oil, balsamic vinegar, and salt.
- Add broccoli to the basket. Cook for 7-8 minutes, shaking up the basket every 2-3 minutes. When broccoli florets start to become golden and brown, broccoli is done.
- Enjoy!

Nutrition

- Calories: 65kcal | Carbohydrates: 7g | Protein: 3g | Fat: 4g | Saturated Fat: 1g | Sodium: 104mg | Potassium: 288mg | Fiber: 2g | Sugar: 2g | Vitamin C: 81mg | Calcium: 43mg | Iron: 1mg

427. Keto Air Fryer Chicken & Veggies

Prep time: 15 minutes

Cook time: 15 minutes

Total time: 30 minutes

Serves: 4

Ingredients

- 1 lb boneless, skinless chicken breast, cut into bite-sized pieces
- 2.5 cups broccoli florets
- 1 medium red bell pepper, chopped
- 1/2 medium onion, chopped
- 1 tbsp olive oil
- 1.5 tsp italian seasoning
- 1 tsp garlic powder
- 1/2 tsp paprika
- 1/2 tsp chili powder
- 1/2 tsp salt
- 1/4 tsp black pepper
- 1/4 tsp onion powder

Direction

- Preheat the air fryer to 400 degrees F (if your air fryer allows).
- Add chicken breast, broccoli, bell pepper, and onion to a large mixing bowl. Coat with olive oil and seasonings, toss to combine.
- Place in air fryer basket and cook for 12-15 minutes, or until chicken is completely cooked through. Stir halfway through cooking time. Serve hot.

Nutrition

- Calories: 189.5
- Fat: 4.9g
- Carbohydrates: 7.8g
- Fiber: 2.7g
- Protein: 24.3g
- Net Carbs: 5.1g

428. Veg Cutlet Recipe (Air Fryer Recipe + No Breadcrumbs)

Prep Time: 15 Mins

Cook Time: 40 Mins

Total Time: 55 Mins

Ingredients For Cutlets

- 2 cups Sweet Potatoes (Boiled, Peeled and Mashed) 1 cup is 250 ml
- 3/4 cup Carrot (finely grated)
- 1/2 cup Sweet Corn (steamed)
- 1/2 cup Capsicum (finely chopped)
- 1/3 cup Green Peas (Steamed)
- 1/2 cup Quick Cooking Oats Or Instant Oats
- 1 tbsp Ginger Paste
- 1 & 1/2 tbsp Oil For Cooking cutlets (1 tbsp oil is 15 ml)
- Salt to taste
- 2 to 3 tbsp Coriander Leaves (finely chopped)
- Spices
- 1 tsp Kashmiri Red chili powder 1 tsp is 5 ml
- 1 & 1/2 tsp Garam Masala Powder
- 1/2 tsp Turmeric Powder
- 1/4 tsp Chaat Masala Powder
- 1/2 tsp Amchur Powder or Dry Mango Powder

Instructions

- In a wide bowl, add boiled and mashed sweet potatoes, cooked peas, steamed sweet corn, grated carrots, and finely chopped capsicum.
- Add all the spices, ginger paste, quick-cooking oats, and salt to taste.
- Now add the finely chopped coriander leaves (I have used stems as well).
- Mix everything together.
- Divide and take an equal portion of the cutlet mixture and shape them into an "oval" shape. Once the cutlets are shaped, preheat the Air Fryer at 200 Degrees C for 5 minutes
- Place around 12 cutlets, brush or spray oil and cook them for 15 minutes at 200 Degree C.
- Turn them after 8 to 10 minutes of cooking, repeat the process of spraying oil or brushing and air fry them until they are golden brown. Serve with the accompaniment of your choice.

Nutritional Value

- Calories: 572kcal | Carbohydrates: 1g | Protein: 46g | Fat: 43g | Saturated Fat: 22g | Cholesterol: 168mg | Sodium: 219mg | Potassium: 606mg | Sugar: 1g | Calcium: 16mg | Iron: 4mg

429. Air-Fried Crispy Vegetables

Prep Time: 10 Mins

Cook Time: 15 Mins

Ingredients

- 2 cups mixed vegetables(bell peppers, cauliflower, mushrooms, zucchini, baby corn)
- For batter
- 1/4 cup cornstarch(cornflour in india)
- 1/4 cup all-purpose flour/maida
- ½ tsp garlic powder
- ½-1 tsp red chilli powder
- ½-1 tsp black pepper powder
- 1 tsp salt or as per taste
- 1 tsp oil

For Sauce Mix

- 2 tbsp soy sauce
- 1 tbsp chilli sauce/
- 1 tbsp tomato ketchup
- 1 tbsp vinegar(rice/synthetic or apple cider)

- 1 tsp brown sugar/coconut sugar

Other
- 1 tbsp sesame oil or any plant-based oil
- 1 tsp sesame seeds
- Spring onion greens for garnish

Instructions
- Cut Cauliflower in small florets, cubed bell peppers, cut mushrooms in half, and carrots and zucchini in circles. Do not cut very thin strips.
- Make a batter with all-purpose flour, cornstarch(sold as cornflour in India), garlic powder, bell pepper powder, red chili powder, and salt.
- Add a tsp of oil and make a smooth lump-free batter. Add and coat all the vegetables nicely in the batter.
- Preheat the air fryer at 350F, then add the veggies when indicated. Air fry the veggies, it takes about 10 minutes.
- Make the sauce mix. In a heavy-bottomed pan, heat a tbsp of oil, add finely chopped garlic, sauté till it gives aroma, and then add the sauce mix and freshly ground black pepper.
- Cook for a minute then add the air fried vegetables and mix well with light hands. Coat all the veggies nicely in sauce.
- Sprinkle Sesame Seeds and finely chopped spring onion greens and serve hot.
- For Sauce Mix.
- Mix all the ingredients together listed under the Sauce section.
- For the deep-fried version.
- Coat vegetables in batter nicely and then deep fry in hot oil, till light brown in color. Oil should be hot enough so that the veggies remain crispy. Take out and cool down and then add to the sauce mix.

Nutritional Value
- Total fat: 3.7g
- sodium: 1820.8mg
- sugar: 11.3g
- Vitamin A: 169.2ug
- Carbohydrates: 33.6mg
- Protein:18g
- Vitamin C: 165.5mg

430. Air Fryer Roasted Brussels Sprouts

Prep Time: 5 Minutes

Cook Time: 18 Minutes

Total Time: 23 Minutes

Ingredients
- 1 pound Brussels sprouts
- 1 ½ tablespoon olive oil
- ½ teaspoon salt
- ½ teaspoon black pepper

Instructions
- Preheat the air fryer to 390 degrees.
- Wash Brussels sprouts and pat dry.
- Remove any loose leaves.
- If the sprouts are larger cut them in half.
- Place Brussels sprouts into a bowl.
- Drizzle olive oil over the vegetables.
- Stir to make sure the Brussels sprouts are fully coated. Place the Brussels sprouts in the basket.
- Season with salt and pepper.
- Cook for 15 to 18 minutes or until the Brussels sprouts soften and begin to brown.
- Serve immediately.

Nutrition Information
- Calories: 172
- Total Fat: 11g
- Saturated Fat: 2g
- Unsaturated Fat: 9g
- Sodium: 577mg
- Carbohydrates: 16g
- Fiber: 6g
- Sugar: 4g
- Protein: 6g

431. Air Fryer Roasted Broccoli (Low Carb + Keto)

Yield: 4

Cook Time: 8 Minutes

Total Time: 8 Minutes

Ingredients
- 5 cups broccoli florets
- 2 tablespoons butter

- 2 teaspoons minced garlic
- 1/3 cup shredded parmesan cheese
- Salt and pepper to taste
- Lemon slices (optional)

Instructions

- Melt the butter and combine with the minced garlic, set aside for later.
- Preheat your air fryer according to the manufactures directions at a temperature of 350 degrees.
- Add the chopped broccoli florets to the basket of the air fryer and spray very lightly with cooking oil.
- Roast the broccoli for 8 minutes total. I remove the basket after 4 minutes and shake or toss with tongs to make sure everything is cooking evenly, then cook for 4 more minutes.
- At this point, the broccoli should be fork tender at the thickest part of the stem and slightly crispy on the outside.
- Remove the broccoli from the basket and toss with the garlic butter, parmesan and add salt and pepper to taste.

Nutrition Information:

- Calories: 106| Total Fat: 7.9g| carbohydrates: 5.2g| fiber: 2.1g| protein: 5.3g

432. Air-Fryer Roasted Veggies

Prep Time: 20 mins

Cook Time: 10 mins

Total Time: 30 mins

Servings: 4

Ingredient

- ½ cup diced zucchini
- ½ cup diced summer squash
- ½ cup diced mushrooms
- ½ cup diced cauliflower
- ½ cup diced asparagus
- ½ cup diced sweet red pepper
- 2 teaspoons vegetable oil
- ¼ teaspoon salt
- ¼ teaspoon ground black pepper
- 1/4 teaspoon seasoning, or more to taste

Instructions

- Preheat the air fryer to 360 degrees F (180 degrees C).
- Add vegetables, oil, salt, pepper, and desired seasoning to a bowl. Toss to coat; arrange in the fryer basket.
- Cook vegetables for 10 minutes, stirring after 5 minutes.

Nutrition Facts

- Calories: 37| Protein: 1.4g| Carbohydrates: 3.4g| Fat: 2.4g| Sodium: 152.2mg.

433. Buttery Garlic Green Beans

Prep Time: 10 mins

Cook Time: 10 mins

Total Time: 20 mins

Servings: 4

Ingredient

- 1 pound fresh green beans, trimmed and snapped in half
- 3 tablespoons butter
- 3 cloves garlic, minced
- 2 pinches lemon pepper
- Salt to taste

Instructions

- Place green beans into a large skillet and cover with water; bring to a boil. Reduce heat to medium-low and simmer until beans start to soften about 5 minutes. Drain water. Add butter to green beans; cook and stir until butter is melted 2 to 3 minutes.
- Cook and stir garlic with green beans until garlic is tender and fragrant for 3 to 4 minutes. Season with lemon pepper and salt.

Nutrition Facts

- Calories: 116; Protein: 2.3g; Carbohydrates: 8.9g;

Fat: 8.8g; Cholesterol: 22.9mg; Sodium: 222.5mg

434. Superb Sauteed Mushrooms

Prep Time: 10 mins

Cook Time: 15 mins

Total Time: 25 mins

Servings: 4

Ingredient

- 3 tablespoons olive oil
- 3 tablespoons butter
- 1 pound button mushrooms, sliced
- 1 clove garlic, thinly sliced
- 1 tablespoon red cooking wine
- 1 tablespoon teriyaki sauce, or more to taste
- ¼ teaspoon garlic salt, or to taste
- Freshly ground black pepper to taste

Instructions

- Heat olive oil and butter in a large saucepan over medium heat. Cook and stir mushrooms, garlic, cooking wine, teriyaki sauce, garlic salt, and black pepper in the hot oil and butter until mushrooms are lightly browned, about 5 minutes. Reduce heat to low and simmer until mushrooms are tender, 5 to 8 more minutes.

Nutrition Facts

- Calories: 199; Protein: 3.9g; Carbohydrates: 5.3g; Fat: 19.2g; Cholesterol: 22.9mg; Sodium: 375.7mg.

435. Pan-Fried Asparagus

Prep Time: 5 mins

Cook Time: 15 mins

Additional Time: 5 mins

Total Time: 25 mins

Servings: 4

Ingredient

- ¼ cup butter
- 2 tablespoons olive oil
- 1 teaspoon coarse salt
- ¼ teaspoon ground black pepper

- 3 cloves garlic, minced
- 1 pound fresh asparagus spears, trimmed

Instructions

- Melt butter in a skillet over medium-high heat. Stir in the olive oil, salt, and pepper. Cook garlic in butter for a minute, but do not brown. Add asparagus, and cook for 10 minutes, turning asparagus to ensure even cooking.

Nutrition Facts

- Calories: 188; Protein 2.8g; Carbohydrates 5.2g; Fat 18.4g; Cholesterol 30.5mg; Sodium 524.6mg.

436. Easy Roasted Broccoli

Prep Time: 10 mins

Cook Time: 20 mins

Total Time: 30 mins

Servings: 4

Ingredient

- 14 ounces broccoli
- 1 tablespoon olive oil
- Salt and ground black pepper to taste

Instructions

- Preheat oven to 400 degrees F (200 degrees C).
- Cut broccoli florets from the stalk. Peel the stalk and slice into 1/4-inch slices. Mix florets and stem pieces with olive oil in a bowl and transfer to a baking sheet; season with salt and pepper.
- Roast in the preheated oven until broccoli is tender and lightly browned, about 18 minutes.

Nutrition Facts

- Calories: 63| Protein: 2.8g| Carbohydrates: 6.5g| Fat: 3.7g| Sodium: 71.2mg.

437. Fried Broccoli

Prep Time: 5 mins

Cook Time: 5 mins

Total Time: 10 mins

Servings: 4

Ingredient

- 1 (16 ounces) package frozen broccoli, thawed
- 1 tablespoon olive oil
- ½ teaspoon crushed red pepper flakes
- Salt, to taste

Instructions

- Rinse and pat dry the broccoli.
- Heat the olive oil in a large skillet over medium heat, add the crushed red pepper, and heat for 1 minute. Cook and stir the broccoli in the skillet until it begins to get crispy, 5 to 7 minutes. Season with salt to serve.

Nutrition Facts

- Calories: 61 | Protein 3.2g | Carbohydrates: 5.6g | Fat: 3.8g | Sodium: 27.4mg.

438. Roasted Garlic Lemon Broccoli

Prep Time: 10 mins

Cook Time: 15 mins

Total Time: 25 mins

Servings: 6

Ingredient

- 2 heads of broccoli, separated into florets
- 2 teaspoons extra-virgin olive oil
- 1 teaspoon sea salt
- ½ teaspoon ground black pepper
- 1 clove garlic, minced
- ½ teaspoon lemon juice

Instructions

- Preheat the oven to 400 degrees F (200 degrees C).
- In a large bowl, toss broccoli florets with extra virgin olive oil, sea salt, pepper, and garlic. Spread the broccoli out in an even layer on a baking sheet.
- Bake in the preheated oven until florets are tender enough to pierce the stems with a fork, 15 to 20 minutes. Remove and transfer to a serving platter. Squeeze lemon juice liberally over the broccoli before serving for a refreshing, tangy finish.

Nutrition Facts

- Calories:124|Protein:2.9g|Carbohydrates:7g|Fat:1.9g| Sodium: 326.5mg.

439. Vegetables And Cabbage Stir-Fry With Oyster Sauce

Prep Time: 15 mins

Cook Time: 5 mins

Total Time: 20 mins

Servings: 6

Ingredient

- 2 tablespoons olive oil
- 1 pound broccoli florets
- 1 pound cauliflower florets
- ½ head cabbage, cut into bite-size pieces
- 2 cloves garlic, minced
- 2 tablespoons oyster sauce

Instructions

- Heat olive oil in a large skillet or wok over medium-high heat; saute broccoli, cauliflower, cabbage, and garlic in the hot oil until tender-crisp, about 5 minutes.
- Remove pan from heat and drizzle oyster sauce over the vegetable mix and toss to coat.

Nutrition Facts

- Calories: 111| Protein: 5g| Carbohydrates: 15.2g; Fat: 5g| Sodium: 102.1mg.

440. Bright And Zesty Broccoli

Prep Time: 15 mins

Cook Time: 10 mins

Total Time: 25 mins

Servings: 4

Ingredient

- 1 tablespoon extra-virgin olive oil
- 1 ½ tablespoon grated orange zest
- ½ teaspoon red pepper flakes
- 1 head broccoli, cut into small pieces with stalks peeled

- ¼ teaspoon sea salt
- ¼ teaspoon freshly ground black pepper
- 2 tablespoons freshly squeezed orange juice

Instructions

Heat the olive oil in a large skillet over medium heat; add the orange zest and red pepper flakes and allow to heat briefly for about 1 minute. Stir the broccoli into the mixture; season with salt and pepper. Continue cooking about 5 minutes more; transfer to a serving bowl. Pour the orange juice over the broccoli and toss to coat. Serve hot.

Nutrition Facts

- Calories: 63| Protein: 2.3g| Carbohydrates: 6.6g| Fat: 3.7g| Sodium: 135.1mg.

441. Spinach & Mushroom Quiche

Active Time: 25 mins

Total Time: 1 hr 5 mins

Servings: 6

Ingredient

- 2 tablespoons extra-virgin olive oil
- 8 ounces sliced fresh mixed wild mushrooms such as cremini, shiitake, button, and/or oyster mushrooms
- 1 ½ cups thinly sliced sweet onion
- 1 tablespoon thinly sliced garlic
- 5 ounces fresh baby spinach (about 8 cups), coarsely chopped
- 6 large eggs
- ¼ cup whole milk
- ¼ cup half-and-half
- 1 tablespoon Dijon mustard
- 1 tablespoon fresh thyme leaves, plus more for garnish
- ¼ teaspoon salt
- ¼ teaspoon ground pepper
- 1 ½ cups shredded Gruyère cheese

Instructions

- Preheat oven to 375 degrees F. Coat a 9-inch pie pan with cooking spray; set aside.
- Heat oil in a large nonstick skillet over medium-high heat; swirl to coat the pan. Add mushrooms;

cook, stirring occasionally until browned and tender, about 8 minutes. Add onion and garlic; cook, stirring often, until softened and tender, about 5 minutes. Add spinach; cook, tossing constantly, until wilted, 1 to 2 minutes. Remove from heat.
- Whisk eggs, milk, half-and-half, mustard, thyme, salt, and pepper in a medium bowl. Fold in the mushroom mixture and cheese. Spoon into the prepared pie pan. Bake until set and golden brown, about 30 minutes. Let stand for 10 minutes; slice. Garnish with thyme and serve.

Nutrition Facts

- Calories: 227| Protein: 17.1g| Carbohydrates: 6.8g| Dietary Fiber: 1.5g| Sugars: 3.2g| Fat: 20g| Saturated Fat: 8.2g| Vitamin C: 10.8mg| Calcium: 357.8mg| Iron: 2mg| Magnesium: 41.8mg| Potassium: 289.1mg| Sodium: 442.5mg

442. Cabbage Diet Soup

Active Time: 35 mins

Total Time: 55 mins

Servings: 6

Ingredient

- 2 tablespoons extra-virgin olive oil
- 1 medium onion, chopped
- 2 medium carrots, chopped
- 2 stalks celery, chopped
- 1 medium red bell pepper, chopped
- 2 cloves garlic, minced
- 1 ½ teaspoon Italian seasoning
- ½ teaspoon ground pepper
- ¼ teaspoon salt
- 8 cups low-sodium vegetable broth
- 1 medium head green cabbage, halved and sliced
- 1 large tomato, chopped
- 2 teaspoons white-wine vinegar

Instructions

- Heat oil in a large pot over medium heat. Add onion, carrots, and celery. Cook, stirring until the vegetables begin to soften, 6 to 8 minutes. Add bell pepper, garlic, Italian seasoning, pepper, and salt and cook, stirring, for 2 minutes.

- Add broth, cabbage, and tomato; increase the heat to medium-high and bring to a boil. Reduce heat to maintain a simmer, partially cover, and cook until all the vegetables are tender, 15 to 20 minutes more. Remove from heat and stir in vinegar.

Nutrition Facts

- Calories: 133| Protein: 3g| Carbohydrates: 19.8g| Dietary Fiber: 7g| Sugars: 11g| Fat: 5.2g| Saturated Fat: 0.7g| Vitamin C: 88.2mg| Calcium: 110.7mg| Iron: 1.5mg| Magnesium: 30.2mg| Potassium: 504.1mg|Sodium: 451.1mg

443. Mexican Cabbage Soup

Total Time: 20 mins

Servings: 8

Ingredient

- 2 tablespoons extra-virgin olive oil
- 2 cups chopped onions
- 1 cup chopped carrot
- 1 cup chopped celery
- 1 cup chopped poblano or green bell pepper
- 4 large cloves garlic, minced
- 8 cups sliced cabbage
- 1 tablespoon tomato paste
- 1 tablespoon minced chipotle chiles in adobo sauce
- 1 teaspoon ground cumin
- ½ teaspoon ground coriander
- 4 cups low-sodium vegetable broth or chicken broth
- 4 cups water
- 2 (15 ounces) cans of low-sodium pinto or black beans, rinsed
- ¾ teaspoon salt
- ½ cup chopped fresh cilantro, plus more for serving
- 2 tablespoons lime juice

Instructions

- Heat oil in a large soup pot (8-quart or larger) over medium heat. Add onions, carrot, celery, poblano (or bell pepper), and garlic; cook, stirring frequently, until softened, 10 to 12 minutes. Add cabbage; cook, stirring

occasionally until slightly softened, about 10 minutes more. Add tomato paste, chipotle, cumin, and coriander; cook, stirring, for 1 minute more.
- Add broth, water, beans, and salt. Cover and bring to a boil over high heat. Reduce heat and simmer, partially covered, until the vegetables are tender about 10 minutes. Remove from heat and stir in cilantro and lime juice. Serve garnished with cheese, yogurt, and/or avocado, if desired.

Nutrition Facts

- Calories: 167; Protein: 6.5g| Carbohydrates: 27.1g| Dietary Fiber: 8.7g| Sugars: 6.6g| Fat: 3.8g| Saturated Fat: 0.6g| Vitamin A: 2968.9IU| Vitamin C: 47.2mg| Folate: 48.4mcg| Calcium: 115mg| Iron: 2.3mg| Magnesium: 50.5mg| Potassium: 623.7mg| Sodium: 408.1mg|

444. Everything Bagel Avocado Toast

Active Time: 5 mins

Total Time: 5 mins

Servings: 1

Ingredient

- ¼ medium avocado, mashed
- 1 slice whole-grain bread, toasted
- 2 teaspoons everything bagel seasoning
- Pinch of flaky sea salt (such as Maldon)

Instructions

- Spread avocado on toast. Top with seasoning and salt.

Nutrition Facts

- Calories: 172; Protein: 5.4g| Carbohydrates: 17.8g| Dietary Fiber: 5.9g| Sugars: 2.3g| Fat: 9.8g| Saturated Fat: 1.4g| Vitamin C: 5.5mg| Calcium: 60.5mg| Iron: 1.3mg| Magnesium: 41.4mg| Potassium: 341.5mg| Sodium: 251.8mg| Added Sugar: 1g.

445. Quick Vegetable Saute

Total Time: 15 mins

Servings: 4

Ingredient

- 1 tablespoon extra-virgin olive oil
- 1 small shallot, minced
- 4 cups mixed frozen vegetables, such as corn, carrots, and green beans
- ½ teaspoon dried dill or tarragon
- ¼ teaspoon salt
- ¼ teaspoon freshly ground pepper

Instructions

- Heat oil in a large skillet over medium heat. Add shallot and cook, stirring, until softened, about 1 minute. Stir in frozen vegetables. Cover and cook, stirring occasionally, until the vegetables are tender, 4 to 6 minutes. Stir in dill (or tarragon), salt, and pepper.

Nutrition Facts

- Calories: 107; Protein: 2.6g| Carbohydrates: 16.8g| Dietary Fiber: 3.5g|Sugars: 4.2g| Fat: 4.2g| Saturated Fat: 0.6g| Vitamin A: 6423.6IU| Vitamin C: 9.6mg| Folate: 28.3mcg| Calcium: 38.8mg| Iron: 0.9mg| Magnesium: 24mg| Potassium: 293.9mg| Sodium: 177.7mg| Thiamin: 0.1mg.

---

446. Air Fryer Frozen Vegetables (No More Mushy Frozen Broccoli!)

Prep Time: 5 Mins

Cook Time: 20 Mins

Total Time: 25 Mins

Ingredients For Air Fryer Frozen Broccoli:

- 1 lb. frozen broccoli (do not thaw)
- 3 tablespoons avocado oil
- 1 teaspoon Trader Joe's Everything But the Bagel Seasoning (other seasoning blends may be substituted)
- cooking oil spray of choice

Ingredients For Air Fryer Frozen Cauliflower:

- 1 lb. frozen cauliflower (do not thaw)
- 3 tablespoons avocado oil

- 1 teaspoon Trader Joe's Everything But the Bagel Seasoning (other seasoning blends may be substituted)
- cooking oil spray of choice

Ingredients For Air Fryer Frozen Brussels Sprouts:

- 12 ounces frozen brussels sprouts (do not thaw)
- 2 tablespoons avocado oil
- 1 teaspoon trader joe's everything but the bagel seasoning (other seasoning blends may be substituted)
- Cooking oil spray of choice

Ingredients For Air Fryer Frozen Spinach:

- 1 lb. Frozen whole leaf spinach (do not thaw)
- 3 tablespoons avocado oil
- 1 teaspoon trader joe's everything but the bagel seasoning (other seasoning blends may be substituted)
- Cooking oil spray of choice

Ingredients For Air Fryer Frozen Okra:

- 12 ounces frozen okra, chopped (do not thaw)
- 2 tablespoons avocado oil
- 1 teaspoon Trader Joe's Everything But the Bagel Seasoning (other seasoning blends may be substituted)
- cooking oil spray of choice

Ingredients For Air Fryer Frozen Butternut Squash:

- 10 ounces frozen butternut squash, chopped small (do not thaw)
- 2 tablespoons avocado oil
- 1 teaspoon trader joe's everything but the bagel seasoning (other seasoning blends may be substituted)
- Cooking oil spray of choice

Instructions

How To Make Air Fryer Frozen Broccoli:

- Cut the frozen broccoli into smaller pieces if some of the pieces are large. (I did not need to do this.) Lightly mist your air fryer baking racks with the cooking spray.
- Drizzle the frozen broccoli with the oil and sprinkle with the seasoning. Stir to distribute it well.

- Spread the broccoli in a single layer on the racks. I used both racks that came with the oven. You may need to cook the broccoli in batches if you have a small air fryer.
- Make sure the drip tray is in place in your air fryer oven. Put the racks in the oven and roast at 400°F for 12 minutes.
- Switch the position of the trays in the oven. Bake an additional 8 minutes. That's it!

How To Make Air Fryer Frozen Cauliflower:

- Cut the frozen cauliflower into smaller pieces if some of the pieces are large. (I did not need to do this.) Lightly mist your air fryer baking racks with the cooking spray.
- Drizzle the frozen cauliflower with the oil and sprinkle with the seasoning. Stir to distribute it well.
- Spread the cauliflower in a single layer on the racks. I used both racks that came with the oven. You may need to cook the cauliflower in batches if you have a small air fryer.
- Make sure the drip tray is in place in your air fryer oven. Put the racks in the oven and roast at 400°F for 12 minutes.
- Switch the position of the trays in the oven. Bake an additional 8 minutes.

How To Make Air Fryer Frozen Brussels Sprouts:

- Lightly mist your air fryer baking racks with the cooking spray.
- Drizzle the frozen Brussels sprouts with the oil and sprinkle with the seasoning. Stir to distribute it well.
- Spread the Brussels sprouts in a single layer on the racks. I used both racks that came with the oven. You may need to cook the Brussels sprouts in batches if you have a small air fryer.
- Make sure the drip tray is in place in your air fryer oven. Put the racks in the oven and roast at 400°F for 10 minutes.
- Switch the position of the trays in the oven. Bake an additional 8 minutes.

How To Make Air Fryer Frozen Spinach:

- Lightly mist your air fryer baking racks with the cooking spray.
- Drizzle the frozen spinach with the oil and sprinkle with the seasoning. Stir to distribute it well.
- Spread the spinach on the air fryer racks. I used both racks that came with the oven. Leave the spinach in frozen clumps for results that are both tender and crispy. Break up the frozen clumps for a spinach side dish that is more crispy.
- Make sure the drip tray is in place in your air fryer oven. Put the racks in the oven and roast at 400°F for 10 minutes.
- Flip and stir the spinach pieces. Switch the position of the trays in the oven. Bake an additional 10 minutes.

How To Make Air Fryer Frozen Okra:

- Lightly mist your air fryer baking racks with the cooking spray.
- Drizzle the frozen okra with the oil and sprinkle with the seasoning. Stir to distribute it well.
- Spread the okra in a single layer on the racks. I used both racks that came with the oven. You may need to cook the okra in batches if you have a small air fryer.
- Make sure the drip tray is in place in your air fryer oven. Put the racks in the oven and roast at 400°F for 12 minutes.
- Switch the position of the trays in the oven. Bake an additional 8 minutes.

How To Make Air Fryer Frozen Butternut Squash:

- Lightly mist your air fryer baking racks with the cooking spray.
- Drizzle the frozen winter squash with the oil and sprinkle with the seasoning. Stir to distribute it well.
- Spread the butternut squash in a single layer on the air fryer racks. I was able to fit it all on a single rack.
- Make sure the drip tray is in place in your air fryer oven. Put the rack in the top rack position in the oven and roast at 400°F for 20 minutes, stirring and flipping the squash after 12 minutes.

Nutrition

Calories: 128kcal | Carbohydrates: 4g | Protein: 2g | Fat: 10.5g | Saturated Fat: 1.2g | Sodium: 100mg | Potassium: 180mg | Fiber: 2g

9. Air Fryer Salad Recipes

447. Air Fryer Healthy Southwestern Salad

Prep Time: 5 mins

Cook Time: 8 mins

Total Time: 13 mins

Ingredients

Kitchen Gadgets:

- Air Fryer
- Air Fryer Grill Pan
- Salad Bowl
- Southwestern Salad Recipe Ingredients:
- 600 g Chickpeas
- 1 Medium Red Pepper
- 200 g Frozen Sweetcorn
- 2 Celery Sticks
- ¼ Medium Cucumber
- ½ Small Red Onion
- 2 Tbsp Extra Virgin Olive Oil
- 1 Tsp Grainy Mustard
- ¼ Tsp Garlic Powder
- 1 Tsp Basil
- 2 Tsp Mexican Seasoning
- Salt & Pepper

Instructions

- Drain and rinse your chickpeas. Chop your red pepper into bite-size cubes. Load into the air fryer basket with the grill attachment the chickpeas, sweetcorn, and pepper. Sprinkle with Mexican seasoning and salt and pepper and cook for 8 minutes at 180c/360f.
- While the air fryer is in action, prep the rest of your salad. Peel and thinly slice your red onion. Clean and thinly dice your cucumber and celery. Load all three into a salad bowl.
- Mix extra virgin olive oil, basil, grainy mustard, and garlic powder. Pour into your salad bowl and mix.
- When the air fryer beeps, load in the ingredients and mix a little more.
- Serve or store into containers for later.

Nutrition

- Calories: 384kcal | Carbohydrates: 58g | Protein: 16g | Fat: 12g | Saturated Fat: 2g | Sodium: 44mg | Potassium: 737mg | Fiber: 15g | Sugar: 12g | | Vitamin C: 45mg | Calcium: 127mg | Iron: 6mg

448. Kale Salad with Air Fryer Herb Chicken Breast

Prep Time: 20 mins

Cook Time: 20 mins

Total Time: 40 mins

Ingredients

- 1 Tablespoon Panko (Bread Crumbs)
- 2 Tablespoons Mixed Dry Herbs Use your favorite blend
- 1 Teaspoon Smoked Paprika
- 1 Teaspoon Salt
- 1 Tablespoon Olive Oil
- 1.5 Pounds Chicken Breast Pounded Evenly
- 1 Cup Corn Kernels From about 2 years, if fresh
- 8 Strawberries, Sliced & Quartered
- 1/2 Ounce Goat Cheese
- 2 Avocados, halved and sliced
- 2 Hard Boiled Eggs, sliced
- 2 Tablespoons Extra Virgin Olive Oil
- 16 Ounce Bag Baby Kale Greens (Washed & Ready)

Instructions

- Combine panko, herbs, smoked paprika, salt, and olive oil in a small bowl to make a paste. Apply this evenly to the chicken breast.
- Cook the chicken in a preheated air fryer for 20 minutes at 370 degrees. Let it rest outside of the air fryer for 5 minutes before slicing for the salad
- In a large salad bowl or serving plate, place your bed of salad greens and then add the corn, strawberries, goat cheese, avocado, hard-boiled eggs, and chicken
- Drizzle the extra virgin olive oil over the top and then season lightly with salt and pepper

Nutrient Value

- Calories: 572kcal | Carbohydrates: 1g | Protein: 46g | Fat: 43g | Saturated Fat: 22g | Cholesterol:

168mg | Sodium: 219mg | Potassium: 606mg | Sugar: 1g | Calcium: 16mg | Iron: 4mg

---

449. Easy Air Fryer Broccoli

Prep Time: 5 Minutes

Cook Time: 6 Minutes

Total Time: 11 Minutes

Ingredients

- 2 heads of broccoli, cut into bite-sized pieces
- 2 tablespoons olive oil
- Sea salt, to taste
- Fresh cracked black pepper, to taste

Instructions

- 2 heads of broccoli, cut into bite-sized pieces
- 2 tablespoons olive oil
- Sea salt, to taste
- Fresh cracked black pepper, to taste

Nutrition Information

- Calories: 126| Total Fat: 8g| Saturated Fat: 1g| Trans Fat: 0g| Unsaturated Fat: 6g| Cholesterol: 0mg| Sodium: 222mg| Carbohydrates: 14g| Fiber: 6g| Sugar: 3g| Protein: 4g

---

450. Roasted Vegetable Pasta Salad

Prep Time: 40 minutes

Cook Time: 1 hour 45 minutes

Total Time: 2 hours 25 minutes

Ingredients

- 3 eggplant (small)
- 1 tablespoon olive oil
- 3 zucchini (medium-sized. Aka courgette.
- 1 tablespoon olive oil
- 4 tomatoes (medium. Cut in eighths)
- 300 g pasta (large, shaped pasta. 4 cups)
- 2 bell peppers (any color)
- 175 g cherry tomatoes (sliced. Or tomatoes cut into small chunks. 1 cup)
- 2 teaspoons salt (or salt sub)
- 8 tablespoons parmesan cheese (grated)
- 125 ml italian dressing (bottled, fat free/ 1/2 cup / 4 oz)
- Basil (few leaves of fresh)

Instructions

- Wash eggplant, slice off and discard the green end. Do not peel. Slice the eggplant into 1 cm (1/2 inch) thick rounds. If using a paddle-type air fryer such as an Actifry™, put in a pan with 1 tablespoon of olive oil. If using a basket-type such as an AirFryer™, toss with 1 tablespoon of olive oil and put in the basket. Cook for about 40 minutes until quite soft and no raw taste left. Set aside.
- Wash zucchini/courgette, slice off and discard the green end. Do not peel. Slice into 1 cm (1/2 inch) thick rounds. If using a paddle-type air fryer such as an Actifry™, put in a pan with 1 tablespoon of olive oil. If using a basket-type such as an AirFryer™, toss with 1 tablespoon of olive oil and put in the basket. Cook for about 25 minutes until quite soft and no raw taste left. Set aside.
- Wash and chunk the tomatoes. If using an Actifry 2 in 1, arranged in a top grill pan. If using a basket-type air fryer, arrange it in the basket. Spray lightly with cooking spray. Roast for about 30 minutes until reduced in size and starting to brown. Set aside.
- Cook the pasta according to pasta directions, empty into a colander, run cold water over it to wash some starch off, drain, set aside to cool.
- Wash, seed, and chop the bell pepper; put into a large bowl. Wash and slice the cherry tomatoes (or small-chunk the regular tomato); add to that bowl. Add the roast veggies, the pasta, the salt, the dressing, the chopped basil, and the parm, and toss all with your (clean) hands to mix well.
- Set in fridge to chill and marinate.
- Serve chilled or room temperature.

Nutrition

- Serving: 1g | Calories: 121kcal | Carbohydrates: 23g | Protein: 5g | Fat: 4g | Saturated Fat: 1g | Sodium: 417mg | Potassium: 471mg | Fiber: 4g | Sugar: 7g | Vitamin C: 34.2mg | Calcium: 53mg | Iron: 0.8mg

451. Air Fryer Buffalo Chicken Salad

Prep Time: 15 Mins

Cook Time: 15 Mins

Total Time: 30 Mins

Ingredients

- 1 pound boneless, skinless chicken breasts, thick sides pounded to make an even thickness
- 1/2 cup WHOLE30 Buffalo Vinaigrette
- 6 cups chopped romaine lettuce
- 1 cup thinly sliced celery
- 1/2 cup shredded carrot
- 3-4 tbsp WHOLE30 Ranch Dressing
- 1 small ripe avocado, peeled, pitted, and sliced
- 1 cup cherry tomatoes, halved
- Freshly ground black pepper
- 2 tsp finely chopped chives

Instructions

- IN a large resealable plastic bag, combine chicken and WHOLE30 Buffalo Vinaigrette. Massage to coat. Seal bag and marinate in the refrigerator for at least 2 hours and up to 4 hours.
- PREHEAT air fryer* to 375°F. Remove chicken from bag; discard marinade. Add the chicken to the air fryer. Cook until chicken is no longer pink and the internal temperature is 170°F, turning once about 15 minutes. Let stand while making the salad.
- IN a large bowl, combine the romaine, celery, and carrot. Add the WHOLE30 Ranch Dressing; toss to combine. Divide salad among four serving plates.
- SLICE the chicken. Top the salads with sliced chicken, avocado, and cherry tomatoes. Season to taste with black pepper. Sprinkle with chives.

Nutrients Value

- Calories: 122| Fat: 8g| Sat fat: 2g| Unsatfat: 5g| Protein: 10g| Carbohydrate| 0g Fiber 0g| Sugars 0g| Added sugars: 0g| Sodium: 254mg

452. Cajun Potato Salad Recipe

Prep Time: 10 Minutes

Cook Time: 20 Minutes

Total Time: 30 Minutes

Ingredients

- 2 1/2 lb red potatoes, quartered
- 2 tablespoons avocado oil (or grapeseed, coconut, or vegetable)
- 3 tablespoons The Fit Cook Southern Creole
- pinch of sea salt & pepper
- 2 slices cooked bacon, chopped and crumbled

Salad Sauce

- 2/3 cup light mayo (I used olive oil mayo)
- 7oz 2% Greek yogurt
- 1/8 cup Dijon mustard (or more to taste)
- 5 BOILED eggs, chopped
- 1 cup diced Dill pickles (OR sweet if you prefer)
- 1/2 medium red onion, diced
- Sea salt & pepper to taste

Steps

- Set the air-fryer to 400F (or oven to 420F).
- In a large bowl, toss the sliced potatoes with oil and seasoning. Add the potatoes to the air-fryer basket. Air-fry for about 20 minutes, or until the potatoes are cooked through and the edges are crispy.
- Air-fried Cajun Potato Salad
- Mix the ingredients for the sauce.
- Cook up some bacon in a skillet until crispy.
- Allow the pieces to cool on a paper towel, then chop into pieces.
- Once the potatoes have finished air-frying, LIGHTLY mash about 40-50% of the potatoes in a bowl, then fold in the remaining potatoes and mix. Add the sauce and the remaining ingredients and fold everything together.
- Season to taste using salt & pepper, dill (or sweet) pickles, mustard, or Greek yogurt. Cover with plastic and store in the fridge for at least 20 minutes, but it's much better overnight.

Nutrient Value

- Calories: 491

- Protein: 20g
- Fat: 16g
- Carbs: 72g
- Fiber: 5g
- Sugar: 9g

453. Air Fryer Squash With Kale Salad

Prep Time: 5 minutes

Cook Time: 10 minutes

Total Time: 15 minutes

Ingredients

- Squash
- 1 medium delicata squash (see note 1)
- Salt and pepper to taste (or other spices)
- Salad
- 8 oz kale or other green, chopped
- 1 cup grape or cherry tomatoes, halved
- 2 cups cucumber, sliced
- 1/2 cup pomegranate seeds
- 1/4 cup squash seeds, roasted, optional
- 1/2 avocado, sliced, optional
- 1/2 cup vegan honey mustard dressing, or any dressing

Instructions

Cut The Squash: If using delicata, cut the top and bottom off, then slice it lengthwise down the middle. Cut the delicata (or other squash) into half-inch thick pieces. You can leave delicate in a half-ring shape, or you can slice it into smaller pieces (especially if feeding littles) (bigger is fine, but will take longer to cook). If you find the squash hard to cut, try microwaving it for a minute or two first.

Save The Seeds: I highly recommend saving the seeds and roasting them! It's so easy, and worth it. I find it easiest to scoop out the seeds and membrane with a grapefruit spoon. Then fill a medium-sized bowl with water, so that the seeds mostly float to the top as I free them from the membrane.

Season: Lightly spray the squash with water, (or oil, if that's your thing) and season with salt, pepper, and whatever else you like (sometimes I use garlic, chili, etc.)

Air Fryer Method: Add to your air fryer. They will get crispier if they are in a single layer. Air fry at 375 degrees F (or 191 degrees C) for about 10 minutes, shaking halfway through. If you like it more browned, you can keep cooking for another 5 minutes or so.

Oven Method: Line a baking tray with a silicone baking mat or parchment paper. Lay the squash pieces out in a single layer with a little breathing room (about an inch) between each piece. Bake at 400 degrees Fahrenheit (or 205 degrees Celsius) for about 20-25 minutes, flipping the pieces halfway through.

Store: Refrigerate leftovers in an airtight container. The salad will keep for about 3 days (if dressed), the squash about 5 days (keep separate from the salad if possible). The seeds should keep on the counter in an airtight container for about 5 days.

Nutrients Value

- Calories: 213
- Total Fat: 5.2g
- Sodium: 419.8mg
- Sugar: 23.6g
- Carbohydrates: 37.1mg
- Protein: 7.1g
- Vitamin C: 165.5mg

454. Fried Chickpeas In The Air Fryer

Prep Time: 2 minutes

Cook Time: 12 minutes

Total Time: 14 minutes

Ingredients

- 1 1/2 cups chickpeas 1 15 ounces can drain & rinse
- Spritz cooking spray
- 2 teaspoons **Nutrition Facts**al yeast flakes
- 1/2 teaspoon granulated onion
- Pinch salt

Instructions

- Put the drained chickpeas into the air fryer basket. Set the air fryer for 400 degrees and 12 minutes.
- Cook the plain chickpeas for the first 5 minutes. This will dry them out.
- Then open the basket, spritz the chickpeas with oil, give a shake, and spritz them again. Sprinkle on **Nutrition Facts**al yeast flakes, granulated onion, and a pinch of salt.

- Return the basket to the air fryer and cook for the remaining 7 minutes.
- Test a chickpea to see if it's done enough for you. Depending on your air fryer, the softness of your chickpeas, and your personal preferences, you may want to cook them for an additional 3 to 5 minutes. If desired, add another pinch of salt before serving.

Nutrition

- Calories: 105kcal | Carbohydrates: 17g | Protein: 5g | Fat: 1g | Sodium: 4mg | Potassium: 198mg | Fiber: 4g | Sugar: 2g | Vitamin A: 15IU | Vitamin C: 0.8mg | Calcium: 30mg | Iron: 1.8mg

---

455. Air Fryer Buffalo Chicken Tenders Salad

Prep Time: 15 minutes

Cook Time: 25 minutes

Total Time: 40 minutes

Ingredients

Chicken Tenders:

- ½ cup blanched almond flour
- 1 tsp sea salt
- 1 tsp paprika
- ¼ tsp ground black pepper
- 2 large chicken breasts, sliced lengthwise into ½" strips
- ¼ cup tapioca flour
- 2 tbsp garlic-infused olive oil
- Avocado oil cooking spray

Salad:

- 2 hearts of romaine, chopped
- 1 cup carrots, coarsely-shredded
- 1 cup grape tomatoes, halved
- 1 bunch scallions, green tops only, chopped
- 1 red pepper, diced
- Your other favorite salad ingredients

Ranch Dressing:

- ½ Batch of my dairy-free homemade ranch dressing recipe (paleo, whole30, low fodmap)

Buffalo Sauce:

- ⅓ cup Paleo Low-FODMAP hot sauce
- 3 tbsp ghee, melted
- 1 tbsp garlic-infused olive oil
- ½ tbsp coconut aminos

Instructions

- Preheat the air fryer to 370° F for 10 minutes. While your air fryer preheats, combine almond flour, sea salt, paprika, and pepper in a large bowl, whisk to combine, and set aside. Place chicken strips in another large bowl. Add tapioca flour to the bowl and toss with your hands to coat the strips evenly. Add the garlic-infused oil and toss again to coat. Dredge each strip in the almond flour mixture, shaking off the excess, and set on a plate.
- Once your air fryer has preheated, spray the pan with cooking spray. Using tongs, place half of the breaded chicken strips in the pan in one layer, ideally not touching one another. Spray the strips lightly with cooking spray. Air fry for 12 minutes, flipping halfway through. Once the first batch has cooked, place it on a clean plate using a clean set of tongs and set aside. Using tongs, take one of the thickest strips out of the air fryer and check its temperature using an instant-read thermometer. The temperature of cooked chicken should be at least 165° F (75° C) to be safely consumed. Once the first batch is at the proper temperature, repeat these steps for the second half of the strips.
- While the chicken strips are frying, prepare a half-batch of my dairy-free homemade ranch dressing recipe, cover, and refrigerate until ready to serve. Chop the ingredients under "salad," place in a large serving bowl, and refrigerate.
- A minute or two before the chicken strips are done, in a large bowl, add the ingredients under "buffalo sauce," whisk to combine, and set aside until all the chicken strips are cooked. If the sauce solidifies, microwave it (covered) for about 20 seconds and whisk again.
- Once the second batch of strips has finished cooking, if desired, place the first batch back in the air fryer on top of the second batch and air fry at 370° F for a minute or so until heated (I typically skip this step as they're going on a cold salad anyway). Using tongs, take each strip out of the air fryer, dip in the buffalo sauce until fully-

coated, and place it on a plate. Chop strips horizontally into small pieces if desired and serve on top of the salad with the ranch dressing.

Nutrient Value

- Total Fat: 30.8gg
- Sodium: 1321.9mg
- Sugar: 6.7g
- Vitamin A: 567.5ug
- Carbohydrates: 21.4g
- Protein:29.8g
- Vitamin C: 56.8mg

456. Roasted Salmon With Fennel Salad In An Air Fryer

Active Time: 15 Mins

Total Time: 25 Mins

How To Make It

- Your air fryer has more up its sleeve than the expected crispy tricks—it's also a fantastic oven for roasting meaty fish fillets like salmon. This recipe serves four, but you can easily cut it in half to make a date night dinner for two.
- Everything comes together so easily—while the salmon cooks, whip up the quick and tangy fennel slaw. By the time you're finished, the salmon will be hot and ready to plate up. For a little extra heft, serve this meal with a side of your favorite quick-cooking brown rice.
- Try it with the air-fryer broccoli with cheese sauce, also pictured.

Ingredients

- 2 teaspoons chopped fresh flat-leaf parsley 1 teaspoon finely chopped fresh thyme 1 teaspoon kosher salt, divided 4 (6-oz.) skinless center-cut salmon fillets 2 tablespoons olive oil 4 cups thinly sliced fennel (from 2 [15-oz.] heads fennel) 2/3 cup 2% reduced-fat Greek yogurt 1 garlic clove, grated 2 tablespoons fresh orange juice (from 1 orange) 1 teaspoon fresh lemon juice (from 1 lemon) 2 tablespoons chopped fresh dill

Nutritional Information

- Calories: 464| Fat: 30g |Sat fat: 7g| Unsatfat: 21g| Protein: 38g |Carbohydrate: 9g| Fiber: 3g| Sugars: 5g| Added sugars: 0g |Sodium: 635mg

457. Air Fryer Taco Salad Bowls

Prep Time: 1 Minute

Cook Time: 7 Minutes

Total Time: 8 Minutes

Ingredients

- 1 burrito sized flour tortilla
- Cooking spray

Instructions

- Spray both sides of the tortilla with cooking spray.
- Fold a piece of foil double thickness the size of the tortilla.
- Fold into the basket of your air fryer.
- Place a larger ramekin (or something similar) into the middle of the shell.
- Air fry for 5 minutes at 400 degrees.
- Carefully remove ramekin (it's HOT!!) and foil. Place ramekin back into the center, air fry 2 minutes more.

Nutrition Information

- Calories: 220| Total Fat: 20g| Saturated Fat: 7g| Trans Fat: 0g| Unsaturated Fat: 11g| Cholesterol: 29mg| Sodium: 1321mg| Carbohydrates: 84g| Fiber: 11g| Sugar: 5g| Protein: 21g

458. Air Fryer, Grilled Chicken Caesar Salad

Prep Time: 5 Minutes

Cook Time: 10 Minutes

Additional Time: 5 Minutes

Total Time: 20 Minutes

Ingredients

Grilled Chicken:

- 2 boneless skinless chicken breast, about 5 ounces each
- 2 tablespoons chicken seasoning (i used lawry's)
- Olive oil spray

Salad:

- 1/2 cup garlic croutons

- 1/4 cup caesar salad dressing
- 2 cups shredded romaine lettuce
- 1/3 cup shredded Parmesan cheese

Instructions

- Rub the chicken seasoning all over the chicken
- As you coat them place them in either a greased air fryer basket or on a greased air fryer tray. Once you are all done coating your chicken, spray them with olive oil spray (the entire chicken breast, otherwise you will get white spots on your chicken)
- Set the temperature to 350 degrees F, for 5-10 minutes. (air fryer setting)
- When the time is up, make sure that the internal temperature reads at least: 165 degrees F.
- In a large mixing bowl, add the lettuce, shredded parmesan cheese, and salad dressing.
- Mix well.
- Cut up the chicken and add it on top.
- Plate, serve, and enjoy!

Nutrients Value

- Calories: 212| Total Fat: 7g| Saturated Fat: 2g| Unsaturated Fat: 0g| Cholesterol: 83mg| Sodium: 282mg| Carbohydrates: 2g| Fiber: 1g| Sugar: 1g| Protein: 33g

459. Air Fryer Brussel Sprout Caesar Salad

PREP TIME: 2 mins

COOK TIME: 15 mins

Ingredients

- 10 oz Brussel sprouts, cut the ends off
- 4 tbsp Caesar dressing, storebought or homemade
- 2 tbsp shaved parmesan
- 1/4 cup garlic croutons

Instructions

- Cut the ends off of the Brussel sprouts and with your hands flake them apart. The more loose pieces, the more crispy crunchy pieces!
- Add to the air fryer basket and drizzle with olive oil, season with salt and pepper.
- Air fry for 15 minutes at 375 until many of the edges and pieces are brown and crispy
- Transfer to a salad bowl, drizzle with caesar dressing, top with parmesan and croutons.

Nutrients Value

- Calories: 122| Fat: 8g| Sat fat: 2g| Unsatfat: 5g| Protein: 10g| Carbohydrate| 0g Fiber 0g| Sugars 0g| Added sugars: 0g| Sodium: 254mg

460. Crispy Chicken Cobb Salad

Prep Time: 15 mins

Total Time: 15 mins

Ingredients

- 3 oz of cooked chicken strips (I like Tyson)
- hard-boiled
- 10 cherry tomatoes, cut in half
- to 3 green onions
- 1/2 cup of cucumbers
- cups of lettuce
- 2 tablespoons of reduced-fat cheese
- Ranch Dressing or Catalina Dressing

Instructions

- Place 3 oz of frozen chicken breast strips in the air fryer basket and cook the chicken breast for 12 minutes at 350.
- While the chicken is cooking slice the cucumbers and cherry tomatoes.
- To make the salad place 2 cups of lettuce, cucumbers, cherry tomatoes, hard-boiled eggs, (optional) cheese, and chopped chicken on top of the lettuce.
- The salad with Catalina or Ranch dressing on top. I typically don't count dressings for points and that is just what works for me.

Nutrition

- Calories: 536| Sugar: 6| Fat: 36| Saturated Fat: 6| Unsaturated Fat: 15|Carbohydrates: 28| Fiber: 13| Protein: 29

461. Egg Salad Poppers Recipe

Prep time: 20mins

Ingredients

- ¼ cup eggs, hard-boiled (chopped)
- 4 ounces Neufchatel cheese
- 2 Tablespoons Mayonnaise
- 2 Tablespoons spinach leaf (chopped)
- 2 Tablespoons green onion (minced)
- For the coating
- 2 Tablespoons THM Oat Fiber
- ¼ cup egg white
- 2 each Low Carb Whole Wheat Tortilla (toasted and crushed)

Instructions

- In a medium bowl mix eggs, cheese, mayonnaise, spinach, and onion together.
- Scoop mixture into 1 TBS mounds on a parchment-lined sheet and freeze for 30 minutes.
- Preheat Air Fryer to 350° F
- Remove egg mounds from the freezer and roll in oat fiber, dip each one into the egg whites, and roll in the crushed low carb tortillas.
- Place coated egg salad balls onto your air fryer rack and bake for 6-8 minutes.
- Be careful when removing from your air fryer as these are delicate and the shell will break easily when they are hot.
- Allow cooling for a few minutes before eating. Can also be eaten cold when stored in the fridge.

Nutrition Information

- Calories: 239
- Fat: 20g
- Carbohydrates: 18g
- Sodium: 458mg
- Fiber: 14g
- Protein: 11g
- Cholesterol: 79mg

---

462. Gluten Free Buffalo Cauliflower Salad

Serves: 4 Salads

Prep Time: 15 Mins

Cook Time: 20 Min

Total Time: 35 Min

Ingredients

- 1/2 cup Frank's red hot sauce
- 1 tablespoon coconut oil (or butter)
- Florets from 1 medium head of cauliflower
- 1/2 cup almond milk
- 1/2 cup water
- 3/4 cup almond flour
- 2 teaspoons garlic powder
- 2 teaspoons onion powder
- 1 teaspoon paprika
- salt and pepper
- 2 celery ribs
- 1 cup halved cherry tomatoes (you can do this while you wait for the cauliflower to cook)
- 1 ripe large avocado
- 2 romaine hearts, chopped
- 1 cup shredded carrots
- to drizzle: ½ cup Ranch dressing

Instructions

- Preheat an air fryer to 400 degrees.
- Place two large bowls next to each other on your workspace. In one bowl, whisk together the hot sauce and coconut oil. In the other bowl, whisk together almond milk, water, flour, garlic powder, onion powder, paprika, salt, and pepper. Add the cauliflower to the bowl. Dredge the cauliflower florets through the mixture and coat them well, patting the mixture into the crevices of the cauliflower. Using tongs (or your hands), transfer the dredged cauliflower into the hot sauce bowl and toss well to coat.
- Add the cauliflower in an even layer in the basket of the air fryer. Set for 10 minutes and halfway through, flip the cauliflower and let cook for an additional 5 minutes.
- While cauliflower cooks, prepare the rest of the recipe. Pour the hot sauce into a large bowl and set aside. Dice the celery, halve the cherry tomatoes, and peel, pit, and slice the avocado. Set everything aside.
- After you're done prepping the salad ingredients, prepare the salads. Divide the romaine lettuce into bowls and drizzle each with 1 tablespoon of Ranch dressing. Divide the

toppings onto the bowls (the celery, tomatoes, avocado, carrots) and once the cauliflower is done cooking, add that to the salad bowls. Drizzle with another tablespoon of Ranch dressing. Serve.

Nutrients Value

- Total Fat: 22g | Saturated Fat: 10g | Trans Fat: 0g | Unsaturated Fat: 12g | Cholesterol: 88mg | Sodium: 789mg | Carbohydrates: 2g | Fiber: 1g | Sugar: 0g | Protein: 29g

463. Air Fryer Coconut Shrimp Salad

Prep Time: 30 minutes

Cook Time: 30 minutes

Servings: 6 servings

Ingredients

Coconut Shrimp

- 2 lbs extra-large shrimp (13-15 per lb), peeled, tail-on
- 1 cup panko bread crumbs* (56 grams)
- 1/2 cup finely shredded sweetened coconut* (40 grams)
- 1/2 cup white whole wheat flour* (60 grams)
- 2 eggs
- 1/2 tsp each: salt and pepper

Salad

- 10 cups baby spinach (325 grams)
- 2 medium mangos, peeled and chopped (650 grams)
- 2 small avocados, peeled and chopped (225 grams)
- 1 1/2 cups cherry tomatoes, halved (225 grams)
- 1/3 cup pickled red onion – recipe below (45 grams)
- 1/4 cup cilantro, chopped (5 grams)

Sweet Chili Dressing

- 1/4 cup sweet Thai chili sauce (2 oz)
- 2 tbsp lime juice (1 oz)
- 2 tbsp coconut milk (1 oz)

Instructions

- Whisk dressing ingredients until combined, set aside.
- Assemble the base of salad with spinach, mango, avocado, tomatoes, pickled red onion, and cilantro. Set aside in the refrigerator while prepping the shrimp.
- Add coconut and breadcrumbs to a bowl and mix until combined. Set aside.
- Add flour, salt, and pepper to a separate bowl and mix. Set aside.
- Add eggs to a third bowl and whisk. Set aside.
- Rinse and dry shrimp on a paper towel, then dip them one at a time into flour, then eggs, then breadcrumb mixture, coating the shrimp completely.
- Air fry shrimp at 380 degrees for 7-8 minutes or until breading is golden brown and shrimp is cooked through.
- Top salad base with shrimp and dressing and serve.

Nutrition Facts

- Calories: 402
- Calories From Fat: 108
- Fat: 12g
- Cholesterol: 289mg
- Sodium: 431mg
- Potassium: 797mg
- Carbohydrates: 37g
- Fiber: 6g
- Sugar: 22g
- Protein: 37g

464. Crispy Keto Air Fryer Pork Chops

Prep Time: 15 minutes

Cook Time: 10 minutes

Total Time: 25 minutes

Ingredients

- Boneless Pork Chops
- 4–6 center-cut boneless pork chops (4–6 oz each, ~ ¾ inch thick)
- Keto Pork Chops Coating
- ⅓ cup almond flour
- ⅓ cup grated parmesan (or sub additional almond flour)
- 1 tsp garlic powder

- 1 tsp paprika
- ½ tsp onion powder
- ½ tsp salt
- ½ tsp black pepper
- 2 eggs

Instructions

How To Air Fry Pork Chops

- Preheat air fryer to 400°F (200°C).
- Mix almond flour, grated parmesan, and seasonings in a shallow dish.
- In a separate dish, beat eggs.
- Coat pork chops in egg, and then coating mixture. Transfer coated chops to a plate.
- Spray both sides of coated chops with cooking spray, then add to the air fryer. Cook 3-4 at a time only. (Don't overcrowd your air fryer!)
- Cook boneless pork chops for 10 minutes, flipping halfway through. (Thicker chops and bone-in chops may need to cook for longer, 12-20 minutes.)
- After flipping, check the internal temperature of the pork every 1-2 minutes, until it reaches 145°F (63°C). To check the internal temperature, insert a meat thermometer straight into the side of the pork chop.
- Allow resting 3 minutes before slicing to reveal a perfect blush pink center.

How To Oven Fry Pork Chops

- Preheat oven to 425°F (210°C).
- Prepare and coat keto pork chops as described above.
- Spray both sides of coated pork chops with cooking spray and add to a baking rack on top of a lined baking sheet.
- Bake for 20 minutes, flipping halfway through. (May need to bake longer for thicker chops or bone-in chops.)
- Near the end of cook time, check oven fried pork chops temperature as explained above.

Nutrition

Calories:273| Sugar: 0.5g| Fat: 15g|Carbohydrates: 1g|Fiber: 0.5g|Protein: 30g

465. Air Fryer Buffalo Salmon Salad

Total Time: 30 mins

Ingredients

- 4 Tbsp. unsalted butter
- ¼ cup hot sauce
- 4 Verlasso salmon fillets (about 1 lb.)
- Cooking spray
- 1 large head romaine lettuce, chopped (about 8 cups)
- 1 ear of corn, kernels removed (or ½ cup frozen corn, thawed)
- ½ cup matchstick carrots
- 1 small red onion, thinly sliced
- 1 bell pepper, thinly sliced
- 3 stalks celery, chopped
- ¼ cup blue cheese crumbles
- Ranch or blue cheese dressing for serving, optional
- Additional hot sauce for serving, optional

Directions

- Melt butter in a small saucepan over medium heat. Remove pan from heat and stir in hot sauce.
- Place salmon in a baking pan and pour the sauce over salmon. Let marinate for 20-30 minutes, turning once halfway through.
- Preheat air fryer to 400°F. Lightly spray the fryer basket with cooking spray. Remove salmon from marinade and pat bottom (skin) dry. Place salmon in basket, skin side down, and cook for 7-10 minutes, or until salmon is cooked to desired doneness.
- While salmon is cooking, assemble the salad. Divide the lettuce among four bowls. Top each bowl with corn, carrots, onion, bell pepper, celery, and blue cheese. Place a salmon fillet on top of each salad.
- Drizzle with dressing and additional hot sauce if desired. Enjoy!

Nutrition

- Calories 360| Total Fat 22g|Cholesterol: 100mg| Sodium: 570mg| Total Carbohydrate: 14g| (Dietary: Fiber 5g| Total Sugars: 6g| Protein: 28g

466. Grilled Romaine Salad

Prep Time: 15 mins

Cook Time: 10 mins

Servings: 4 servings

Ingredients

- 2 medium heads of romaine lettuce, cut lengthwise into wedges
- Olive oil for brushing the romaine lettuce
- 1/2 cup crumbled or grated cheese (choose your favorite!)
- Lemon wedges for serving and squeezing over salad

For The Dressing

- 2 cloves garlic, crushed or fine mince
- 3 tablespoons olive oil for the dressing
- Zest of 1 fresh lemon
- 2 tablespoons fresh lemon juice
- 1 tablespoon balsamic vinegar
- 1/2 teaspoon dijon mustard
- 1 teaspoon soy sauce (use tamari for gluten free)
- 1 teaspoon brown sugar
- 1/2 teaspoon paprika
- 1/2 teaspoon kosher salt, or to taste
- Black pepper to taste

Instructions

Make The Dressing

- Whisk together the dressing ingredients (garlic, olive oil, lemon zest, lemon juice, balsamic, mustard, soy sauce, brown sugar, paprika, salt, and black pepper). Set aside.
- Heat the grill to medium-high to high heat (depending on the grill's heat intensity). Make sure to scrape the grill grates so they are clean & food won't stick as easily.
- Lightly coat the romaine lettuce heads with oil. Grill the romaine until they're gently cooked and slightly charred.
- Allow grilled romaine to cool. Lay on a serving tray, drizzle dressing on top, and sprinkle with cheese. Serve with lemon wedges and enjoy!

Nutrition

- Calories: 165kcal | Carbohydrates: 4g | Protein: 4g | Fat: 15g | Saturated Fat: 4g | Cholesterol: 15mg | Sodium: 472mg | Potassium: 48mg | Fiber: 1g | Sugar: 2g | Vitamin C: 4mg | Calcium: 109mg | Iron: 0.3mg

467. Air Fryer Sesame Ginger Salmon With Spicy Cucumber Salad

Prep time: 10mins

Cook time: 8mins

Ingredients

- 1/ 3 cup Annie's Organic Sesame Ginger Vinaigrette
- 1 pound salmon, cut into 4 portions
- 2 hothouse cucumbers, thinly sliced
- 1 jalapeño, thinly sliced
- A handful of fresh mint leaves, chopped
- 1/ 2 cup seasoned rice vinegar
- 1/ 2 teaspoon salt
- 1 teaspoon sugar

Method

- Pour ¼ cup Annie's Sesame Ginger Vinaigrette into the bottom of a medium bowl or baking dish
- Marinate salmon portions skin side facing up in dish for 5 minutes
- Mix cucumber slices, hot pepper, mint, vinegar, salt, + sugar in a large mason jar or medium bowl. Chill cucumber salad in the refrigerator, stirring every 5 minutes while salmon is cooking.
- After salmon has marinated for 5 minutes, place skin side down in air fryer
- Air Fry at 400°F for 8 minutes
- Drizzle salmon with remaining vinaigrette and air fry an additional 1-2 minutes until cooked through, browned, and crispy on the edges
- Using a slotted spoon to eliminate excess pickling juices, place ¼ cucumber salad topped with 1 salmon portion on each plate. Serve immediately!

Nutrient Value

- Calories: 122| Fat: 8g| Sat fat: 2g| Unsatfat: 5g| Protein: 10g| Carbohydrate| 0g Fiber 0g| Sugars 0g| Added sugars: 0g| Sodium: 254mg

468. Citrus & Avocado Salad

Prep Time: 10 Mins

Total Time: 10 minutes

Ingredients

- 1/2 red grapefruit
- 1 blood orange
- 1 Navel orange
- 1/2 avocado
- 1/4 cup chopped roasted pistachios
- 2 Tbsp. chives
- 1 Tbsp. blood orange infused olive oil
- Sea salt & black pepper to taste!

Instructions

- Slice all citrus in whole circular thin slices.
- Arrange citrus on a large plate and top with avocado slices.
- Garnish with chopped chives, pistachios, blood orange olive oil, sea salt, and pepper.

Nutrient Value

- Total Fat: 22g | Saturated Fat: 10g | Trans Fat: 0g | Unsaturated Fat: 12g | Cholesterol: 88mg | Sodium: 789mg | Carbohydrates: 2g | Fiber: 1g | Sugar: 0g | Protein: 29g

469. Radicchio Salad With Cashew Ricotta Dressing

Prep Time: 10 Minutes

Cook Time: 20 Minutes

Total Time: 30 Minutes

Dressing

- 1/2 cup raw cashews, soaked in hot water for 10 minutes (or sub unroasted macadamia nuts)
- 2 cloves garlic
- 2 Tbsp lemon juice
- 1 ½ Tbsp nutritional yeast
- 1/3 tsp sea salt, plus more to taste
- 1 dash onion powder (optional)
- Water to thin

Beets

- 1 medium beet, thinly sliced into rounds
- 7 cloves garlic, peeled + roughly chopped
- 1 tsp avocado oil (if oil-free, sub maple syrup)
- 1 healthy pinch of each sea salt and black pepper

Candied Walnuts

- 2/3 cup raw walnuts
- 2 tsp maple syrup
- 1 ½ tsp coconut sugar
- 1 pinch sea salt
- 1 dash ground cinnamon

Salad

- 1 head radicchio, rinsed, dried, bottom trimmed, unpeeled, and roughly chopped (~6 cups as the recipe is written)
- 1/2 medium lemon, juiced
- 1 healthy pinch of each sea salt and black pepper
- 1/2 cup chopped fresh parsley

Instructions

- Heat oven to 425 degrees F (218 C) and line a baking sheet with parchment paper.
- Add cashews to a small bowl and cover with very hot water. Soak for 10 minutes.
- Add sliced beets and chopped garlic to the prepared baking pan and toss in a bit of oil and salt and pepper. Roast for 10-15 minutes, or until the beets are caramelized and the garlic is golden brown (being careful not to burn).
- In the meantime, add walnuts to a skillet (we prefer cast iron) and heat over medium heat to toast for 5 minutes, stirring frequently, being careful not to burn. Then add maple syrup, coconut sugar, salt, and cinnamon and toss to combine. Turn off heat and allow to cool in the pan.
- In the meantime, prepare the dressing. Drain cashews and add to a small blender (we use this small spice grinder that also has a cup for blending small-batch sauces) along with other dressing ingredients.
- Taste and adjust flavor as needed, adding more garlic for zing, lemon for acidity, salt to taste, or nutritional yeast for cheesiness. It should be zingy, salty, and lemony with a bit of cheesiness. It needs to be quite flavorful, so don't be shy!
- Add radicchio to a serving bowl or platter and toss with lemon juice, salt, and pepper. Then add cashew dressing and toss to coat.
- Top with roasted beets, garlic, and candied walnuts. Garnish with fresh parsley. Serve.

Nutrition Value

- Calories: 274
- Carbohydrates: 20.4 g
- Protein: 9 g
- Fat: 19.6 g
- Saturated Fat: 2.5 g
- Polyunsaturated Fat: 9.44 g
- Monounsaturated Fat: 6.2 g
- Trans Fat: 0 g
- Cholesterol: 0 mg
- Sodium: 286 mg
- Potassium: 579 mg
- Fiber: 4 g
- Sugar: 7.1 g
- Vitamin A: 660 IU
- Vitamin C: 23.46 mg
- Calcium: 67.4 mg
- Iron: 2.82 mg

470. Air Fryer Croutons

Total Time: 30 mins

Ingredients

- 4 slices bread
- 2 tablespoons melted butter
- 1 teaspoon parsley
- 1/2 teaspoon onion powder
- 1/2 teaspoon seasoned salt
- 1/2 teaspoon garlic salt

Instructions

- Preheat the air fryer to 390 degrees.
- Cut 4 slices of bread into bite-sized pieces.
- Melt butter, and place butter into a medium-sized bowl.
- Add 1 teaspoon parsley, 1/2 teaspoon seasoned salt, 1/2 teaspoon garlic salt, 1/2 teaspoon of onion powder to the melted butter. Stir well.
- Add bread to the bowl and carefully stir to coat the bread so that it is coated by the seasoned butter.
- Place buttered bread into the air fryer basket.
- Cook for 5 to 7 minutes or until the bread is toasted.
- Serve immediately.

Nutrition Value

- Calories: 127kcal | Carbohydrates: 14g | Protein: 3g | Fat: 7g | Saturated Fat: 4g | Cholesterol: 15mg | Sodium: 777mg | Potassium: 51mg | Fiber: 1g | Sugar: 2g | Vitamin A: 175IU | Calcium: 39mg | Iron: 1mg

471. Instant Pot Southern-Style Potato Salad

Prep Time: 15 minutes

Cook Time: 4 minutes

Chill Time: 1 hour

Total Time 1 hour 19 minutes

Ingredients

- 1 1/2 cups water
- 5 (about 2 pounds total) russet potatoes peeled and sliced into 1 1/2 inch cubes
- 4 eggs
- 1 large bowl of cold water ice added to the water is optional
- 1 cup mayo
- 1/2 cup white onions chopped
- 1/4 cup pickle relish
- 1 tablespoon yellow mustard
- salt and pepper to taste
- Lawry's seasoning salt to taste optional
- 1 teaspoon paprika

Instructions

- Add the water to the Instant Pot. Place the Instant Pot on the saute' function. This will allow the water to warm so that it comes to pressure sooner.
- While the water heats up slice the potatoes.
- Add the steamer basket to the pot. Place the potatoes on top of the basket. Season the potatoes with about 1/4 teaspoon of salt.
- Place the eggs on the very top of the potatoes.
- Close the pot and seal. Cook for 4 minutes on Manual > High-Pressure Cooking.
- When the Instant Pot indicates it has finished cooking, quick release the steam.
- Remove the eggs and place them in the bowl of cold water for 5 minutes.
- Remove the potatoes and transfer to a large bowl.

- Peel the eggs and slice them into small cubes.
- Add the cooked eggs, mayo, mustard, relish, white onions, paprika, and salt and pepper to taste to the mixture. Taste repeatedly. You may need to add additional salt and pepper.
- (If you prefer sweet potato salad add a little more relish and maybe sugar.)
- Stir to combine.
- Cover and chill for at least an hour to two hours before serving.

Nutrition Value

- Calories: 247kcal | Carbohydrates: 13g | Protein: 4g | Fat: 20g

---

472. Grilled Romaine Salad

Prep Time: 10 Minutes

Cook Time: 2 Minutes

Total Time: 12 Minutes

Ingredients

- 2 heads of romaine lettuce
- 6 slices of bacon
- 6 oz. pomegranate seeds
- 6 oz. of blue cheese crumbles
- 12 oz. of blue cheese dressing (see recipe card below)
- 4 tbsp of olive oil
- 1 tbsp balsamic glaze

Instructions

- Cook the bacon in an air fryer at 370°F for 8-12 minutes until crispy and slice into crumbles. Check out the recipe for the best air fryer bacon.
- Slice the heads of romaine in half, lengthwise.
- Brush the romaine lettuce with olive oil.
- Place the romaine cut side down on the medium-hot grill.
- Flip the heads of romaine after 1-2 minutes and cook on for equal time on the other side.
- Transfer the romaine cut side up to a serving platter and pile on the bacon, pomegranate seeds, and blue cheese crumbles.
- Finish by drizzling the amazing blue cheese salad dressing over the grilled romaine (see recipe below)

- Drizzle with a sweet balsamic glaze, and serve.

Nutrition Information

- Total Fat: 51g
- Saturated Fat: 13g
- Trans Fat: 1g
- Unsaturated Fat: 36g
- Cholesterol: 50mg
- Sodium: 901mg
- Carbohydrates: 17g
- Fiber: 6g
- Sugar: 10g
- Protein: 14g

---

473. Roasted Sumac Cauliflower Mediterranean Salad

Prep Time: 20 mins

Cook Time: 5 mins

Ingredients

- 4 tbsp Hummus
- 1 cup cooked chickpeas

Roasted Cauliflower

- 1 small head cauliflower
- 1 tsp Cured Sumac I used Burlap & Barrel
- 1 tsp garlic powder
- 2 tbsp extra virgin olive oil

Mediterranean Tomato-Cucumber-Mint Salad

- 2 Persian cucumbers chopped into 1/2 inch pieces
- 1/4 cup red onion diced
- 1 cup cherry tomatoes or mini San Marzano Tomatoes sliced in half
- 2 sprigs mint Julienned
- 2 tsp lemon juice
- 1 tbsp extra virgin olive oil

Instructions

Prepare the Hummus

Roast The Cauliflower

- In a mixing bowl, coat the florets in a few drizzles of olive oil and about 1 tsp cured sumac and 1 tsp garlic powder. Add salt and pepper to taste.
- Mix well to combine.

- Set Air Fryer to 400° and air fry the cauliflower for 7 minutes.
- Remove the basket and shake and air fry for an additional 7 minutes until the edges are brown and crispy.
- If you don't have an air fryer, lay florets on a baking tray and roast at 425° for 20-25 minutes

Prepare The Tomato-Cucumber-Mint Salad

- Assemble all ingredients in a small bowl and mix well.
- Assemble the Bowl
- Layer some salad greens into a large bowl.
- Add a handful of cauliflower, some tomato-cucumber-mint salad, a few tablespoons of hummus, and a handful of chickpeas.
- Serve with lemon wedges or with some balsamic vinegar and olive oil and some toasted pita bread.

474. Salade Niçoise | Air Fryer Recipe

Prep Time: 15 minutes

Cook Time: 20 minutes

Total Time: 35 minutes

Ingredients

- 6 Baby New Potatoes, quartered
- 2 teaspoons Vegetable Oil, plus additional for tuna
- salt and ground black pepper
- 1 cup slender green beans, trimmed and snapped in half
- 2 4 ounce tuna fillets, about 1 inch thick, cut in half
- 1 cup Cherry Tomatoes, halved
- 6 butter lettuce leaves
- 2 hard-boiled eggs, peeled and halved
- 10 Nicoise olives

For The Vinaigrette

- 2 tablespoons Olive Oil
- 1 tablespoon Red Wine Vinegar
- 1/8 teaspoon, salt
- 1 teaspoon Dijon mustard
- 1/4 teaspoon Herbes de Provence, (optional)
- Ground Black Pepper

Instructions

- **For The Salad:** In a small bowl, toss potatoes, green beans, and grape tomatoes with 2 teaspoons of vegetable oil, salt, and pepper. Arrange the vegetables in a single layer in an air fryer basket. Set fryer to 400°F for 10 minutes, shaking halfway through cook time.
- After 10 minutes of cook time, brush tuna on both sides with 1 tablespoon vegetable oil and season to taste with salt and coarsely ground pepper. Press the salt and pepper into the tuna so they will stay put. Add tuna to the basket on top of the vegetables. Cook for 5 minutes for tuna that is cooked medium-well.
- At end of cook time, remove the tuna and let it rest for 5 minutes. Slice tuna thinly across the grain.
- Meanwhile, for the vinaigrette: Combine vinegar, salt, mustard, olive oil, black pepper, and Herbes de Provence to taste in a small jar with a lid. Shake to combine.
- Place 3 lettuce leaves on each of two dinner plates. Arrange tuna, green beans, tomatoes, and potatoes in small piles on lettuce. Place 2 egg halves on each plate. Scatter olives over. Drizzle all with the vinaigrette. Serve immediately.

Nutrition Value

- Calories: 601kcal | Carbohydrates: 49g | Protein: 41g | Fat: 27g | Fiber: 8g | Sugar: 7g

475. Air Fryer Kale

Prep Time: 5 mins

Cook Time: 3 mins

Ingredients

- 3.5 ounces kale leaves 100 grams or 2-3 cups
- Oil spray
- Salt to taste optional

Instructions

- Preheat air fryer to 350 degrees F (175 C) for at least 5 minutes
- While the air fryer preheats, wash and dry the kale leaves thoroughly. Remove the stems from the leaves if desired (see note). Slice the leaves into very thin strips.
- When the air fryer has finished preheating, add the sliced kale into the basket. Spray the leaves with oil as you shake the basket. Season lightly with salt (if using). Make sure the leaves are spread evenly across the basket before you put the basket back in the fryer.
- Air fry for 3 minutes, pausing briefly after 1.5 or 2 minutes to shake and agitate the kale. Serve immediately.

Nutrient Value

- Total Fat: 22g | Saturated Fat: 10g | Trans Fat: 0g | Unsaturated Fat: 12g | Cholesterol: 88mg | Sodium: 789mg | Carbohydrates: 2g | Fiber: 1g | Sugar: 0g | Protein: 29g

---

476. Chopped Salad With Japanese Sweet Potato Croutons

Total Time: 30 mins

Ingredients

- 1 pound salad mixture including greens and vegetables of your choice
- 1 each crisp sweet apple, cored and diced
- 2 each mandarin oranges, peeled, segmented & cut in half
- 1/3 cup pomegranate seeds
- 1 8-12 ounce baked Japanese Sweet Potato cold, cut into pieces with skin on
- 2 tbsp Sweet Balsamic Vinegar 4% acidity Nappa Valley Naturals Grand Reserve or California Balsamic Simply Lemon are two of my favorites for this salad.

Instructions

- To make the JSP croutons, place the cold diced sweet potato pieces in a cold air fryer set to 400 degrees. Air fry for about 20 minutes or until golden brown. If You don't have an air fryer you can crisp them up under the broiler. Watch them carefully as they go from lightly brown to burnt in a hurry.

- While the croutons are in the air fryer, chop the salad with a mezzaluna knife in a wood bowl or you can use a large knife and a large cutting board or one of the other methods I show in my video on how to chop a salad without a wood bowl.
- Add the diced apple, mandarin oranges, pomegranate seeds, JSP croutons, and the balsamic vinegar of your choice. Gently stir all of the ingredients together and place it in a pretty bowl to serve. Many different flavors would work well with this salad. Don't add the vinegar until you are ready to serve the salad as it is best served freshly tossed.

Nutritional Value

- Total fat: 30.8gg
- Sodium: 1321.9mg
- Sugar: 6.7g
- Vitamin A: 567.5ug
- Carbohydrates: 21.4g
- Protein: 29.8g
- Vitamin C: 56.8mg

---

477. Crisp Pork Belly With Coriander Salad

Prep Time: 1 day

Cook Time: 40 minutes

Ingredients

- Pork Belly
- 1 kg pork belly
- Salt

Coriander Salad Ingredients

- 1 cup washed coriander leaves including stems roughly chopped
- ½ medium red onion very finely sliced
- 1 medium red chili finely chopped or to taste
- ¼ cup toasted white sesame seeds
- ⅓ cup roasted chopped unsalted peanuts

Coriander Salad Dressing Ingredients

- 2 tablespoons sesame oil or EVOO- extra virgin olive oil
- 2 tablespoons rice wine vinegar or apple cider vinegar (ACV)/white vinegar

- ½ tablespoon tamari or soy sauce
- 1 teaspoon stevia blend or sweetener of choice

Instructions

- Prepare the pork belly by washing and drying with a paper towel. Rub with salt and leave it in the fridge overnight to dry out covered with paper toweling or a cloth.
- Just before cooking removes the pork from the fridge and score the fat horizontally and vertically about 1 cm/.4 " or visually score it so that the score lines will coincide with the cutting line when you slice the pork belly to serve. Rub some additional salt into the pork rind.

Air Fryer Pork Belly Method

- Preheat the air fryer to 200 C/390 F.
- Cook the pork belly rind side down for 10 minutes. This helps prevent the pork belly from curling up.
- Turn the heat down to 180 C/ 360 F and turn the pork belly over so the rind side is on top. Continue to cook for a further 30 minutes or until the pork belly is cooked and tender. Allow the pork to rest for about 20 minutes before slicing into approximately 2cm/.8" slices or as you prefer.

Conventional Oven Pork Belly Method

- Preheat the oven to 200 C/ 290 F.
- Place the pork rind side in a baking dish. Cook the pork for 20-25 minutes. If your oven is baking unevenly, turn your pork belly around and bake for a further 20-25 minutes or until the pork belly is cooked and tender. Allow the pork to rest for about 20 minutes before slicing into approximately 2cm/.8" slices or as you prefer.

Coriander Salad Instructions

- Combine the dressing ingredients and mix them so the sweetener dissolves.
- Mix all of the salad ingredients in a medium bowl.
- Mix the dressing through the salad and serve on the side of the pork belly.

Nutritional Information

- Calories: 476kcal | Carbohydrates: 4g | Protein: 54g | Fat: 25g | Fiber: 2g

---

478. Air Fried Chicken Cordon Bleu Salad

Prep Time: 10 Minutes

Cook Time: 12 Minutes

Total Time: 22 Minutes

Ingredients

- 2 boneless, skinless chicken breasts
- 2 tablespoons flour
- 1 egg, beaten
- 1/4 cup seasoned bread crumbs
- 4 tablespoons white wine vinegar
- 2 tablespoons nonfat plain Greek yogurt
- 2 Tablespoons Dijon mustard
- 2 Tablespoons honey
- 4 tablespoons olive oil
- 8 slices deli ham
- 4 slices Swiss cheese, cut in half
- 12 cups lettuce
- 1 seedless cucumber, chopped
- 1 cup tomatoes, halved
- 1/4 cup thinly sliced red onion

Instructions

- Lightly coat the chicken with flour, then dip it into the egg. Dredge in bread crumbs to coat. Spritz with oil.
- Air fry at 400 degrees for 12 minutes, or until cooked through. Slice into bite-sized pieces.
- Meanwhile, make the dressing by whisking together the vinegar, yogurt, mustard, and honey until smooth. Drizzle in the olive oil. Season with salt and pepper.
- Layer together one piece of ham and one piece of cheese. Roll together, then slice into 4 pinwheels. Repeat with remaining ham and cheese.
- Pile the lettuce onto a platter. Top with cucumber, tomatoes, onion, chicken, and ham and cheese pinwheels. Drizzle with dressing.

Nutrition Information

- Total Fat: 28g
- Saturated Fat: 8g
- Trans Fat: 0g

- Unsaturated Fat: 17g
- Cholesterol: 139mg
- Sodium: 909mg
- Carbohydrates: 27g
- Fiber: 5g
- Sugar: 13g
- Protein: 39g

479. Southwest Tortilla Crusted Tilapia Salad

Cook Time: 15 mins

Total Time: 15 mins

Ingredients

- 6 c. mixed greens
- 1 c. cherry tomatoes
- 1/3 c. diced red onion
- 1 avocado
- 2 Tortilla Crusted Tilapia fillets I used Sea Cuisine frozen fillets
- 1/2 c. Chipotle Lime Dressing

Instructions

- Spray your frozen tilapia fillets with cooking spray on both sides. Place in your Airfryer and cook for 15-18 minutes at 390° until crispy. (If you don't have an air fryer, you can bake the fillets in the oven according to the directions.)
- While the fish is baking, in two bowls, add half of the greens, tomatoes, and red onion. Toss the mixture with the Chipotle Lime Dressing.
- Top the greens with the baked fish and sliced avocado. Serve immediately.

Nutritional Value

- Calories: 572kcal | Carbohydrates: 1g | Protein: 46g | Fat: 43g | Saturated Fat: 22g | Cholesterol: 168mg | Sodium: 219mg | Potassium: 606mg | Sugar: 1g | Calcium: 16mg | Iron: 4mg

480. Pecan Chicken Salad Sandwiches

Prep Time: 15 minutes

Cook Time: 15 minutes

Ingredients

- 1 pound Chicken Breasts Boneless/Skinless Air Fried or Poached
- sprinkling Salt & Pepper
- 1/2 cup Red Grapes diced
- 1/2 cup Apples (Honeycrisp, Braeburn, or Red Delicious) peeled and diced
- 1/4 cup Celery Stalks strings peeled away and diced
- 1/4 cup Whole Pecans chopped
- 1/2 cup Olive Oil Mayonnaise Light or Regular
- 1/2 teaspoon Sea Salt
- Romaine Lettuce
- 8 slices Honey Wheat Bread
- 1 Avocado sliced into 8 slices

Instructions

- Air Fryer - Season Chicken Breasts with Salt and Pepper and place into Air Fryer. Cook at 340 degrees for 15 minutes. When time is up, wait 5 minutes and then remove Chicken from the Basket.

OR

- Pressure Cooker - Season Chicken Breasts with Salt and Pepper and place into Pressure Cooker. Add just enough liquid (broth/water) to cover the chicken. Lock-on lid, close Pressure Valve, and cook on Low Pressure for 3 minutes. When Beep sounds, wait 10 minutes and then slowly release the rest of the pressure.
- Allow Chicken to fully cool and then dice into cubes.
- Remove the threads from the Celery and then dice.
- Dice up the Grapes, Apples, and Pecans and add to a Bowl.
- Add Salt and Mayonnaise and combine. Add diced chicken and combine. Taste and add more Mayonnaise or Salt, as needed.
- Place in refrigerator for one hour.
- Lightly toast bread and pile on Pecan Chicken Salad.
- Top with sliced Avocados and place top slice of Bread

Nutrient Value

- Total Fat: 22g | Saturated Fat: 10g | Trans Fat: 0g | Unsaturated Fat: 12g | Cholesterol: 88mg | Sodium: 789mg | Carbohydrates: 2g | Fiber: 1g |

Sugar: 0g| Protein: 29g

481. Amazing Potato Salad

Prep Time: 5 minutes

Cook Time: 20 minutes

Ingredients

- 2 1/2 lbs red potatoes or gold, cut into bite-sized pieces
- 4 eggs
- 1 tbsp distilled white vinegar
- 1/2 cup mayonnaise
- 2 tsp Dijon mustard
- 1/2 cup diced celery
- 2 scallions thinly sliced
- 2 tbsp flat-leaf parsley chopped
- 1 cup crispy crumbled bacon
- 1/2 cup parmesan grated
- 1 tbsp pepper
- Additional chopped parsley and scallions for garnish optional

Instructions

- Pour 1 1/2 cups of water into the Instant Pot and insert the steam rack. Place cubed potatoes in a steamer basket and lower the steamer basket onto the steam rack. Add eggs on top of the potatoes.
- Secure the lid, making sure the vent is closed.
- Using the display panel select the MANUAL or PRESSURE COOK function*. Use the +/- keys and program the Instant Pot for 5 minutes.
- When the time is up, quick-release the pressure.
- Remove eggs and place in an ice bath. Sprinkle 1 tbsp vinegar over the potatoes and allow to cool.
- Keep eggs in an ice bath for 5 minutes, then peel and chop.
- Meanwhile, in a large bowl whisk together mayonnaise and dijon. Mix in celery, scallions, and parsley.
- Fold in cooked potatoes, chopped eggs, crumbled bacon, parmesan, and pepper. Season to taste.
- Serve chilled garnished with additional chopped parsley and scallions (optional).

Nutritional Value

- Calories: 212| Total Fat: 7g| Saturated Fat: 2g| Unsaturated Fat: 0g| Cholesterol: 83mg| Sodium: 282mg| Carbohydrates: 2g| Fiber: 1g| Sugar: 1g| Protein: 33g

482. All Kale Caesar

Prep: 15 mins

Total: 15 mins

Ingredients

- ½ Cup lemon juice
- 2 anchovy fillets
- 2 cloves garlic, peeled
- ½ teaspoon dijon mustard
- ½ cup olive oil
- ¼ teaspoon salt
- Ground black pepper to taste
- 6 cups kale leaves
- 1 cup croutons
- ¼ cup grated parmesan cheese

Directions

- Combine lemon juice, anchovies, garlic, and mustard in a blender or food processor fitted with a steel blade. Process until thoroughly combined. Pour in olive oil very gradually through the feed tube while the machine is running, first 1 tablespoon at a time, then gradually increasing the amount. Season with salt and pepper.
- Stack and bunch the kale leaves together on a cutting board and cut across the stack into skinny slivers.
- Place the kale, croutons, and Parmesan cheese in the bowl and drizzle with about 1/4 of the dressing. Toss and taste the salad and add more dressing if desired, then toss again.

Nutrition Facts

- Protein: 6.8g|Carbohydrates:17.6g|Fat 31.1g| Cholesterol: 6.1mg| Sodium: 437.3mg.

483. Spinach Salad with Warm Bacon-Mustard Dressing

Prep Time: 15 mins

Cook Time: 5 mins

Total Time: 20 mins

Ingredient

- 1 (10 ounces) bag baby spinach leaves
- 4 hard-cooked eggs, peeled and sliced
- 1 cup sliced mushrooms
- 4 strips crisply cooked bacon, crumbled
- 10 ounces swiss cheese, shredded
- ½ cup toasted sliced almonds
- 1 tablespoon olive oil
- 1 large shallot, minced
- 1 teaspoon garlic, minced
- ⅓ cup white wine vinegar
- ⅓ cup dijon mustard
- ⅓ cup honey
- 2 strips crisply cooked bacon, crumbled
- Salt and pepper to taste

Instructions

- Place spinach into a large serving bowl, top with hard-cooked eggs, mushrooms, 4 crumbled strips of bacon, Swiss cheese, and almonds.
- Heat olive oil in a small skillet over medium heat. Stir in shallots and garlic, and cook until softened and translucent, about 2 minutes. Whisk in the vinegar, Dijon mustard, honey, and 2 crumbled strips of bacon; season to taste with salt and pepper, then cook until hot.
- Pour hot dressing over spinach and toss to coat.

Nutrition Facts

Calories; protein 36.1g; carbohydrates 40.1g; fat 40.6g; cholesterol 292.6mg; sodium 1123.4mg.

484. Fennel And Watercress Salad

Prep Time: 20 mins

Total Time: 20 mins

Ingredient

- ½ cup chopped dried cranberries
- ¼ cup red wine vinegar
- ¼ cup balsamic vinegar
- 1 tablespoon minced garlic
- 1 ¼ teaspoons salt

- 1 cup extra virgin olive oil
- 6 bunches watercress - rinsed, dried, and trimmed
- 3 bulbs fennel - trimmed, cored, and thinly sliced
- 3 small heads radicchio, cored and chopped
- 1 cup pecan halves, toasted

Instructions

- In a bowl, combine the cranberries, red wine vinegar, balsamic vinegar, garlic, and salt. Whisk in the olive oil.
- In a large salad bowl, combine the watercress, fennel, radicchio, and pecans. Stir the vinaigrette and pour over the salad. Toss well and serve at once.

Nutrition Facts

- Calories: 178| Protein: 3.1g| Carbohydrates: 8.9g| Fat: 15.4g| Sodium: 201.8mg

485. Juicy Fruit Salad

Prep: 5 mins

Total: 5 mins

Ingredients

- 1 (15 ounces) can pineapple chunks with juice
- 1 apple - peeled, cored, and diced
- 1 orange - peeled, diced and juice reserved
- 1 banana, sliced
- 1 cup seedless green grapes, halved

Instructions

- In a large bowl, toss together the pineapple, apple, orange, banana, and grapes. Add the juice from the pineapple and orange and let chill until serving.

Nutrition Facts

- Calories: 104| protein: 1g| carbohydrates: 26.8g| fat: 0.3g| sodium: 1.7mg.

486. Fabulous Fruit Salad

Prep: 20 mins

Total: 20 mins

Ingredient

- 1 red apple, cored and chopped
- 1 Granny Smith apple, cored and chopped
- 1 nectarine, pitted and sliced
- 2 stalks celery, chopped
- ½ cup dried cranberries
- ½ cup chopped walnuts
- 1 (8 ounces) container nonfat lemon yogurt

Instructions

- In a large bowl, combine red apple, Granny Smith apple, nectarine, celery, dried cranberries, and walnuts. Mix in yogurt. Chill until ready to serve.

Nutrition Facts

- Calories:243| Protein: 5.8g| Carbohydrates: 37.4g| Fat: 9.8g| Cholesterol: 0.9mg| Sodium: 55.3mg

487. Holiday Salad Wreath

Prep: 20 mins

Total: 20 mins

Ingredient

- ½ (10 ounces) package fresh spinach, or more to taste
- ½ (5 ounces) package arugula leaves or more to taste
- 2 canned beets, cut into 1/4-inch pieces, or more to taste
- 1 (4 ounces) log soft goat cheese, or to taste
- 3 tablespoons unsalted shelled pistachios
- kosher salt and ground black pepper to taste

Instructions

- Neatly arrange spinach in a 10- to a 12-inch circle with leaf tips facing outward. Arrange arugula on top of spinach, leaving the outer tips of the spinach exposed. Scatter beets over the arugula. Arrange pieces of goat cheese around the wreath. Sprinkle pistachios on top. Season salad lightly with salt and pepper.

Nutrition Facts

- Calories: 152| Protein: 8.9g| Carbohydrates: 5.1g| Fat: 11.4g| Cholesterol: 22.4mg| Sodium: 241.4mg.

488. Autumn Salad With Caramel-Sesame Dressing

Prep: 20 mins

Total: 20 mins

Ingredient

- 1 ½ cups chopped fresh spinach
- 1 ½ cups chopped romaine lettuce
- ½ ripe Bartlett pear - skinned, cored, and diced into medium chunks
- ½ Fuji apple - skin on, cored and diced into medium chunks
- ¼ cup halved seedless red grapes (Optional)
- 3 tablespoons rice vinegar
- 1 tablespoon caramel topping (such as Hershey's®)
- ¼ teaspoon sesame oil
- ¼ teaspoon toasted sesame seeds

Instructions

- Arrange spinach, romaine lettuce, pear, apple, and grapes on a plate.
- Mix vinegar, caramel topping, sesame oil, and sesame seeds together in a bowl. Pour dressing over salad.

Nutrition Facts

- Calories: 233| Protein: 4.5g| Carbohydrates: 52g| Fat 2.6g| Cholesterol: 0.2mg| Sodium: 140.1mg.

489. Simple Herb Salad Mix

Prep: 20 mins

Total: 20 mins

Ingredient

- 1 (5 ounces) bag mesclun lettuce salad mix
- 1 (5 ounces) package baby spinach
- 1 (5 ounces) package baby arugula
- 1 small head endive, sliced
- ¼ cup coarsely chopped parsley
- ¼ cup coarsely chopped dill
- ¼ cup coarsely chopped tarragon (optional)

Instructions

- Place mesclun lettuce, baby spinach, baby arugula, endive, parsley, dill, and tarragon in a large bowl; fold gently to mix.
- Transfer mixture to a gallon-size resealable plastic bag and seal, pressing out as much air as possible to avoid condensation. Store in the refrigerator.

Nutrition Facts

- Calories: 35| Protein: 3.2g| Carbohydrates: 6g| Fat 0.6g| Sodium: 57.6mg.

490. Pomegranate Spinach Salad

Prep Time: 10 mins

Cook Time: 5 mins

Total Time: 15 mins

Ingredient

- 1 tablespoon butter
- ⅓ cup sliced almonds
- ¼ cup vegetable oil
- 2 tablespoons white sugar
- 2 tablespoons white wine vinegar
- 2 tablespoons cider vinegar
- 1 tablespoon sesame seeds, toasted
- 1 ½ teaspoons poppy seeds
- 1 teaspoon minced onion
- ⅛ teaspoon paprika
- 1 (10 ounces) package fresh spinach
- ½ cup pomegranate arils
- 1 tablespoon toasted sesame seeds

Instructions

- Melt butter in a small saucepan over medium heat. Add almonds; cook, stirring frequently, until lightly toasted.
- Whisk oil, sugar, vinegar, sesame seeds, poppy seeds, onion, and paprika together in a bowl for the dressing.
- Toss spinach, toasted almonds, and pomegranate arils together in a large bowl. Drizzle with dressing and toss to coat.

Nutrition Facts

- Calories: 103| Protein: 1.9g| Carbohydrates:

5.4g| Fat 8.5g| Cholesterol 2.5mg| Sodium: 26mg.

491. Fresh Broccoli Salad

Prep Time: 15 mins

Cook Time: 15 mins

Total Time: 30 mins

Ingredient

- 2 heads of fresh broccoli
- 1 red onion
- ½ pound bacon
- ¾ cup raisins
- ¾ cup sliced almonds
- 1 cup mayonnaise
- ½ cup white sugar
- 2 tablespoons white wine vinegar

Instructions

- Place bacon in a deep skillet and cook over medium-high heat until evenly brown. Cool and crumble.
- Cut the broccoli into bite-size pieces and cut the onion into thin bite-size slices. Combine with the bacon, raisins, your favorite nuts, and mix well.
- To prepare the dressing, mix the mayonnaise, sugar, and vinegar until smooth. Stir into the salad, let chill, and serve.
-

Nutrition Facts

- Calories: 374| Protein: 7.3g| Carbohydrates: 28.5g| Fat: 27.2g| Cholesterol: 18.3mg| Sodium: 352.9mg.

492. The Best Vegetable Salad

Prep Time: 30 mins

Total Time: 30 mins

Ingredient

- 1 cucumber, peeled and chopped
- 2 fresh tomatoes, chopped
- 2 green onion, minced
- 1 red bell pepper, chopped
- 5 radishes, chopped

- 1 small jicama, peeled and julienned
- 5 romaine lettuce leaves, torn into bite-size pieces
- 1 clove garlic, minced
- 1 ½ tablespoon lemon juice
- 2 tablespoons olive oil
- 1 tablespoon pomegranate juice
- 1 teaspoon salt
- 1 teaspoon ground black pepper
- 1 teaspoon chopped fresh dill
- 1 teaspoon chopped fresh basil
- 1 ½ teaspoons water

Instructions

- Toss together the cucumber, tomato, onion, pepper, radish, jicama, and lettuce in a large salad bowl. Whisk together the garlic, lemon juice, olive oil, pomegranate juice, salt, pepper, dill, basil, and water in a small bowl. Drizzle dressing over the salad just before serving.

Nutrition Facts

- Calories: 88| Protein: 1.5g| Carbohydrates: 10.9g| Fat 4.8g| Sodium 397.9mg.

493. Caprese Salad With Balsamic Reduction

Prep Time: 15 mins

Cook Time: 10 mins

Total Time: 25 mins

Ingredient

- 1 cup balsamic vinegar
- ¼ cup honey
- 3 large tomatoes, cut into 1/2-inch slices
- 1 (16 ounces) package fresh mozzarella cheese, cut into 1/4-inch slices
- ¼ teaspoon salt
- ¼ teaspoon ground black pepper
- ½ cup fresh basil leaves
- ¼ cup extra-virgin olive oil

Instructions

- Stir balsamic vinegar and honey together in a small saucepan and place over high heat. Bring to a boil, reduce heat to low, and simmer until the vinegar mixture has reduced to 1/3 cup,

about 10 minutes. Set the balsamic reduction aside to cool.

- Arrange alternate slices of tomato and mozzarella cheese decoratively on a serving platter. Sprinkle with salt and black pepper, spread fresh basil leaves over the salad, and drizzle with olive oil and the balsamic reduction.

Nutrition Facts

Calories: 580| Protein: 22g| Carbohydrates: 34.8g| Fat: 38.8g| Cholesterol: 89.3mg| Sodium: 330.9mg.

494. Sichuan Smashed Cucumber Salad

Total Time: 25 Mins

Ingredients

- 4 cups (532 g) Smashed Cucumber, see the recipe for directions
- 2 Tablespoons (2 Tablespoons) Chinese Black Vinegar
- 1 Tablespoon (1 Tablespoon) Sesame Oil
- 1.5 teaspoon (1.5 teaspoons) Chili Crisp Oil, or toasted Sichuan peppercorns, smashed
- 1/2 teaspoon (1) Splenda, (or sugar)
- 1 teaspoon (1 teaspoon) Kosher Salt

For Finishing

- 1/4-1/3 cup (4 g) chopped Cilantro
- 1/4 cup (36.5 g) crushed peanuts

Instructions

- Peel the cucumber into long strips such that you're alternating one long peeled length with one long unpeeled length. When you're done, you should have a cucumber zebra, so to speak You're doing this to add a little color variation, and also to allow the sauce to flavor but not water-log the outside of the cucumber. This is a tiny affectation that you could skip entirely.
- Cut the cucumber into fourths lengthwise and then cut into chunks.
- Using the flat of your knife--or a cleaver if you trust yourself with one, I can't be trusted with one--roughly smash the cucumber on the side to smoosh it a bit. You want it to crack but not turn into a cucumber purée.

- In a bowl mix all the sauce ingredients. Taste and adjust as needed.
- 15-20 minutes before serving, pour the sauce over the cucumbers.
- Add cilantro and crushed peanuts (which just totally complete this dish!) and mix well before serving.

Nutrition Value

- Calories: 77kcal | Carbohydrates: 3g | Protein: 2g | Fat: 6g | Fiber: 1g | Sugar: 1g

---

495. Spinach And Strawberry Salad

Prep Time: 10 mins

Total Time: 10 mins

Ingredient

- 2 bunches of spinach, rinsed and torn into bite-size pieces
- 4 cups sliced strawberries
- ½ cup vegetable oil
- ¼ cup white wine vinegar
- ½ cup white sugar
- ¼ teaspoon paprika
- 2 tablespoons sesame seeds
- 1 tablespoon poppy seeds

Instructions

- In a large bowl, toss together the spinach and strawberries.
- In a medium bowl, whisk together the oil, vinegar, sugar, paprika, sesame seeds, and poppy seeds. Pour over the spinach and strawberries, and toss to coat.

Nutrition Facts

- Calories: 235; Protein: 3.6g; Carbohydrates: 22.8g; Fat: 15.9g; Sodium: 69.3mg.

---

496. Cucumber Salad With Dill Vinaigrette

Prep Time: 20 mins

Total Time: 20 mins

Ingredients

- 1-pint grape tomatoes halved

- 3 cucumbers - peeled, seeded, and chopped
- 1 red onion, chopped
- 2 yellow bell peppers, chopped
- ¼ cup cider vinegar
- ¼ cup olive oil
- 1 (4 ounces) jar capers, drained
- 2 teaspoons dried dill

Instructions

- Mix tomatoes, cucumbers, red onion, and yellow bell peppers in a bowl; add vinegar, olive oil, capers, and dill. Toss to evenly coat vegetables with dressing.

Nutrition Facts

- Calories: 193; Protein: 3.2g; Carbohydrates: 15.4g; Fat: 14.7g; Sodium: 855.6mg.

10. Air Fryer Meatless Recipes

497. Soy And Onion Sugar Snap Peas

Prep Time: 3 mins

Cook Time: 7 mins

Ingredients

- 1 tablespoon melted butter
- 2 tablespoon finely chopped onion
- 2 teaspoon minced garlic
- 1/2 tablespoon soy sauce
- 1/2 teaspoon onion powder
- 1/4 teaspoon black pepper or to taste
- 8 ounces sugar snap peas (about 250g)

Instructions

- Remove and discard the stem end and string from each pea pod.
- In a cake barrel, mix butter, onion, and garlic. Air fry at 380F (190C) for 2 minutes.
- Add in sugar snap peas and the rest of the ingredients. Stir to make sure the snap peas are coated with butter.
- Air fry at 360F (180C) for about 5-7 minutes, stirring once in the middle.

Nutrition

- Calories: 56kcal | Carbohydrates: 6g | Protein: 2g | Fat: 3g | Saturated Fat: 2g | Cholesterol: 8mg | Sodium: 154mg | Potassium: 113mg | Fiber: 2g | Sugar: 3g | Vitamin C: 35mg | Calcium: 27mg | Iron: 1mg

498. Korean BBQ Chickpeas

Prep Time: 5 mins

Cook Time: 25 mins

Ingredients

- 1 can of garbanzo (chickpeas) beans drained
- 2 tablespoon Korean BBQ sauce
- 1/2 teaspoon gochujang Korean hot pepper paste or to taste
- 1/2 teaspoon honey

Instructions

- Line the fryer basket with a sheet of lightly greased aluminum foil.
- In a medium-sized bowl, mix the Korean BBQ sauce, gochujang, and honey until homogenous.
- Add in the garbanzo beans. Gently mix everything until all the beans are coated with the sauce.
- Transfer all the garbanzo beans and the sauce in the bowl to the fryer basket. Spread the beans out so they are not stacked on top of each other.
- Air fry at 320F (160C) for 23-25 minutes, string a few times in the middle until the sauce on the bean's surface caramelized.
- Let cool for about 5 minutes before serving.

Nutrition

- Calories: 190kcal | Carbohydrates: 33g | Protein: 10g | Fat: 3g | Saturated Fat: 1g | Sodium: 147mg | Potassium: 309mg | Fiber: 8g | Sugar: 8g | Vitamin C: 1mg | Calcium: 52mg | Iron: 3mg

499. Easy Roasted Asparagus

Prep Time: 5 mins

Cook Time: 8 mins

Ingredients

- 1 pound asparagus ends trimmed (about 500g)
- 1/4 tsp sea salt or to taste
- 1/8 teaspoon black pepper or to taste
- 1 tablespoon extra virgin olive oil

Instructions

- Rinse the asparagus and drain.
- Put the asparagus on a large plate and drizzle olive oil on it and season with salt, pepper. Mix gently.
- Line the fryer basket with a grill mat or a sheet of lightly greased aluminum foil.
- Put the asparagus in the fryer basket, without stacking if possible, and air fry at 360F (180C) for about 6-8 minutes until tender.

Nutrition

- Calories: 54kcal | Carbohydrates: 4g | Protein: 3g | Fat: 4g | Saturated Fat: 1g | Sodium: 148mg | Potassium: 229mg | Fiber: 2g | Sugar: 2g |Vitamin C: 6mg | Calcium: 27mg | Iron: 2mg

500. Blueberry Cream Cheese Croissant Bake

Prep Time: 10 mins

Cook Time: 20 mins

Ingredients

- 1/2 tube crescent dough (4 crescents) (or puff pastry sheets)
- 1/2 cup blueberry
- 4 oz cream cheese (約 113g)
- 1/3 cup sugar
- 1 egg
- 1/2 teaspoon vanilla
- 2 tablespoon milk

Instructions

- Roll the crescent dough into the shape of a crescent and set it aside.
- Lightly grease a shallow baking dish and set it aside.
- In an electric mixer, cream together cream cheese and sugar until fluffy.
- Add in milk, egg, and vanilla and mix until well combined and pour the mixture into the baking dish.
- Place the crescents on top and sprinkle the blueberries into the dish.
- Air fry at 280F (140C) for 18-20 minutes until the egg is set and the crescent rolls are golden brown.

Nutrition

- Calories: 206kcal | Carbohydrates: 22g | Protein: 4g | Fat: 12g | Saturated Fat: 6g | Cholesterol: 73mg | Sodium: 138mg | Potassium: 78mg | Fiber: 1g | Sugar: 20g | Vitamin C: 2mg | Calcium: 42mg | Iron: 1mg

501. Garlic And Herb Artisan Bread

Prep Time: 2 hrs

Cook Time: 20 mins

Ingredients

- 1 cup water about 95F (35C)
- 1/2 tablespoon instant dry yeast
- 1/2 tablespoon salt
- 2 1/4 cup all-purpose flour
- 2 teaspoon garlic powder or to taste
- 1/2 teaspoon onion powder
- 1 teaspoon thyme
- 1/2 teaspoon dried parsley

Instructions

- In a medium bowl, gently stir the water and yeast.
- In a large mixing bowl, combine all dry ingredients and mix well.
- Pour the yeast and water mixture into the mixing bowl containing the dry ingredients and mix well. Cover the mixing bowl with a damp towel and let rise for about 2 hours or until the dough rose and double in size.
- Line a 7-inch cake barrel with parchment paper. Sprinkle a little flour onto the parchment paper.
- Use a spatula to punch down the dough then transfer the dough to the cake barrel. Sprinkle some flour on top and let it rise for about 30 minutes.
- If the air fryer you use has a detachable basket, pour about 3 tablespoons of water into the bottom of the outer basket. Preheat the air fryer at 400F (200C) for about 4 minutes.
- Put the cake barrel inside the fryer basket and air fryer at 400F (200C) for about 10-12 minutes until the bread has a nice golden-brown crust.
- Turn the bread over and air fry again at 400F (200C) for another 4-6 minutes until the crust is golden brown. Try knocking on the bread, if it sounds hollow then it is cooked through on the inside.
- Let cool on a wired rack for about 10-15 minutes before slicing.

Nutrition

Calories: 176kcal | Carbohydrates: 37g | Protein: 5g | Fat: 1g | Saturated Fat: 1g | Sodium: 585mg | Potassium: 62mg | Fiber: 1g | Sugar: 1g | Vitamin C: 1mg | Calcium: 7mg | Iron: 2mg

502. Hilton DoubleTree Hotel Chocolate Chip Cookies

Prep Time: 10 mins

Cook Time: 1 hr

Ingredients

- 1/2 cup butter softened
- 1/3 cup granulated sugar
- 1/4 cup packed brown sugar
- 1 egg
- 1/2 teaspoons vanilla extract
- 1/8 teaspoon lemon juice
- 1 cup and 2 tablespoons all-purpose flour
- 1/4 cup rolled oats
- 1/2 teaspoon baking soda
- 1/2 teaspoon salt
- Pinch cinnamon
- 1 1/4 cup semi-sweet chocolate chips
- 1 cup chopped walnuts

Instructions

- Cream butter, sugar, and brown sugar in the bowl of a stand mixer on medium speed for about 2 minutes.
- Add eggs, vanilla, and lemon juice, blending with mixer on low speed for 30 seconds, then medium speed for about 2 minutes, or until light and fluffy, scraping down bowl.
- With the mixer on low speed, add flour, oats, baking soda, salt, and cinnamon, blending for about 45 seconds. Don't overmix.
- Remove bowl from mixer and stir in chocolate chips and walnuts.
- Line the fryer basket with a grill mat or a sheet of parchment paper.
- Scoop about one tablespoon of dough onto a baking sheet lined with parchment paper about 2 inches apart.
- Air fry at 260F (130C) for 18-20 minutes.
- Remove from the air fryer and cool on a wired rack for about 1/2 hour.

Nutrition

- Calories: 397kcal | Carbohydrates: 30g | Protein: 5g | Fat: 29g | Saturated Fat: 15g | Cholesterol: 55mg | Sodium: 154mg | Potassium: 182mg | Fiber: 3g | Sugar: 17g | Vitamin C: 1mg | Calcium:

34mg | Iron: 2mg

503. Korean Air Fried Green Beans

Prep Time: 5 mins

Cook Time: 15 mins

Ingredients

- 1 pound green beans (about 500g) washed and dried in a colander
- 1/3 cup Korean BBQ sauce
- 1/2 teaspoon black pepper or to taste
- 2 teaspoon toasted sesame seeds

Instructions

- Line the fryer basket with a grill mat or a sheet of lightly greased aluminum foil.
- In a mixing bowl, mix and coat the green beans with the seasoning ingredients.
- Transfer all contents in the mixing bowl into the fryer basket.
- Air fry at 400F (200C) for 14-16 minutes, stirring a few times in between until the surface is slightly caramelized. When you see the BBQ sauce starts drying up, keep an eye on it, as you don't want the beans to get charred. Therefore, check more frequently towards the end.
- Sprinkle some sesame seeds to serve.

Nutrition

- Calories: 74kcal | Carbohydrates: 15g | Protein: 3g | Fat: 1g | Saturated Fat: 1g | Sodium: 379mg | Potassium: 250mg | Fiber: 3g | Sugar: 9g | Vitamin C: 14mg | Calcium: 52mg | Iron: 1mg

504. General Tso Tofu

Prep Time: 2 hrs

Cook Time: 15 mins

Ingredients

- 10 oz firm tofu (about 285g)
- 2 tablespoon thinly sliced green onion
- 1 teaspoon sesame seeds
- Ingredients for the sauce:
- 1 Tablespoon chili oil
- 2 Tablespoon minced garlic

- 1 Tablespoon grated ginger
- 2 Tablespoon soy sauce
- 1 Tablespoon vinegar
- 1 1/2 Tablespoon sugar
- 2 teaspoon corn starch mix with 4 teaspoon water

Instructions

- Place a kitchen towel on the counter and place the tofu on top. Put a heavy item, such as a small pot, on top of the tofu for one hour to squeeze out excess water.
- Line the fryer basket with a grill mat or a sheet of lightly greased aluminum foil.
- Cut tofu into bite-size pieces and put them in a fryer basket without stacking. Spritz them with some oil and air fry at 400F (200C) for about 10-12 minutes, flip them once in the middle.
- In the meantime, prepare the sauce by mixing chili oil, minced garlic, grated ginger, soy sauce, vinegar, and sugar.
- Heat the sauce in a wok and bring it to a boil. Mix corn starch with water and add it to the sauce in the wok. Stir constantly until the sauce thickens.
- When the tofu is done, toss them in the wok to coat.
- Sprinkle some sesame seeds and green onion to serve.

Nutrition

- Calories: 129kcal | Carbohydrates: 10g | Protein: 8g | Fat: 7g | Saturated Fat: 1g | Sodium: 507mg | Potassium: 35mg | Fiber: 1g | Sugar: 5g | Vitamin C: 2mg | Calcium: 101mg | Iron: 1mg

505. Roasted Barley Tea

Prep Time: 5 mins

Cook Time: 35 mins

Ingredients

1/2 cup round or pressed barley

Instructions

- Rinse the barley, drain and let dry a bit in a colander.
- Put barley in a cake barrel and air fry at 400F (175C) for 30-35 minutes, stirring 3-4 times in

the middle, until the color turns dark brown.
- Let cool completely before use.
- In a teapot put one tablespoon of roasted barley with one cup of boiling water. Let sit for at least 10 minutes for it to become fragrant and flavorful.

Nutrition

- Calories: 41kcal | Carbohydrates: 8g | Protein: 1g | Fat: 1g | Saturated Fat: 1g | Sodium: 1mg | Potassium: 52mg | Fiber: 2g | Sugar: 1g | Calcium: 4mg | Iron: 1mg

506. Roasted Cinnamon Sugar Orange

Prep Time: 5 mins

Cook Time: 5 mins

Ingredients

- 4 Oranges
- 1/2 tsp cinnamon
- 2 tsp brown sugar
- **Instructions**
- Mix cinnamon and sugar and set aside.
- Cut each half of the orange in half. Then, take a serrated knife to cut along the inner edges of the orange rind.
- Sprinkle the cinnamon sugar the orange.
- Air fry at 400F (200C) for about 4-5 minutes.
- Serve warm by itself or over ice cream.

Nutrition

- Calories: 70kcal | Carbohydrates: 18g | Protein: 1g | Fat: 1g | Saturated Fat: 1g | Sodium: 1mg | Potassium: 237mg | Fiber: 3g | Sugar: 14g | Vitamin A: 295IU | Vitamin C: 70mg | Calcium: 52mg | Iron: 1mg

507. Air Fryer Sweet Potato Fries

Prep Time: 5 mins

Cook Time: 15 mins

Ingredients

- 1 pound sweet potatoes peeled (about 500g)
- 1 tablespoon olive oil
- 1/2 teaspoon garlic powder

- 1/2 teaspoon onion powder
- 1/2 teaspoon paprika
- 1/2 teaspoon salt or to taste
- 1/4 teaspoon white pepper powder
- 1/2 teaspoon dried basil flakes to garnish

Instructions

- Line the fryer basket with a grill mat or a sheet of lightly greased aluminum foil.
- Cut the sweet potato into 1/4 inch sticks.
- In a large mixing bowl, toss the sweet potato sticks with all other ingredients, except dried basil flakes.
- Place the sweet potato sticks inside the fryer basket without stacking, if possible. Air fry at 380F (190C) for 14-16 minutes, stirring once in the middle until the edges look nice and crisp.
- Sprinkle some dried basil to serve.

Nutrition

- Calories: 132kcal | Carbohydrates: 24g | Protein: 2g | Fat: 4g | Saturated Fat: 1g | Sodium: 354mg | Potassium: 382mg | Fiber: 3g | Sugar: 5g |Vitamin C: 3mg | Calcium: 34mg | Iron: 1mg

508. Blueberry Cream Cheese Muffins

Prep Time: 10 mins

Cook Time: 10 mins

Ingredients

- 1 1/2 cups all-purpose flour
- 1/2 cup white sugar
- 1/2 teaspoon salt
- 2 teaspoons baking powder
- 1/4 cup vegetable oil
- 8 oz cream cheese (about 225g) softened at room temperature
- 1 egg
- 1/2 teaspoon vanilla extract
- 1/3 cup milk
- 1 cup fresh blueberries

Instructions

- Grease muffin cups or line with muffin liners.
- In a large bowl, combine flour, sugar, salt, and

baking powder.
- In a large mixing bowl, cream together vegetable oil, cream cheese, egg, and vanilla extract. Then, add in milk and all the dried ingredients and mix until well combined.
- Fold in blueberries. Scoop the mixture into the muffin tins, about 3/4 full.
- Air fry at 320F (160C) for about 12-14 minutes until done, and the toothpick comes out clean.

Nutrition

- Calories: 421kcal | Carbohydrates: 47g | Protein: 7g | Fat: 24g | Saturated Fat: 15g | Cholesterol: 70mg | Sodium: 334mg | Potassium: 267mg | Fiber: 1g | Sugar: 21g | Vitamin C: 2mg | Calcium: 119mg | Iron: 2mg

509. Air Fryer BBQ Brussels Sprouts

Prep Time: 5 mins

Cook Time: 25 mins

Ingredients

- 1 pound Brussels sprouts about 500g
- 2 tsp olive oil
- 1/8 tsp black pepper or to taste
- 1/4 cup BBQ sauce American-style BBQ sauce (such as the Sweet Baby Ray's BBQ sauce)
- 1/4 cup Parmesan cheese or to taste

Instructions

- Rinse the Brussels sprouts with cold water and let dry in a colander. Trim off the ends and cut them in half.
- In a large mixing bowl, toss the Brussels sprouts, olive oil, and black pepper. Then, wrap them in aluminum foil and air fry at 380F (190C) for about about 16 minutes.
- Mix in the BBQ sauce and air fry again at 360F (180C) for 5-6 minutes, stirring once in the middle until the surface is slightly caramelized.
- Sprinkle some Parmesan cheese to serve.

Nutrition

- Calories: 122kcal | Carbohydrates: 18g | Protein: 6g | Fat: 4g | Saturated Fat: 1g | Cholesterol:

4mg | Sodium: 312mg | Potassium: 483mg | Fiber: 4g | Sugar: 8g | Vitamin C: 96mg | Calcium: 128mg | Iron: 2mg

510. Hotteok Korean Sweet Pancakes

Prep Time: 2 hrs 30 mins

Cook Time: 10 mins

Ingredients

Ingredients For The Dough:

- 1 1/4 cup all-purpose flour
- 1/2 tsp salt
- 1 tsp white sugar
- 1 tsp instant dry yeast
- 1/2 cup lukewarm milk
- Ingredients for the filling:
- 1/4 cup brown sugar
- 1/4 tsp cinnamon powder
- 1/4 cup chopped walnuts

Instructions

- In a mixing bowl, mix all the dough ingredients with a spatula.
- Lightly cover the bowl with saran wrap and let the dough rise for about 1-2 hours or until the dough doubles in size.
- Punch the dough down several times to release the air in the dough. Then, cover with saran wrap again and let it rest for about 20 minutes.
- In the meantime, mix all the filling ingredients in a bowl and set aside.
- Line the fryer basket with a grill mat or a sheet of lightly greased aluminum foil.
- Rub some cooking oil in your hands and take the dough out from the bowl. Roll the dough into a cylinder shape on the counter surface then cut it into six equal pieces. Roll each piece into a ball.
- Take one ball of dough and flatten it between the palms of your hand. Scoop about 1 tablespoon of filling and wrap it inside the dough. Place the dough inside the fryer basket, leaving about 2 inches between the balls. Repeat until done.
- Press the balls down with the palm of your hand. Spritz some oil on top and air fry at 300F (150C) for 8-10 minutes, flip once in the middle until the surface is golden brown.

Nutrition

- Calories: 137kcal | Carbohydrates: 24g | Protein: 4g | Fat: 3g | Saturated Fat: 1g | Cholesterol: 2mg | Sodium: 155mg | Potassium: 81mg | Fiber: 1g | Sugar: 8g | Calcium: 29mg | Iron: 1mg

511. Parmesan Sugar Snap Peas

Prep Time: 5 mins

Cook Time: 10 mins

Ingredients

- 1/2 pound sugar snap peas (about 250g)
- 1 tsp olive oil
- 1/4 cup panko breadcrumbs (optional)
- 1/4 cup parmesan cheese
- Salt and pepper to taste
- 2 tbsp minced garlic

Instructions

- Remove and discard the stem end and string from each pea pod. Then, rinse and drained in a colander.
- Line the fryer basket with a grill mat or a sheet of lightly greased aluminum foil.
- In a large mixing bowl, toss the snap peans with olive oil, panko breadcrumbs, half of the parmesan cheese, and salt and pepper.
- Put the snap pea mixture into the fryer basket and air fry at 360F for about 4 minutes.
- Stir in the minced garlic then air fry again at 360F (180C) for another 4-5 minutes.
- Sprinkle the rest of the parmesan cheese to serve.

Nutrition

Calories: 78kcal | Carbohydrates: 9g | Protein: 5g | Fat: 3g | Saturated Fat: 1g | Cholesterol: 4mg | Sodium: 131mg | Potassium: 129mg | Fiber: 2g | Sugar: 3g | Vitamin C: 35mg | Calcium: 112mg | Iron: 1mg

512. Air Fryer Roasted Almonds

Prep Time: 1 min

Cook Time: 15 mins

Ingredients

- 1 cup raw almonds

Instructions

- Put raw almonds in bakeware, air fry at 320F (160C) for 10-12 minutes, stirring twice in the middle to ensure they roast evenly.
- Let cool completely before serving.

Nutrition

- Calories: 206kcal | Carbohydrates: 8g | Protein: 8g | Fat: 18g | Saturated Fat: 1g | Sodium: 1mg | Potassium: 252mg | Fiber: 4g | Sugar: 1g | Calcium: 94mg | Iron: 1mg

513. Gochujang Lotus Root

Prep Time: 10 mins

Cook Time: 10 mins

Ingredients

- 1/2 pound lotus root sliced about 1/4 inch thick (about 250g)
- 1 tablespoon Gochujang Korean hot pepper paste
- 1 tablespoon soy sauce
- 4 tablespoon honey
- 2 teaspoon apple cider vinegar
- 1 teaspoon sesame seed

Instructions

- In a Ziploc bag, mix Gochujang, soy sauce, honey, and apple cider vinegar. Add lotus roots to the bag and mix. Seal the bag and marinate for at least one hour or best overnight.
- Line the fryer basket with a grill mat or a sheet of lightly greased aluminum foil.
- Put the lotus root slices in the fryer basket without stacking. Air fry at 380F (190C) for about 10 minutes, flip once in the middle until the surface looks slightly caramelized.
- In the meantime, transfer the marinade from the bag to a wok or saucepan and bring it to a boil. Stir constantly until the sauce thickens.
- Toss the lotus root with the sauce. Then, sprinkle some sesame seeds and scallion to serve.

Nutrition

- Calories: 116kcal | Carbohydrates: 29g | Protein: 2g | Fat: 1g | Saturated Fat: 1g | Sodium: 276mg | Potassium: 351mg | Fiber: 3g | Sugar: 18g | Vitamin C: 26mg | Calcium: 30mg | Iron: 1mg

514. Korean BBQ Lotus Root

Prep Time: 5 mins

Cook Time: 10 mins

Ingredients

- 1/3 cup Korean BBQ Sauce
- 1/2 pound Lotus root cut into 1/4 inch slices (about 250g)
- 1 teaspoon sesame seeds
- 2 tablespoon scallion

Instructions

- Marinate lotus in Korean BBQ sauce for at least 1 hour or best overnight.
- Line the fryer basket with a grill mat or a sheet of lightly greased aluminum foil.
- Put the lotus root slices in the fryer basket without stacking. Air fry at 380F (190C) for about 6-8 minutes, flip once in the middle until the surface looks slightly caramelized.
- In the meantime, transfer the marinade from the bag to a wok or saucepan and bring it to a boil. Stir constantly until the sauce thickens.
- Toss the lotus root with the sauce. Then, sprinkle some sesame seeds and scallion to serve.

Nutrition

- Calories: 79kcal | Carbohydrates: 17g | Protein: 3g | Fat: 1g | Saturated Fat: 1g | Sodium: 396mg | Potassium: 326mg | Fiber: 3g | Sugar: 6g | Vitamin A: 30IU | Vitamin C: 26mg | Calcium: 30mg | Iron: 1mg

515. Honey Sesame Tofu

Prep Time: 1 hr

Cook Time: 30 mins

Ingredients

- 1 box firm tofu about 1 pound or 500g
- 1/3 cup honey

- 1/3 cup soy sauce
- 1/4 cup ketchup
- 1/4 cup brown sugar
- 1/4 cup rice vinegar
- 1 tsp sesame oil
- 2 Tbsp minced garlic
- 1 Tbsp sesame seeds for garnish or to taste
- 1/4 cup scallions for garnish or to taste

Instructions

- Wrap the tofu in a cheesecloth. Place a heavy pan on top for about 30 minutes.
- Then, place the tofu in the freezer for at least 6 hours.
- Remove the tofu from the freezer and use the defrost function of the microwave for about 10 minutes. After that, repeat step one to squeeze out excess water.
- In the meantime, take a large bowl to mix and combine honey, soy sauce, ketchup, brown sugar, vinegar, sesame oil, and garlic. Scoop about 1/2 cup of the marinade and set aside.
- Use hands to break the tofu into bite-size pieces and put them inside the large bowl containing the marinade. Stir and let the tofu marinate for at least 30 minutes.
- Line the fryer basket with a grill mat or sheet of lightly greased aluminum foil.
- Put the tofu pieces inside the fryer basket without stacking and air fry at 400F (200C) for 14-16 minutes, stir once in the middle until the edges of tofu looks a bit caramelized.
- While air frying, use a wok or a frying pan to bring the sauce to a boil. Stir constantly until the sauce thickens.
- When the tofu is done, toss in the wok to coat. Sprinkle some sesame seeds and scallions to serve.

Nutrition

- Calories: 281kcal | Carbohydrates: 46g | Protein: 12g | Fat: 6g | Saturated Fat: 1g | Sodium: 1227mg | Potassium: 164mg | Fiber: 1g | Sugar: 41g | Vitamin C: 3mg | Calcium: 170mg | Iron: 2mg

516. Raspberry Nutella Toast Cups

Prep Time: 5 mins

Cook Time: 10 mins

Ingredients

- 6 pieces of bread
- 2 tbsp unsalted butter melted
- 1/4 cup Nutella or to taste
- 1/2 cup Raspberry or to taste
- 2 tbsp powdered sugar optional

Instructions

- Trim off the sides of the toast and save for them for other uses such as croutons or bread pudding. Flatten the toast with a rolling pin and brush a thin layer of butter to both sides.
- Place each of the toast inside a muffin tin and press down against the walls of the tin. Air fry at 320F (160C) for about 7-8 minutes until the toast becomes golden brown.
- Spoon some Nutella into the bread cup and spread it inside of the cup. Finally, place the raspberries inside the cup. Dust the cups with powdered sugar if desired.

Nutrition

- Calories:196kcal | Carbohydrates: 24g | Protein: 2g | Fat: 10g | Saturated Fat: 9g | Cholesterol: 7mg | Sodium: 21mg | Potassium: 132mg | Fiber: 3g | Sugar: 20g | Vitamin C: 5mg | Calcium: 32mg | Iron: 1mg

517. Turnip Fries

Prep Time: 30 mins

Cook Time: 15 mins

Ingredients

- 1/2 pound turnip peeled and cut into sticks
- 1/4 tsp salt
- 2 teaspoon olive oil
- 1/4 tsp paprika
- 1/4 tsp onion powder
- 1/8 tsp white pepper powder or to taste
- 1/8 tsp cayenne pepper or to taste (optional)

Instructions

- In a mixing bowl, toss the turnip sticks with salt. Let it rest for about 20 minutes to draw some of the water out. Discard the excess water in the bowl.
- Toss the turnips sticks in olive oil to coat. Then, add in the rest of the ingredients and toss. Put the turnip sticks into the fryer basket and try to spread them out as much as possible.
- Air fry at 380F (190C) for 10-12 minutes, shake basket a couple of times in between until the surface looks crisp and golden brown.
- Serve immediately. Sprinkle some dried basil if desired.

Nutrition

- Calories: 69kcal | Carbohydrates: 8g | Protein: 1g | Fat: 4g | Saturated Fat: 1g | Sodium: 367mg | Potassium: 217mg | Fiber: 2g | Sugar: 4g | Vitamin A: 175IU | Vitamin C: 24mg | Calcium: 34mg | Iron: 1mg

518. Home Fries

Prep Time: 5 mins

Cook Time: 10 mins

Ingredients

- 1 russet potato
- 1 tbsp olive oil
- 1/2 tsp salt or to taste
- 1/2 tsp paprika
- 1/4 tsp black pepper
- 1/4 tsp cayenne pepper (optional)

Instructions

- Peel and dice the potato into 1/2 inch pieces. Soak the potato in cold water for about 10-15 minutes. Drain.
- Toss the potato in olive oil. Then, add the remaining ingredients and toss.
- Line the fryer basket with a grill mat or a sheet of lightly greased aluminum foil.
- Spread the diced potato inside the fryer basket. Air fry at 380F (190C) for about 10-12 minutes, stir twice in the middle until the surface is crispy and golden brown.

Nutrition

- Calories: 84kcal | Carbohydrates: 9g | Protein: 2g | Fat: 5g | Saturated Fat: 1g | Sodium: 395mg | Potassium: 293mg | Fiber: 2g | Sugar: 1g | Vitamin C: 8mg | Calcium: 21mg | Iron: 2mg

519. BBQ Baby Corn

Prep Time: 5 mins

Cook Time: 10 mins

Ingredients

- 1 can baby corn drained and rinse with cold water
- 1/4 cup Korean BBQ sauce or to taste **
- 1/2 tsp Sriracha or to taste optional

Instructions

- Line the fryer basket with a grill mat or a sheet of lightly greased aluminum foil.
- In a large bowl, mix the Korean BBQ sauce and Sriracha. Roll the baby corn in the sauce and place them inside the fryer basket without stacking.
- Air fry at 400F (200C) for about 8-10 minutes, brush some more sauce onto baby corn if necessary until the sauce on the surface is slightly caramelized.

Nutrition

- Serving: 0.5cup | Calories: 98kcal | Carbohydrates: 18g | Protein: 2g | Fat: 1g | Sodium: 325mg | Sugar: 8g | Vitamin C: 1mg

520. Air Fried Banana

Prep Time: 5 mins

Cook Time: 10 mins

Ingredients

- 1 ripe banana cut into 1/2 inch slices
- 1/4 tsp cinnamon
- 1/2 tsp brown sugar
- 1 tbsp Granola to taste
- 1 tbsp Chopped toasted nuts to taste

Instructions

- In a small bowl, mix the cinnamon and brown sugar and set aside.
- Lightly grease a shallow baking pan. Place the banana slices into the pan. Spray some oil onto the banana and sprinkle some cinnamon sugar. Air fry at 400F (200C) for about 4-5 minutes.
- Sprinkle some granola and nuts over the banana to serve.

Nutrition

Calories: 113kcal | Carbohydrates: 19g | Protein: 2g | Fat: 4g | Saturated Fat: 1g | Sodium: 3mg | Potassium: 253mg | Fiber: 2g | Sugar: 9g | Vitamin A: 38IU | Vitamin C: 5mg | Iron: 1mg

521. Sweet And Sour Brussel Sprouts

Prep Time: 5 mins

Cook Time: 20 mins

Ingredients

- 1 pound Brussels sprouts (about 500g)
- 1 tsp olive oil
- 1 tbsp minced garlic
- 1/4 tsp salt or to taste
- 2 tbsp Thai Sweet Chili Sauce
- 2-3 tsp lime juice

Instructions

- Rinse the Brussels sprouts with cold water and let dry in a colander. Trim off the ends and cut them in half.
- In a large mixing bowl, toss the Brussels sprouts and garlic with olive oil and wrap them in aluminum foil. Air fry at 380F (190C) for about about 18 minutes.
- In a mixing bowl, toss the Sprouts with Thai Sweet Chili Sauce and lime juice to serve.

Nutrition

- Calories: 79kcal | Carbohydrates: 15g | Protein: 4g | Fat: 1g | Saturated Fat: 1g | Sodium: 259mg | Potassium: 441mg | Fiber: 4g | Sugar: 7g | Vitamin A: 855IU | Vitamin C: 98mg | Calcium: 51mg | Iron: 2mg

522. Mozzarella Stuffed Mushrooms

Prep Time: 5 mins

Cook Time: 10 mins

Ingredients

- 8 medium to large button mushrooms wiped clean and stem removed
- 3-4 tbsp Korean BBQ sauce
- 1/3 cup mozzarella cheese
- Olive oil spray
- 1/2 tsp basil flakes

Instructions

- Line the fryer basket with a grill mat or a sheet of lightly greased aluminum foil.
- Scoop about 1/2 teaspoon of Korean BBQ sauce into the mushroom. Then, stuff the mushroom with the desired amount of mozzarella cheese.
- Place the mushrooms inside the fryer basket. Spray the mushrooms with some olive oil and air fry at 380F (190C) for about 4-5 minutes until the cheese is golden brown.
- Sprinkle some basil flakes to serve if desired.

Nutrition

- Calories: 74kcal | Carbohydrates: 7g | Protein: 5g | Fat: 3g | Saturated Fat: 2g | Cholesterol: 10mg | Sodium: 360mg | Potassium: 170mg | Fiber: 1g | Sugar: 5g | Vitamin C: 1mg | Calcium: 67mg | Iron: 1mg

523. Red Bean Wheel Pie (Imagawayaki)

Prep Time: 10 mins

Cook Time: 10 mins

Ingredients

- 2 tbsp melted butter
- 2 eggs
- 2 tbsp sugar
- 1 tbsp honey
- 1/4 tsp vanilla extract
- 1/4 cup milk
- 1 cupcake flour
- 3/4 tsp baking powder
- 6 tbsp mashed sweetened red bean canned or homemade filling to taste

Instructions

- Lightly grease 4 ramekins with butter and place them in the fryer basket. Preheat at 400F (200C) for 2 minutes.
- In a large bowl, use a whisk to mix the egg, sugar, vanilla extract, and honey. Add in milk and whisk until the mixture is homogeneous. Finally, add in the sifted cake flour and baking powder. Continue to mix until everything is well blended.
- The total weight of the batter is about 280g. Spoon about 30g into the ramekin. Air fry at 300F (150C) for about 3 minutes.
- Take the desired amount of red bean (about 1 1/2 Tablespoon for mine) and roll it into a ball using the palms of your hand. Flatten it into a circular disc that is smaller than the diameter of the ramekin. Place it in the center of the ramekin on top of the pancake. Scoop about 40g of the batter into the ramekins to cover the red beans.
- Air fry again at 300F (150C) for about 3 minutes. Brush some butter on top and air fry again at 300F (150C) for 1-2 minutes until the top is slightly golden brown.

Nutrition

- Calories: 284kcal | Carbohydrates: 47g | Protein: 8g | Fat: 9g | Saturated Fat: 5g | Cholesterol: 98mg | Sodium: 101mg | Potassium: 157mg | Fiber: 2g | Sugar: 20g | Vitamin A: 318IU | Calcium: 67mg | Iron: 1mg

524. Crispy Curry Chickpeas

Prep Time: 5 mins

Cook Time: 25 mins

Ingredients

- 2 cups canned chickpeas drained
- 1 teaspoon olive oil
- 1/2 teaspoon curry powder
- 1/4 teaspoon onion powder
- 1/4 teaspoon paprika
- 1/4 teaspoon salt or to taste
- 1/8 teaspoon garlic powder
- 1/8 teaspoon cayenne pepper optional
- 1/8 teaspoon mushroom essence or Hondashi optional

Instructions

- Mix all the dry ingredients and set aside.
- In a large bowl, toss the chickpeas with olive oil. Then, add in the dry ingredients and toss, making sure all chickpeas are coated with seasoning.
- In a lightly greased cake pan or bakeware, air fry the chickpeas at 360F (180C) for about 23-25 minutes, shake the basket 3-4 times in the middle, until the surface is crisp and lightly golden brown.
- Pour the chickpeas onto a plate. Let cool completely before serving.

Nutrition

- Calories: 166kcal | Carbohydrates: 23g | Protein: 8g | Fat: 5g | Saturated Fat: 1g | Sodium: 747mg | Potassium: 236mg | Fiber: 7g | Sugar: 1g | Vitamin A: 175IU | Calcium: 57mg | Iron: 2mg

525. Cheesy Cauliflower Croquettes

Prep Time: 15 mins

Cook Time: 10 mins

Ingredients

- 2 cups of cauliflower rice preparation see instruction
- 2 eggs beaten
- 1/2 cup Mexican blend cheese or your favorite cheese
- 1/4 cup grated Parmesan cheese
- 1/4 cup Mozzarella cheese
- 1/3 cup breadcrumbs
- 1 teaspoon garlic powder
- 1 teaspoon dried basil
- 1/2 teaspoon onion powder
- 1/4 teaspoon salt or to taste
- 1/4 teaspoon black pepper or to taste

Instructions

- Pulse the cauliflower in the food processor a few

times until it is about the size of a grain of rice. Transfer the cauliflower rice to a microwave-safe bowl and microwave for about 5-6 minutes.

- In a large bowl, combine the cauliflower rice with all the other ingredients (except sriracha mayonnaise). Shape the mixture into the desired shape.
- Line the fryer basket with a grill mat or a sheet of lightly greased aluminum foil.
- Place the croquettes in the fryer basket and air fry at 400F (200C) for 8-9 minutes, flip once in the middle, until the surface is golden brown.
- Serve with sriracha mayo or your favorite dipping sauce.

Nutrition

- Calories: 182kcal | Carbohydrates: 11g | Protein: 12g | Fat: 10g | Saturated Fat: 5g |Sodium: 495mg | Potassium: 218mg | Fiber: 2g | Sugar: 2g | Vitamin C: 24mg | Calcium: 242mg | Iron: 1mg

526. Curry Roasted Cauliflower

Prep Time: 10 mins

Cook Time: 10 mins

Ingredients

- 1/2 head cauliflower break them into small florets
- 2 teaspoon olive oil
- 1/2 teaspoon curry powder
- 1/4 teaspoon paprika
- 1/4 teaspoon cumin
- 1/4 teaspoon garlic powder
- 1/4 teaspoon sea salt or to taste

Instructions

- Put the cauliflower florets in a large microwave-safe bowl and microwave for about 4-5 minutes.
- When done, transfer the florets to a large mixing bowl. Add in olive oil and toss. Then, add the rest of the ingredients to the mixing bowl and toss again to coat.
- Air fry at 350F (175C) for about 5-6 minutes, shake the basket once in between. until you start seeing browning of the edges.

Nutrition

- Calories: 38kcal | Carbohydrates: 4g | Protein: 1g | Fat: 2g | Saturated Fat: 1g | Sodium: 167mg | Potassium: 215mg | Fiber: 2g | Sugar: 1g | Vitamin C: 35mg | Calcium: 16mg | Iron: 1mg

31. Vietnamese Vegetarian Egg Meatloaf

Prep Time: 30 mins

Cook Time: 20 mins

Ingredients

- 15 g wood ear mushrooms
- 20 g dried shiitake mushrooms
- 4 eggs
- 1/4 cup milk
- small carrot shredded or grated
- 1 tablespoon minced garlic
- 60 g mung bean noodles glass noodles
- tablespoon fish sauce
- 1/4 teaspoon sugar
- 1/4 teaspoon salt
- 1/4 teaspoon black pepper

Instructions

- Soak the shiitake mushrooms and wood ear mushrooms in warm water for about 20 minutes. Once they are softened, squeeze out excess water in the shiitake mushrooms and thinly slice both mushrooms.
- Soak mung bean noodles in cold water for about 15 minutes then cut them into 2-inch sections.
- Crack 2 whole eggs and 2 egg whites into a large bowl and save the 2 egg yolks in a small bowl for later use.
- Add milk into the large bowl and use a whisk to mix until homogenous. Add all the ingredients, except for the egg yolks, into the large bowl and mix.
- Spray some oil in a mini loaf pan and pour the egg mixture into the pan. Smooth out the top surface as much as possible since anything that sticks out of the surface will likely be charred during the air frying process.
- Air fry at 280F (140C) for 16-18 minutes until the egg is set.
- In the meantime, add a pinch of salt into the small bowl containing the egg yolks and mix.

- When the egg loaf is done, pour the egg yolk on top and spread it evenly over the egg loaf. Air fry again at 400F (200C) for about 2 minutes until the egg yolks are hardened.
- When cool enough to handle, remove the egg loaf from the pan and cut them into 3/4 inch thick slices. Spoon some sauce over it to serve.

Nutrition

- Calories: 167kcal | Carbohydrates: 24g | Protein: 8g | Fat: 5g | Saturated Fat: 2g | Cholesterol: 165mg | Sodium: 783mg | Potassium: 300mg | Fiber: 2g | Sugar: 2g | Vitamin C: 2mg | Calcium: 61mg | Iron: 1mg

527. Broccoli And Mushroom Omelette

Prep Time: 10 mins

Cook Time: 10 mins

Ingredients

- 2 eggs beaten
- 1/4 cup broccoli florets steamed
- 1/4 cup buttoned mushroom sliced
- 1/4 cup shredded cheese Mexican Blend
- 2-3 Tablespoon milk
- 1/8 teaspoon salt and pepper or to taste
- 4-5 slices of pickled jalapeno or to taste (optional)
- Extra cheese to sprinkle

Instructions

- Lightly grease a shallow baking pan and set it aside.
- In a large bowl, mix the eggs, broccoli, mushroom, 1/4 cup shredded cheese, milk, salt, and pepper, and pour it into the pan. Then, place the jalapeno slices on top (or can be chopped up and mix with the egg mixture).
- Air fry at 320F (160C) for about 6-8 minutes. Sprinkle some more cheese on top and air fry again at 320F (160C) for another 2 minutes or so until the eggs are set.

Nutrition

- Calories: 121kcal | Carbohydrates: 3g | Protein: 10g | Fat: 8g | Saturated Fat: 4g | Cholesterol: 176mg | Sodium: 323mg | Potassium: 155mg |

Fiber: 1g | Sugar: 2g | Vitamin C: 10mg | Calcium: 118mg | Iron: 1mg

528. Taro Balls With Salted Egg Yolks

Prep Time: 20 mins

Cook Time: 10 mins

Ingredients

- 6 salted egg yolk
- 1 teaspoon rice wine
- 500 g taro steamed
- 50 g corn starch
- 80 g sugar
- 1/4 teaspoon salt
- 2 Tablespoon coconut oil

Instructions

- Coat the egg yolk with rice wine and let sit for 10 minutes. Put the egg yolks in shallow bakeware and air fry at 380F (190C) for about 3-4 minutes.
- Put all other ingredients in a mixing bowl. Mush and mix all ingredients until the texture is dough-like and without lumps. Alternatively, a food processor can be used as well.
- When done, divide this taro dough into 6 equal portions and roll them into round balls. Flatten each ball and put an egg yolk in the middle. Wrap the dough around the egg yolk and roll it into a ball again, making sure there are no cracks or openings.
- Line the fryer basket with a grill mat or lightly greased aluminum foil.
- Place the taro balls inside the fryer basket. Air fry at 380F (190C) for 8-10 minutes, shake the basket once in the middle until the surface is golden brown.

Nutrition

- Calories: 276kcal | Carbohydrates: 44g | Protein: 4g | Fat: 10g | Saturated Fat: 6g | Cholesterol: 195mg | Sodium: 116mg | Potassium: 512mg | Fiber: 3g | Sugar: 14g | Vitamin C: 4mg | Calcium: 59mg | Iron: 1mg

529. Black Pepper Mushroom

Prep Time: 5 mins

Cook Time: 10 mins

Ingredients

- 8 oz button mushrooms (about 250g) wiped clean, halved, or quartered
- 1 Tablespoon butter melted
- 2 cloves of garlic thinly sliced
- 1 Tablespoon oyster sauce or to taste
- 3/4 teaspoon black pepper or to taste
- 1/4 cup green onion finely sliced

Instructions

- Put melted butter and garlic in a cake pan and air fry at 380F (190C) for 2 minutes.
- Add the mushroom into the pan and stir. Air fry at 360F (180C) for 3 minutes. Stir in the oyster sauce and black pepper. Air fry again at 360F (180C) for 2-3 minutes.
- Sprinkle some green onion to serve.

Nutrition

- Calories: 90kcal | Carbohydrates: 7g | Protein: 4g | Fat: 6g | Saturated Fat: 4g | Cholesterol: 15mg | Sodium: 255mg | Potassium: 395mg | Fiber: 2g | Sugar: 3g | Vitamin C: 6mg | Calcium: 14mg | Iron: 1mg

530. Vegetarian Grilled Unagi

Prep Time: 10 mins

Cook Time: 5 mins

Ingredients

- 1 Chinese eggplant cut in half
- 2 Tablespoon Unagi sauce or Teriyaki sauce or to taste
- 1 teaspoon toasted sesame seeds
- 2 tablespoon thinly sliced green onion

Instructions

- Steam the eggplants until tender.
- When cool enough to handle, cut the eggplant vertically without cutting through. Then, score the flesh of the eggplants so they look like tiny squares or rectangles.
- Line the fryer basket with a grill mat or lightly greased aluminum foil.
- Brush both sides of the eggplants with Unagi

sauce (or Teriyaki sauce). Place the eggplant into the fryer basket skin side down and air fry at 400F (200C) for about 4-5 minutes.
- Sprinkle some sesame seeds and green onion to serve.

Nutrition

- Calories: 81kcal | Carbohydrates: 17g | Protein: 4g | Fat: 1g | Saturated Fat: 1g | Sodium: 405mg | Potassium: 565mg | Fiber: 7g | Sugar: 11g | Vitamin C: 6mg | Calcium: 30mg | Iron: 1mg

531. Air Fried Button Mushrooms

Prep Time: 5 mins

Cook Time: 10 mins

Ingredients

- 10 medium button mushrooms wiped clean with a paper towel and quartered
- 1 egg beaten
- 1/2 cup breadcrumbs
- 1/2 teaspoon garlic powder
- 1/2 teaspoon onion powder
- 1/4 teaspoon dried basil
- 1/4 teaspoon black pepper
- 1/4 teaspoon salt
- Ranch dressing optional

Instructions

- Put all the dry ingredients in a large Ziploc bag and shake well.
- Dip the mushroom pieces in the egg then drop them into the Ziploc bag. Shake the bag to coat the mushroom pieces with bread crumb mixture.
- Shake off excess bread crumbs from the mushroom and place them in the fryer basket. Spray some oil onto the mushrooms and air fry at 400F (200C) for about 3 minutes. Flip the mushrooms and spray some oil again. Air fry at 400F (200C) for another 2-3 minutes.
- Serve immediately with ranch dressing or the sauce of your choice.

Nutrition

- Calories: 330kcal | Carbohydrates: 48g | Protein: 19g | Fat: 8g | Saturated Fat: 2g | Cholesterol: 164mg | Sodium: 659mg | Potassium: 590mg |

Fiber: 4g | Sugar: 8g | Vitamin C: 4mg | Calcium: 123mg | Iron: 5mg

532. Marinated Korean BBQ Tofu

Prep Time: 2 hrs

Cook Time: 15 mins

Ingredients

- 8 oz firm tofu cut into bite-size cubes
- 1 cup Korean BBQ Sauce
- 2-3 Tablespoon minced garlic
- Thinly sliced scallions and sesame optional

Instructions

- In a Ziploc bag or a container with a lid, marinate the tofu with Korean BBQ sauce and grated garlic for at least 2 hours.
- Line the fryer basket with a Grill mat or a sheet of lightly greased aluminum foil.
- Place the tofu cube inside the fryer basket and air fry at 400F (200C) for 10-12 minutes, flip once in the middle, until the surface is caramelized.
- Garnish with scallions and sesame seeds to serve if desired.

Nutrition

- Calories: 152kcal | Carbohydrates: 22g | Protein: 9g | Fat: 3g | Saturated Fat: 1g | Sodium: 638mg | Potassium: 49mg | Fiber: 1g | Sugar: 17g | Vitamin C: 1mg | Calcium: 78mg | Iron: 1mg

533. Buttered Green Beans

Prep Time: 5 mins

Cook Time: 10 mins

Ingredients

- 1 pound green beans (about 500g) rinsed and dried
- 1 1/2 Tablespoon unsalted butter melted
- 1/2 teaspoon sea salt
- 1/4 teaspoon black pepper
- 2 Tablespoon chopped garlic

Instructions

- Toss the green beans with melted butter, salt,

and pepper. Air fry at 350F (175C) for about 4 minutes.
- Add in the garlic, stir, and air fry again at 350F (175C) for another 3-4 minutes.

Nutrition

- Calories: 62kcal | Carbohydrates: 5g | Protein: 2g | Fat: 4g | Saturated Fat: 3g | Cholesterol: 11mg | Sodium: 321mg | Potassium: 211mg | Fiber: 1g | Sugar: 1g | Vitamin C: 28mg | Calcium: 22mg | Iron: 1mg

534. Matcha Red Bean Toast

Prep Time: 5 mins

Cook Time: 10 mins

Ingredients

- 4 pieces of bread
- 1 Tablespoon unsalted butter softened
- Canned Japanese sweetened red bean (mashed), to taste
- 3 tablespoon matcha green tea powder
- 1 1/4 Tablespoon water

Instructions

- In a small bowl, matcha mixes green tea powder with water until it forms a thickened paste. Spread the paste on one piece of bread and the mashed red bean on the other piece (one side only).
- Put the two pieces together to make a sandwich.
- Spread the softened butter onto the outside of the sandwich on both sides. Stick one toothpick through the sandwich to prevent the displacement of bread during the air frying process.
- Air fry at 400F (200C) for about 7-8 minutes, flip once until the surface is golden brown.

Nutrition

- Calories: 123kcal | Carbohydrates: 1g | Protein: 12g | Fat: 6g | Saturated Fat: 4g | Cholesterol: 15mg | Sodium: 12mg | Sugar: 1g | Vitamin A: 1300IU | Iron: 4mg

535. Cumin Spiced Tofu Skewers

Prep Time: 1 hr 10 mins

Cook Time: 15 mins

Ingredients

- 8 oz firm tofu
- 2 Tablespoon soy paste
- 1 Tablespoon olive oil
- 1 Tablespoon cumin
- 1 teaspoon brown sugar
- 1/4 teaspoon cayenne pepper or to taste
- 1/4 Sichuan peppercorn powder or to taste
- 2 tablespoon thinly sliced green onion
- 1 teaspoon toasted sesame seeds

Instructions

- Place a kitchen towel on the counter and place the tofu on top. Put a heavy item, such as a small pot, on top of the tofu for one hour to squeeze out excess water.
- Soak bamboo skewers in water for at least 10 minutes. Take a metal steamer rack and brush olive oil onto the surface of the rack and put it inside the fryer basket.
- In a small bowl, prepare the sauce by mixing all the seasoning ingredients and set aside.
- Cut tofu into bite-size pieces and thread them on 2 skewers parallel to each other. Generously brush both sides of the tofu with a layer of the seasoning mixture and place the skewers on top of the steamer rack.
- Air fry at 400F (200C) for about 10-12 minutes, brushing more sauce in the middle if necessary, until the surface of the tofu is slightly caramelized.
- Sprinkle some sesame seeds and green onion to serve.

Nutrition

- Calories: 107kcal | Carbohydrates: 6g | Protein: 6g | Fat: 7g | Saturated Fat: 1g | Sodium: 198mg | Potassium: 27mg | Fiber: 1g | Sugar: 3g | Vitamin A: 101IU | Vitamin C: 1mg | Calcium: 90mg | Iron: 2mg

536. Maple Banana French Toast Bake

Prep Time: 5 mins

Cook Time: 20 mins

Ingredients

- Ingredients: makes two loaves using 5.75 in x 3 in mini loaf pans
- 2 eggs beaten
- 1/4 cups milk
- 1 Tablespoon brown sugar
- 3 Tablespoon maple syrup
- 1 Tablespoon butter melted
- 1 teaspoon vanilla extract
- 1/4 teaspoon ground cinnamon
- 1 small banana sliced
- 4 slices of bread cubed
- 1/3 cup raw walnut chopped
- Raw chop walnuts to top

Instructions

- In a large mixing bowl, mix the eggs, milk, brown sugar, maple syrup, butter, vanilla extract, and cinnamon. When the mixture is well combined, gently stir in bread cubes, banana, and chopped pecans.
- Scoop the mixture into a lightly greased mini loaf pan and top it with the whole pecan.
- Air fry at 280F (140C) for about 12 minutes. Then, carefully remove the loaf from the pan, flip, and place the bread loaf directly on parchment paper (now bottom side up). Air fry at 280F (140C) again for about 6 minutes more.

Nutrition

- Calories: 287kcal | Carbohydrates: 36g | Protein: 8g | Fat: 13g | Saturated Fat: 4g | Cholesterol: 91mg | Sodium: 211mg | Potassium: 284mg | Fiber: 3g | Sugar: 18g | Vitamin C: 3mg | Calcium: 94mg | Iron: 2mg

537. Wasabi Avocado Fries

Prep Time: 5 mins

Cook Time: 10 mins

Ingredients

- 1 avocado pitted and diced
- 1 egg
- 1 1/2 Tablespoon wasabi paste or to taste
- 1/2 teaspoon salt

- 1/2 cup breadcrumbs or Japanese panko
- Lime wedges optional

Instructions

- Put the breadcrumbs in a Ziploc bag and set them aside.
- In a medium bowl, use a whisk to mix the egg, wasabi paste, and salt until homogenous.
- Put all the avocado chunks in the egg mixture to coat.
- Carefully transfer the avocado into the bag. Shake the bag to coat the avocado with breadcrumbs.
- Place the avocado pieces into the fryer basket, spray them with some oil, and air fry at 400F (200C) for about 3 minutes.
- Squeeze some lime juice to serve.

Nutrition

- Calories: 160kcal | Carbohydrates: 16g | Protein: 5g | Fat: 9g | Saturated Fat: 2g | Cholesterol: 41mg | Sodium: 511mg | Potassium: 325mg | Fiber: 5g | Sugar: 1g | Vitamin C: 8mg | Calcium: 47mg | Iron: 1mg

538. Roasted Garlic

Prep Time: 5 mins

Cook Time: 30 mins

Ingredients

- 3-4 head of garlic
- 2 tbsp Olive oil
- A pinch of salt

Instructions

- Slice off the top of garlic. Drizzle some olive oil over it and sprinkle with some salt and pepper. Wrap the garlic with aluminum foil and air fry at 400F (200C) for 25-30 minutes until the garlic is tender and slightly golden brown.

Nutrition

- Calories: 65kcal | Carbohydrates: 1g | Protein: 1g | Fat: 7g | Saturated Fat: 1g | Sodium: 1mg | Potassium: 9mg | Sugar: 1g | Vitamin C: 1mg | Calcium: 4mg

539. Tofu with Bamboo Shoots

Prep Time: 10 mins

Cook Time: 15 mins

Ingredients

Ingredients For Tofu:

- 1 1/4 cup bean curd cut into 1/4 inch thick strips
- 1 teaspoon olive oil

Other Ingredients:

- 2 cups bamboo shoots
- 2 Tablespoon garlic minced
- 2 Tablespoon oyster sauce
- 2 Tablespoon soy sauce
- 1 Tablespoon rice wine
- 1 Tablespoon brown sugar
- 1/2 teaspoon Sriracha optional
- 2 green onions cut into one-inch pieces.

Instructions

- Line the fryer basket with lightly greased aluminum foil. Toss tofu strips with olive oil then put them into the basket. Air fry at 380F (190C) for about 5 minutes. Add in the bamboo shoots, stir, and air fry again at 380F (190C) for another 3 minutes.
- In a frying pan or wok, stir fry the garlic in olive oil. Then, add in all other ingredients (except green onions) and continue to stir until the sauce thickens a little.
- Add in the tofu strips, bamboo shoots, and green onion and toss. Enjoy!

Nutrition

- Calories: 123kcal | Carbohydrates: 11g | Protein: 10g | Fat: 5g | Saturated Fat: 1g | Sodium: 773mg | Potassium: 112mg | Fiber: 2g | Sugar: 5g | C: 4mg | Calcium: 117mg | Iron: 2mg

540. Oyster Sauce Mushroom

Prep Time: 5 mins

Cook Time: 10 mins

Ingredients

- 8 ounces large button mushrooms cleaned and quartered. For smaller ones, keep whole or cut in half
- 1 Tablespoon melted butter
- 1 Tablespoon oyster sauce
- 1/4 teaspoon black pepper or to taste
- 1 Tablespoon green onion thinly sliced optional

Instructions

- In a large bowl, toss the mushroom with melted butter, oyster sauce, and black pepper.
- Put the mushroom in a lightly greased cake pan, ait fry the mushroom at 380F (190C) for about 6-7 minutes, stir once in between.
- Garnish with some green onion to serve.

Nutrition

- Calories: 80kcal | Carbohydrates: 5g | Protein: 4g | Fat: 6g | Saturated Fat: 4g | Cholesterol: 15mg | Sodium: 302mg | Potassium: 361mg | Fiber: 1g | Sugar: 2g | Vitamin C: 2mg | Iron: 1mg

541. Fried Okra With Sriracha Mayo

Prep Time: 5 mins

Cook Time: 10 mins

Ingredients

- 15 okra
- 1 egg beaten
- 1/2 cup Japanese panko
- 3 Tablespoon freshly chopped Thai basil
- 1/4 cup mayonnaise
- 1 Tablespoon Sriracha or to taste
- 2-3 Tablespoon Mirin

Instructions

- Mix chopped basil with panko and set aside.
- Line the fryer basket with lightly greased aluminum foil. Dip the okra in the egg wash, roll them in panko mix, and put them in the fryer basket without stacking. Air fry at 380F (190C)

for about 8 minutes, shake the basket once in between.
- In the meantime, mix the mayo, sriracha, and mirin and set aside.
- Serve the fried okra with sriracha mayo when done.

Nutrition

- Calories: 337kcal | Carbohydrates: 25g | Protein: 7g | Fat: 24g | Saturated Fat: 4g | Cholesterol: 94mg | Sodium: 627mg | Potassium: 329mg | Fiber: 4g | Sugar: 7g | Vitamin C: 26mg | Calcium: 119mg | Iron: 2mg

542. Miso Tofu

Prep Time: 10 mins

Cook Time: 20 mins

Ingredients

- 1 box firm tofu
- 2 tablespoon miso paste
- 1 teaspoon Sriracha Hot Sauce optional
- 4 teaspoon brown sugar
- 2 teaspoon sesame oil
- 2 teaspoon soy sauce
- 1 green onion thinly sliced
- 1 Tablespoon sesame seeds

Instructions

- Place a kitchen towel on the counter and place the tofu on top. Put a heavy item, such as a small pot, on top of the tofu for one hour to squeeze out excess water.
- In the meantime, prepare the sauce by mixing miso, Sriracha, brown sugar, sesame oil, and soy sauce.
- Cut tofu into 1/2-3/4 inches thick slices then cut the surface of the tofu in a crisscrossed fashion without cutting through.
- Carefully put the tofu pieces into the parchment-lined fryer basket. Brush a thick layer of sauce onto the tofu and lightly dab the surface so the sauce can get into the crevices. Air fry at 400F (200C) for 10-12 minutes, brushing a layer of the sauce every 3-4 minutes until the sauce is caramelized.
- Sprinkle some green onion and sesame seeds to

serve.

Nutrition

- Calories: 147kcal | Carbohydrates: 9g | Protein: 11g | Fat: 8g | Saturated Fat: 1g | Sodium: 517mg | Potassium: 27mg | Fiber: 2g | Sugar: 5g |Vitamin C: 1mg | Calcium: 151mg | Iron: 2mg

543. Maple Walnut Biscotti

Prep Time: 10 mins

Cook Time: 40 mins

Ingredients

- 1 cup all-purpose flour
- 1/3 cup packed brown sugar
- 1 1/4 teaspoons baking powder
- 1/4 teaspoon salt
- 1 egg
- 2 Tablespoon maple syrup
- 2 Tablespoon melted unsalted butter
- 1 cups coarsely chopped walnuts

Instructions

- In a parchment-lined fryer basket, air fry the walnuts at 300F (150C) for 6 minutes.
- In the meantime, take a large and bowl and mix all the dry ingredients. Then, add in the wet ingredients until everything is well combined. Finally, fold in the chopped walnuts and form the batter into a ball shape.
- Place the ball-shaped dough on parchment paper and press it down with the palm of your hand to mold the dough into a rectangular shape with a thickness of about 1/2 inch. Air fry at 360F (180C) for 15 minutes.
- Remove the rectangular cookie along with the parchment paper from the fryer basket and let cool for a few minutes. When cool enough to handle, cut it into 3/4 inch wide pieces.
- Place all the pieces back into the fryer basket with the cut side up and air fry at 360 for about 10 minutes, flipping once in between with the other cut side facing up.
- When done, carefully remove the biscotti from the fryer basket and let them cool completely on a cooling rack before serving.

Nutrition

- Calories: 234kcal | Carbohydrates: 27g | Protein: 5g | Fat: 13g | Saturated Fat: 3g | Sodium: 85mg | Potassium: 175mg | Fiber: 1g | Sugar: 12g | Vitamin C: 1mg | Calcium: 60mg | Iron: 1mg

544. Kimchi Tofu Stir Fry

Prep Time: 5 mins

Cook Time: 10 mins

Ingredients

- 8 oz firm tofu (about 250g) cut into cubes
- 4 Tablespoon honey
- 2 Tablespoon Korean hot pepper paste Gochujang or to taste
- 2 Tablespoon soy sauce
- 1 Tablespoon oyster sauce
- 1 Tablespoon sesame oil
- 2 Tablespoon minced garlic
- 1/2 cup kimchi chopped
- 2 green onions cut into one-inch pieces
- 1 teaspoon sesame seeds

Instructions

- Line the fryer basket with parchment paper and place the tofu cubes inside the basket without stacking. Spray the surface of the tofu with some oil and air fry at 400F (200C) for 10 minutes, flipping once in the middle.
- In the meantime, in a saucepan, saute the minced garlic with sesame oil. Then, add honey, soy sauce, oyster sauce, and kimchi into the sauce to the pan and bring to boil, stirring frequently until the sauce thickens a bit.
- When the tofu is done, toss the tofu in the sauce along with the green onion for about a minute. Sprinkle some sesame seeds over the tofu to serve.

Nutrition

- Calories: 338kcal | Carbohydrates: 48g | Protein: 14g | Fat: 13g | Saturated Fat: 2g | Sodium: 1264mg | Potassium: 184mg | Fiber: 2g | Sugar: 37g | Vitamin C: 7mg | Calcium: 175mg | Iron: 3mg

Prep Time: 20 mins

Cook Time: 20 mins

Ingredients

1 potato peeled and cubed

2 Tablespoon olive oil

1/2 teaspoon garlic powder

1/2 teaspoon paprika

1/4 teaspoon salt

1/2 teaspoon dried parsley flakes

1/3 cup shredded cheese

Instructions

- Soak the potato cubes in cold water for at least 15 minutes then drained.
- Combine all ingredients, except parsley flakes and cheese, and toss. Air fry, without stacking, in a lightly greased aluminum foil-lined fryer basket at 360F (180C) for 15-17 minutes. Stir a couple of times in between until the potato cubes are tender.
- Pull the fryer basket out, sprinkle the parsley flakes and mix. Top the potato with cheese and push the basket into the air fryer unit for about a minute for the cheese to melt. Serve immediately.

Nutrition

- Calories: 123kcal | Carbohydrates: 7g | Protein: 4g | Fat: 9g | Saturated Fat: 2g | Cholesterol: 7mg | Sodium: 210mg | Potassium: 220mg | Fiber: 1g | Sugar: 1g Vitamin C: 6mg | Calcium: 63mg | Iron: 2mg

54

To

In

about 500g
- 1/4 cup yellow onion finely chopped
- 1/2 cup Panko breadcrumb
- 1/2 tablespoon Italian seasoning
 grated Parmesan cheese
 soy sauce
 orn starch
 arlic powder
 nion powder
 black pepper or to taste

 n olive oil
 y diced
 n garlic chopped
 low onion diced
 nato ketchup
 rrot diced
 chini diced
 ne I used rice wine
 hed tomatoes
 orn kernels
 h I used chicken
 oon Italian seasoning
 on garlic powder
 pepper to taste

 fryer basket with a grill mat or a sheet of
 reased aluminum foil.
 rge bowl, combine all the meatball
 ents. Take about 1 tablespoonful of the
 e and roll it into a ball. Place the meatballs
 e fryer basket. Spritz the meatballs with oil
 fry at 380F (190C) for about 8 minutes,
 the basket once in the middle.

 meantime, pour olive oil into a pot and
 garlic, celery, and onion until fragrant. Add
 rest of the soup ingredient and bring it to

- When the meatballs are done, transfer them to the pot. Fill the pot with water just enough to cover all the ingredients. Let it simmer for about 30 minutes.
- Serve on its own or with pasta or bread.

Handwritten note:

Plain low-fat Greek yogurt
Unsweet Almond Milk
Bananas
Spinch
Frozen Raspberries
Avocado
Tomato Paste
Tomato Puree
Kideny beans + Pinto beans
Green bell peppers
Extra Virgen Oil
Shredded low-fat cheese
Diced tomato
Oregano
Shredded low-fat
Scallions
Parmesan cheese

547. Hearty Meatball Soup

Prep Time: 10 mins

Cook Time: 45 mins

Ingredients

Meatball Ingredients:

- 1 pound ground meat I used ground turkey,

Nutrition

- Calories: 476kcal | Carbohydrates: 22g | Protein: 24g | Fat: 31g | Saturated Fat: 10g | Cholesterol: 83mg | Sodium: 1047mg | Potassium: 659mg | Fiber: 3g | Sugar: 8g | Vitamin C: 13mg | Calcium: 112mg | Iron: 4mg

548. Easy Swedish Meatballs

Prep Time: 15 mins

Cook Time: 25 mins

Ingredients

- Ingredients for meatballs: (makes about 30 meatballs)
- 1 1/2 pound ground meat or ground meat mixtures (about 750g) I used ground turkey
- 1/3 cup Panko breadcrumbs
- 1/2 cup milk
- 1/2 of an onion finely chopped
- 1 large egg
- 2 tablespoon parsley dried or fresh
- 2 tablespoon minced garlic
- 1/3 teaspoon salt
- 1/4 teaspoon black pepper or to taste
- 1/4 teaspoon paprika
- 1/4 teaspoon onion powder

Ingredients For Sauce:

- 1/3 cup butter
- 1/4 cup all-purpose flour
- 2 cups broth I used chicken broth
- 1/2 cup milk
- 1 tablespoon soy sauce
- Salt and pepper to taste

Instructions

- Line the fryer basket with a grill mat or a sheet of lightly greased aluminum foil.
- In a large bowl, combine all the meatball ingredients and let it rest for 5-10 minutes.
- Using the palm of your hands, roll the meat mixture into balls of the desired size. Place them in the fryer basket and air fry at 380F (190C) for 8-12 minutes (depending on the size of the meatballs) until they are cooked through and internal temperature exceeds 165F or 74C)

- In the meantime, melt the butter in a wok or a pan. Whisk in flour until it turns brown. Pour in the broth, milk, and soy sauce and bring it to a simmer. Season with salt and pepper to taste. Stir constantly until the sauce thickens.
- Serve meatballs and sauce over pasta or mashed potato. Sprinkle some parsley if desired.

Nutrition

- Calories: 299kcal | Carbohydrates: 12g | Protein: 31g | Fat: 15g | Saturated Fat: 8g | Cholesterol: 121mg | Sodium: 723mg | Potassium: 443mg | Fiber: 1g | Sugar: 3g | Vitamin C: 3mg | Calcium: 71mg | Iron: 2mg

549. Garlicky Honey Sesame Ribs

Prep Time: 3 hrs

Cook Time: 15 mins

Ingredients

- 2 pounds pork ribs about 1000g
- 1/3 cup honey
- 1/4 cup soy sauce
- 1/4 cup ketchup
- 1/4 cup brown sugar
- 2 tbsp rice vinegar
- 2 tbsp lemon juice
- 2 tsp sesame oil
- 2 Tbsp minced garlic
- 1 Tbsp sesame seeds for garnish or to taste
- 1/4 cup scallions for garnish or to taste

Instructions

- In a medium-size bowl, prepare the marinade by mixing honey, soy sauce, ketchup, brown sugar, vinegar, and lemon juice.
- Take a Ziploc bag, put the ribs in the bag. Pour about 2/3 of the marinade into the bag, mix with the ribs, and marinate in the refrigerator for at least 3 hours or best overnight. Save the rest of the marinade for later use.
- Take the pork ribs out from the refrigerator 30 minutes before air frying.
- Line the fryer basket with a grill mat or a sheet of lightly greased aluminum foil.
- Put the ribs inside the fryer basket without stacking. Air fry at 380F (190C) for about 10-12

minutes, flip once in the middle until the edges are slightly caramelized.

- In the meantime, use a wok to saute garlic in sesame oil until fragrant, about one minute. Then, add in the rest of the marinade. Stir constantly until the sauce thickens.
- When the ribs are done, toss the ribs in the wok along with sesame seeds. Sprinkle some scallions on top to serve.

Nutrition

- Calories: 429kcal | Carbohydrates: 30g | Protein: 18g | Fat: 27g | Saturated Fat: 8g | Cholesterol: 85mg | Sodium: 721mg | Potassium: 359mg | Fiber: 1g | Sugar: 27g | Vitamin C: 4mg | Calcium: 46mg | Iron: 2mg

---

550. Chinese BBQ Pork Pastry

Prep Time: 20 mins

Cook Time: 10 mins

Ingredients

- 1/2 pound char siu Chinese BBQ pork diced (about 250g)
- 2 tsp olive oil
- 1/4 onion diced
- 1 1/2 tbsp ketchup
- 1/2 tbsp oyster sauce
- 1 tbsp sugar
- 1 tbsp honey
- 1/4 cup water
- 1 1/2 tbsp corn starch
- 1 1/2 tbsp water
- 1 roll of store-bought pie crust thawed according to package instruction
- 1 egg beaten

Instructions

- In a wok or frying pan, saute diced onion in olive oil until translucent. Then, add in ketchup, oyster sauce, sugar, honey, and 1/4 cup water. Stir and bring to boil
- In the meantime, take a small bowl and mix the corn starch with 1 1/2 tablespoon of water. Add the mixture to the wok and stir constantly until the sauce thickens.
- Add the diced BBQ pork and stir. Wait for it to

cool, then put it in the refrigerator for at least 30 minutes. The refrigeration will cause the mixture to harden and will make it easier to handle later.
- Line the fryer basket with a grill mat or lightly greased aluminum foil.
- Roll out pie crusts. Use a bowl size of your choice to trace circles onto the pie crust and cut them into circular pieces. Mix the leftover pie crust, use a rolling pin to roll them out. Repeat the above process to get as many circular crusts as you can.
- Lay the circular pieces of pie crust on the counter and put the desired amount of BBQ pork filling in the center. Fold pie crust in half and keep the fillings inside. Use the back of a fork to press down on the edges of the pie crust to seal.
- Carefully transfer the pork pastry into the fryer basket. Brush the top surface with egg and air fry at 340F (170C) for about 5-6 minutes. Flip the pastries over and brush the top side with egg. Air fry again at 340F (170C) for another 5-6 minutes until the surface is golden brown.

Nutrition

- Calories: 225kcal | Carbohydrates: 17g | Protein: 2g | Fat: 7g | Saturated Fat: 2g | Polyunsaturated Fat: 1g | Monounsaturated Fat: 1g | Trans Fat: 1g | Cholesterol: 100mg | Sodium: 395mg | Potassium: 345mg | Fiber: 1g | Sugar: 17g | Vitamin C: 1mg | Calcium: 8mg | Iron: 1mg

---

551. Vietnamese Style Pork Chops

Prep Time: 2 hrs

Cook Time: 10 mins

Ingredients

- 1 pound pork shoulder blade steak (about 500g)
- 3 tbsp dark soy sauce
- 3 tbsp fish sauce
- 2 tbsp minced garlic
- 2 tbsp grated ginger
- 2 tbsp brown sugar
- 1 Lime juice and zest
- 1 tbsp olive oil
- Chopped cilantro to garnish optional

Instructions

- Mix the pork with all the pork ingredients, except olive oil and cilantro, and marinate in the refrigerator for at least 2 hours or best overnight. Take the meat out of the refrigerator 30 minutes before air frying.
- Pat dry the pork steaks with a paper towel. Brush both sides of the meat with olive oil and place them in the fryer basket without stacking. Air fry at 400F (200C) for 8-10 minutes, flip once in the middle until the pork is cooked through when the temperature exceeds 145F or 63C.
- Garnish with chopped cilantro if desired.

Nutrition

- Calories: 229kcal | Carbohydrates: 23g | Protein: 15g | Fat: 9g | Saturated Fat: 2g | Cholesterol: 46mg | Sodium: 1359mg | Potassium: 322mg | Fiber: 1g | Sugar: 17g | Vitamin C: 7mg | Calcium: 33mg | Iron: 1mg

552. Meatballs With Gochujang Mayo

Prep Time: 15 mins

Cook Time: 10 mins

Ingredients

Ingredients For Meatballs:

- 1 pound ground pork (about 500g) or meat of your choice
- 1/4 cup onion finely chopped
- 2 Tablespoon soy sauce
- 2 teaspoon corn starch
- 1 teaspoon dried basil
- 1 teaspoon garlic powder
- 1 teaspoon onion powder
- 1/4 teaspoon white pepper powder

Ingredients For Sauce:

- 1 teaspoon Gochujang (Korean hot pepper paste)
- 2 Tablespoon Mayonnaise
- 2 Tablespoon mirin

Instructions

- Line the fryer basket with a grill mat or a sheet of lightly greased aluminum foil.

- Mix all the meatball ingredients then form them into about 1 inch balls. Put the meatballs in the fryer basket without stacking. Spray some oil onto the meatballs and air fry at 380F (190C) for 8-10 minutes until the meat is cooked through at its proper temperature.
- In the meantime, take a small bowl and mix all the sauce ingredients.
- Dip the meatballs in the Gochujang mayo to serve.

Nutrition

- Calories: 378kcal | Carbohydrates: 7g | Protein: 21g | Fat: 29g | Saturated Fat: 10g | Cholesterol: 85mg | Sodium: 677mg | Potassium: 368mg | Fiber: 1g | Sugar: 3g | Vitamin C: 2mg | Calcium: 21mg | Iron: 1mg

553. Five Spices Salt And Pepper Pork

Prep Time: 1 hr 15 mins

Cook Time: 15 mins

Ingredients

Ingredients For Pork:

- 1/2 pound pork shoulder cut into thick slices (about 250g)
- 2 Tablespoon soy sauce
- 1/2 Tablespoon rice wine
- 1 teaspoon corn starch
- 1 Tablespoon minced garlic
- 1 teaspoon sesame oil
- 1/2 teaspoon sugar
- 1/2 teaspoon Chinese five spices powder
- 1/4 cup tapioca starch

Instructions

- Marinate the meat with all the pork ingredients, except tapioca flour, for at least 1 hour.
- Dredge the pork slices in tapioca flour, shake off excess, and let sit for about 5-10 minutes until you don't see dry flour.
- Place the meat in the fryer basket and spray some oil. Air Fry at 380F for 12-14 minutes, flip once in the middle until the surface appears to be nice and crisp.
- Toss in the pork slices with chili pepper and

chopped cilantro. Then, sprinkle some salt and pepper to serve.

Nutrition

- Calories: 100kcal | Carbohydrates: 9g | Protein: 8g | Fat: 3g | Saturated Fat: 1g | Cholesterol: 23mg | Sodium: 529mg | Potassium: 137mg | Fiber: 1g | Sugar: 1g | Vitamin C: 1mg | Calcium: 8mg | Iron: 1mg

554. Seasoned Pork Chops With Avocado Salsa

Prep Time: 5 mins

Cook Time: 15 mins

Ingredients

- 2 pork chops or pork shoulder blade steaks
- 2 Tablespoon olive oil
- 1 teaspoon sea salt
- 1 teaspoon black pepper
- 1/2 teaspoon paprika
- 1/2 teaspoon garlic powder
- 1/2 teaspoon cumin

Ingredients For Salsa:

- 1 avocado pitted and diced
- 1 large tomato seeded and diced
- 1/3 cup cilantro chopped
- 1 lime juiced
- 1/4 yellow onion finely chopped
- Pickled or fresh jalapeno to taste chopped (optional)
- Salt to taste

Instructions

- In a small bowl, mix all the dry seasonings in the pork ingredients and set them aside.
- Use a paper towel to pat dry the pork chop then rub both sides with olive oil. Generously season both sides of the meat and air fry at 380F (190C) for 10-12 minutes, flip once in the middle until the internal temperature exceeds 145F (63C).
- In the meantime, combine all the ingredients for the salsa in a large bowl.
- When the pork chops are done, let them rest for a few minutes. Scoop some salsa over the pork chops to serve.

Nutrition

- Calories: 528kcal | Carbohydrates: 18g | Protein: 32g | Fat: 38g | Saturated Fat: 7g | Cholesterol: 90mg | Sodium: 1242mg | Potassium: 1187mg | Fiber: 9g | Sugar: 4g | Vitamin C: 30mg | Calcium: 39mg | Iron: 2mg

555. Chinese Style Ground Meat Patties

Prep Time: 5 mins

Cook Time: 10 mins

Ingredients

- 1 pound ground pork about 500g
- 1 egg
- 1 teaspoon corn starch
- 1/3 cup green onion chopped
- 1/4 cup cilantro stems chopped
- 1/4 cup yellow onion finely diced
- 2 1/2 Tablespoon oyster sauce
- 2 Tablespoon minced garlic
- 1/4 teaspoon black pepper

Instructions

- Mix all the ingredients and making sure everything is well combined.
- Line the fryer basket with lightly greased aluminum foil. Form patties of equal size and place them into the fryer basket. Air fry at 380F (190C) for 8-10 minutes until fully cooked when the internal temperature exceeds 160F (72C).

Nutrition

- Calories: 335kcal | Carbohydrates: 5g | Protein: 21g | Fat: 25g | Saturated Fat: 9g | Cholesterol: 123mg | Sodium: 390mg | Potassium: 394mg | Fiber: 1g | Sugar: 1g | Vitamin C: 5mg | Calcium: 39mg | Iron: 1mg

556. Pork Satay Skewers

Prep Time: 1 hr

Cook Time: 15 mins

Ingredients

Ingredients For Pork:

- 1 pound pork shoulder (about 500g) cut into 1/2

inch cubes
- 1/4 cup soy sauce
- 2 Tablespoons brown sugar
- 2 tablespoons Thai sweet chili sauce
- 1 Tablespoon sesame oil
- 1 Tablespoon minced garlic
- 1 Tablespoon fish sauce

Ingredients For The Sauce:

- 1/3 cup peanut butter
- 3 Tablespoon coconut milk or milk or water
- 2 Tablespoon Thai Sweet Chili Sauce
- 2 teaspoon minced garlic
- 2 teaspoon brown sugar
- 1 teaspoon fish sauce

Instructions

- Combine all the ingredients for the pork and marinate for at least 1 hour or overnight.
- In the meantime, soak the wooden skewers in water for at least 15 minutes. Also, combine all the ingredients for the dipping sauce and set aside.
- Thread the pork cubes onto skewers and place them in the fryer basket. Air fry at 380F (190C) for about 8-10 minutes, flip once in between until the meat is cooked through.

Nutrition

- Calories: 363kcal | Carbohydrates: 23g | Protein: 21g | Fat: 22g | Saturated Fat: 7g | Cholesterol: 46mg | Sodium: 1607mg | Potassium: 444mg | Fiber: 1g | Sugar: 18g | Vitamin C: 2mg | Calcium: 33mg | Iron: 2mg

557. Pork Chop Marinated With Fermented Bean Curd

Prep Time: 2 hrs

Cook Time: 15 mins

Ingredients

Ingredients For Pork:

- 1 pound pork shoulder cut into chunks.
- 1-2 pieces fermented bean curd chunk
- 2 teaspoon rice wine
- 1 Tablespoon dark soy sauce
- 1 Tablespoon brown sugar

- 2 Tablespoon garlic minced
- Other ingredients:
- Fried garlic chips to taste
- Thinly sliced green onions to taste

Instructions

- Marinate the pork with all the pork ingredients for at least 2 hours or best overnight in the refrigerator.
- Leave the pork out at room temperature 30 minutes before air frying.
- Line the fryer basket with a sheet of lightly greased aluminum foil. Put the pork inside without stacking and air fry at 380F (190C) for about 10-12 minutes until the temperature exceeds 160F (71C).
- Sprinkle some fried garlic and green onion to serve.

Nutrition

- Calories: 143kcal | Carbohydrates: 9g | Protein: 14g | Fat: 5g | Saturated Fat: 2g | Cholesterol: 46mg | Sodium: 194mg | Potassium: 267mg | Fiber: 1g | Sugar: 6g | Vitamin C: 3mg | Calcium: 20mg | Iron: 1mg

558. Pork And Bean Curd Strips

Prep Time: 1 hr

Cook Time: 15 mins

Ingredients

Ingredients For Pork:

- 1/2 pound pork shoulder cut into strips (about 250g)
- 2 teaspoon sesame oil
- 2 teaspoon corn starch
- 1 teaspoon sugar
- 1 Tablespoon rice wine
- Other ingredients:
- 8 ounces bean curd cut into strips
- 1 teaspoon olive oil
- 4-5 cloves of garlic
- 1/4 cup chicken broth
- 3-4 green onion cut into thin slices
- 1 teaspoon black vinegar optional

Instructions

- Marinate the pork strips with all the pork ingredients for at least one hour or overnight.
- In the meantime, mix 1 teaspoon of olive oil with bean curd strips. In a lightly greased cake pan, air fry the bean curd at 380F (190C) for 6 minutes, stir once in between. Remove and set aside when done.
- Put the garlic on the bottom of the cake pan put pork strips over it. Air fry at 380F (190C) for about 8 minutes, stir once in between.
- Add in the chicken broth, bean curd strips, and half of the green onion and mix. Air fry at 380F (190C) for 4-5 minutes until the pork is cooked through.
- Mix in the remaining green onion and black vinegar to serve.

Nutrition

- Calories: 143kcal | Carbohydrates: 4g | Protein: 12g | Fat: 8g | Saturated Fat: 2g | Cholesterol: 23mg | Sodium: 83mg | Potassium: 142mg | Fiber: 1g | Sugar: 1g | Vitamin C: 2mg | Calcium: 81mg | Iron: 1mg

559. Marinated Korean Style Pork With Mushroom

Prep Time: 35 mins

Cook Time: 15 mins

Ingredients

Ingredients For The Pork:

- 1/2 pound pork shoulder (about 250g) cut into thin slices
- 1/4 cup Korean BBQ sauce

Other Ingredients:

- 1 Tablespoon garlic minced
- 1/2 cup button mushroom cut into slices
- 1/3 cup carrots sliced
- 1 Tablespoon Korean BBQ sauce
- 1 teaspoon corn starch
- 1/3 cup green onion cut into 1-inch pieces

Instructions

- Marinate the pork with Korean BBQ sauce and set aside for 30 minutes.

- In a lightly greased cake barrel, put the garlic and carrots on the bottom then put pork slices on top. Air fry at 380F (190C) for about 8-9 minutes, stir once in between.
- Mix the rest of the ingredients into the cake pan and air fry again 380F (190C) for 3-4 minutes until pork is cooked through.

Nutrition

- Calories: 193kcal | Carbohydrates: 19g | Protein: 17g | Fat: 5g | Saturated Fat: 2g | Cholesterol: 46mg | Sodium: 770mg | Potassium: 426mg | Fiber: 1g | Sugar: 12g | Vitamin C: 7mg | Calcium: 36mg | Iron: 1mg

560. Cilantro Lime Spiced Pork

Prep Time: 1 hr 10 mins

Cook Time: 15 mins

Ingredient:

- 12 Ounces pork shoulder thinly sliced
- 1 Tablespoon soy sauce
- 1/4 teaspoon cumin
- 1/2 teaspoon curry
- 1/4 teaspoon salt

Other Ingredients:

- 1/4 cup cilantro chopped
- 3-4 Tablespoon of lime juice or to taste

Instructions

- Marinate the pork slices with all the ingredients for at least 1 hour.
- Line the fryer basket with lightly greased aluminum foil. Place the pork slices in the basket and air fry at 380F (190C) for 10-12 minutes until the pork is cooked through.
- When done, mix in cilantro and lime juice to serve.

Nutrition

- Calories:162kcal | Carbohydrates: 1g | Protein: 21g | Fat: 8g | Saturated Fat: 3g | Cholesterol: 70mg | Sodium: 874mg | Potassium: 373mg | Sugar: 1g | Vitamin C: 1mg | Calcium: 15mg | Iron: 2mg

561. Chinese Style Meatloaf With Pickled Cucumber

Prep Time: 5 mins

Cook Time: 20 mins

Ingredients For Pork:

- 1 pound ground pork about 500g
- 1 egg
- 1/4 cup pickled cucumber chopped
- 1 Tablespoon minced garlic
- 1 Tablespoon soy sauce
- 3 Tablespoon juice from pickled cucumber
- 2 teaspoon of rice wine
- 1 teaspoon sesame oil
- 1 teaspoon sugar
- 2 teaspoon corn starch
- White pepper powder to taste

Other Ingredients:

- Chicken or beef stock
- 1/4 cup thinly sliced scallions to garnish.

Instructions

- Mix all the pork ingredients and scoop the meatloaf into each ramekin and put them inside the fryer basket.
- Fill the stock up to almost to the rim of the ramekins as the fluid may dry up during the air frying process. Put a sheet of aluminum foil over the ramekins and place a steamer rack on top. Air fry at 360F (170C) for about 15-18 minutes until the meat temperature exceeds 160F (72C).
- Sprinkle some green onion on top to serve.

Nutrition

- Calories: 336kcal | Carbohydrates: 3g | Protein: 21g | Fat: 26g | Saturated Fat: 9g | Cholesterol: 123mg | Sodium: 331mg | Potassium: 350mg | Sugar: 1g | Vitamin C: 1mg | Calcium: 26mg | Iron: 1mg

562. Honey Garlic Pork

Prep Time: 35 mins

Cook Time: 15 mins

Ingredients For Pork:

- 1/2 pound pork shoulder thinly sliced
- 1 Tablespoon soy sauce
- 1 teaspoon garlic powder
- 1 teaspoon corn starch
- 1 teaspoon rice wine
- 3 Tablespoon tapioca starch

Ingredients For Sauce:

- 1 Tablespoon sesame oil
- 3 Tablespoon minced garlic
- 2 Tablespoon honey
- 2 Tablespoon Chinese black vinegar
- 1 Tablespoon soy sauce

Instructions

- In a Ziploc bag, combine all the ingredients for the pork, except for tapioca starch, and marinate for 30 minutes. Before air frying, add tapioca starch to the bag and shake well. The goal is to have all the pork slices coat with some tapioca starch.
- Place a sheet of lightly greased aluminum foil in the fryer basket. Put the pork slices in and try to separate them as much as possible. Air fry at 400F (200C) for about 15 minutes, stir 2-3 times in between until the edges are crispy.
- In the meantime, saute garlic with sesame oil in a saucepan for about one minute. Then combine the rest of the ingredients and stir constantly until the sauce thickens.
- When the pork is done, toss the pork slices in the sauce to serve.

Nutrition

- Calories: 154kcal | Carbohydrates: 17g | Protein: 8g | Fat: 6g | Saturated Fat: 1g | Cholesterol: 23mg | Sodium: 531mg | Potassium: 170mg | Fiber: 1g | Sugar: 9g | Vitamin C: 2mg | Calcium: 16mg | Iron: 1mg

563. General Tso's Pork

Prep Time: 15 mins

Cook Time: 20 mins

Ingredients For Pork:

- 1 pound pork shoulder cut into slices
- 1 egg beaten
- 2 Tablespoon soy sauce
- 1/4 teaspoon salt
- 1/4 teaspoon black pepper
- 1 teaspoon corn starch
- 1/4 cup tapioca starch
- Ingredients for sauce:
- 1 1/2 Tablespoon chili oil
- 2-3 Tablespoon minced garlic
- 1 Tablespoon grated ginger
- 2 Tablespoon soy sauce
- 2 Tablespoon vinegar
- 2 Tablespoon sugar
- 2 teaspoon corn starch mix with 4 teaspoon water

Instructions

- In a Ziploc bag, mix all the ingredients for the pork, except tapioca starch, and marinate in the refrigerator for at least one hour. Add the tapioca starch into the bag. Shake the bag or mix gently.
- Line the fryer basket with lightly greased aluminum foil. Put the pork slices in and spread them out as much as possible. Air fry at 400F (200C) for 15-17 minutes until the outside is crispy and the meat is cooked through, stir 2-3 times in between.
- In the meantime, use a saucepan to saute the garlic and ginger in chili oil for one minute. Add in the rest of the ingredients and bring them to a boil. Add in the corn starch and water mixture, stir until the sauce thickens.
- When the pork is done, toss in the sauce to coat. Sprinkle some chopped green onion to serve.

Nutrition

- Calories: 235kcal | Carbohydrates: 16g | Protein: 17g | Fat: 11g | Saturated Fat: 3g | Cholesterol: 87mg | Sodium: 1220mg | Potassium: 305mg | Fiber: 1g | Sugar: 6g | Vitamin A: 59IU | Vitamin C: 2mg | Calcium: 23mg | Iron: 2mg

564. Korean Marinated Pork Belly

Prep Time: 35 mins

Cook Time: 15 mins

Ingredients

- 1 pound pork belly with or without skin, (about 500g) cut into thin slices
- 2 Tablespoon minced garlic
- 2 Tablespoon minced ginger
- 1/2 tablespoon Korean hot pepper paste Gochujang, or to taste
- 3 tablespoon honey
- 3 tablespoon soy sauce
- 1 tablespoon sesame oil
- 1/2 tablespoon apple cider vinegar
- 3 tablespoon toasted white sesame seeds

Instructions

- Prepare the marinade by mixing all other ingredients. Use 3/4 of the marinade to marinate the pork belly for at least 30 minutes and save the rest for later use.
- On a lightly greased aluminum foil, air fry the pork belly slices at 380F (190C) for about 12 minutes, stir about 2 times in between, until the meat is cooked through.
- In the meantime, use a saucepan to heat the remaining marinade on the stovetop. Stir constantly until the sauce thickens. When the pork is done, toss with the sauce.
- To serve, sprinkle some sesame seeds and garnish with cilantro leaves or chopped green onion.

Nutrition

- Calories: 360kcal | Carbohydrates: 9g | Protein: 7g | Fat: 33g | Saturated Fat: 11g | Cholesterol: 41mg | Sodium: 397mg | Potassium: 149mg | Fiber: 1g | Sugar: 7g | Vitamin C: 1mg | Calcium: 37mg | Iron: 1mg

565. Korean Style Pork Chops

Prep Time: 3 hrs

Cook Time: 15 mins

Ingredients

- 1 pound pork chops (about 500g)
- 1/2 cup soy sauce
- 1/3 cup brown sugar
- 1/3 cup onion thinly sliced
- 2 Tablespoon grated ginger
- 2 Tablespoon minced garlic
- 2 teaspoon sesame oil
- 1 teaspoon black pepper
- 1-2 teaspoon Sriracha hot sauce optional
- 3 Tablespoon sliced green onions
- 1 Tablespoon toasted sesame seeds

Instructions

- Marinate the pork chops in all the ingredients (except sesame seeds and green onion) in the refrigerator for at least 3 hours. Take the pork chops out of the refrigerator about 30 minutes before air frying.
- Put the pork chops in the parchment paper-lined fryer basket without stacking. Air fry at 380F (190C) for about 15 minutes until the meat temperature is at least 165F (64C).
- Sprinkle some green onion and sesame seeds to serve.

Nutrition

- Calories: 309kcal | Carbohydrates: 24g | Protein: 28g | Fat: 11g | Saturated Fat: 3g | Cholesterol: 76mg | Sodium: 1709mg | Potassium: 581mg | Fiber: 1g | Sugar: 19g | Vitamin C: 4mg | Calcium: 62mg | Iron: 2mg

566. Char Siu Pork Chops

Prep Time: 3 hrs

Cook Time: 15 mins

Ingredients

- 1 pound pork chop about 500g
- 1/3 cup of store-bought char siu sauce see notes for substitution
- 2 Tablespoon soy sauce

Instructions

- Marinate the pork chops in all the ingredients. Refrigerate for at least 3 hours. Take the pork

chops out of the refrigerator 30 minutes before air frying.
- Place the pork chops in the parchment paper-lined fryer basket and air fry at 380F (190C) for about 15 minutes until the meat temperature is at least 165F (64C).

Nutrition

- Calories: 206kcal | Carbohydrates: 7g | Protein: 25g | Fat: 8g | Saturated Fat: 3g | Polyunsaturated Fat: 1g | Monounsaturated Fat: 1g | Trans Fat: 1g | Cholesterol: 76mg | Sodium: 1032mg | Potassium: 442mg | Fiber: 1g | Sugar: 1g | Calcium: 8mg | Iron: 1mg

567. Wasabi Lime Steak

Prep Time: 1 hr 15 mins

Cook Time: 15 mins

Ingredients for the steak:

- 1 pound flank steak (about 500g) thinly sliced
- 1 tablespoon wasabi paste
- 2 Tablespoon soy sauce
- 2 Tablespoon lime juice
- 1/2 Tablespoon Sesame oil
- 1 Tablespoon grated ginger

Wasabi Mayonnaise:

- 1/4 cup mayonnaise
- 1 Tablespoon water
- 1 Tablespoon mirin non-alcohol
- 1 Tablespoon lime juice
- 1 teaspoon wasabi paste
- Other ingredients:
- 1/3 cup cilantro chopped

Instructions

- Combine all the ingredients for the steak and mix well. Marinate for at least one hour or overnight in the refrigerator.
- Line the fryer basket with a sheet of lightly greased aluminum foil. Spread the beef slices out as much as possible and air fry at 380F (190C) for about 8-10 minutes, stir 1-2 times in between.
- In the meantime, mix the mayonnaise, water, mirin, lime juice, and wasabi paste in a medium bowl.

- Drizzle the wasabi mayo over the steak and garnish with some cilantro to serve.

Nutrition

- Calories: 288kcal | Carbohydrates: 5g | Protein: 26g | Fat: 18g | Saturated Fat: 4g | Cholesterol: 74mg | Sodium: 686mg | Potassium: 427mg | Fiber: 1g | Sugar: 2g | Vitamin C: 6mg | Calcium: 29mg | Iron: 2mg

568. Korean Beef With Veggie

Prep Time: 40 mins

Cook Time: 15 mins

Ingredients For Beef:

12 ounces flank steak cut into thin slices

1 teaspoon corn starch

1/4 cup Korean BBQ sauce

Other Ingredients:

- 2 cups mung bean sprouts
- 3 cups baby spinach or spinach cut into 2-inch length
- 1 Tablespoon sesame oil
- 1 Tablespoon minced garlic
- 1 Tablespoon freshly grated ginger
- 1 Tablespoon rice wine
- 2-3 Tablespoon Korean BBQ sauce
- 1 teaspoon jalapeno pepper sliced (optional)
- 1 teaspoon toasted sesame seeds

Instructions

- In a large bowl, marinate the beef with Korean BBQ sauce and corn starch for about 30 minutes.
- In a small pot, boil the mung bean sprouts until tender. Remove and set aside. Then, boil the spinach for about one minute and set aside.
- In a lightly greased cake pan, air fry the marinated beef at 380F (190C) for about 7-8 minutes, stir once in between.
- In the meantime, stir fry the garlic, grated ginger, and jalapeno pepper with sesame oil in a wok for about 1-2 minutes until fragrant. Add in the Korean BBQ sauce and rice wine and bring to a boil then turn the stove off.
- Toss the spinach, bean sprouts, and beef slices in

the sauce. Sprinkle some sesame seeds over the dish to serve.

Nutrition

- Calories: 220kcal | Carbohydrates: 13g | Protein: 22g | Fat: 8g | Saturated Fat: 2g | Cholesterol: 51mg | Sodium: 486mg | Potassium: 493mg | Fiber: 1g | Sugar: 9g | Vitamin C: 15mg | Calcium: 55mg | Iron: 2mg

569. Mongolian Beef

Prep Time: 15 mins

Cook Time: 10 mins

Ingredients For The Beef:

- 1 pound flank steak cut into 1/4 inch thick pieces (about 500g)
- 2 teaspoon soy sauce
- 1 teaspoon sesame oil
- 2 teaspoon cornstarch
- 1/4 cup tapioca starch

Ingredients For The Sauce:

- 2 Tablespoon olive oil
- 1 Tablespoon grated ginger
- 1 Tablespoon minced garlic
- 2 Tablespoon soy sauce
- 3 Tablespoon brown sugar
- 3-4 green onion green parts only, cut into 1-2 inch pieces
- 1-2 teaspoon sesame seeds optional

Instructions

- In a Ziploc back, marinate the steak pieces with soy sauce, sesame oil, and corn starch for at least 15 minutes. Add in the tapioca starch and shake, making sure all the pieces are coated.
- Line the fryer basket with a sheet of lightly greased aluminum foil. Put the steak pieces in, preferably without stacking, and air fry at 400F (200C) for about 8 minutes, flip once until the edges look slightly crispy.
- In the meantime, in a frying pan or a wok, saute the garlic and grated ginger in olive oil for about 1-2 minutes until fragrant. Add in the soy sauce and brown sugar and stir constantly until the sauce thickens.

- When the beef is done, toss the beef in the sauce, followed by the green onion. To serve, sprinkle the dish with sesame seeds if desired.

Nutrition

- Calories: 306kcal | Carbohydrates: 19g | Protein: 26g | Fat: 14g | Saturated Fat: 4g | Cholesterol: 68mg | Sodium: 735mg | Potassium: 443mg | Fiber: 1g | Sugar: 9g | Vitamin A: 90IU | Vitamin C: 2mg | Calcium: 46mg | Iron: 2mg

570. Beef Wrapped Cheesy Mushroom

Prep Time: 10 mins

Cook Time: 10 mins

Ingredients

- 12 pieces of thinly sliced beef
- 12 button mushrooms
- 1/3 cup cheddar cheese
- 1/4 cup Korean BBQ sauce
- 2 Tablespoon sesame seeds optional
- 6 pieces of pickled jalapeno peppers chopped (optional)

Instructions

- Marinate the beef with Korean BBQ sauce for 15 minutes.
- Use a paper towel to wipe the button mushroom clean and remove the stems. Fill the mushroom with cheese and some chopped jalapeno pepper.
- Take a slice of beef and wrap it around the mushroom. Air fry at 380F (190C) for about 5 minutes (depending on the thickness of the meat).
- Sprinkle some sesame seeds to serve.

Nutrition

- Calories: 330kcal | Carbohydrates: 16g | Protein: 29g | Fat: 17g | Saturated Fat: 7g | Cholesterol: 73mg | Sodium: 800mg | Potassium: 718mg | Fiber: 2g | Sugar: 11g | Vitamin C: 3mg | Calcium: 214mg | Iron: 4mg

571. Cumin Beef

Prep Time: 3 hrs

Cook Time: 15 mins

Ingredients

- 1 pound beef flank steak thinly sliced (about 500g)
- 3 Tablespoon Soy sauce
- 2 Tablespoon chopped garlic
- 1 tablespoon Shaoxing wine
- 1 1/2 Tablespoon cumin
- 1 Tablespoon paprika
- 1 1/2 teaspoon corn starch
- 1/4 teaspoon salt
- 1/2 teaspoon black pepper
- 1/2 teaspoon hot pepper flakes optional
- 1/3 cup chopped cilantro
- 1/2 cup chopped green onion

Instructions

- Marinate the beef slices with all of the ingredients, except cilantro and green onion, in the refrigerator for at least 3 hours. Remove from the refrigerator about 30 minutes before air frying.
- In a lightly greased foiled lined fryer basket, air fry the beef slices at 380F (190C), stir 2-3 times in between, about 10-12 minutes, or until the desired degree of doneness is reached.
- When done, toss the beef with cilantro and green onion to serve.

Nutrition

- Calories: 196kcal | Carbohydrates: 6g | Protein: 27g | Fat: 6g | Saturated Fat: 2g | Cholesterol: 68mg | Sodium: 968mg | Potassium: 546mg | Fiber: 1g | Sugar: 1g | Vitamin A: 1105IU | Vitamin C: 4mg | Calcium: 68mg | Iron: 4mg

572. Meatballs With Gochujang Mayo

Prep Time: 15 mins

Cook Time: 10 mins

Ingredients For Meatballs:

- 1 pound ground pork (about 500g) or meat of your choice

- 1/4 cup onion finely chopped
- 2 Tablespoon soy sauce
- 2 teaspoon corn starch
- 1 teaspoon dried basil
- 1 teaspoon garlic powder
- 1 teaspoon onion powder
- 1/4 teaspoon white pepper powder
- Ingredients for sauce:
- 1 teaspoon Gochujang (Korean hot pepper paste)
- 2 Tablespoon Mayonnaise
- 2 Tablespoon mirin

Instructions

- Line the fryer basket with a grill mat or a sheet of lightly greased aluminum foil.
- Mix all the meatball ingredients then form them into about 1 inch balls. Put the meatballs in the fryer basket without stacking. Spray some oil onto the meatballs and air fry at 380F (190C) for 8-10 minutes until the meat is cooked through at its proper temperature.
- In the meantime, take a small bowl and mix all the sauce ingredients.
- Dip the meatballs in the Gochujang mayo to serve.

Nutrition

- Calories:378kcal | Carbohydrates: 7g | Protein: 21g | Fat: 29g | Saturated Fat: 10g | Cholesterol: 85mg | Sodium: 677mg | Potassium: 368mg | Fiber: 1g | Sugar: 3g | Vitamin C: 2mg | Calcium: 21mg | Iron: 1mg

---

573. Pie Crust Beef Empanadas

Prep Time: 30 mins

Cook Time: 15 mins

Ingredients

- 1 pound ground beef

- 1-2 Tablespoon pickled jalapeno chopped (optional)
- 1 teaspoon corn starch
- 1 teaspoon cumin
- 1 teaspoon chili powder
- 1/4 teaspoon salt or to taste
- 1/4 teaspoon pepper or to taste
- 1 teaspoon olive oil
- 2 Tablespoon minced garlic
- 1/4 cup diced onions
- 2 rolls of pie crust thawed according to package instruction
- 1 cup Mexican blend cheese or to taste
- 1 egg beaten

Instructions

- In a large bowl, mix the ground beef with jalapeno (optional), corn starch, cumin, chili powder, salt, and pepper, and let it sit for about 5-10 minutes.
- Line the fryer basket with a grill mat or lightly greased aluminum foil.
- In a large skillet, saute garlic and onion for about 1 minute until fragrant. Add in the ground beef and stir fry until beef is cooked through and the onion is translucent.
- Roll out pie crusts. Use a bowl size of your choice to trace circles onto the piecrust and cut them into circular pieces. Mix the leftover pie crust, use a rolling pin to roll them out. Repeat the above process to get as many circular crusts as you can.
- Lay the circular pieces of pie crust on the counter and put the desired amount of filling and cheese in the center. Fold pie crust in half and keep the fillings inside. Use the back of a fork to press down on the edges of the pie crust.
- Carefully transfer the empanadas into the fryer basket. Brush the top surface with egg and air fry at 350F (175C) for about 4-5 minutes. Flip the empanadas over and brush the top side with egg. Air fry again at 350F (175C) for another 3-4 minutes until the surface is golden brown.

Nutrition

- Calories: 545kcal | Carbohydrates: 30g | Protein: 22g | Fat: 37g | Saturated Fat: 14g | Cholesterol: 99mg | Sodium: 554mg | Potassium: 318mg |

Fiber: 2g | Sugar: 1g | Vitamin C: 1mg | Calcium: 159mg | Iron: 4mg

574. Tri-tip Roast

Prep Time: 1 hr 10 mins

Cook Time: 30 mins

Ingredients

- 2 pound tri-tip roast excess fat trimmed
- 6-8 garlic cloves
- 1/4 cup olive oil
- 2 1/2 tsp salt
- 1 tsp garlic powder
- 1/2 tsp black pepper

Instructions

- In a food processor or a blender, pulse the seasoning ingredient several times.
- Pat dry the tri-tip roast with a paper towel and put it inside a large Ziploc bag.
- Put the seasoning mixture inside the bag, squeeze out as much air as possible and seal the bag. Spread the seasoning and massage the meat at the same time, making sure all surfaces are covered with the mixture. Leave it at room temperature for about one hour.
- Insert a meat thermometer into the center of the roast. Air fry at 400F (200C) for about 20-25 minutes until the desired temperature is reached, 125F (52C) for rare, 135F (57C) for medium-rare and 145F (63C) for medium.
- Let the roast rest for about 10 minutes before serving.

Nutrition

- Calories:323kcal | Carbohydrates: 1g | Protein: 31g | Fat: 21g | Saturated Fat: 6g | Cholesterol: 98mg | Sodium: 1050mg | Potassium: 503mg | Fiber: 1g | Sugar: 1g | Vitamin C: 1mg | Calcium: 42mg | Iron: 2mg

575. Cheese Stuffed Meatballs

Prep Time: 10 mins

Cook Time: 15 mins

Ingredients

- 1 lb ground beef (about 500g)
- 3/4 cup crushed saltine crackers or breadcrumb
- 1/4 cup onion chopped
- 1/4 cup Parmesan cheese
- 1 tsp onion powder
- 1 tsp garlic powder
- 1 tsp parsley
- 1/2 tsp salt
- 1/4 tsp pepper
- 2 eggs
- 3 sticks mozzarella cheese cut into 4-5 pieces each

Other Ingredients:

- Spaghetti sauce

Instructions

- Line the fryer basket with a grill mat or lightly greased aluminum foil.
- Mix all the ingredients, except mozzarella cheese. Scoop about 2 Tablespoons of the meat mixture and wrap one piece of the cheese in the middle to form a ball. Place the meatballs inside the air fryer.
- Spray the meatballs with some oil. Air fry at 380F (190C) for about 6 minutes. Flip, spray some oil again, and air fry at 380F (190C) for another 4-5 minutes.
- Take a pot to heat the spaghetti sauce. When the meatballs are done, simmer the meatballs in the sauce for a few minutes.
- Serve the meatballs and sauce with your favorite pasta.

Nutrition

- Calories: 312kcal | Carbohydrates: 9g | Protein: 20g | Fat: 21g | Saturated Fat: 9g | Cholesterol: 119mg | Sodium: 532mg | Potassium: 254mg | Fiber: 1g | Sugar: 1g | Vitamin A: 112IU | Vitamin C: 1mg | Calcium: 83mg | Iron: 2mg

576. Asian Meatball Stuffed Zucchini

Prep Time: 15 mins

Cook Time: 15 mins

Ingredients

- 1 pound ground beef (about 500g)
- 1 egg beaten
- 1/4 cup minced onion
- 2 tbsp chopped basil
- 2 tbsp oyster sauce
- 1 tsp corn starch
- 1/4 tsp black pepper or to taste
- 2 large zucchinis peeled

Instructions

- Combine all the ingredients, except zucchini, and let it marinate at room temperature for about 15 minutes.
- Line the fryer basket with a large sheet of aluminum and spray it with some oil.
- Cut zucchini into 1-inch sections and hollow out the center with a sharp knife. Then, fill the zucchini with the beef mixture and put them into the fryer basket without stacking.
- Air fry at 360F (180C) for 10-12 minutes. Flip sides about halfway through and continue to air fry until the ground meat is cooked through when then internal temperature exceeds 160F (72C).

Nutrition

- Calories: 221kcal | Carbohydrates: 4g | Protein: 15g | Fat: 16g | Saturated Fat: 6g | Cholesterol: 81mg | Sodium: 231mg | Potassium: 394mg | Fiber: 1g | Sugar: 2g | Vitamin C: 12mg | Calcium: 30mg | Iron: 2mg

577. Air Fried Bulgogi

Prep Time: 30 mins

Cook Time: 10 mins

Ingredients

- 1 pound thinly sliced beef rib-eye
- 1/4 cup thinly sliced onion
- 1/3 cup Korean BBQ Sauce or to taste
- 2 tbsp grated ginger
- 1/4 cup thinly sliced green onion
- 2 tsp sesame seed

Instructions

- In a large Ziploc bag, combine the meat, onion,

Korean BBQ sauce, and ginger and mix well. Marinate for at least 30 minutes.
- Lin the fryer basket with a grill mat or a sheet of lightly greased aluminum foil.
- Spread the beef out inside the basket as much as possible and air fry at 380F (190C) for 8-10 minutes, stir once in the middle until the meat is cooked through.
- Sprinkle with sesame seeds and green onion to serve.

Nutrition

Calories: 283kcal | Carbohydrates: 9g | Protein: 24g | Fat: 17g | Saturated Fat: 7g | Cholesterol: 69mg | Sodium: 433mg | Potassium: 361mg | Fiber: 1g | Sugar: 6g | Vitamin C: 2mg | Calcium: 22mg | Iron: 2mg

578. Black Pepper Steak And Mushroom

Prep Time: 1 hr 15 mins

Cook Time: 15 mins

Ingredients For Steak:

- 1 pound rib eye steak about 500g, cubed (about 1/2 inch pieces)
- 1 tsp cornstarch
- 1 tbsp rice wine
- 1 tbsp lime juice
- 2 tsp light soy sauce
- 2 tsp dark soy sauce
- 2 tbsp grated ginger
- 1/4 tsp black pepper or to taste

Other Ingredients:

- 8 button mushrooms thinly sliced
- 1 tbsp garlic finely chopped
- 1 tbsp oyster sauce

Instructions

- In a Ziploc bag, mix all the ingredients for the steak and marinate for about one hour.
- Line the fryer basket with a sheet of lightly greased aluminum foil.
- Put the steak inside the fryer basket and air fry at 380F (190C) for about 5 minutes.
- Add all other ingredients to the steak and stir. Air

fry at 380F (190C) for another 4-5 minutes or until the desired doneness is reached.

- Carefully pour the drippings from aluminum foil into a wok and bring it to a boil. Stir constantly until the sauce thickens.
- Toss the steak cubes in the wok to coat. Serve immediately.

Nutrition

- Calories:275kcal | Carbohydrates: 7g | Protein: 25g | Fat: 16g | Saturated Fat: 7g | Cholesterol: 69mg | Sodium: 407mg | Potassium: 446mg | Fiber: 1g | Sugar: 3g | Vitamin C: 3mg | Calcium: 12mg | Iron: 2mg

579. Marinated Rib-Eye Steak

Prep Time: 2 hrs

Cook Time: 10 mins

Ingredients

- 1 pound rib-eye steak (or any cut you prefer) 500g
- 2 Tablespoon grated Ginger
- 2 Tablespoon Honey
- 1 Tablespoon minced garlic
- 1 Tablespoon sesame oil
- 2 teaspoon apple cider vinegar
- 1/4 cup soy sauce
- 1 teaspoon scallion optional
- 1 teaspoon dried minced garlic optional

Instructions

- Combine all the seasoning ingredients, except scallions and fried minced garlic, and marinate the steak in a Ziploc bag for at least 2 hours or best overnight in the refrigerator.
- If refrigerated, remove from the fridge about 30 minutes before air frying.
- Preheat air fryer for 400F (200C) for 3-4 minutes.
- Place the steak in the preheated air fryer and air fry at 400F (200C) for 6-8 minutes, flip once in the middle, until the desired doneness is reached.
- Let the steak rest for about 10 minutes before cutting. Sprinkle some fried minced garlic and scallions to serve if desired.

Nutrition

- Calories: 317kcal | Carbohydrates: 11g | Protein: 25g | Fat: 20g | Saturated Fat: 8g | Cholesterol: 69mg | Sodium: 870mg | Potassium: 349mg | Fiber: 1g | Sugar: 9g | Vitamin C: 1mg | Calcium: 19mg | Iron: 2mg

580. Asian Flavored Ribs

Prep Time: 2 hrs 15 mins

Cook Time: 10 mins

Ingredients

- 1 pound beef short ribs about 500g
- 1/3 cup brown sugar
- 1/4 cup oyster sauce
- 1/4 cup soy sauce
- 2 tbsp rice wine
- 3 cloves garlic minced
- 1 tbsp fresh grated ginger
- 1 tbsp scallions

Instructions

- Put the short ribs in a large Ziploc bag.
- In a large bowl, mix all other ingredients, except scallions. Pour the mixture into the Ziploc bag and mix it with the ribs. Marinate the ribs for about 2 hours.
- Line the fryer basket with a sheet of lightly greased aluminum foil.
- Place the ribs inside the fryer basket, without stacking. Air fry at 380F (190C) for 8-10 minutes, flip once in the middle until the surface is slightly caramelized.
- Sprinkle some scallions to garnish.

Nutrition

Calories: 244kcal | Carbohydrates: 22g | Protein: 18g | Fat: 9g | Saturated Fat: 4g | Cholesterol: 49mg | Sodium: 867mg | Potassium: 360mg | Fiber: 1g | Sugar: 18g | Vitamin C: 1mg | Calcium: 33mg | Iron: 2mg

581. Korean Ground Beef Stir Fry

Prep Time: 5 mins

Cook Time: 10 mins

Ingredients

- 1/2 pound ground beef (or ground meat of your choice) about 500g
- 1 teaspoon corn starch
- 1/4 cup Korean BBQ sauce (**see note) or to taste
- 1/4 cup zucchini julienned
- 1/4 cup steamed carrots julienned
- 1 tablespoon sesame seeds
- 1/4 cup scallions

Instructions

- In a large bowl, mix the ground beef, corn starch, and Korean BBQ sauce. Marinate for about 5 minutes.
- Add the carrots and zucchini to the bowl, and gently mix.
- Transfer the mixture to a lightly greased cake barrel and use a spatula to spread them out a bit. Air fry at 380F (190C) for 8-10 minutes, stirring twice in the middle until the ground beef is cooked through.
- Sprinkle some sesame seeds and scallions to serve.

Nutrition

- Calories: 189kcal | Carbohydrates: 7g | Protein: 11g | Fat: 12g | Saturated Fat: 5g | Cholesterol: 40mg | Sodium: 325mg | Potassium: 226mg | Fiber: 1g | Sugar: 5g | Vitamin C: 3mg | Calcium: 37mg | Iron: 1mg

582. Easy Swedish Meatballs

Prep Time: 15 mins

Cook Time: 25 mins

Ingredients For Meatballs: (Makes About 30 Meatballs)

- 1 1/2 pound ground meat or ground meat mixtures (about 750g) I used ground turkey
- 1/3 cup Panko breadcrumbs
- 1/2 cup milk
- 1/2 of an onion finely chopped
- 1 large egg
- 2 tablespoon parsley dried or fresh
- 2 tablespoon minced garlic
- 1/3 teaspoon salt

- 1/4 teaspoon black pepper or to taste
- 1/4 teaspoon paprika
- 1/4 teaspoon onion powder

Ingredients For Sauce:

- 1/3 cup butter
- 1/4 cup all-purpose flour
- 2 cups broth I used chicken broth
- 1/2 cup milk
- 1 tablespoon soy sauce
- Salt and pepper to taste

Instructions

- Line the fryer basket with a grill mat or a sheet of lightly greased aluminum foil.
- In a large bowl, combine all the meatball ingredients and let it rest for 5-10 minutes.
- Using the palm of your hands, roll the meat mixture into balls of the desired size. Place them in the fryer basket and air fry at 380F (190C) for 8-12 minutes (depending on the size of the meatballs) until they are cooked through and internal temperature exceeds 165F or 74C)
- In the meantime, melt the butter in a wok or a pan. Whisk in flour until it turns brown. Pour in the broth, milk, and soy sauce and bring it to a simmer. Season with salt and pepper to taste. Stir constantly until the sauce thickens.
- Serve meatballs and sauce over pasta or mashed potato. Sprinkle some parsley if desired.

Nutrition

- Calories: 299kcal | Carbohydrates: 12g | Protein: 31g | Fat: 15g | Saturated Fat: 8g | Cholesterol: 121mg | Sodium: 723mg | Potassium: 443mg | Fiber: 1g | Sugar: 3g | Vitamin C: 3mg | Calcium: 71mg | Iron: 2mg

583. Korean Kimchi Beef

Prep Time: 30 mins

Cook Time: 10 mins

Ingredients For Beef:

- 1 pound tri-tip strip about 500g, thinly sliced
- 1/4 cup kimchi juice
- 1 tablespoon oyster sauce

- 1 tablespoon soy sauce
- 1 tablespoon freshly grated ginger
- 1 teaspoon sesame oil
- 1 teaspoon corn starch

Other Ingredients:

- 1/2 cup kimchi or to taste
- 1/4 cup thinly sliced green onion
- 1 teaspoon sesame seeds optional

Instructions

- In a large bowl, combine all the beef ingredients and marinate for at least 30 minutes.
- Line the fryer basket with a sheet of lightly greased aluminum foil.
- Transfer the content of the bowl to the fryer basket and air fry at 380F (190C) for 5 minutes. Stir once in the middle.
- Add the kimchi and green onion to the beef and stir. Air fry again at 380F (190C) for about 3 minutes.
- Sprinkle some toasted sesame seeds to serve if desired.

Nutrition

- Calories: 200kcal | Carbohydrates: 2g | Protein: 24g | Fat: 10g | Saturated Fat: 3g | Cholesterol: 74mg | Sodium: 436mg | Potassium: 391mg | Fiber: 1g | Sugar: 1g | Vitamin C: 1mg | Calcium: 37mg | Iron: 2mg

584. A Minnesotan's Beef And Macaroni Hotdish

Prep: 15 mins

Cook: 25 mins

Total: 40 mins

Ingredient

- 1 pound ground beef
- 2 cups elbow macaroni
- ½ large green bell pepper, coarsely chopped
- ½ large onion, chopped
- 1 (16 ounces) can tomato sauce
- 1 pound tomatoes, coarsely chopped
- 2 teaspoons Worcestershire sauce
- 1 teaspoon soy sauce
- 1 teaspoon salt

- ¾ teaspoon dried basil
- ¾ teaspoon dried oregano
- ½ teaspoon ground black pepper
- ½ teaspoon chili powder
- ¼ teaspoon garlic powder
- ⅛ teaspoon hot pepper sauce (such as Tabasco®)
- 1 cup beef broth

Instructions

- Cook beef in a large skillet over medium heat, stirring occasionally, until browned, about 5 minutes. Transfer beef to a bowl.
- Cook macaroni, bell pepper, and onion in the same skillet over medium heat for 3 minutes. Add cooked beef, tomato sauce, tomatoes, Worcestershire sauce, soy sauce, salt, basil, oregano, ground black pepper, chili powder, garlic powder, and hot pepper sauce. Pour in beef broth. Cover skillet and simmer until macaroni is tender about 15 minutes. Remove lid and simmer, stirring occasionally, until thickened, 5 to 10 minutes.

Nutrition Facts

- Calories: 336 | Protein: 19.6g | Carbohydrates: 35.9g | Fat: 12.8g | Cholesterol: 46.4mg | Sodium: 1039.5mg.

585. Tennessee Meatloaf

Prep Time: 40 mins

Cook Time: 1 hr

Additional Time: 15 mins

Total Time: 1 hr 55 mins

Ingredients

Brown Sugar Glaze:

- ½ cup ketchup
- ¼ cup brown sugar
- 2 tablespoons cider vinegar

Meatloaf:

- Cooking spray
- 1 onion, chopped
- ½ green bell pepper, chopped
- 2 cloves garlic, minced

- 2 large eggs, lightly beaten
- 1 teaspoon dried thyme
- 1 teaspoon seasoned salt
- ½ teaspoon ground black pepper
- 2 teaspoons prepared mustard
- 2 teaspoons worcestershire sauce
- ½ teaspoon hot pepper sauce (such as tabasco®)
- ½ cup milk
- ⅔ cup quick-cooking oats
- 1 pound ground beef
- ½ pound ground pork
- ½ pound ground veal

Instructions

- Combine ketchup, brown sugar, and cider vinegar in a bowl; mix well.
- Preheat oven to 350 degrees F (175 degrees C). Spray two 9x5-inch loaf pans with cooking spray or line with aluminum foil for easier cleanup (see Cook's Note).
- Place onion and green pepper in a covered microwave container and cook until softened, 1 to 2 minutes. Set aside to cool.
- In a large mixing bowl, combine garlic, eggs, thyme, seasoned salt, black pepper, mustard, Worcestershire sauce, hot sauce, milk, and oats. Mix well. Stir in cooked onion and green pepper. Add ground beef, pork, and veal. With gloved hands, work all ingredients together until completely mixed and uniform.
- Divide meatloaf mixture in half and pat half of mixture into each prepared loaf pan. Brush loaves with half of the glaze; set the remainder of glaze aside.
- Bake in preheated oven for 50 minutes. Remove pans from oven; carefully drain fat. Brush loaves with remaining glaze. Return to oven and bake for 10 minutes more. Remove pans from the oven and allow the meatloaf to stand for 15 minutes before slicing.

Nutrition Facts

- Calories: 233| Protein: 17.1g| Carbohydrates: 15.9g| Fat: 11.2g|Cholesterol: 92mg|

12. Air Fryer Soup And Stew Recipes

586. Peruvian Roast Chicken With Green Sauce

Prep Time: 8 hrs

Cook Time: 20 mins

Ingredients

For The Chicken

- 4 pieces of skin-on chicken thighs
- 3 tablespoon olive oil
- 1/4 cup lime juice
- 4 garlic cloves chopped
- 1 tablespoon salt
- 2 teaspoon paprika
- 1 teaspoon black pepper
- 1 tablespoon cumin
- 1 teaspoon dried oregano
- 2 teaspoons sugar
- 1 teaspoon black pepper

For The Green Sauce

- 3 jalapeno peppers seeded and chopped
- 1 cup cilantro leaves
- 2 cloves garlic chopped
- 1/2 cup mayonnaise
- 1/4 cup sour cream
- 1 tablespoon lime juice
- 1/2 teaspoon salt
- 1/8 teaspoon black pepper
- 2 tablespoon olive oil

Instructions

- Blend all the seasoning ingredients for the chicken in the food processor until smooth to make the marinade.
- Put the chicken thighs in a large Ziploc bag and pour in the marinade. Marinate the thighs in the refrigerator overnight.
- Air fry at 380F (190C) skin side down for about 8-10 minutes. Turn the thighs over and air fry again at 380F (190C) for another 6-8 minutes until temp at 165F (74C).
- To make the green sauce, first, blend everything (except olive oil) until smooth. Then, drizzle olive

oil slowly and blend to thicken. Refrigerate until ready to serve.

- Drizzle the sauce over the chicken or serve it on the side.

Nutrition

- Calories:725kcal | Carbohydrates: 9g | Protein: 25g | Fat: 66g | Saturated Fat: 14g | Cholesterol: 161mg | Sodium: 2343mg | Potassium: 443mg | Fiber: 1g | Sugar: 4g | Vitamin C: 21mg | Calcium: 60mg | Iron: 3mg

---

587. Chicken Pasta In Creamy Chimichurri Sauce

Prep Time: 1 hr 30 mins

Cook Time: 15 mins

Ingredients

- 4 pieces of skinless boneless chicken thighs
- 1/4 cup bacon bits
- 2 tbsp butter bacon grease, or olive oil
- 1 tbsp all-purpose flour
- 2/3 cup milk or heavy creamer
- 1 pound cooked spaghetti about 500g or to taste

For The Chimichurri Sauce:

- 1 1/2 cup cilantro minced
- 1/4 cup thinly sliced chives or green onions
- 2 Tablespoon minced garlic
- 2 limes zested and juiced
- 1/2 cup olive oil
- 3 Tablespoon chopped pickled jalapenos
- 1/2 teaspoon sea salt
- 1/4 teaspoon black pepper

Instructions

- Use the food processor or a blender to mix all the ingredients for chimichurri sauce for about 10 seconds. Pour about 3/4 cup out and set aside.
- In a Ziploc bag, put the chicken pieces in the bag along with the rest of the sauce. Seal the bag, mix, and let them marinate in the refrigerator for at least one hour.
- Take the chicken out of the refrigerator 30 minutes before air frying.
- Line the fryer basket with a grill mat or a sheet of lightly greased aluminum foil.

- Place the chicken inside the fryer basket without stacking. Air fry at 380F (190C) for 10-12 minutes until fully cooked through when the internal temperature exceeds 165F (74C)
- In the meantime, heat butter in a wok or a frying pan. Add in flour and stir constantly until it bubbles and thickens. Then, add in milk and 3/4 cup of chimichurri sauce and stir until thickens.
- When done, stir in the chicken and serve over pasta.
- Sprinkle some bacon bits to serve.

Nutrition

- Calories:760kcal|Carbohydrates:49g | Protein: 41g | Fat: 45g | Saturated Fat: 10g | Cholesterol: 154mg | Sodium: 829mg | Potassium: 585mg | Fiber: 5g | Sugar: 4g | Vitamin C: 15mg | Calcium: 108mg |Iron: 4mg

---

588. Air Fryer Cashew Chicken

Prep Time: 40 mins

Cook Time: 10 mins

Ingredients

- 1 lb boneless and skinless chicken thigh or breast (about 500g) cut into bite-size pieces

Ingredients For Marinade:

- 1/4 cup hoisin sauce
- 1/4 cup soy sauce
- 1 tablespoon white vinegar
- 1 tablespoon sugar
- 2 tablespoon freshly grated ginger
- 1 teaspoon corn starch
- Other ingredients:
- 1 teaspoon olive oil
- 2 tablespoon minced garlic
- 1/4 cup steamed carrots diced
- 2 tablespoon scallions
- 1/3 cup roasted cashew halves

Instructions

- Mix all the marinade ingredients.
- Put the chicken pieces in a Ziploc bag along with 2/3 of the sauce and mix. Marinade the chicken for about 30 minutes. If longer, refrigerate it

until cooking.

- Line the fryer basket with a grill mat or a sheet of lightly greased aluminum foil.
- Spread the chicken out in the fryer basket and air fry at 380F (190C) for 10-12 minutes until cooked through.
- In the meantime, use a wok or a frying pan to saute garlic in olive oil until fragrant, about 1 minute.
- Add the remaining 1/3 of the marinade and stir constantly until the sauce thickens.
- Toss the chicken, carrots, and cashew in the wok to coat. Then, sprinkle some scallions to serve.

Nutrition

- Calories: 271kcal | Carbohydrates: 18g | Protein: 29g | Fat: 9g | Saturated Fat: 2g | Cholesterol: 73mg | Sodium: 1228mg | Potassium: 598mg | Fiber: 1g | Sugar: 9g | Vitamin C: 4mg | Calcium: 28mg | Iron: 2mg

589. Air Fryer Roasted Curry Chicken

Prep Time: 2 hrs

Cook Time: 20 mins

Ingredients For Chicken:

- 5 pieces skin-on bone-in chicken thighs
- 1/4 cup mayonnaise
- 1 Tablespoon brown sugar
- 1 Tablespoon garlic minced
- 2 Tablespoon soy sauce
- 2 Tablespoon grated ginger
- 1 teaspoon curry powder
- 1/4 teaspoon paprika
- 1/4 teaspoon cumin
- Other ingredients:
- 1/2 teaspoon curry powder
- 1/4 teaspoon cumin
- 1/4 teaspoon paprika
- 1/4 cup scallion

Instructions

- Mix all the ingredients for chicken. Marinate the chicken in this marinade for at least 2 hours or overnight in the refrigerator.
- Mix 1/2 teaspoon of curry, 1/4 teaspoon of

cumin, and 1/4 teaspoon of paprika and set aside for later.

- Take the chicken out of the refrigerator 30 minutes before air frying.
- Line the fryer basket with a grill mat or a sheet of lightly greased aluminum foil.
- Put the chicken thighs into the basket skin side down, without stacking, and air fry at 380F (190C) for 10 minutes.
- Flip the chicken thigh over, now ski side up, and sprinkle some dry seasoning mix over the skin.
- Air fry at 380F (190C) for another 6-7 minutes until the meat is cooked through, internal temperature exceeds 170F (77C).
- Sprinkle some scallion to serve

Nutrition

- Calories: 101kcal | Carbohydrates: 5g | Protein: 1g | Fat: 9g | Saturated Fat: 1g | Cholesterol: 6mg | Sodium: 477mg | Potassium: 41mg | Fiber: 1g | Sugar: 3g | Vitamin C: 1mg | Calcium: 6mg | Iron: 1mg

590. Yakitori Japanese Skewered Chicken

Prep Time: 1 hr 10 mins

Cook Time: 10 mins

Ingredients

- 1 pound skinless and boneless chicken thigh (about 500g) cut into 1 inch cubes
- 1/4 cup dark soy sauce
- 1/4 cup mirin
- 2 tbsp rice wine
- 2 tbsp brown sugar
- 2 tbsp minced garlic
- 2 tbsp freshly grated ginger
- 1/4 cup scallions for garnish

Instructions

- In a large bowl, mix dark soy sauce, mirin, rice wine, brown sugar, garlic, and ginger. Save about 1/3 of the sauce in a small bowl and set aside for later.
- Put the chicken thigh cubes in the bowl and mix. Marinate for about 1 hour.
- Soak the bamboo skewers in water for at least 15 minutes.

- Line the fryer basket with a grill mat or a sheet of lightly greased aluminum foil.
- Thread the skewers through the chicken pieces then put the skewers in the fryer basket. Spritz some oil over the skewers and air fry at 380F (190C) for 10-12 minutes, flip once in the middle, until the surface is slightly caramelized and the meat is cooked through.
- In the meantime, use a saucepan to bring the previously set-aside sauce to boil. Stir constantly until the sauce thickens. Put the sauce in a small bowl to be used for dipping.
- Sprinkle the yakitori with scallions and serve with dipping sauce on the side.

Nutrition

- Calories:258kcal | Carbohydrates: 28g | Protein: 22g | Fat: 5g | Saturated Fat: 1g | Cholesterol: 108mg | Sodium: 479mg | Potassium: 326mg | Fiber: 1g | Sugar: 20g | Vitamin C: 2mg | Calcium: 27mg | Iron: 1mg

591. Chicken With Scallion And Ginger Sauce

Prep Time: 5 mins

Marinate At Least One Hour: 20 mins

Ingredients

- 4 pieces of skinless boneless thighs
- 1/2 tsp salt
- 2 tbsp rice wine
- 3 tbsp olive oil
- 1/4 cup dripping from the chicken
- 1/4 cup scallions
- 2 tbsp freshly grated ginger
- 1 tbsp minced garlic
- Salt to taste

Instructions

- Marinate the chicken with 1/2 teaspoon of salt and rice wine for at least one hour.
- Wrap the thighs in a large, lightly greased aluminum foil (without stacking) and air fry at 380F (190C) for about 15 minutes until the internal temperature exceeds 165F (74C).
- When the chicken is done, pour about 1/4 cup of drippings from the foil into a saucepan. Combine it with the rest of the ingredients and bring it to a boil.
- Pour the sauce over the chicken to serve.

Nutrition

- Calories: 112kcal | Carbohydrates: 2g | Protein: 1g | Fat: 11g | Saturated Fat: 1g | Cholesterol: 1mg | Sodium: 294mg | Potassium: 32mg | Fiber: 1g | Sugar: 1g | Vitamin C: 2mg | Calcium: 8mg | Iron: 1mg

592. Chicken And Kimchi Fritters

Prep Time: 10 mins

Cook Time: 10 mins

Ingredients For Chicken:

- 2 cups of chicken fully cooked and shredded
- 1/3 cup kimchi finely shopped
- 1/3 cup Japanese Panko
- 1/4 cup shredded cheese I used Mexican blend
- 2 Tablespoon green onion finely chopped
- 1 Egg beaten
- Other ingredients:
- Mayonnaise to taste
- Thinly sliced green onions to taste
- Kimchi to taste

Instructions

- Line the fryer basket with a grill mat or a sheet of lightly greased aluminum foil.
- Combine all the ingredients. Then, form them into round patties and place them in the fryer basket without stacking.
- Air fry at 380F (190C) for about 7-8 minutes, flip once in the middle until the surface is slightly golden brown.

Nutrition

- Calories:358kcal | Carbohydrates: 8g | Protein: 28g | Fat: 23g | Saturated Fat: 8g | Cholesterol: 178mg | Sodium: 272mg | Potassium: 264mg | Fiber: 1g | Sugar: 1g | Vitamin C: 3mg | Calcium: 114mg | Iron: 2mg

593. Thai Chicken Drumsticks

Prep Time: 10 mins

Cook Time: 20 mins

Ingredients For Chicken:

- 8 chicken drumsticks
- 2-3 tablespoon minced garlic
- 3 tablespoon fish sauce
- 2 tablespoon rice wine
- 1 teaspoon sesame oil
- 1 teaspoon black pepper or to taste
- 1/2 teaspoon sriracha hot sauce optional
- 1/4 cup brown sugar
- Juice of one lime

Instructions

- Marinate the chicken drumsticks with all the chicken ingredients in a Ziploc bag and refrigerate for at least 3-4 hours, preferably overnight.
- Remove the chicken from the refrigerator 30 minutes before air frying.
- Line the fryer basket with a grill mat or a sheet of lightly greased aluminum foil.
- Air fry at 360F (180C) for about 18-20 minutes until the chicken is cooked through when the internal temperature exceeds 170F (77C).
- Drizzle some Thai sweet chili sauce over drumsticks and sprinkle some chopped cilantro to serve.

Nutrition

- Calories:324kcal|Carbohydrates:16g | Protein: 28g | Fat: 15g | Saturated Fat: 4g | Cholesterol: 139mg | Sodium: 645mg | Potassium: 411mg | Fiber: 1g | Sugar: 14g | Vitamin C: 2mg | Calcium: 40mg | Iron: 1mg

594. Curry Chicken Tenderloins

Prep Time: 5 mins

Cook Time: 15 mins

Ingredients

- 4 pieces of chicken tenderloin
- 2 teaspoon coconut oil melted
- 1/2 teaspoon curry powder
- 1/4 teaspoon paprika
- 1/4 teaspoon garlic powder
- 1/4 teaspoon sea salt

Instructions

- In a small bowl, mix all the dry ingredients.
- Dap dry the tenderloins with a paper towel. Brush coconut oil to both sides of tenderloins. Then, sprinkle the dry ingredients to both sides of the chicken.
- Place the tenderloins in the fryer basket. Air fry at 380F (190C) for 10-12 minutes, flip once in the middle until the meat is cooked through when internal temperature exceeds 165F (74C).
- Serve the chicken over a bed of greens or rice.

Nutrition

- Calories:40kcal | Carbohydrates: 1g | Protein: 3g | Fat: 4g | Saturated Fat: 3g | Cholesterol: 1mg | Sodium: 294mg | Fiber: 1g | Sugar: 1g | Iron: 1mg

595. Keto Chicken And Kimchi Rice Bake

Prep Time: 10 mins

Cook Time: 10 mins

Ingredients

- 1 small head of cauliflower
- 2 cups chicken cooked and chopped
- 1 cup kimchi chopped, or to taste
- 2/3 cup juice from kimchi jar or to taste
- 1 cup shredded mozzarella cheese divided, or to taste
- 1 green onion cut into 1/2 inch pieces
- 1/4 cup green onion thinly sliced to garnish (optional)

Instructions

- Put the cauliflower into a food processor and pulse it a few times so the cauliflower becomes the size of a grain of rice. Transfer it to a large microwavable bowl and microwave for about 4-5 minutes.
- In the meantime, lightly grease a cake pan and set it aside.

- When the cauliflower is done, stir in chicken, kimchi, kimchi juice, 2/3 cup of mozzarella cheese, and large green onion pieces. Then, transfer the mixture to the cake pan.
- Put the cake pan in the fryer basket and air fry at 360F (180C) for about 4 minutes. Then, sprinkle the rest of the mozzarella cheese over the top and air fry again at 360F (180C) for 3-4 minutes until the cheese melts.
- Sprinkle some green onion on to serve.

Nutrition

- Calories:181kcal | Carbohydrates: 8g | Protein: 14g | Fat: 11g | Saturated Fat: 5g | Cholesterol: 42mg | Sodium: 239mg | Potassium: 520mg | Fiber: 3g | Sugar: 3g | Vitamin C: 71mg | Calcium: 181mg | Iron: 1mg

596. Roast Chicken Stuffed Avocados

Prep Time: 5 mins

Cook Time: 10 mins

Ingredients

- 2 avocados pitted
- 2 cups roast chicken shredded
- 1/3 cup tomato seeded and diced
- 1/4 cup shredded cheese Mexican blend
- 1/4 cup cilantro stems chopped
- 2 Tablespoon mayonnaise
- 1 Tablespoon Sriracha optional
- Mozzarella cheese to top

Instructions

- Preheat the air fryer at 400F (200C) for 2 minutes.
- Mix all the ingredients, except Mozzarella cheese, and them on top of avocados. Place them inside the fryer basket.
- Sprinkle some mozzarella cheese over the chicken mixture and let the cheese melt for 1 minute in the preheated air fryer.
- Air fry at 360F (180C) for 4-5 minutes until the cheese is slightly golden brown.

Nutrition

- Calories:349kcal | Carbohydrates: 9g | Protein: 21g | Fat: 26g | Saturated Fat: 5g | Cholesterol:

61mg | Sodium: 235mg | Potassium: 677mg | Fiber: 7g | Sugar: 1g | Vitamin C: 14mg | Calcium: 56mg | Iron: 1mg

12. Kimchi Chicken

Prep Time: 35 mins

Cook Time: 15 mins

Ingredients

- 1/2 pound of chicken thigh cut into thin slices
- 1/3 cup kimchi juice from kimchi jar
- 2 Tablespoon of grated ginger
- 1 teaspoon soy sauce
- 1/2 teaspoon corn starch
- 1/4 cup kimchi sliced or to taste
- 1 green onion thinly sliced

Instructions

- Mix the chicken slices with corn starch, kimchi sauce, grated ginger, and soy sauce. Marinate for at least 30 minutes.
- In a lightly greased cake pan, air fry the chicken at 380F (190C) for about 10-12 minutes until the meat is cooked through. When done, add in chopped kimchi and stir. Air fry at 380F (190C) for 2 more minutes.
- Garnish with green onion to serve.

Nutrition

- Calories: 146kcal | Carbohydrates: 2g | Protein: 22g | Fat: 5g | Saturated Fat: 1g | Cholesterol: 108mg | Sodium: 270mg | Potassium: 307mg | Fiber: 1g | Sugar: 1g | Vitamin C: 1mg | Calcium: 10mg | Iron: 1mg

597. Garlic Parmesan Chicken Tenderloins

Prep Time: 10 mins

Cook Time: 15 mins

Ingredients

- 4-6 pieces of chicken tenderloins defrosted and pat dry
- 1 egg beaten
- 1 Tablespoon Italian seasoning
- 1/2 cup shredded Parmesan cheese
- 1 teaspoon garlic powder

- 1/2 teaspoon paprika
- 1/4 teaspoon cayenne pepper or to taste

Instructions

- In a shallow plate, mix all the dry ingredients and set aside.
- Dip the tenderloins into egg then dredge them in seasoning mix.
- Place the tenderloins in the fryer basket and air fry at 380F (190C) for 10-12 minutes, flip once in the middle, until the chicken is cooked through at 165F (74C) and the surface is golden brown.

Nutrition

- Calories: 384kcal | Carbohydrates: 58g | Protein: 16g | Fat: 12g | Saturated Fat: 2g | Sodium: 44mg | Potassium: 737mg | Fiber: 15g | Sugar: 12g | | Vitamin C: 45mg | Calcium: 127mg | Iron: 6mg

598. Easy Chicken With Creamed Spinach

Prep Time: 5 mins

Cook Time: 15 mins

Ingredients For Chicken:

- 4 boneless skinless chicken (thighs, breasts, or tenderloins)
- 1 tablespoon olive oil
- 1/2 teaspoon paprika
- 1/2 teaspoon garlic powder
- 1/2 teaspoon onion powder
- 1/2 teaspoon dried basil
- Salt and pepper to taste

Ingredients For Creamed Spinach:

- 2 cans of Campbell Cream of Chicken Soup
- 1 can of water using the soup cans
- 1 Tablespoon olive oil
- 1/2 yellow onion diced
- 4 garlic cloves minced
- 8 ounces baby spinach or chopped spinach
- 1/3 cup grated Parmesan cheese or to taste

Instructions

- In a small bowl, mix all the dry ingredients for the chicken and set aside.

- Use a paper towel to pat dry the chicken pieces and rub them with olive oil. Season both sides of the chicken with the seasoning mixture and place them inside the fryer basket. Air fry at 380F (190C) for 10-12 minutes, flip once in the middle until the chicken is fully cooked and the internal meat temperature exceeds 165F (74C).
- In the meantime, use a skillet to saute the onion and garlic in olive oil until the onion is translucent. Stir in two cans of soup and one can of water and bring it to boil. Then, turn the heat to low and stir in the cheese.
- When the chicken is done, transfer the chicken to the skillet and add in the spinach. Let it simmer for 2-3 minutes until the spinach wilts.

Nutrition

- Calories: 250kcal | Carbohydrates: 5g | Protein: 29g | Fat: 12g | Saturated Fat: 3g | Cholesterol: 78mg | Sodium: 313mg | Potassium: 767mg | Fiber: 2g | Sugar: 1g | Vitamin C: 19mg | Calcium: 172mg | Iron: 2mg

599. Easy Dry Rub Chicken

Prep Time: 5 mins

Cook Time: 15 mins

Ingredients

- 4 skin-on boneless chicken thighs
- 2 Tablespoon olive oil
- 1 Tablespoon Italian seasoning
- 2 teaspoons paprika
- 2 teaspoons garlic powder
- 2 teaspoons onion powder
- 1/2 teaspoon salt
- 1/2 teaspoon black pepper

Instructions

- Mix all the dry ingredients and set aside.
- Make a few slices on the flesh part of the chicken thigh without cutting through. Use a paper towel to pat dry the thighs.
- Rub both sides of the chicken with olive oil. Then, rub both sides of the chicken generously with the dry mix.
- Line the fryer basket with lightly greased aluminum foil. Put the chicken thighs into the

basket without stacking. Air fry at 360F (180C) for about 8 minutes. Then, air fry again at 400F (200C) for about 4 minutes until cooked through at 165F (74C).

Nutrition

- Calories: 324kcal | Carbohydrates: 4g | Protein: 19g | Fat: 26g | Saturated Fat: 6g | Cholesterol: 111mg | Sodium: 381mg | Potassium: 298mg | Fiber: 1g | Sugar: 1g | Vitamin A: 602IU | Vitamin C: 1mg | Calcium: 33mg | Iron: 2mg

600. Breaded Parmesan Chicken

Prep Time: 10 mins

Cook Time: 15 mins

Ingredients

- 4 boneless skinless chicken thighs
- 1 egg
- 2 Tablespoon milk
- Salt and pepper to taste
- 3/4 cups Italian breadcrumbs. If using regular breadcrumbs, add 2 teaspoons of Italian seasoning to the bread crumbs.
- 1/3 cup freshly grated Parmesan cheese
- 1 1/2 teaspoon garlic powder
- Olive oil in a spritzer

Instructions

- Mix egg and milk in a shallow dish and season with salt and pepper.
- In a shallow dish, mix bread crumbs, Parmesan cheese, and garlic powder.
- Dab dry the chicken thighs with paper towels. Dip chicken thighs in the egg mixture and dredge both sides with bread crumbs mix.
- Place thighs inside the fryer basket without stacking and spray some olive oil on chicken thighs.
- Air fry at 380F (190C) for 10-12 minutes until the thighs are fully cooked through when the internal temperature exceeds 165F (74C).

Nutrition

- Calories: 281kcal | Carbohydrates: 17g | Protein: 30g | Fat: 10g | Saturated Fat: 3g | Cholesterol: 157mg | Sodium: 548mg | Potassium: 378mg |

Fiber: 1g | Sugar: 2g | Vitamin A: 202IU | Vitamin C: 1mg | Calcium: 158mg | Iron: 2mg

601. Fusion Chicken Wrap

Prep Time: 5 mins

Cook Time: 15 mins

Ingredients For Chicken:

- 3 pieces of skinless boneless chicken thighs or breast, thinly sliced
- 3 Tablespoon soy sauce
- 1 Tablespoon garlic powder
- 1 teaspoon corn starch
- 1 teaspoon Chinese five spices powder
- 1/4 teaspoon black pepper

Other Ingredients:

- 4 Tortillas
- 1/3 cup Hoisin sauce or to taste
- 1/2 cup thinly sliced green onion
- Green salad optional

Instructions

- Mix all the ingredients for the chicken and marinate for at least one hour in the refrigerator. Air fry at 380F (190C) for 10-12 minutes, stir 1-2 times in between until chicken is fully cooked through.
- To assemble, spread some Hoisin sauce onto a piece of tortilla. Put some green onion, chicken, and come green salad (optional) on the tortilla and wrap it up.

Nutrition

- Calories: 163kcal | Carbohydrates: 29g | Protein: 5g | Fat: 3g | Saturated Fat: 1g | Cholesterol: 1mg | Sodium: 454mg | Potassium: 160mg | Fiber: 2g | Sugar: 8g | Vitamin A: 125IU | Vitamin C: 2mg | Calcium: 51mg | Iron: 2mg

602. Honey Ginger Chicken

Prep Time: 3 hrs

Cook Time: 15 mins

Ingredients For Chicken:

- 4 pieces skin-on boneless chicken thighs
- 2 Tablespoon minced garlic
- 2 Tablespoons soy sauce
- 2 Tablespoons rice wine
- 2 Tablespoons honey
- 2 Tablespoon grated ginger

Instructions

- In a Ziploc bag, combine all the ingredients for the chicken and marinate in the refrigerator for at least 3 hours or overnight. Remove from the refrigerator 30 minutes before air frying.
- Line the fryer basket with a sheet of lightly greased aluminum foil. Put the chicken thighs in the basket skin side down without stacking. Air fry at 380F (190C) for about 7 minutes.
- Turn the chicken thighs over so they are skin side up. Air fry again at 380F (190C) for 5-6 minutes until the chicken is cooked through when the internal temperature exceeds 165F (74C). Save the juices on the foil to drizzle over rice if desired.
- Sprinkle some green onion and sesame seeds to serve.

Nutrition

- Calories: 63kcal | Carbohydrates: 12g | Protein: 2g | Fat: 1g | Saturated Fat: 1g | Cholesterol: 1mg | Sodium: 506mg | Potassium: 67mg | Fiber: 1g | Sugar: 9g | Vitamin A: 62IU | Vitamin C: 2mg | Calcium: 17mg | Iron: 1mg

603. Three Cup Chicken

Prep Time: 40 mins

Cook Time: 20 mins

Ingredients For The Chicken:

- 1 pound boneless skinless thighs (about 500g) cut into one inch pieces
- 2 Tablespoon sesame oil
- 4 Tablespoon soy paste
- 3 Tablespoon rice wine
- 2 Tablespoon mirin
- 2 Tablespoon grated ginger

Other Ingredients:

- 2 teaspoon olive oil

- 5 cloves of garlic
- 6-7 slices of ginger
- Red chili pepper optional
- 1 teaspoon sesame oil
- 1 bunch of basil
- 2 green onion cut into one-inch pieces

Instructions

- Mix all of the seasonings in the chicken ingredients and marinate the chicken with half of the marinade for about 30 minutes
- Put the garlic cloves and ginger slices into the cake pan and drizzle them with 2 teaspoons of olive oil. Air fry at 400F (200C) for about 2-3 minutes.
- Add in the chicken along with its marinade and air fry at 380F (190C) for 10 minutes, stir two times in between. Add the rest of the marinade, 3/4 of the green onion, 3/4 of the basil, and chili pepper (optional), and stir. Air fry at 380F (190C) for 6-7 minutes stirring once in between until the chicken is cooked through.
- When done, mix the rest of the basil and green onion and drizzle 1 teaspoon of sesame oil to serve.

Nutrition

- Calories: 291kcal | Carbohydrates: 12g | Protein: 24g | Fat: 15g | Saturated Fat: 3g | Cholesterol: 108mg | Sodium: 553mg | Potassium: 324mg | Fiber: 1g | Sugar: 5g | Vitamin A: 87IU | Vitamin C: 3mg | Calcium: 21mg | Iron: 1mg

604. Mushroom Chicken

Prep Time: 35 mins

Cook Time: 15 mins

Ingredients For Chicken:

- 1 tablespoon soy sauce
- 1 tablespoon Shaoxing wine
- 1 tablespoon corn starch
- Ingredients for the sauce:
- 3 tablespoons oyster sauce
- 1 tablespoon Shaoxing wine
- 1 Tablespoon soy sauce
- 2 Tablespoon chicken stock
- 2 teaspoon grated ginger

- 1 teaspoon sugar
- 1/4 teaspoon black pepper

Other Ingredients:

- 1/4 lbs button mushroom
- 3 cloves garlic chopped
- 1 green onion cut into 1-inch pieces
- 1 teaspoon sesame oil

Instructions

- Marinate the chicken with soy sauce, Shaoxing wine, and corn starch for at least 30 minutes.
- In a small bowl, mix all the ingredients for the sauce,
- In a lightly greased cake, pan put garlic on the bottom of the pan then put in the marinated chicken. Air fry at 380F (190C) for 10 minutes stirring once in the middle.
- Stir in the sauce and air and mushroom and air fry at 380F (190C) for about 4 minutes until the chicken is cooked through.
- When done, stir in the sesame oil and green onion to serve.

Nutrition

- Calories: 57kcal | Carbohydrates: 8g | Protein: 2g | Fat: 1g | Saturated Fat: 1g | Cholesterol: 1mg | Sodium: 885mg | Potassium: 118mg | Fiber: 1g | Sugar: 2g | Vitamin C: 2mg | Calcium: 8mg | Iron: 1mg

605. Thai Basil Chicken

Prep Time: 45 mins

Cook Time: 15 mins

Ingredients For Chicken:

- 1/2 pound boneless skinless chicken thighs thinly sliced
- 3 tablespoons minced garlic
- 1 tablespoons fish sauce
- 1/2 tablespoons olive oil
- 1 teaspoon sugar or to taste
- 1 teaspoon corn starch
- 1/2 Tablespoon dark soy sauce
- 1/2 teaspoon light soy sauce
- 1/2 tablespoon oyster sauce

- 1/4 teaspoon white pepper powder

Instructions

- Marinate the chicken in all the meat ingredients for about 30 minutes.
- In a lightly greased cake pan, air fry the onion at 320F (160C) for about 3-4 minutes. Put the marinated chicken over the onion and air fry at 380F (190C) for about 10 minutes until the meat is cooked through, stirring twice in between.
- Finally, stir in the basil leaves, jalapeno, and chicken broth into the cake pan. Air fry again at 380F (190C) for 2 minutes.
- Serve over rice or when done.

Nutrition

- Calories:132kcal | Carbohydrates: 10g | Protein: 13g | Fat: 4g | Saturated Fat: 1g | Cholesterol: 54mg | Sodium: 572mg | Potassium: 259mg | Fiber: 1g | Sugar: 5g | Vitamin C: 5mg | Calcium: 30mg | Iron: 1mg

606. Salt And Pepper Wings

Prep Time: 30 mins

Cook Time: 25 mins

Ingredients For The Wings:

- 18 chicken wings
- 3 Tablespoon soy sauce
- 1 Tablespoon minced garlic
- 2 teaspoon sugar
- 2 teaspoon rice wine
- 1 teaspoon sesame oil
- 2 egg yolks
- Other ingredients:
- 1/2 cup tapioca starch
- Thinly sliced red chili pepper or jalapeno optional
- 2 tablespoon thinly sliced green onion
- Salt to taste
- White pepper powder to taste
- Chopped cilantro for garnish

Instructions

- In a Ziploc bag, marinate the wings with all the other wing ingredients combined for at least 30 minutes in the refrigerator.

- Add the tapioca starch into the bag and shake. Let the bag sit at room temperature. When you see the tapioca starch appears to be moist (no longer white), put them in the fryer basket. Air fry at 380F (190C) for 20-22 minutes, turn the wings twice in between. During the second turn, put in the hot chili peppers and continue to air fry until the wings exceed 165F (74C) and the skin is crispy.
- Place the wings in a large mixing bowl and toss with the salt, pepper, green onion, and cilantro. Serve the wings while still hot.

Nutrition

- Calories: 394kcal | Carbohydrates: 11g | Protein: 28g | Fat: 25g | Saturated Fat: 7g | Cholesterol: 176mg | Sodium: 611mg | Potassium: 251mg | Fiber: 1g | Sugar: 2g | Vitamin C: 2mg | Calcium: 29mg | Iron: 2mg

607. Roasted Cornish Hen

Prep Time: 5 mins

Cook Time: 40 mins

Ingredients

- 1 Cornish hen completely defrosted and pat dry
- 1/2 teaspoon salt
- 1/2 teaspoon Italian seasoning
- 1/2 teaspoon paprika
- 1/2 teaspoon garlic powder
- 1/4 teaspoon black pepper

Instructions

- Combine all the dried ingredients and set them aside. Put a steamer rack inside an aluminum lined fryer basket.
- Generously rub the surface of the Cornish hen with seasoning mix and place the Cornish hen on the rack with the breast side facing up. Spray some oil on the Cornish hen. Stick the thermometer probe inside the breast and covered the hen with a sheet of aluminum foil. If possible, use another steamer rack to hold the foil down.
- Air fry at 390F (195C) for about 30 minutes. Remove the foil and air fry again at 390F (195C) for another 7-8 minutes until the temperature of the breast exceeds 170F (77C).
- Leave the Cornish hen in the air fryer for 10 minutes before serving.

Nutrition

- Calories:228kcal | Carbohydrates: 1g | Protein: 19g | Fat: 16g | Saturated Fat: 4g | Cholesterol: 114mg | Sodium: 360mg | Potassium: 266mg | Fiber: 1g | Sugar: 1g | Vitamin C: 1mg | Calcium: 16mg | Iron: 1mg

Miso Marinated Chicken

Prep Time: 3 hrs

Total Time: 20 mins

Ingredients

- 3 boneless chicken thighs
- 3 Tablespoon miso
- 1 Tablespoon soy sauce
- 1 Tablespoon mirin
- 1 Tablespoon rice wine

Instructions

- Combine miso, soy sauce, mirin, and rice wine and mix well. Marinate the chicken with the sauce mixture in the refrigerator for at least 3 hours or overnight.
- Take the chicken out of the refrigerator 30 minute before air frying.
- Place the chicken thighs skin-side down in the fryer basket lined with lightly greased aluminum foil. Air fry at 380F (190C) for about 12 minutes. Flip, then air fry again at 380F (190C) for 6-7 minutes or until the meat temperature exceeds 165 (74C).

Nutrition

- Calories:225kcal | Carbohydrates: 6g | Protein: 16g | Fat: 15g | Saturated Fat: 4g | Cholesterol: 83mg | Sodium: 825mg | Potassium: 210mg | Fiber: 1g | Sugar: 2g | Vitamin A: 66IU | Calcium: 14mg | Iron: 1mg

608. Black Bean Sauce Marinated Chicken

Prep Time: 4 mins

Cook Time: 20 mins

Ingredients

- 3 boneless chicken thighs
- 1 Tablespoon Black Bean Sauce
- 1 Tablespoon oyster sauce
- 1 Tablespoon mirin
- 1 Tablespoon rice wine
- Thinly sliced green onion to garnish

Instructions

- Combine the black bean sauce, oyster sauce, mirin, and rice wine. Marinate the chicken with the sauce mixture and refrigerate for at least 3 hours or overnight.
- Take the chicken out of the refrigerator 30 minute before air frying. Line the fryer basket with lightly greased aluminum foil.
- Place the chicken thighs in the fryer basket skin side down and air fry at 380F (190C) for about 12 minutes. Flip, then air fry again at 380F (190C) for 6-7 minutes or until the meat temperature exceeds 165 (74C). Save the drippings.
- Thinly slice the chicken, garnish with green onion, and drizzle with some drippings to serve.

Nutrition

- Calories: 204kcal | Carbohydrates: 3g | Protein: 14g | Fat: 14g | Saturated Fat: 4g | Cholesterol: 83mg | Sodium: 357mg | Potassium: 174mg | Fiber: 1g | Sugar: 1g | Calcium: 7mg | Iron: 1mg

609. Tomato And Pesto Chicken

Prep Time: 5 mins

Cook Time: 20 mins

Ingredients

- 2 skinless and boneless chicken thighs
- 1-2 Roma tomatoes cut into 1/4 inch slices
- 1/4 cup pesto sauce
- 1/3 cup shredded Mozzarella cheese
- black pepper to taste
- 1/2 teaspoon parsley flakes

Instructions

- Cover the chicken thighs with a large piece of saran wrap. Use a heavy object or a rolling pin to lightly pound the chicken so the thighs are somewhat flattened and even in thickness throughout.
- Line the fryer basket with a sheet of lightly greased aluminum foil. Place the thighs in the basket and sprinkle with some black pepper.
- Scoop and spread about 2 tablespoons of pesto sauce onto the chicken thighs and top them with a layer of tomato slices. Air fry at 360F (180C) for 14 minutes.
- Sprinkle Mozzarella cheese over the tomato slices and air fry at 380F (190C) for about 4-5 minutes until meat temperature exceeds 165F (74C).
- Garnish with some parsley to serve.

Nutrition

- Calories: 429kcal | Carbohydrates: 4g | Protein: 24g | Fat: 34g | Saturated Fat: 10g | Cholesterol: 128mg | Sodium: 496mg | Potassium: 305mg | Fiber: 1g | Sugar: 2g | Vitamin C: 4mg | Calcium: 153mg | Iron: 1mg

610. Chicken Fajitas

Prep Time: 45 mins

Cook Time: 20 mins

Ingredients For The Chicken:

- 1 1/2 pound skinless boneless chicken thighs (about 750g) cut into strips
- 1/2 cup chopped onion
- 1 Tablespoon olive oil
- 1 lime juiced
- 1 teaspoon salt
- 1 1/2 teaspoon ground cumin
- 1 1/2 teaspoon garlic powder
- 1 teaspoon chili powder
- 1/2 teaspoon paprika

Instructions

- Combine all the ingredients for the chicken and marinate it in the refrigerator for at least 30 minutes.
- Cut the bell peppers into thin slices and microwave for about 2-3 minutes.

- Air fry chicken strips on a lightly greased aluminum foil or a baking pan at 320F (160C) for about 16-18 minutes until all the meat is cooked through, stirring every 3-4 minutes. During the last stir, mix in the bell pepper and continue to air fry until completion.
- To serve, wrap the chicken with tortilla and top it with chopped green onion, cilantro, cheese, and sour cream if desired.

Nutrition

- Calories: 265kcal | Carbohydrates: 7g | Protein: 34g | Fat: 11g | Saturated Fat: 2g | Cholesterol: 162mg | Sodium: 747mg | Potassium: 574mg | Fiber: 2g | Sugar: 2g | Vitamin C: 39mg | Calcium: 37mg | Iron: 2mg

611. Keto Muffins

Prep Time: 5 mins

Cook Time: 15 mins

Ingredients

- 8 oz ground turkey or chicken
- 1 teaspoon garlic powder
- 1/4 cup shredded cheese
- 1/4 teaspoon black pepper
- 1 egg beaten
- 1/4 cup chopped basil
- 1/4 cup chopped green onion
- 2 Tablespoon chopped pickled jalapeno optional
- 1/4 teaspoon salt

Instructions

- In a large bowl, mix the ground turkey, garlic powder, shredded cheese, and black pepper. Divide the ground meat mixture into four portions.
- Lightly grease the muffin cups. Scoop one portion of the ground meat into each cup then press it against the walls and form it into a cup shape. Air fry at 380F (190C) for 6 minutes.
- In the meantime, mix the egg with basil, green onion, and salt. Then, scoop the egg mixture into each cup and air fry again at 380F (190C) for another 6-7 minutes until the egg is cook through.

Nutrition

- Calories: 107kcal | Carbohydrates: 2g | Protein: 17g | Fat: 4g | Saturated Fat: 2g | Cholesterol: 78mg | Sodium: 319mg | Potassium: 218mg | Fiber: 1g | Sugar: 1g | Vitamin C: 2mg | Calcium: 49mg | Iron: 1mg

612. Basil Chicken Zucchini Wrap

Prep Time: 10 mins

Cook Time: 15 mins

Ingredients

- 1 large chicken breast butterflied
- 1 medium zucchini cut into 1/4 inch thick slices
- 7-8 basil leaves
- 1/4 teaspoon black pepper
- 4 strips of bacon

Instructions

- On a cutting board, cover the butterflied chicken breast with a large sheet of saran wrap. Use a rolling pin or a heavy object to pound the chicken so the thickness is even throughout. Then, cut the chicken into 4 pieces.
- Sprinkle some black pepper onto the chicken. Then, put the zucchini slice and 1 or 2 basil leaves on top of each chicken and roll it up. Finally, take one strip of bacon and wrap it around the chicken roll. Secure it with toothpicks if necessary.
- Place a metal steamer rack inside the fryer basket and place the wraps on the rack. Air fry at 400F (200C) for 10-12 minutes or until the internal meat temp exceeds 165F (74C).

Nutrition

- Calories:165kcal | Carbohydrates: 2g | Protein: 15g | Fat: 10g | Saturated Fat: 3g | Cholesterol: 51mg | Sodium: 215mg | Potassium: 381mg | Fiber: 1g | Sugar: 1g | Vitamin C: 9mg | Calcium: 11mg | Iron: 1mg

613. Garlic Chicken Roll

Prep Time: 45 mins

Cook Time: 20 mins

Ingredients

- 4 pieces of chicken breast or thigh
- 1/4 cup of minced garlic divided
- 4 teaspoon of rice wine divided
- 1 teaspoon of pink Himalayan salt divided
- white pepper powder to taste
- 2 Tablespoons of chopped fresh Thai basil optional

Instructions

- Butterfly the chicken breast to make the breast into one large thinner piece and cover it with saran wrap. Use a rolling pin or a heavy pan to pound the meat so the chicken is uniform in thickness. Sprinkle 1 teaspoon rice wine, 1/4 teaspoon salt, 1 Tablespoon minced garlic, and some white pepper powder over each piece of chicken.
- Roll the chicken up. Then, use a sheet of aluminum foil to wrap the chicken tightly the way one would wrap a candy (like Tootsie Roll). Refrigerate for at least 30 minutes.
- Place the foil-wrapped chicken rolls in the fryer basket and air fry at 320F (160C) for 18-20 minutes. Check the internal meat temperature by inserting a food thermometer directly through the aluminum foil. The chicken is done when the temperature exceeds 165F (74C). Let cool before cutting it into slices.
- This dish is usually served chilled. Sprinkle some chopped fresh Thai basil to serve.

Nutrition

- Calories: 181kcal | Carbohydrates: 3g | Protein: 31g | Fat: 4g | Saturated Fat: 1g | Cholesterol: 91mg | Sodium: 747mg | Potassium: 559mg | Fiber: 1g | Sugar: 1g | Vitamin C: 4mg | Calcium: 22mg | Iron: 1mg

Prep Time: 10 mins

Cook Time: 15 mins

Ingredients

- 10 oz Ground chicken or turkey 300g
- 1 egg
- 1/4 cup minced yellow onion
- 1/2 teaspoon garlic powder
- 1/2 teaspoon parsley flakes
- 1/4 teaspoon salt
- 1/4 teaspoon black pepper
- Cheddar cheese cubes or take the slices of cheese together
- 1/4 cup Japanese Panko about 14g carbs (Optional)
- 1/4 cup mayo
- 2 Tablespoon Sriracha hot sauce or to taste
- 1-2 Tablespoon honey optional

Instructions

- Mix ground chicken, egg, onion, garlic powder, parsley flakes, salt, and black pepper together.
- Take a cube of cheddar and wrap the ground meat around it. Roll it in the Panko and place it inside the parchment-lined fryer basket. Air fry at 360F (180C) for 12-14 minutes, turn the chicken cheese balls once in the middle until the meat is cooked through.
- in the meantime, mix the mayo, Sriracha, and honey. To serve, drizzle the sriracha mayo over the chicken cheese balls or use it as a dip.

Nutrition

- Calories: 273kcal | Carbohydrates: 9g | Protein: 22g | Fat: 17g | Saturated Fat: 5g | Cholesterol: 98mg | Sodium: 556mg | Potassium: 259mg | Fiber: 1g | Sugar: 5g | Vitamin C: 6mg | Calcium: 94mg | Iron: 1mg

---

614. Cheesy Chicken Balls

615. Chicken Zucchini Boats

Prep Time: 30 mins

Cook Time: 15 mins

Ingredients

- 3 Medium Zucchini
- 8 oz ground or finely chopped chicken (about 250g)
- 1/4 cup finely chopped kimchi optional
- 1 Tablespoon oyster sauce
- 1 teaspoon Gochujang Korean hot pepper sauce
- 1 teaspoon sesame seeds
- 1 teaspoon sesame oil
- 1/2 teaspoon corn starch
- 1/3 cup Mozzarella cheese
- 2-3 tablespoon thinly sliced fresh basil

Instructions

- Marinate the chicken with all the ingredients, except Mozzarella cheese and basil, for at least 30 minutes.
- Line the fryer basket with a grill mat or a sheet of lightly greased aluminum foil. Cut zucchini lengthwise to about 1/4-1/2 inch thickness and put them side by side inside the fryer basket. Top the zucchini slices with ground meat mixture and air fry at 360F (180C) for about 8 minutes.
- Sprinkle cheese over ground chicken and let it melt in the air fryer unit for about 1 minute. Then, air fry at 380F (190C) for about 3 minutes until the cheese is lightly golden brown.
- Sprinkle with some thinly sliced fresh basil leaves to serve.

Nutrition

- Calories: 183kcal | Carbohydrates: 4g | Protein: 14g | Fat: 12g | Saturated Fat: 4g | Cholesterol: 50mg | Sodium: 229mg | Potassium: 363mg | Fiber: 1g | Sugar: 3g | Vitamin C: 18mg | Calcium: 74mg | Iron: 1mg

616. Air Fryer Chicken Tenders

Prep Time: 5 Mins

Cook Time: 30 Mins

Total Time: 35 Mins

Yield: 4 Servings

Ingredients

- 12 chicken tenders, (1 1/4 lbs)
- 2 large eggs, beaten
- 1 teaspoon kosher salt
- Black pepper, to taste
- 1/2 cup seasoned breadcrumbs
- 1/2 cup seasoned panko
- Olive oil spray
- Lemon wedges, for serving

Instructions

- Season chicken with salt and pepper.
- Place egg in a shallow bowl. In a second shallow bowl, combine the bread crumbs and panko.
- Dip chicken in the egg, then into the breadcrumb mixture and shake off excess, and place on a large dish or cutting board. Spray both sides of the chicken generously with oil.
- Preheat air fryer to 400F.
- In batches, cook the chicken 5 to 6 minutes on each side, until the chicken is cooked through and crispy and golden on the outside. Serve with lemon wedges.

Nutrient Value

- Calories: 291kcal| Carbohydrates: 16.5g| Protein: 38.5g| Fat: 7g| Saturated Fat: 2g| Cholesterol: 197mg| Sodium: 653mg| Fiber: 1g| Sugar: 1.5g

617. Air Fryer Fried Chicken

Prep Time: 10 minutes

Cook Time: 25 minutes

Total Time: 35 minutes

Ingredients

- Marinade
- ½ whole chicken cut into separate pieces (breast, thigh, wing, and leg)
- ½ cup hot sauce
- ½ cup buttermilk
- Seasoning

- ¾ cup All-Purpose Flour
- 2 tsp seasoning salt
- 1 tsp garlic powder
- 1 tsp onion powder
- 1 tsp Italian seasoning
- ½ tsp cayenne pepper
- Oil for spraying Canola or Vegetable

Instructions

- Place chicken pieces in buttermilk and hot sauce. Place in refrigerator and allow to marinate anytime from 1-24 hours.
- Whisk together all-purpose flour, seasoning salt, garlic powder, onion powder, Italian seasoning, and cayenne pepper in a bowl. Set aside.
- Place a parchment liner in the Air Fryer basket.
- Remove a piece of chicken from the buttermilk mixture and place in the flour mixture, coating all sides of the chicken and shaking off any excess flour. Place the chicken pieces in the basket in a single layer.
- Close the Air Fryer basket and set the temperature to 390 degrees Fahrenheit and the timer to 25 minutes. Start the Air Fryer.
- After 13 minutes, open the air fryer and spray any flour spots on the chicken. Flip the chicken and spray the other side with oil, ensuring all the flour spots are covered. Close the air fryer and cook for 12 more minutes.
- Once the timer is up, open the Air Fryer and check chicken pieces with a quick read thermometer. Chicken is done when it reaches an internal temperature of 165 degrees at the thickest part of the chicken.

Nutrition

- Calories:318kcal | Carbohydrates:21g | Protein21g | Fat: 15g | Saturated Fat: 4g | Cholesterol: 74mg | Sodium: 2055mg | Potassium: 297mg | Fiber: 1g | Sugar: 2g | Vitamin C: 23.9mg | Calcium: 56mg | Iron: 2.3mg

---

618. Crispy Air Fryer Chicken Breast

American Prep Time: 10 minutes

Cook Time: 10 minutes

Total Time: 20 minutes

Servings: 4

Ingredients

- 2 large boneless skinless chicken breasts sliced into cutlets
- 1 tablespoon oil olive oil, canola, or vegetable oil
- ½ cup (25g) dried bread crumbs
- ½ teaspoon paprika
- ¼ teaspoon dried chili powder
- ¼ teaspoon ground black pepper
- ¼ teaspoon garlic powder
- ¼ teaspoon onion powder
- ¼ teaspoon cayenne pepper
- ½ teaspoon salt

Instructions

Breaded Version:

- Put the chicken breasts in a bowl and drizzle with oil. Make sure that they're well coated.
- In a shallow dish, mix the dried bread crumbs with the spices until well combined.
- Coat each chicken breast in bread crumbs, and transfer to your air fryer basket.
- Air fry in the air fryer at 390°F or 200°C for 10-12 minutes. After the first 7 minutes, open the air fryer and flip the chicken on the other side then continue cooking (cook for 3 minutes, depending on the size of the chicken breast used).

Unbreaded Version:

- Drizzle oil over your boneless skinless chicken breasts, and season with your favorite seasonings.
- Place the seasoned chicken breasts in the Air Fryer basket breast side down, and air fry for 12-15 minutes flipping halfway through using kitchen tongs.
- When the cooking time is up, remove from the Air Fryer immediately so that the chicken does not dry out. Allow resting for 5 minutes before serving.

Nutrition

- Calories: 163kcal | Carbohydrates: 1g | Protein: 24g | Fat: 7g | Saturated Fat: 1g | Cholesterol: 72mg | Sodium: 423mg | Potassium: 418mg |

Fiber: 1g | Sugar: 1g | Vitamin A: 220IU | Vitamin C: 1.3mg | Calcium: 6mg | Iron: 0.5mg

619. Air Fryer Chicken & Broccoli

Prep Time: 10 mins

Cook Time: 15 mins

Total Time: 25 mins

Servings: 4 Servings

Ingredients

- 1 pound (454 g) boneless skinless chicken breast, cut into bite-sized pieces
- 1/4-1/2 pound (113-226 g) broccoli, cut into florets (1-2 cups)
- 1/2 medium (0.5 medium) onion, sliced thick
- 2 tablespoons (30 ml) olive oil or grapeseed oil
- 1/2 teaspoon (2.5 ml) garlic powder
- 1 tablespoon (15 ml) fresh minced ginger
- 1 tablespoon (15 ml) low sodium soy sauce, or to taste (use tamari for gluten free)
- 1 teaspoon (5 ml) sesame seed oil
- 2 teaspoons (10 ml) rice vinegar (use distilled white vinegar for gluten free)
- 2 teaspoons (10 ml) hot sauce (optional)
- Additional salt, to taste
- Additional black pepper, to taste
- Serve with lemon wedges

Instructions

- In a large bowl, combine chicken breast, broccoli, and onion. Toss ingredients together.

Make The Marinade:

- In a bowl, combine oil, garlic powder, ginger, soy sauce, sesame oil, rice vinegar, and hot sauce. Add the chicken, broccoli, and onions to the marinade. Stir thoroughly to combine the marinade with chicken, broccoli, and onions.
- Air Fry: Add ingredients to the air fry basket. Air fry 380°F for 16-20 minutes, shaking and gently tossing halfway through cooking. Make sure to toss so that everything cooks evenly.
- Check chicken to make sure it's cooked through. If not, cook for additional 3-5 minutes.
- Add additional salt and pepper, to taste. Squeeze fresh lemon juice on top and serve warm.

Nutrition

- Calories: 191kcal | Carbohydrates: 4g | Protein: 25g | Fat: 7g | Saturated Fat: 1g | Cholesterol: 72mg | Sodium: 328mg | Potassium: 529mg | Sugar: 1g | Vitamin C: 29.1mg | Calcium: 22mg | Iron: 0.7mg

620. Air-fried General Tso's Chicken

Active Time: 20 Mins

Total Time: 35 Mins

Ingredients

- 1 large egg 1 pound boneless, skinless chicken thighs, patted dry and cut into 1 to 1 1/4-inch chunk 1/3 cup plus 2 tsp. cornstarch, divided 1/4 teaspoon kosher salt 1/4 teaspoon ground white pepper 7 tablespoons lower-sodium chicken broth 2 tablespoons lower-sodium soy sauce 2 tablespoons ketchup 2 teaspoons sugar 2 teaspoons unseasoned rice vinegar 1 1/2 tablespoons canola oil 3 to 4 chiles de árbol, chopped and seeds discarded 1 tablespoon finely chopped fresh ginger 1 tablespoon finely chopped garlic 2 tablespoons thinly sliced green onion, divided 1 teaspoon toasted sesame oil 1/2 teaspoon toasted sesame seeds

Ingredients

- Beat egg in a large bowl, add chicken, and coat well. In another bowl, combine 1/3 cup cornstarch with salt and pepper. Transfer chicken with a fork to cornstarch mixture, and stir with a spatula to coat every piece.
- Transfer chicken to air-fryer oven racks (or fryer basket, in batches), leaving a little space between pieces. Preheat the air-fryer at 400°F for 3 minutes. Add the battered chicken; cook for 12 to 16 minutes, giving things a shake midway. Let dry for 3 to 5 minutes. If chicken is still damp on one side, cook for 1 to 2 minutes more.
- Whisk together the remaining 2 teaspoons cornstarch with broth, soy sauce, ketchup, sugar, and rice vinegar. Heat canola oil and chiles in a large skillet over medium heat. When gently sizzling, add the ginger and garlic; cook until fragrant, about 30 seconds.
- Re-whisk cornstarch mixture; stir into mixture in

skillet. Increase heat to medium-high. When sauce begins to bubble, add chicken. Stir to coat; cook until sauce thickens and nicely clings to chicken, about 1 1/2 minutes. Turn off heat; stir in 1 tablespoon green onion and sesame oil. Transfer to a serving plate, and top with sesame seeds and remaining 1 tablespoon green onion.

Nutritional Information

- Calories: 302| Fat: 13g | Sat fat: 3g | Unsatfat: 10g | Protein: 26g| Carbohydrate: 18g | Fiber: 0g | Sugars: 4g | Added sugars: 2g | Sodium: 611mg

621. Air Fryer Chicken Wings

Prep Time: 10 Mins

Cook Time: 30 Mins

Total Time: 40 Mins

Ingredients

- 2 pounds (907 g) chicken wings
- Kosher salt, or sea salt, to taste
- Black pepper, to taste
- Garlic powder, optional

Instructions

- If needed, pat dries the chicken wings. Season with salt, pepper, and optional garlic powder.
- For an oil-free version, place an even layer in the air fryer basket/tray. Follow the air fry instructions below.

Air Fry

- Air Fry wings at 400°F/205°C for 30-35 minutes or until crispy and cooked through. You must flip the wings over after the first 20 minutes of cooking. Or you might need an extra flip to get the wings crispy to your personal preference.
- If using a sauce, toss with a little sauce, then air fry for another 2-4 minutes. Or you can just toss or dip the wings in the sauce after they are finished cooking.

Nutrient Value

- Calories: 271kcal |Protein: 22g | Fat: 19g | Saturated Fat: 5g |Cholesterol: 94mg| Sodium: 89mg | Potassium: 191mg | Vitamin A: 180IU |

Vitamin C: 0.8mg | Calcium: 15mg | Iron: 1.2mg

622. Air Fryer Nashville Hot Chicken Tender

Prep Time: 10 mins

Cook Time: 30 mins

Total Time: 40 mins

Ingredients

- 1 lb chicken tenders
- ¾ cup milk
- 2 tbsp hot sauce
- ¾ cup panko bread crumbs
- 1 tsp paprika
- ½ tsp italian seasoning
- ½ tsp salt
- ½ garlic powder
- ½ onion powder
- ¼ tsp black pepper
- Salt and pepper to taste
- Oil for spraying canola, olive oil, or any oil with a high smoke point
- Hot paste
- ½ cup peanut oil
- 2 tbsp brown sugar
- 1 ½ tbsp cayenne pepper
- 1 tsp paprika
- 1 tsp dry mustard
- 1 tsp garlic powder
- ½ tsp salt

Instructions

- Season tenders with a little salt and pepper. Set aside. Create a dredging station by whisking milk and hot sauce in one bowl. In a separate bowl, mix panko bread crumbs, paprika, Italian seasoning, salt, garlic powder, onion powder, and black pepper.
- Preheat your air fryer to 375 degrees Fahrenheit.
- Start by coating chicken tenders with milk mixture and drain off excess milk, then coat chicken in panko bread crumbs mixture, ensuring all of the chicken is coated.
- Place chicken in greased air fryer basket or use a parchment sheet liner. Cook on 375 degrees for 14-16 minutes, flipping and spraying chicken

halfway through cooking, until chicken is fully cooked and has reached a temperature of at least 165 degrees Fahrenheit.

- Meanwhile, when there are about 5 minutes left on the chicken, create the hot paste. Add peanut oil, brown sugar, cayenne pepper, paprika, dry mustard, garlic powder, and salt to a medium-sized saucepan over medium heat and whisk to combine. Once your mixture starts to bubble and simmer, remove from heat.
- Once chicken tenders are done, remove from air fryer and add them to a large bowl. Pour the hot paste over the chicken and toss to combine, making sure hot sauce covers all of the chicken. Serve and enjoy.

Nutrition

- Calories:488kcal|Carbohydrates:19g | Protein: 28g | Fat: 34g | Saturated Fat: 7g | Cholesterol: 77mg | Sodium: 998mg | Potassium: 583mg | Fiber: 2g | Sugar: 9g | Vitamin C: 8mg | Calcium: 89mg | Iron: 1mg

623. Air Fryer Sesame Chicken

Prep Time: 10 Minutes

Cook Time: 25 Minutes

Total Time: 35 Minutes

Ingredients

Chicken

- 6 Boneless, Skinless Chicken Thighs
- 1/2 Cup Cornstarch
- Olive Oil Spray

Sauce

- 1/4 Cup Soy Sauce or Gluten-Free Soy Sauce
- 2 Tbsp Brown Sugar
- 2 Tbsp Orange Juice
- 5 Tsp Hoisin Sauce or Gluten-Free Sauce
- 1/2 Tsp Ground Ginger
- 1 Garlic Clove, Crushed
- 1 Tbsp Cold Water
- 1 Tbsp Cornstarch
- 2 Tsp Sesame Seeds

Instructions

- Cut the chicken into cubed chunks, then toss in a bowl with Cornstarch or Potato Starch. Use enough to coat the chicken evenly.
- Place in the Air Fryer and cook according to your Air Fryer Manual for chicken. (Note - I cooked ours on 390* for 24 minutes, 12 minutes on each side.)When the chicken is in the air fryer, add a nice even coat of olive oil cooking spray, once it's in the air fryer, it works best to mix it up halfway through cook time and add a coat of spray.
- While the chicken is cooking, in a small saucepan, begin to make the sauce.
- Add the soy sauce, brown sugar, orange juice, hoisin sauce, ground ginger, and garlic to the saucepan on medium-high heat. Whisk this up until well combined.
- Once the sugar has fully dissolved and a low boil is reached, whisk in the water and cornstarch.
- Mix in the sesame seeds. (The sauce should only take about 5 minutes or less to make on the stove and then an additional 5 minutes to thicken up.)
- Remove the sauce from the heat and set aside for 5 minutes to thicken.
- Once the chicken is done, remove it from the air fryer and place it in a bowl, and then coat it with the sauce.
- Serve topped over rice and beans.

Nutrition Information

- Calories: 335| Total Fat: 12g| Saturated Fat: 3g| Trans Fat: 0g| Unsaturated Fat: 9g| Cholesterol: 137mg| Sodium: 1100mg| Carbohydrates: 28g| Fiber: 1g| Sugar: 6g| Protein: 30g

624. Air Fryer Chicken Parmesan

Prep Time: 10 min

Cook Time: 20 min

Ready in 30 min

Ingredients

Chicken

- 4 boneless skinless chicken breasts (4 oz./125 g each)
- ¼ tsp (2 ml) salt
- ½ cup (125 ml) all-purpose flour

- 2 eggs
- 2 tbsp (30 ml) milk
- 1½ oz. (45 g) fresh parmesan cheese (⅓ cup/75 ml grated)
- ⅔ cup (150 ml) panko breadcrumbs
- 1 tbsp (15 ml) italian seasoning mix
- 8 oz. (250 g) fresh mozzarella cheese
- Pasta
- 3 cups (750 ml) cherry tomatoes
- 1 pkg (9 oz./275 g) refrigerated cheese-filled tortellini
- 1 oz. (30 g) fresh parmesan cheese (¼ cup/60 ml grated)
- ½ cup (125 ml) fresh basil leaves, loosely packed
- 1 tbsp (15 ml) olive oil
- 1 tbsp (15 ml) balsamic vinegar
- ¼ tsp (1 ml) salt

Directions

- Season the chicken with salt. Add the flour to one Coating Tray. Whisk the eggs and milk together in a second coating tray. Grate the Parmesan with the Microplane Adjustable Coarse Grater and combine with the panko and seasoning in the third coating tray.
- Coat each chicken breast in flour first, then the eggs, then the panko mixture.
- Divide the chicken onto two cooking trays of the Deluxe Air Fryer. Place the trays on the top and middle racks.
- Cut the tomatoes in half with the Close & Cut; place them on the drip tray of the air fryer. Turn the wheel to select the setting; press the wheel to select AIR FRY. Turn the wheel to adjust the time to 18 minutes. Press the wheel to start. Switch the trays with the chicken halfway through cooking (you'll hear beeps as a reminder). Cook until the internal temperature reaches 165°F (74°C).
- Slice the mozzarella with the Quick Slice. When the chicken is halfway through cooking, add the tortellini to the 3-qt. (3-L) Micro-Cooker Plus with enough water to cover the pasta. Microwave, covered, on HIGH, for 8 minutes.
- Drain the pasta and transfer it to a medium mixing bowl. Grate the Parmesan cheese into the bowl with the Microplane® Adjustable Fine Grater. Grate the basil into the bowl with the

Herb Mill. Add the remaining pasta ingredients and toss to combine.
- When the timer is up, top each chicken breast with the mozzarella. Turn the wheel to select the AIR FRY setting; press the wheel to select. Turn the wheel to adjust the time to 2 minutes. Press the wheel to start.
- Add the tomatoes to the pasta mixture and serve with the chicken.

Nutrients Value

- Calories: 620 | Total Fat: 21 g | Saturated Fat: 7 g | Cholesterol: 160 mg | Sodium: 930 mg | Carbohydrate: 60g | Fiber: 1g | Total Sugars: 5g | Protein: 47g

---

625. Air Fryer Chicken Breast

Prep Time: 5 mins

Cook Time: 20 mins

Resting Time: 5 mins

Total Time: 30 mins

Ingredients

- 1.5 tbsp cornstarch
- 1.5 tsp garlic powder
- 1 tsp smoked paprika
- 1.5 tsp dried oregano
- 4 chicken breasts boneless
- Oil

Instructions

- Prepare the chicken breasts by trimming off any excess fat and unwanted pieces.
- Mix the spices and cornstarch in a bowl.
- Coat the chicken breasts with oil or cooking spray.
- Sprinkle the spice & cornstarch mixture on the chicken.
- Place a piece of parchment or foil in the bottom of your air fryer basket. Place the chicken on top of that.
- Air fry the chicken for 16-18 minutes at 350 degrees F, flipping the chicken breasts halfway through. Cook until the internal temperature in the thickest part of the chicken reaches a minimum of 165 degrees F.

- Let the chicken rest for 5 minutes before slicing & plating.

Nutrition

- Calories: 276kcal | Carbohydrates: 4g | Protein: 48g | Fat: 6g | Saturated Fat: 1g | Cholesterol: 145mg | Sodium: 264mg | Potassium: 871mg | Fiber: 1g | Sugar: 1g | Vitamin C: 3mg | Calcium: 23mg | Iron: 1mg

626. Garlic Parmesan Chicken Wings In An Air Fryer

Prep Time: 5 min

Cook Time: 20 min

Total Time: 25 min

Ingredients

- 2 pounds chicken wings (or drumsticks)
- 3/4 cup grated Parmesan cheese
- 2 teaspoons minced garlic
- 2 teaspoons fresh parsley (chopped)
- 1 teaspoon salt
- 1 teaspoon pepper

Instructions

- Preheat your air fryer to 400 degrees for 3-4 minutes
- Pat chicken pieces dry with a paper towel.
- Mix Parmesan cheese, garlic, parsley, salt, and pepper together in a bowl.
- Toss chicken pieces in cheese mixture until coated.
- Place chicken in the bottom of the air fryer basket and set the timer to 10-12 minutes.
- After 12 minutes, use tongs to flip the chicken.
- Fry again for 12 minutes.
- Remove chicken from the basket with tongs and sprinkle with more Parmesan cheese and parsley.
- Serve with your favorite dipping sauce. We like ranch and buffalo.

Nutrient Value

- Calories: 460 | Total Fat: 20g | Saturated Fat: 6g | Cholesterol: 94mg | Sodium: 840mg | Carbohydrates: 47g | Dietary Fiber:1g | Sugar: 22g | Protein: 23g |

627. Air fryer marinated chicken breasts (no breading)

Total Time: 5 Hours

Ingredients

- Chicken marinade
- ¼ cup olive oil
- ¼ cup freshly squeezed lemon juice
- 3 tbsp worcestershire sauce
- 3 medium cloves garlic minced
- ½ tsp salt
- ½ tsp black pepper
- 2 tbsp fresh oregano minced or 2 teaspoons dried oregano
- ¼ cup fresh parsley minced and lightly packed or 4 teaspoons dried parsley
- ¼ cup fresh basil minced and lightly packed or 4 teaspoons dried basil
- Chicken
- 4 8 oz boneless, skinless chicken breasts
- Olive oil cooking spray

Instructions

- In a large bowl, whisk together ingredients for the marinade. Add chicken breast to a large container or resealable bag, pour marinade over chicken, seal, or cover.
- Chill in the refrigerator for up to 4 hours.
- Remove from the refrigerator and let your chicken reach room temperature. (20-30 minutes)
- Preheat your air fryer to 370° F for 5 minutes.
- Remove the air fryer basket and place chicken breasts inside, leaving room between the breasts, so they cook evenly.
- Spray each chicken breast with olive oil.
- Place back into the preheated air fryer and cook for 10 minutes
- Remove the basket and flip breasts over, spray again with olive oil and cook for another 6-8 minutes; chicken is done when the internal temperature reaches 160° F when checked with an instant-read thermometer.
- Remove your chicken from the air fryer basket and allow it to rest for 5 minutes before serving!
- Garnish chicken with fresh oregano, parsley, and/or basil.

Nutrition

- Calories:274kcal | Carbohydrates: 5g | Protein: 25g | Fat: 17g | Saturated Fat: 3g | Cholesterol: 72mg | Sodium: 550mg | Potassium: 597mg | Fiber: 1g | Sugar: 2g | Vitamin C: 15mg | Calcium: 71mg | Iron: 2mg

628. Amazing Buttermilk Air Fried Chicken

Prep Time:15 mins

Cook Time: 20 mins

Total Time:35 mins

Ingredient

- 1 cup buttermilk
- ½ teaspoon hot sauce
- ⅓ cup tapioca flour
- ½ teaspoon garlic salt
- ⅛ teaspoon ground black pepper
- 1 egg
- ½ cup all-purpose flour
- 2 teaspoons salt
- 1 ½ teaspoons brown sugar
- 1 teaspoon garlic powder
- ½ teaspoon paprika
- ½ teaspoon onion powder
- ¼ teaspoon oregano
- ¼ teaspoon black pepper
- 1 pound skinless, boneless chicken thighs

Instructions

- Combine buttermilk and hot sauce in a shallow dish; mix to combine.
- Combine tapioca flour, garlic salt, and 1/8 teaspoon black pepper in a resealable plastic bag and shake to combine.
- Beat egg in a shallow bowl.
- Mix flour, salt, brown sugar, garlic powder, paprika, onion powder, oregano, and 1/4 teaspoon black pepper in a gallon-sized resealable bag and shake to combine.
- Dip chicken thighs into the prepared ingredients in the following order: buttermilk mixture, tapioca mixture, egg, and flour mixture, shaking off excess after each dipping.
- Preheat an air fryer to 380 degrees F (190 degrees C). Line the air fryer basket with parchment paper.
- Place coated chicken thighs in batches into the air fryer basket and fry for 10 minutes. Turn chicken thighs and fry until chicken is no longer pink in the center and the juices run clear for an additional 10 minutes.

Nutrition Facts

- Calories: 335| Protein: 24.3g| Carbohydrates: 27.4g| Fat: 13.6g| Cholesterol 113.8mg| Sodium: 1549.8mg.

629. Crumbed Chicken Tenderloins (Air Fried)

Prep Time: 15 mins

Cook Time: 12 mins

Total Time: 27 mins

Ingredient

- 1 egg
- ½ cup dry bread crumbs
- 2 tablespoons vegetable oil
- 8 chicken tenderloins

Instructions

- Preheat an air fryer to 350 degrees F (175 degrees C).
- Whisk egg in a small bowl.
- Mix bread crumbs and oil in a second bowl until the mixture becomes loose and crumbly.
- Dip each chicken tenderloin into the bowl of an egg; shake off any residual egg. Dip chicken into the crumb mixture, making sure it is evenly and fully covered. Lay chicken tenderloins into the basket of the air fryer. Cook until no longer pink in the center, about 12 minutes. An instant-read thermometer inserted into the center should read at least 165 degrees F (74 degrees C).

Nutrition Facts

- Calories: 253| protein: 26.2g| carbohydrates: 9.8g| fat: 11.4g| cholesterol: 109mg| sodium: 170.7mg.

630. Air Fryer Blackened Chicken Breast

Prep Time: 10 mins

Cook Time: 20 mins

Additional Time: 10 mins

Total Time: 40 mins

Ingredient

- 2 teaspoons paprika
- 1 teaspoon ground thyme
- 1 teaspoon cumin
- ½ teaspoon cayenne pepper
- ½ teaspoon onion powder
- ½ teaspoon black pepper
- ¼ teaspoon salt
- 2 teaspoons vegetable oil
- 2 (12 ounces) skinless, boneless chicken breast halves

Instructions

- Combine paprika, thyme, cumin, cayenne pepper, onion powder, black pepper, and salt in a bowl. Transfer spice mixture to a flat plate.
- Rub oil over each chicken breast until fully coated. Roll each piece of chicken in a blackening spice mixture, making sure to press down so spice sticks on all sides. Let sit for 5 minutes while you preheat the air fryer.
- Preheat an air fryer to 360 degrees F (175 degrees C) for 5 minutes.
- Place chicken in the basket of the air fryer and cook for 10 minutes. Flip and cook for an additional 10 minutes. Transfer chicken to a plate and let rest for 5 minutes before serving.

Nutrition Facts

- Calories: 432| Protein: 79.4g| Carbohydrates: 3.2g| Fat: 9.5g; Cholesterol: 197.7mg| Sodium: 515.8mg.

---

631. Air Fryer BBQ Cheddar-Stuffed Chicken Breasts

Prep Time:10 mins

Cook Time: 25 mins

Total Time: 35 mins

Ingredients

- 3 strips bacon, divided

- 2 ounces cheddar cheese, cubed, divided
- ¼ cup barbeque sauce, divided
- 2 (4 ounces) skinless, boneless chicken breasts
- Salt and ground black pepper to taste

Instructions

- Preheat an air fryer to 380 degrees F (190 degrees C). Cook 1 strip of bacon in the air fryer for 2 minutes. Remove from air fryer and cut into small pieces. Line the air fryer basket with parchment paper and increase the temperature to 400 degrees F (200 degrees C).
- Combine cooked bacon, Cheddar cheese, and 1 tablespoon barbeque sauce in a bowl.
- Use a long, sharp knife to make a horizontal 1-inch cut at the top of each chicken breast, creating a small internal pouch. Stuff each breast equally with the bacon-cheese mixture. Wrap remaining strips of bacon around each chicken breast. Coat chicken breast with remaining barbecue sauce and place into the prepared air fryer basket.
- Cook for 10 minutes in the air fryer, turn and continue cooking until chicken is no longer pink in the center and the juices run clear about 10 more minutes. An instant-read thermometer inserted into the center should read at least 165 degrees F (74 degrees C).

Nutrition Facts

- Calories: 379| Protein: 37.7g| Carbohydrates: 12.3g| Fat: 18.9g| Cholesterol: 114.3mg| Sodium: 986.7mg.

---

49. Air-Fried Buffalo Chicken

Prep Time: 20 mins

Cook Time: 16 mins

Total Time: 36 mins

Ingredients

- ½ cup plain fat-free Greek yogurt
- ¼ cup egg substitute
- 1 tablespoon hot sauce (such as Frank's®)
- 1 teaspoon hot sauce (such as Frank's®)
- 1 cup panko bread crumbs
- 1 tablespoon sweet paprika

- 1 tablespoon garlic pepper seasoning
- 1 tablespoon cayenne pepper
- 1 pound skinless, boneless chicken breasts, cut into 1-inch strips

Instructions

- Whisk Greek yogurt, egg substitute, and 1 tablespoon plus 1 teaspoon hot sauce in a bowl.
- Mix panko bread crumbs, paprika, garlic pepper, and cayenne pepper in a separate bowl.
- Dip chicken strips into yogurt mixture; coat with panko bread crumb mixture.
- Arrange coated chicken strips in a single layer in an air fryer. Cook until evenly browned, about 8 minutes per side.

Nutrition Facts

- Calories: 234| Protein: 31.2g| Carbohydrates: 22.1g| Fat: 4.6g| Cholesterol: 64.8mg| Sodium: 696.2mg.

---

632. Crispy Ranch Air Fryer Nuggets

Prep Time: 15 mins

Cook Time: 10 mins

Additional Time: 15 mins

Total Time: 40 mins

Ingredients

- 1 pound chicken tenders, cut into 1.5 to 2-inch pieces
- 1 (1 ounce) package dry ranch salad dressing mix
- 2 tablespoons flour
- 1 egg, lightly beaten
- 1 cup panko bread crumbs
- 1 serving olive oil cooking spray

Instructions

- Place chicken in a bowl, sprinkle with ranch seasoning and toss to combine. Let sit for 5-10 minutes.
- Place flour in a resealable bag. Place egg in a small bowl and panko bread crumbs on a plate. Preheat air fryer to 390 degrees F (200 degrees C).
- Place chicken into the bag and toss to coat. Lightly dip chicken into the egg mixture, letting

excess drip off. Roll chicken pieces in panko, pressing crumbs into the chicken.

- Spray basket of the air fryer with oil and place chicken pieces inside, making sure not to overlap. You may have to do two batches, depending on the size of your air fryer. Lightly mist chicken with cooking spray.
- Cook for 4 minutes. Turn chicken pieces and cook until chicken is no longer pink on the inside, about 4 more minutes. Serve immediately.

Nutrition Facts

- Calories: 244| Protein: 31g| Carbohydrates: 25.3g| Fat: 3.6g| Cholesterol: 112.3mg| Sodium: 713.4mg.

13. Air Fryer Dessert And Snacks Recipes

633. Hilton DoubleTree Hotel Chocolate Chip Cookies

Prep Time: 10 mins

Cook Time: 1 hr

Ingredients

- 1/2 cup butter softened
- 1/3 cup granulated sugar
- 1/4 cup packed brown sugar
- 1 egg

- 1/2 teaspoons vanilla extract
- 1/8 teaspoon lemon juice
- 1 cup and 2 tablespoons all-purpose flour
- 1/4 cup rolled oats
- 1/2 teaspoon baking soda
- 1/2 teaspoon salt
- Pinch cinnamon
- 1 1/4 cup semi-sweet chocolate chips
- 1 cup chopped walnuts

Instructions

- Cream butter, sugar, and brown sugar in the bowl of a stand mixer on medium speed for about 2 minutes.
- Add eggs, vanilla, and lemon juice, blending with mixer on low speed for 30 seconds, then medium speed for about 2 minutes, or until light and fluffy, scraping down bowl.
- With the mixer on low speed, add flour, oats, baking soda, salt, and cinnamon, blending for about 45 seconds. Don't overmix.
- Remove bowl from mixer and stir in chocolate chips and walnuts.
- Line the fryer basket with a grill mat or a sheet of parchment paper.
- Scoop about one tablespoon of dough onto a baking sheet lined with parchment paper about 2 inches apart.
- Air fry at 260F (130C) for 18-20 minutes.
- Remove from the air fryer and cool on a wired rack for about 1/2 hour.

Nutrition

- Calories:397kcal| Carbohydrates: 30g | Protein: 5g | Fat: 29g | Saturated Fat: 15g | Cholesterol: 55mg | Sodium: 154mg | Potassium: 182mg | Fiber: 3g | Sugar: 17g | Vitamin C: 1mg | Calcium: 34mg | Iron: 2mg

---

634. Hotteok Korean Sweet Pancakes

Prep Time: 2 hrs 30 mins

Cook Time: 10 mins

Ingredients For The Dough:

- 1 1/4 cup all-purpose flour

- 1/2 tsp salt
- 1 tsp white sugar
- 1 tsp instant dry yeast
- 1/2 cup lukewarm milk
- Ingredients for the filling:
- 1/4 cup brown sugar
- 1/4 tsp cinnamon powder
- 1/4 cup chopped walnuts

Instructions

- In a mixing bowl, mix all the dough ingredients with a spatula.
- Lightly cover the bowl with saran wrap and let the dough rise for about 1-2 hours or until the dough doubles in size.
- Punch the dough down several times to release the air in the dough. Then, cover with saran wrap again and let it rest for about 20 minutes.
- In the meantime, mix all the filling ingredients in a bowl and set aside.
- Line the fryer basket with a grill mat or a sheet of lightly greased aluminum foil.
- Rub some cooking oil in your hands and take the dough out from the bowl. Roll the dough into a cylinder shape on the counter surface then cut it into six equal pieces. Roll each piece into a ball.
- Take one ball of dough and flatten it between the palms of your hand. Scoop about 1 tablespoon of filling and wrap it inside the dough. Place the dough inside the fryer basket, leaving about 2 inches between the balls. Repeat until done.
- Press the balls down with the palm of your hand. Spritz some oil on top and air fry at 300F (150C) for 8-10 minutes, flip once in the middle until the surface is golden brown.

Nutrition

- Calories: 137kcal | Carbohydrates: 24g | Protein: 4g | Fat: 3g | Saturated Fat: 1g | Cholesterol: 2mg | Sodium: 155mg | Potassium: 81mg | Fiber: 1g | Sugar: 8g | Calcium: 29mg | Iron: 1mg

---

635. Cinnamon Pear Slices

Prep Time: 5 mins

Cook Time: 15 mins

Ingredients

1 medium-sized Asian pear peeled and cored

2 tbsp butter melted

1 tbsp brown sugar

1/2 tsp cinnamon

Granola for garnish optional

Instructions

- Thinly cut the pear into 1/4 inch thick wedges.
- In a mixing bowl, combine and toss all the ingredients.
- Lightly grease a shallow baking pan. Place the pear wedges in the pan, pour whatever is left in the bowl over the pear, and air fry at 340F (170C) for 14-16 minutes until tender.
- Pair them with ice cream or sprinkle some granola over them to serve.

Nutrition

- Calories: 175kcal | Carbohydrates: 20g | Protein: 1g | Fat: 11g | Saturated Fat: 7g | Cholesterol: 30mg | Sodium: 4mg | Potassium: 103mg | Fiber: 3g | Sugar: 15g | Vitamin C: 4mg | Calcium: 8mg | Iron: 1mg

636. Rice Cake Spring Rolls

Prep Time: 10 mins

Cook Time: 10 mins

Ingredients

- Spring roll wrapper
- Chinese sweet rice cake
- A small bowl of water
- Melted butter

Instructions

- Cut the rice cake into rectangles, about 1/4 inch thick.
- Cut the spring roll wrappers to the appropriate size, enough to wrap around the rice cake.
- Wrap the rice cake with spring roll paper. Smear a little water at the end of the wrapper so the wrapper will stick onto itself.
- Line the fryer basket with a grill mat or a sheet of lightly greased aluminum foil.
- Place the wrapped rice cake inside the fryer basket. Brush melted butter onto the wraps and

air fry at 400F (2000C) for about 4-5 minutes.

- Flip the rolls over and brush them with butter again. Air fry again at 400F (200C) for another 4-5 minutes until the surface looks crispy and golden brown.
- Let cool about 5 minutes before serving.

637. Candied Kumquats

Prep Time: 5 mins

Cook Time: 10 mins

Ingredients

- 2 cup kumquat
- 2 tbsp melted unsalted butter
- 1/4 cup brown sugar or to taste depending on the sweetness

Instructions

- Cut kumquats in half and pick out all the visible seeds. (Kumquat seeds are edible, therefore it is okay if the seeds cannot be removed completely.)
- In a large mixing bowl, gently stir and mix all the ingredients. Then, transfer the kumquats to a lightly greased bakeware.
- Air fry at 300F (150C) for 10-12 minutes, stirring a couple of times in the middle until there is a slightly thickened sauce.

Nutrition

- Calories: 143kcal | Carbohydrates: 22g | Protein: 1g | Fat: 6g | Saturated Fat: 4g | Cholesterol: 15mg | Sodium: 10mg | Potassium: 123mg | Fiber: 4g | Sugar: 19g | Vitamin C: 25mg | Calcium: 46mg | Iron: 1mg

638. Pastry Wrapped Rice Cakes

Prep Time: 10 mins

Cook Time: 10 mins

Ingredients

- Chinese rice cake (nian-ago)
- Pie crust or puff pastry
- Egg wash

Instructions

- Line the fryer basket with lightly greased aluminum foil.
- Cut rice cake into 1/2 inch thick pieces. Wrap the rice cake with pie crust or puff pastry. Lightly press down on the overlapping pie crust to prevent it from opening up. Then, place them in the fryer basket.
- Brush the top side with egg wash. Air fry at 350F (175C) for 4 minutes.
- Flip the rice cake over and brush with egg wash. Air fry again at 350F (175C) for another 4-5 minutes until the surface is golden brown.
- The rice cake hardens when they are cold, so it is best to serve them warm.

Nutrient Value

- Calories: 384kcal | Carbohydrates: 58g | Protein: 16g | Fat: 12g | Saturated Fat: 2g | Sodium: 44mg | Potassium: 737mg | Fiber: 15g | Sugar: 12g | | Vitamin C: 45mg | Calcium: 127mg | Iron: 6mg

639. Peanut Butter Cupcake Swirl

Prep Time: 10 mins

Cook Time: 15 mins

Ingredients

- 1/4 cup butter softened
- 1/3 cup creamy peanut butter
- 2 tbsp sugar
- 1 egg
- 3/4 cup milk
- 1/2 tsp vanilla extract
- 3/4 cup cake flour
- 1 tsp baking soda
- 1/2 tsp baking powder
- 1/2 tsp salt
- 1/4 cup Nutella divided warmed

Instructions

- Line the muffin tins with cupcake liners and set them aside.
- Cream together the butter, sugar, and peanut butter using a whisk or an electric mixer. Then, add the egg, milk, and vanilla extract. Mix until homogenous. Finally, add the rest of the dry ingredients and mix until well combined.

- Scoop the batter into the liners about 2/3 full. Then, use a spoon to drop about 1/2 teaspoon of Nutella into the center of the cupcake. Insert a toothpick into the center of the Nutella and create a swirl by making circles in the batter.
- Air fry at 300F (150C) for about 12-14 minutes. Insert a toothpick to test. When the toothpick comes out clean, then the cupcake is cooked through.

Nutrition

- Calories: 215kcal | Carbohydrates: 18g | Protein: 5g | Fat: 14g | Saturated Fat: 7g | Cholesterol: 34mg | Sodium: 378mg | Potassium: 168mg | Fiber: 1g | Sugar: 9g | Calcium: 54mg | Iron: 1mg

640. Chocolate Sponge Cake

Prep Time: 10 mins

Cook Time: 15 mins

Ingredients

- 3 large eggs
- 1 1/2 tbsp melted butter let cool until almost to room temperature
- 2 tbsp milk
- 2 tbsp sugar
- 1/4 tsp vanilla extract
- 1/3 cup cake flour
- 1/2 tsp baking powder
- 1 1/2 tbsp cocoa powder

Instructions

- Crack 3 eggs. Put the egg whites in a mixing bowl and egg yolks in a large bowl.
- To the egg yolks, add in the cooled butter, milk, sugar, and vanilla extract and mix until well combined. Sieve the cake flour, baking powder, and cocoa powder and whisk to combine the wet and dry ingredients to form a thick batter.
- In the meantime, use the electric mixer (or a whisk) to beat the egg whites until they can form a stiff peak. When done, pour this fluffy egg whites into the batter and gently combine them with a spatula until it is almost homogenous.
- Lightly grease the ramekins and put them inside the fryer basket. Preheat the air fryer at 400F (200C) for about 2 minutes.

pan. Pour the batter into the pan and air fry at 300F (150C) for about 8 minutes.

- Let cool on a cooling rack. When cooled, cut it into 1-inch squares to serve.

Nutrition

- Calories:307kcal | Carbohydrates: 16g | Protein: 7g | Fat: 26g | Saturated Fat: 8g | Cholesterol: 1mg | Sodium: 194mg | Potassium: 92mg | Fiber: 4g | Sugar: 8g | Vitamin C: 2mg | Calcium: 72mg | Iron: 1mg

646. Marshmallow Chocolate Chip Explosion Cookies

Prep Time: 10 mins

Cook Time: 10 mins

Ingredients

- 2/3 cup all-purpose flour
- 1/4 teaspoon baking soda
- 1/8 teaspoon salt
- 1/4 cup unsalted butter softened at room temperature
- 1/3 cup brown sugar
- 1 egg yolk
- 1/2 teaspoon vanilla extract
- 1/2 cup chocolate chips or to taste
- 1/4 cup marshmallow or to taste chopped into about 1/4 inch cubes

Instructions

- Preheat the air fryer at 350F (175C) for about 3-4 minutes.
- Line a small cookie sheet or bakeware with parchment paper and set it aside. This step is crucial. Without some kind of bakeware under the parchment paper, the edges of the paper may be lifted off during the air frying process which may cause the cookies to bunch together.
- In a medium bowl, combine the flour, baking soda, and salt.
- In a large bowl, whisk together the butter and brown sugar until smooth. Add in the egg yolk and vanilla extract and whisk again.
- Combine the two bowls and mix well. Scoop one tablespoonful of the dough and roll it into a ball. Flatten it with the palm of your hand and put the desired amount of marshmallow and chocolate

chip in the middle. Wrap the dough around to form a ball again. Place the balls of dough on the parchment paper, making sure they are about 2 inches apart from each other.

- Air fry at 350F (175C) for 5-6 minutes until the cookies look crispy. Remove the cookies and let them cool on a rack. Repeat the same process for the remaining dough if necessary.
- For your enjoyment, my little baker recommends the cookies to be warmed up a bit and topped with a scoop of ice cream.

Nutrition

- Calories: 257kcal | Carbohydrates: 35g | Protein: 3g | Fat: 12g | Saturated Fat: 7g | Cholesterol: 55mg | Sodium: 112mg | Potassium: 31mg | Fiber: 1g | Sugar: 23g | Calcium: 36mg | Iron: 1mg

647. Coffee Cake

Prep Time: 15 mins

Cook Time: 30 mins

Ingredients

- 1/2 cup oil
- 1 egg beaten
- 1/2 teaspoon vanilla extract
- 1/2 cup milk
- 1/2 cup sugar
- 1 1/2 cup cake flour
- 1 1/2 teaspoon baking powder
- 1/4 teaspoon salt
- 1/2 cup brown sugar
- 1 teaspoon cinnamon
- 1/4 cup melted butter

Instructions

- In a medium bowl, prepare streusel by combining brown sugar and cinnamon. Divide the streusel into two equal portions.
- In a large mixing bowl, combine oil, eggs, vanilla,

and milk. In a medium bowl, blend sugar, flour, baking powder, and salt. Then, combine egg mixture with flour mixture, mix well, then divide the batter into two equal parts.

- Lightly grease the loaf pans. Pour 1/2 of the batter into each pan. Sprinkle 1/2 of streusel into the pan and top it off with the remaining batter
- Sprinkle the remaining streusel on top and drizzle with melted butter.
- Air fry at 320F (160C) for about 30 minutes until the toothpick comes out clean.

Nutrition

- Calories: 379kcal | Carbohydrates: 44g | Protein: 4g | Fat: 21g | Saturated Fat: 5g | Cholesterol: 37mg | Sodium: 143mg | Potassium: 145mg | Fiber: 1g | Sugar: 27g | Calcium: 72mg | Iron: 1mg

648. Apple French Toast Cups

Prep Time: 10 mins

Cook Time: 15 mins

Ingredients

- 1 apple peeled and cubed
- 1 Tablespoon butter
- 6 oz bread or bread ends cut into one-inch cubes
- 1/3 cup brown sugar
- 1 teaspoons cornstarch
- 3 eggs
- 2/3 cups milk
- 1/2 teaspoon vanilla extract
- 1/2 teaspoon cinnamon
- 2 Tablespoon maple syrup

Instructions

- In a microwave-safe bowl, microwave the apple cubes with butter for about 3 minutes until the apples are tender. Let cool for a few minutes.
- Combine the bread, sugar, and cornstarch in a large mixing bowl.
- In a separate bowl, mix the eggs, milk, vanilla, cinnamon, apple (and its juices) and maple syrup then pour this mixture into the bread bowl and gently combine all ingredients.
- Scoop the mixture into a lightly greased muffin tin and air fry at 320F (160C) for about 12-14

minutes until the surface is golden brown.

Nutrition

- Calories:336kcal | Carbohydrates: 55g | Protein: 10g | Fat: 9g | Saturated Fat: 4g | Cholesterol: 134mg | Sodium: 292mg | Potassium: 272mg | Fiber: 3g | Sugar: 33g | Vitamin C: 2mg | Calcium: 152mg | Iron: 2mg

649. Maple Walnut Biscotti

Prep Time: 10 mins

Cook Time: 40 mins

Ingredients

- 1 cup all-purpose flour
- 1/3 cup packed brown sugar
- 1 1/4 teaspoons baking powder
- 1/4 teaspoon salt
- 1 egg
- 2 Tablespoon maple syrup
- 2 Tablespoon melted unsalted butter
- 1 cups coarsely chopped walnuts

Instructions

- In a parchment-lined fryer basket, air fry the walnuts at 300F (150C) for 6 minutes.
- In the meantime, take a large and bowl and mix all the dry ingredients. Then, add in the wet ingredients until everything is well combined. Finally, fold in the chopped walnuts and form the batter into a ball shape.
- Place the ball-shaped dough on parchment paper and press it down with the palm of your hand to mold the dough into a rectangular shape with a thickness of about 1/2 inch. Air fry at 360F (180C) for 15 minutes.
- Remove the rectangular cookie along with the parchment paper from the fryer basket and let cool for a few minutes. When cool enough to handle, cut it into 3/4 inch wide pieces.
- Place all the pieces back into the fryer basket with the cut side up and air fry at 360 for about 10 minutes, flipping once in between with the other cut side facing up.
- When done, carefully remove the biscotti from the fryer basket and let them cool completely on a cooling rack before serving.

- Calories: 297| Protein: 5.5g| Carbohydrates: 64.9g| Fat: 2.1g| Cholesterol: 48mg| Sodium: 248.6mg.

654. Air Fryer Roasted Bananas

Prep Time: 2 mins

Cook Time: 7 mins

Total Time: 9 mins

Ingredients

- 1 banana, sliced into 1/8-inch thick diagonals
- Avocado oil cooking spray

Instructions

- Line air fryer basket with parchment paper.
- Preheat an air fryer to 375 degrees F (190 degrees C).
- Place banana slices into the basket, making sure that they are not touching; cook in batches if necessary. Mist banana slices with avocado oil.
- Cook in the air fryer for 5 minutes. Remove the basket and flip banana slices carefully (they will be soft). Cook until banana slices are browning and caramelized, an additional 2 to 3 minutes. Carefully remove from basket.

Nutrition Facts

- Calories:107| Protein:1.3g| Carbohydrates:27g| Fat:0.7g|Sodium: 1.2mg.

655. Air Fryer Triple-Chocolate Oatmeal Cookies

Prep Time: 15 mins

Cook Time: 10 mins

Total Time: 25 mins

Ingredient

- 3 cups quick-cooking oatmeal
- 1 ½ cups all-purpose flour
- ¼ cup cocoa powder
- 1 (3.4 ounces) package instant chocolate pudding mix

- 1 teaspoon baking soda
- 1 teaspoon salt
- 1 cup butter, softened
- ¾ cup brown sugar
- ¾ cup white sugar
- 2 eggs
- 1 teaspoon vanilla extract
- 2 cups chocolate chips
- 1 cup chopped walnuts (optional)
- Nonstick cooking spray

Instructions

- Preheat an air fryer to 350 degrees F (175 degrees C) according to the manufacturer's instructions. Spray the air fryer basket with nonstick cooking spray.
- Mix oatmeal, flour, cocoa powder, pudding mix, baking soda, and salt in a bowl until well combined. Set aside.
- Cream butter, brown sugar, and white sugar together in another bowl using an electric mixer. Add eggs and vanilla extract. Add oatmeal mixture and mix well. Stir in chocolate chips and walnuts.
- Drop dough into the air fryer using a large cookie scoop; flatten out and leave about 1 inch between each cookie.
- Cook until lightly browned, 6 to 10 minutes. Cool on a wire rack before serving.

Nutrition Facts

- Calories: 199| Protein: 2.9g| Carbohydrates: 24.7g| Fat: 10.9g| Cholesterol: 23.9mg| Sodium: 180.4mg.

656. Air Fryer Beignets

Prep Time: 10 mins

Cook Time: 15 mins

Total Time: 25 mins

Ingredient

- Cooking spray
- ½ cup all-purpose flour
- ¼ cup white sugar
- ⅛ cup water
- 1 large egg, separated

- 1 ½ teaspoon melted butter
- ½ teaspoon baking powder
- ½ teaspoon vanilla extract
- 1 pinch salt
- 2 tablespoons confectioners' sugar, or to taste

Instructions

- Preheat air fryer to 370 degrees F (185 degrees C). Spray a silicone egg-bite mold with nonstick cooking spray.
- Whisk flour, sugar, water, egg yolk, butter, baking powder, vanilla extract, and salt together in a large bowl. Stir to combine.
- Beat egg white in a small bowl using an electric hand mixer on medium speed until soft peaks form. Fold into batter. Add batter to the prepared mold using a small hinged ice cream scoop.
- Place filled silicone mold into the basket of the air fryer.
- Fry in the preheated air fryer for 10 minutes. Remove mold from the basket carefully; pop beignets out and flip over onto a parchment paper round.
- Place parchment round with beignets back into the air fryer basket. Cook for an additional 4 minutes. Remove beignets from the air fryer basket and dust with confectioners' sugar.

Nutrition Facts

- Calories: 88| Protein: 1.8g| Carbohydrates: 16.2g| Fat: 1.7g| Cholesterol: 28.9mg| Sodium: 73.5mg.

---

657. Air-Fried Banana Cake

Prep Time: 10 mins

Cook Time: 30 mins

Total Time: 40 mins

Ingredient

- Cooking spray
- ⅓ cup brown sugar
- 3 ½ tablespoons butter, at room temperature
- 1 banana, mashed

- 1 egg
- 2 tablespoons honey
- 1 cup self-rising flour
- ½ teaspoon ground cinnamon
- 1 pinch salt

Instructions

- Preheat an air fryer to 320 degrees F (160 degrees C). Spray a small fluted tube pan with cooking spray.
- Beat sugar and butter together in a bowl using an electric mixer until creamy. Combine banana, egg, and honey in a separate bowl. Whisk banana mixture into butter mixture until smooth.
- Sift flour, cinnamon, and salt into the combined banana-butter mixture. Mix batter until smooth. Transfer to the prepared pan; level the surface using the back of a spoon.
- Place the cake pan in the air fryer basket. Slide the basket into the air fryer and set the timer for 30 minutes. Bake until a toothpick inserted into the cake comes out clean.

Nutrition Facts

- Calories: 497| Protein: 5.2g| Carbohydrates: 56.9g| Fat: 11.8g| Cholesterol: 73.2mg| Sodium: 530.6mg.

---

658. Air-Fried Butter Cake

Prep Time: 10 mins

Cook Time: 15 mins

Additional Time: 5 mins

Total Time: 30 mins

Ingredient

- Cooking spray
- 7 tablespoons butter, at room temperature
- ¼ cup white sugar
- 2 tablespoons white sugar
- 1 egg
- 1 ⅔ cups all-purpose flour
- 1 pinch salt, or to taste
- 6 tablespoons milk

Instructions

- Preheat an air fryer to 350 degrees F (180

Made in the USA
Las Vegas, NV
18 July 2021